STOP!

This is the back of the book.
You wouldn't want to spoil a great ending!

This book is printed "manga-style," in the authentic Japanese right-to-left format. Since none of the artwork has been flipped or altered, readers get to experience the story just as the creator intended. You've been asking for it, so TOKYOPOP® delivered: authentic, hot-off-the-press, and far more fun!

DIRECTIONS

If this is your first time reading manga-style, here's a quick guide to help you understand how it works.

It's easy... just start in the top right panel and follow the numbers. Have fun, and look for more 100% authentic manga from TOKYOPOP®!

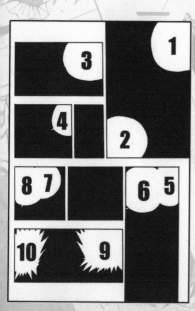

P9-DFO-635

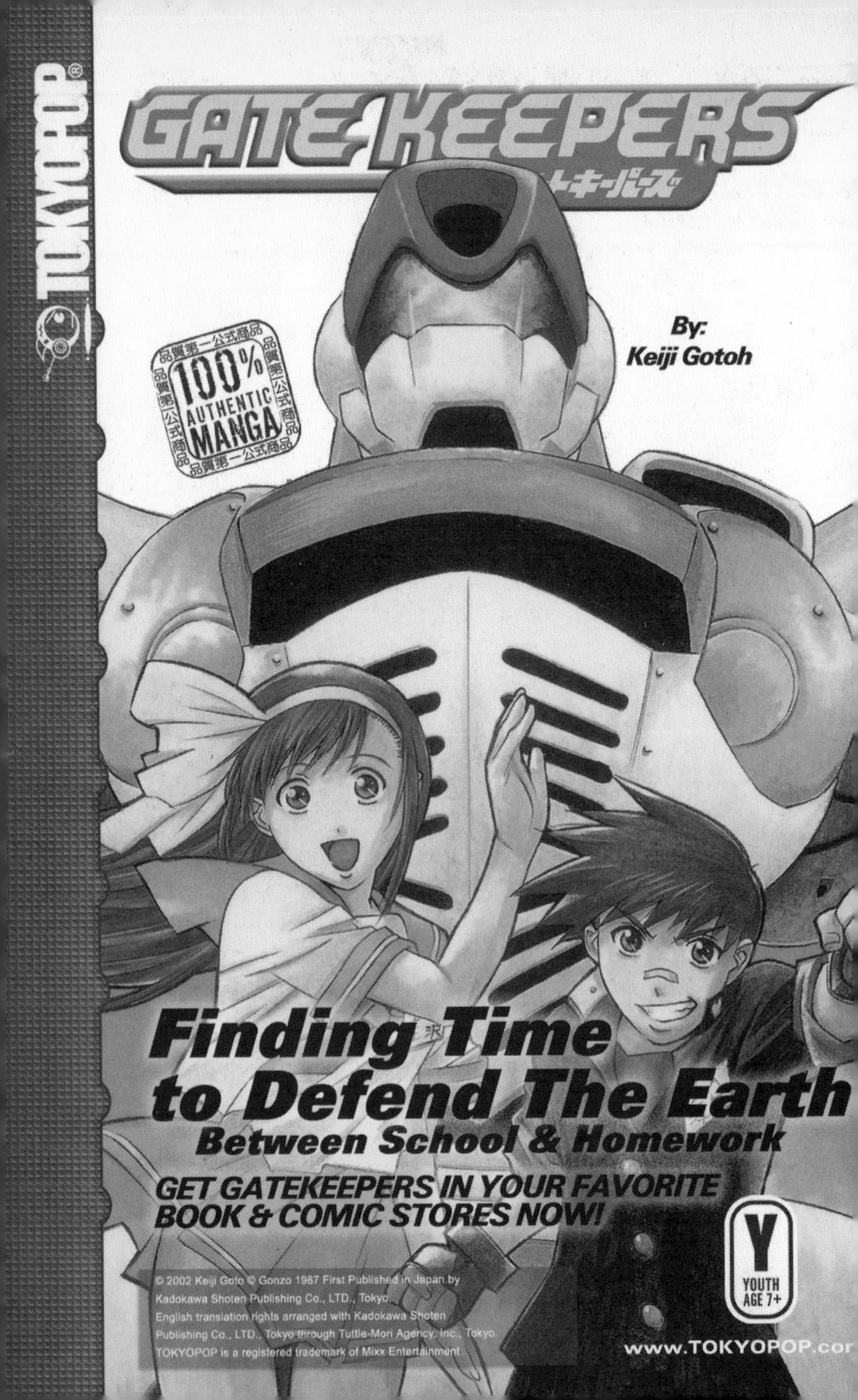
TOKYOPOP®
GATE KEEPERS
ゲートキーパーズ
By:
Keiji Gotoh
品質第一公式商品
100% AUTHENTIC MANGA
Finding Time
to Defend The Earth
Between School & Homework
GET GATEKEEPERS IN YOUR FAVORITE
BOOK & COMIC STORES NOW!
Y
YOUTH
AGE 7+
© 2002 Keiji Goto © Gonzo 1987 First Published in Japan by
Kadokawa Shoten Publishing Co., LTD., Tokyo.
English translation rights arranged with Kadokawa Shoten
Publishing Co., LTD., Tokyo through Tuttle-Mori Agency, Inc., Tokyo.
TOKYOPOP is a registered trademark of Mixx Entertainment
www.TOKYOPOP.com

.hack 1

// LEGEND OF THE TWILIGHT

MANGA: REI IZUMI

ORIGINAL CONCEPTS: TATSUYA HAMAZAKI

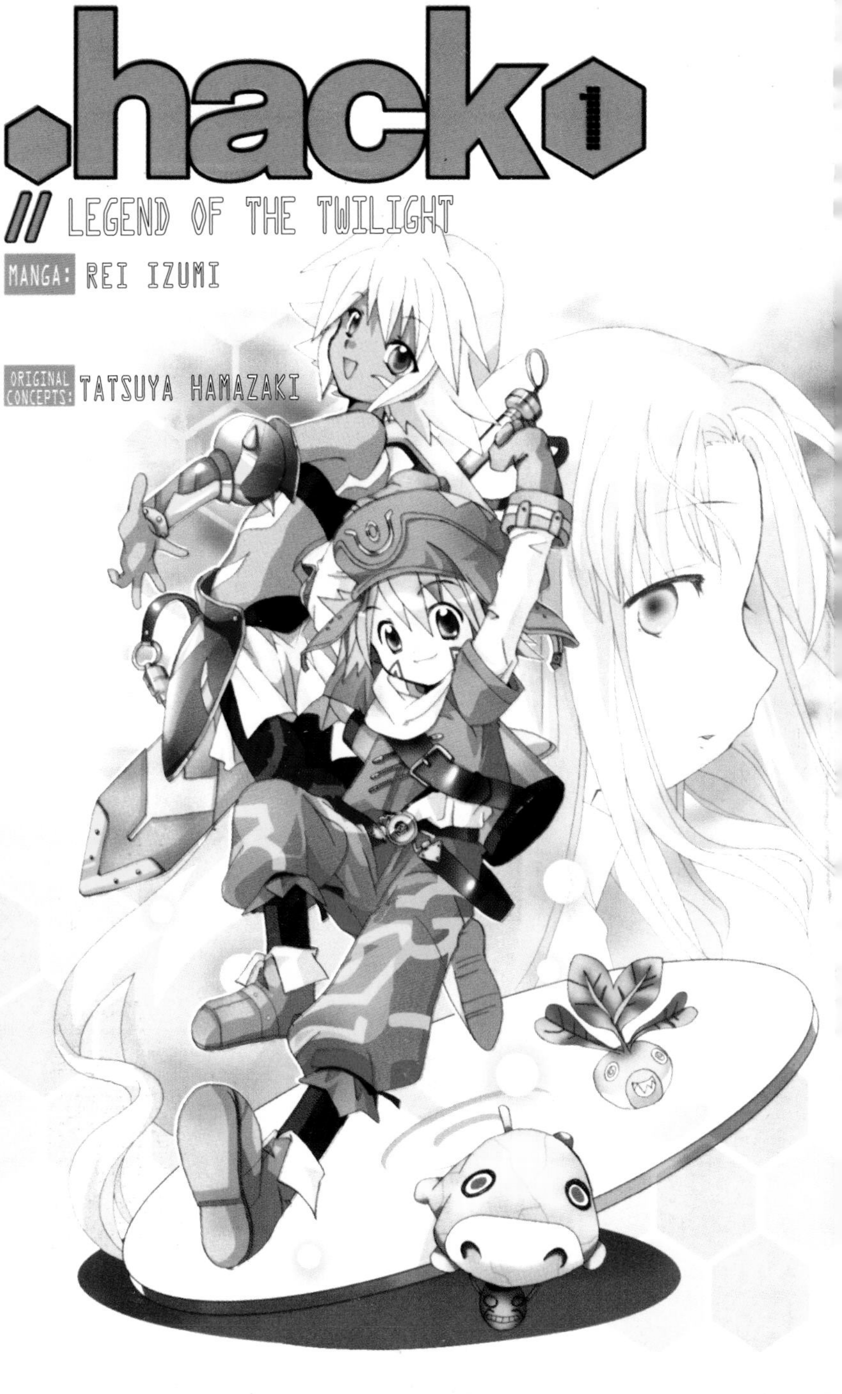

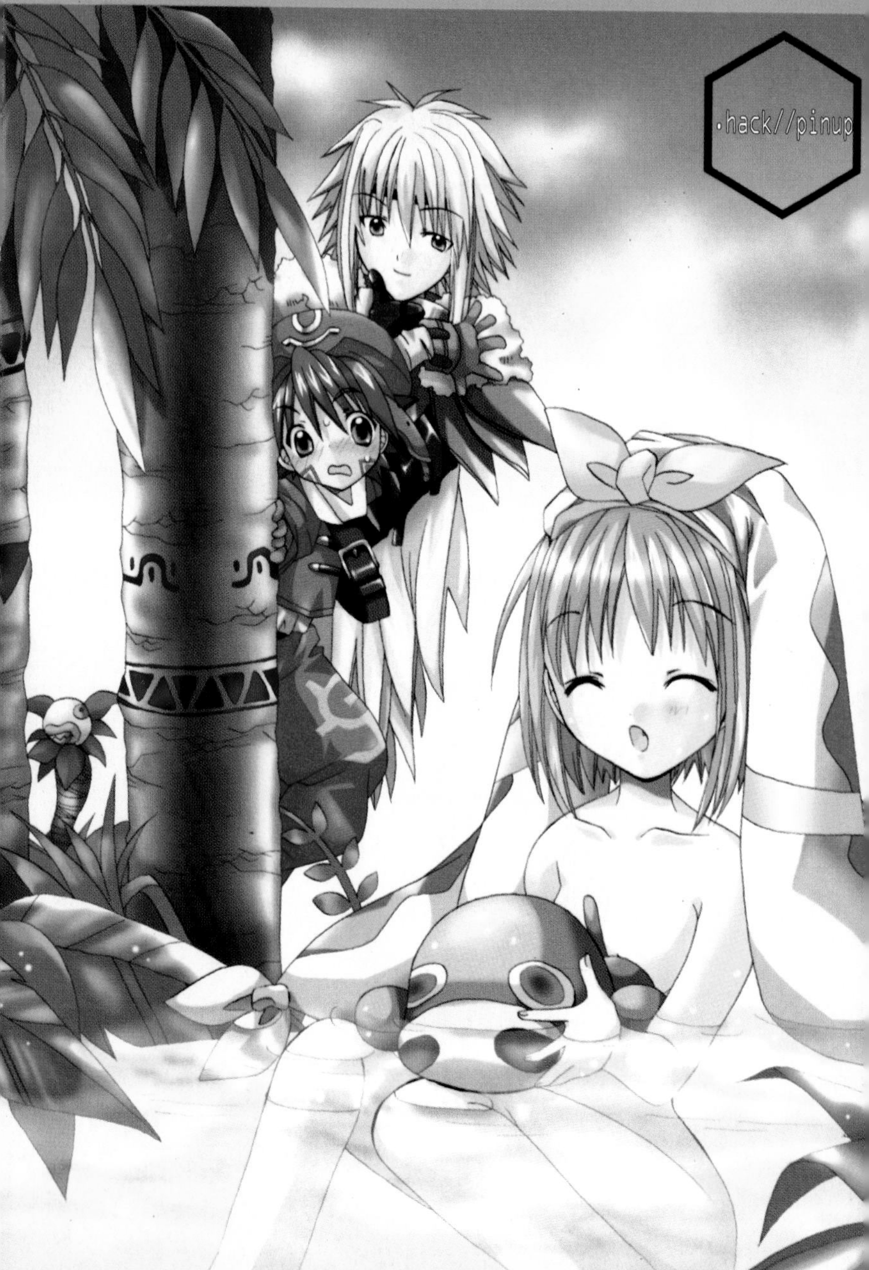
.hack//pinup

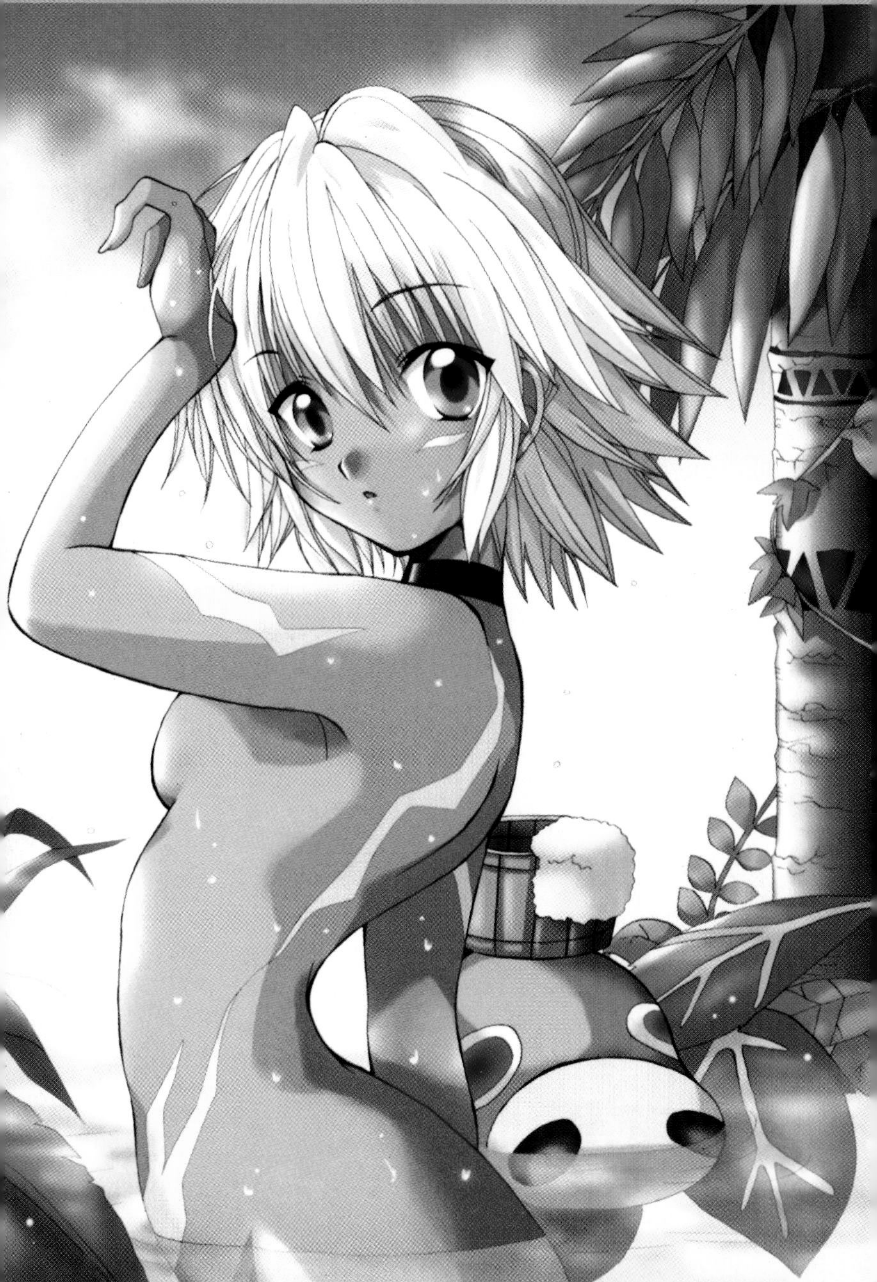

.hack//table of contents

.hack
// LEGEND OF THE TWILIGHT

Art by Rei Izumi
Story by Tatsuya Hamazaki

Volume 1

Los Angeles • Tokyo • London

Translator - Naomi Kokubo
English Adaptation - Jake Forbes
Associate Editor - Carol Fox
Copy Editor - Paul Morrissey
Retouch - Joe Llamazord
Lettering & Layout - Jake Forbes
Cover Layout - Aaron Suhr

Editor - Jake Forbes
Managing Editor - Jill Freshney
Production Coordinator - Antonio DePietro
Production Manager - Jennifer Miller
Art Director - Matt Alford
Editorial Director - Jeremy Ross
VP of Production - Ron Klamert
President & C.O.O. - John Parker
Publisher & C.E.O. - Stuart Levy

Email: editor@TOKYOPOP.com
Come visit us online at www.TOKYOPOP.com

A **TOKYOPOP** Manga

TOKYOPOP Inc.
5900 Wilshire Blvd. Suite 2000
Los Angeles, CA 90036

ISBN: 1-59182-414-1

First TOKYOPOP® printing: September 2003

10 9 8 7 6 5 4 3 2 1
Printed in the USA

ALSO AVAILABLE FROM TOKYOPOP®

MANGA

For more information visit www.TOKYOPOP.com

*INDICATES 100% AUTHENTIC MANGA (RIGHT-TO-LEFT FORMAT)

CINE-MANGA™

NOVELS

TOKYOPOP KIDS

ART BOOKS

ANIME GUIDES

062703

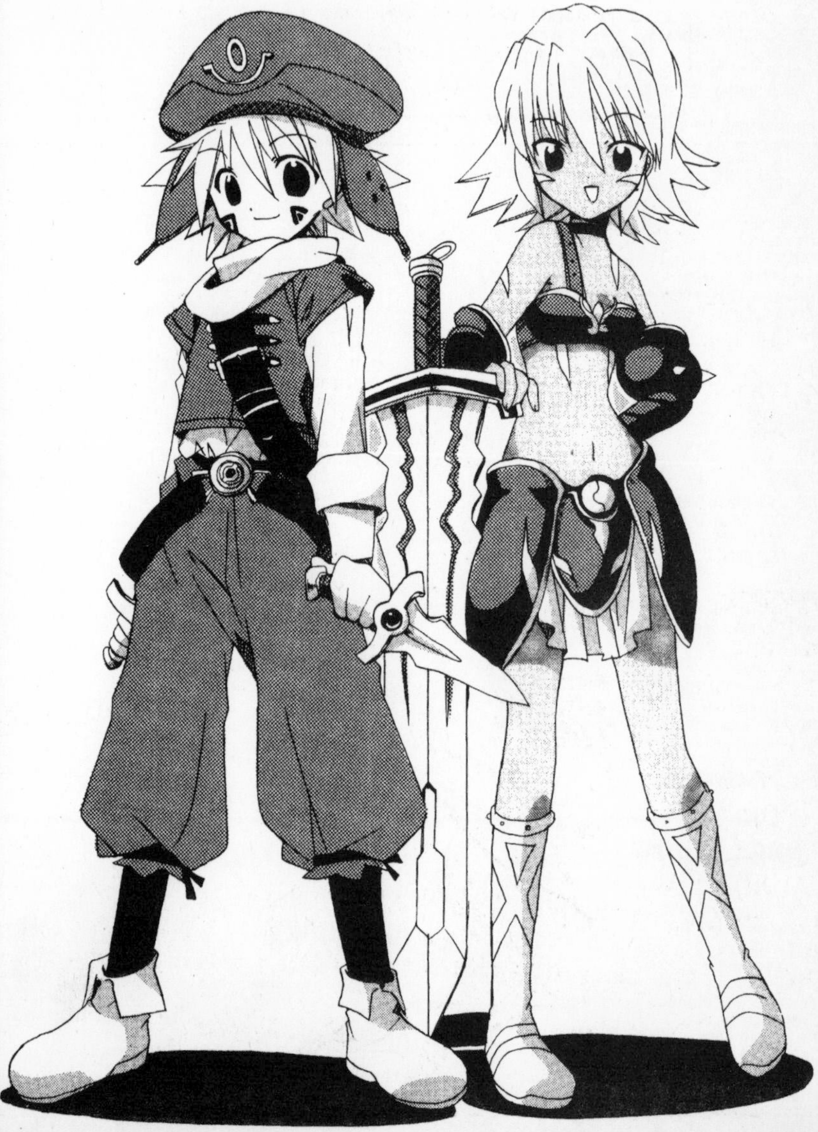

LOGIN 0
PROLOGUE

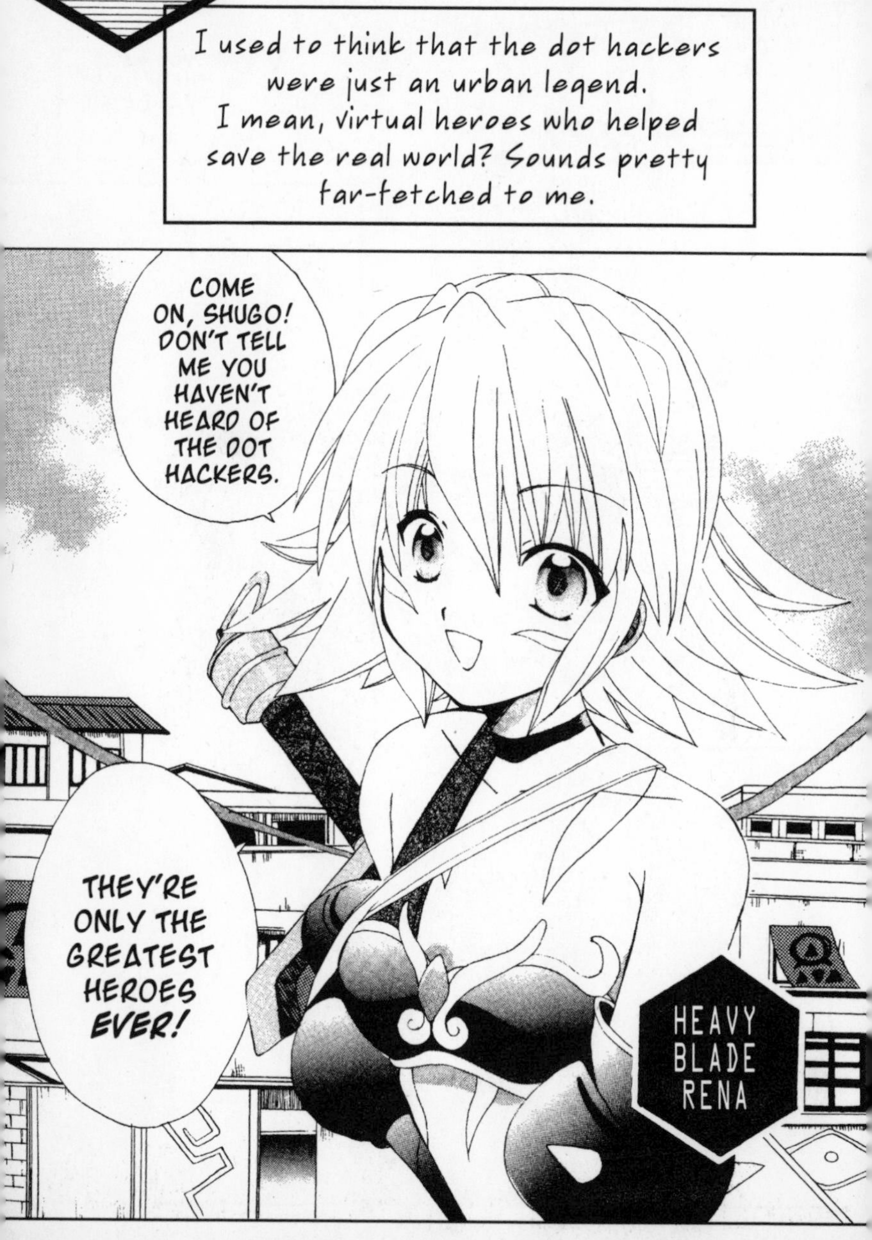
I used to think that the dot hackers were just an urban legend. I mean, virtual heroes who helped save the real world? Sounds pretty far-fetched to me.
COME ON, SHUGO! DON'T TELL ME YOU HAVEN'T HEARD OF THE DOT HACKERS.
THEY'RE ONLY THE GREATEST HEROES EVER!
HEAVY BLADE RENA

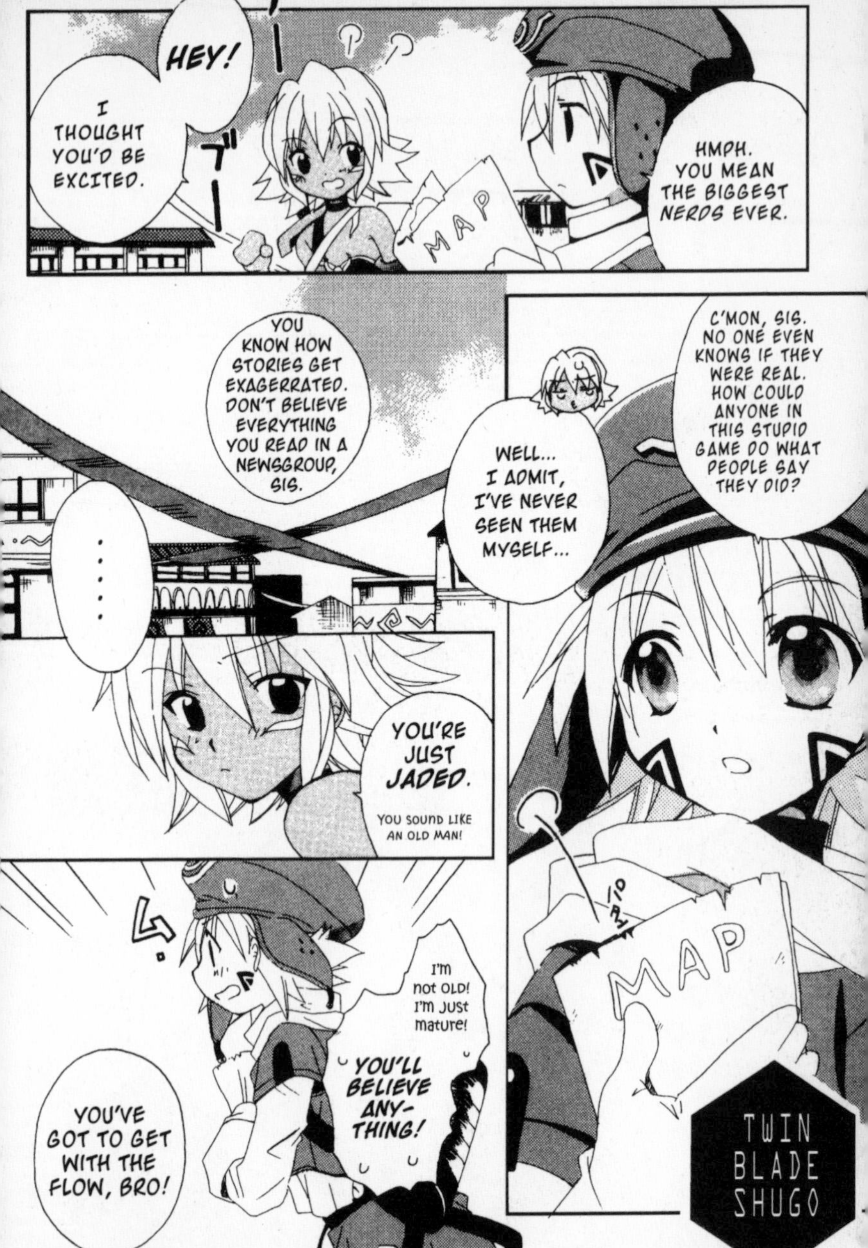
HMPH. YOU MEAN THE BIGGEST NERDS EVER.
ブー
HEY!
ブー
I THOUGHT YOU'D BE EXCITED.
MAP
C'MON, SIS. NO ONE EVEN KNOWS IF THEY WERE REAL. HOW COULD ANYONE IN THIS STUPID GAME DO WHAT PEOPLE SAY THEY DID?
WELL... I ADMIT, I'VE NEVER SEEN THEM MYSELF...
MAP
TWIN BLADE SHUGO
YOU KNOW HOW STORIES GET EXAGERRATED. DON'T BELIEVE EVERYTHING YOU READ IN A NEWSGROUP, SIS.
......
YOU'RE JUST JADED.
YOU SOUND LIKE AN OLD MAN!
I'm not OLD! I'm JUST mature!
YOU'LL BELIEVE ANY-THING!
YOU'VE GOT TO GET WITH THE FLOW, BRO!

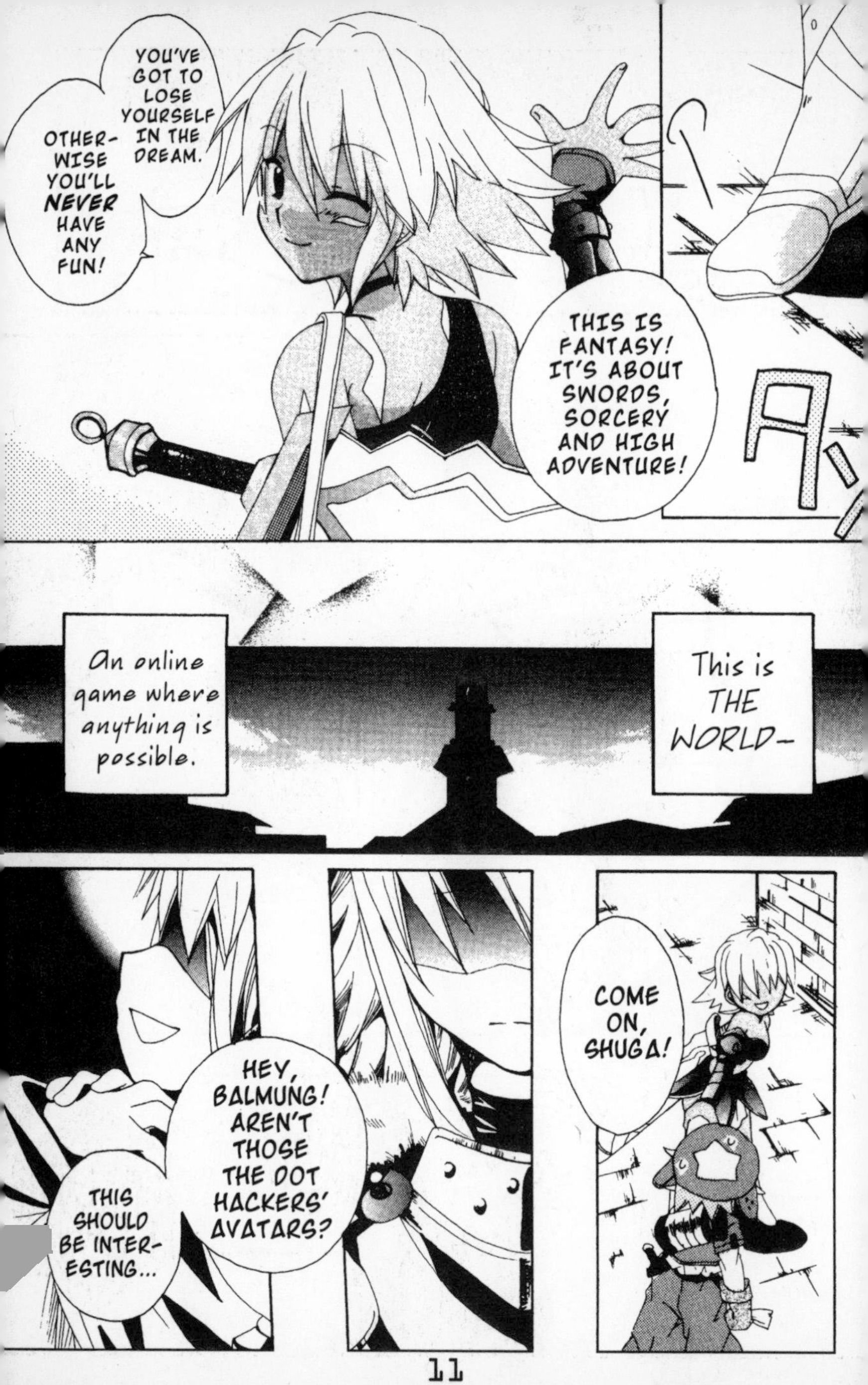
THIS IS FANTASY! IT'S ABOUT SWORDS, SORCERY AND HIGH ADVENTURE!
YOU'VE GOT TO LOSE YOURSELF IN THE DREAM. OTHER-WISE YOU'LL **NEVER** HAVE ANY FUN!
This is THE WORLD-
An online game where anything is possible.
COME ON, SHUGA!
HEY, BALMUNG! AREN'T THOSE THE DOT HACKERS' AVATARS?
THIS SHOULD BE INTER-ESTING...

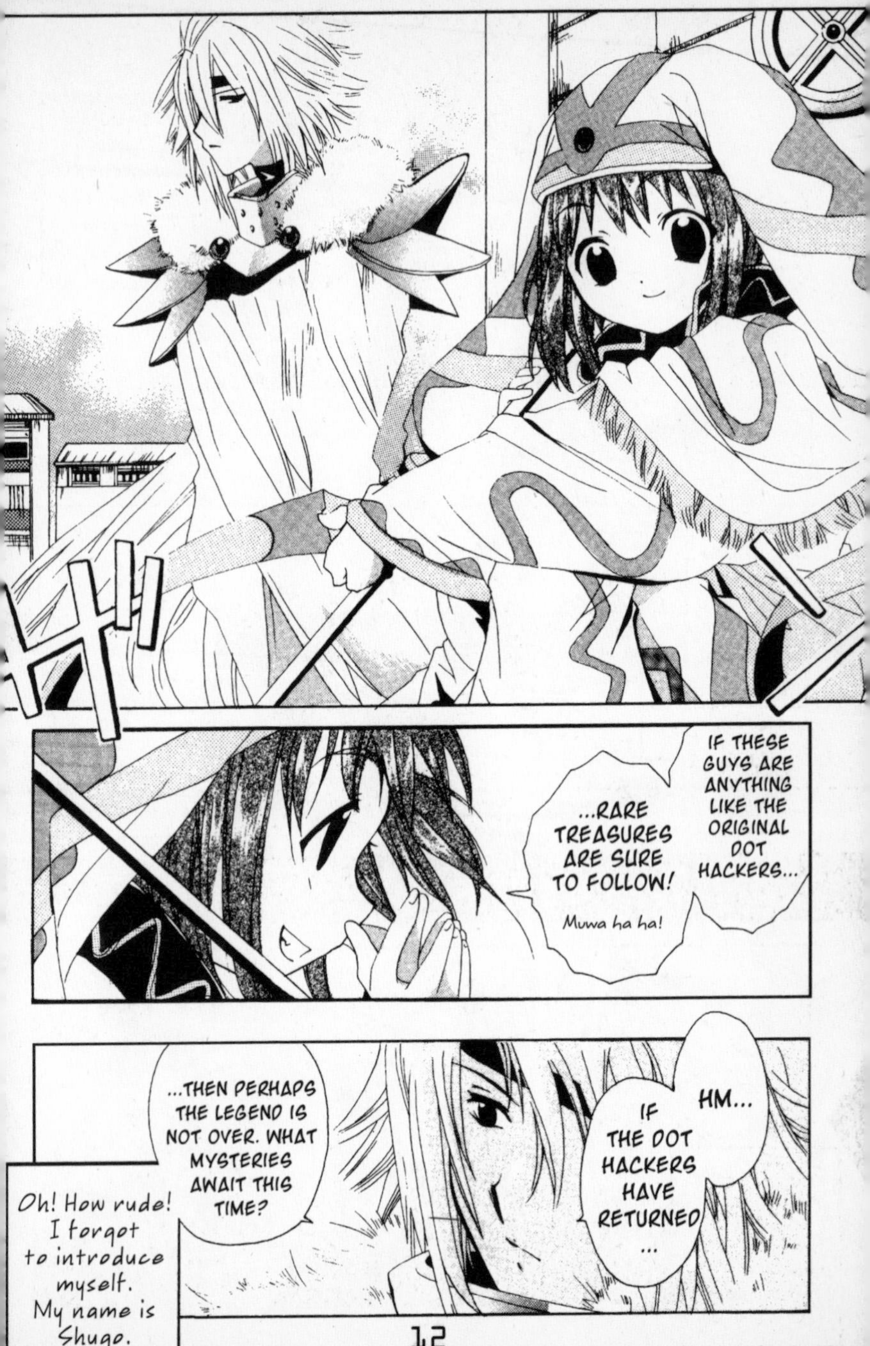
IF THESE GUYS ARE ANYTHING LIKE THE ORIGINAL DOT HACKERS...
...RARE TREASURES ARE SURE TO FOLLOW!
Muwa ha ha!
HM...
IF THE DOT HACKERS HAVE RETURNED...
...THEN PERHAPS THE LEGEND IS NOT OVER. WHAT MYSTERIES AWAIT THIS TIME?
Oh! How rude! I forgot to introduce myself. My name is Shugo.

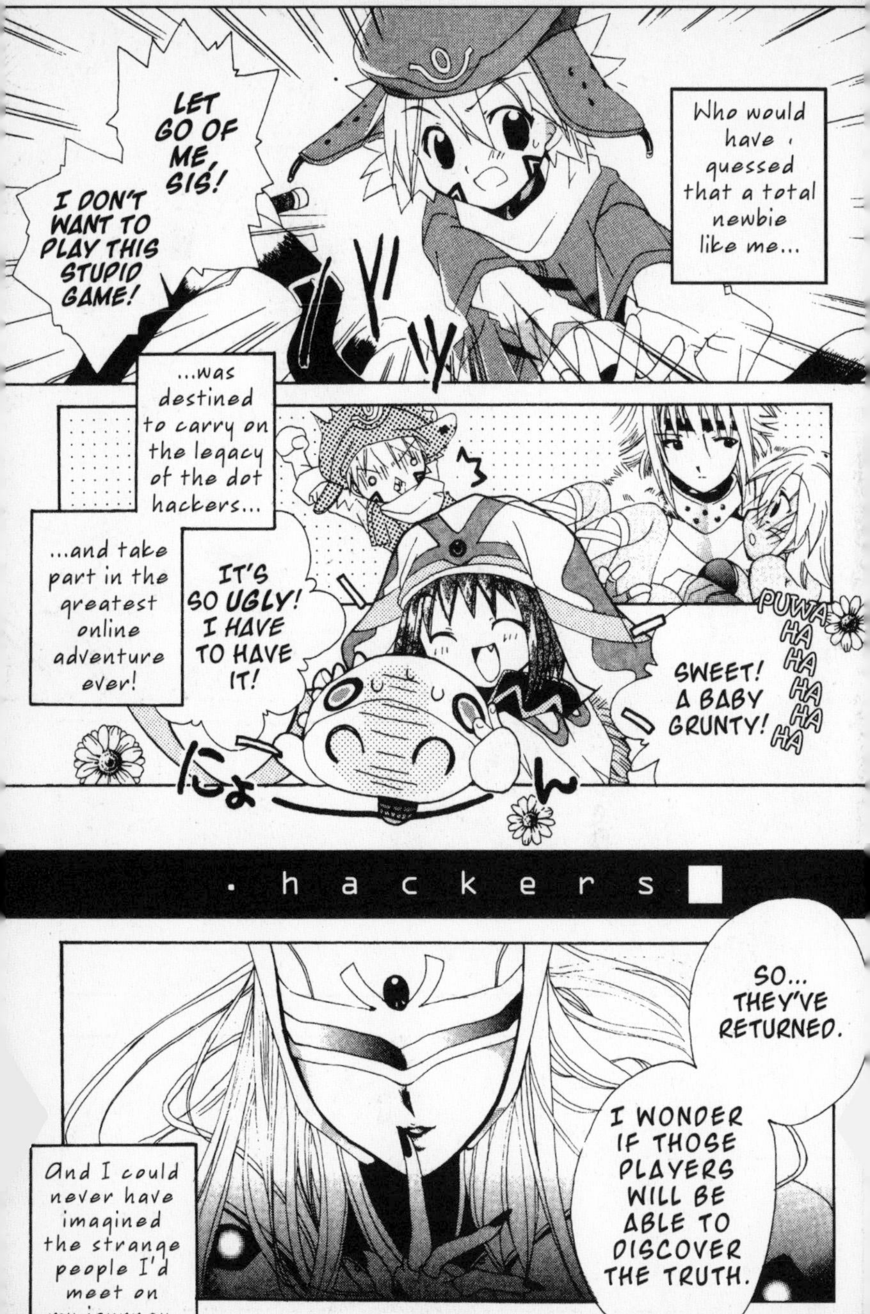

Who would have guessed that a total newbie like me...
LET GO OF ME, SIS!
I DON'T WANT TO PLAY THIS STUPID GAME!
...was destined to carry on the legacy of the dot hackers...
...and take part in the greatest online adventure ever!
PUWA HA HA HA HA HA
SWEET! A BABY GRUNTY!
IT'S SO UGLY! I HAVE TO HAVE IT!
にょん
.hackers
SO... THEY'VE RETURNED.
I WONDER IF THOSE PLAYERS WILL BE ABLE TO DISCOVER THE TRUTH.
And I could never have imagined the strange people I'd meet on my journey.

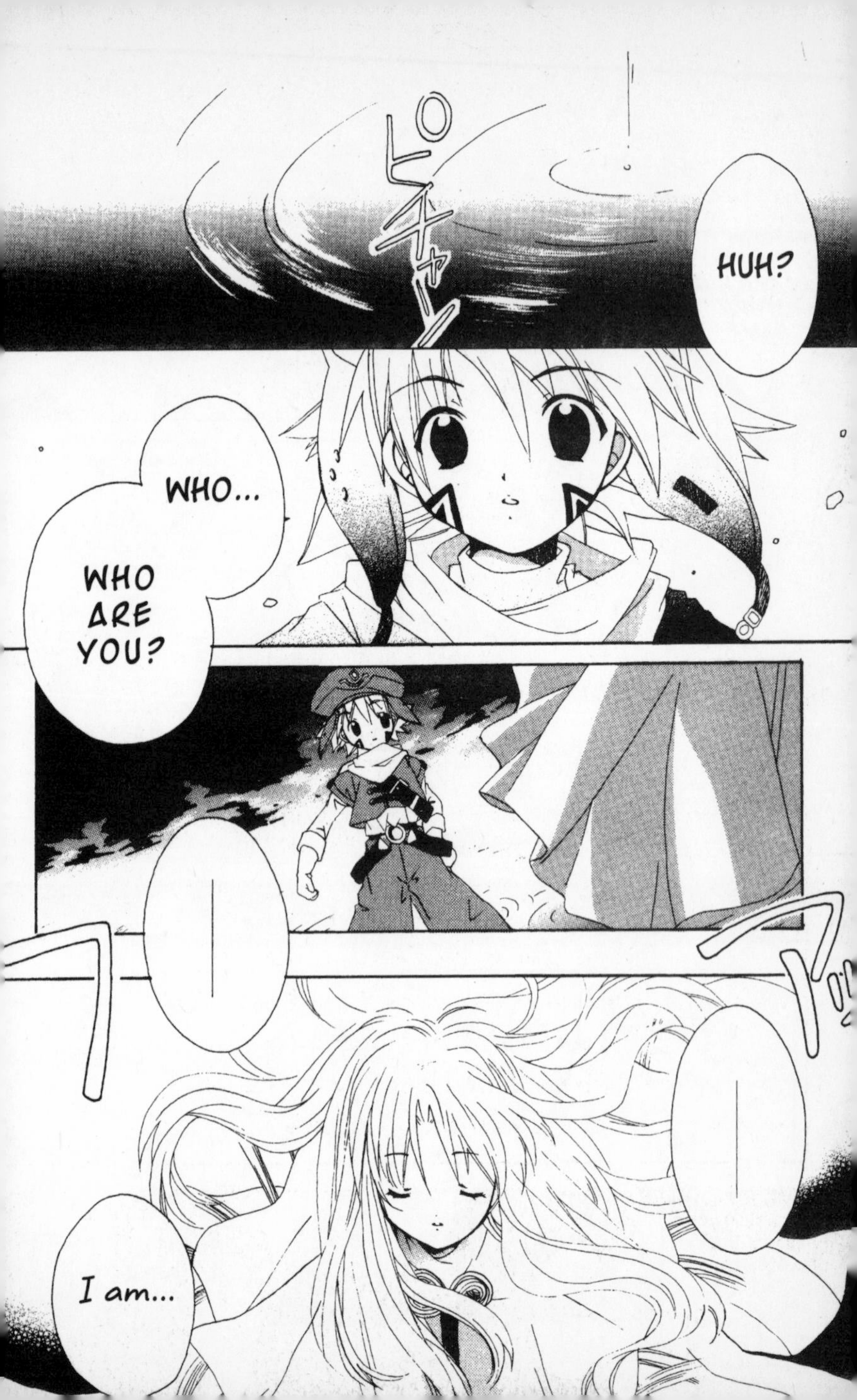
ピチャーン
HUH?
WHO...
WHO ARE YOU?
I am...

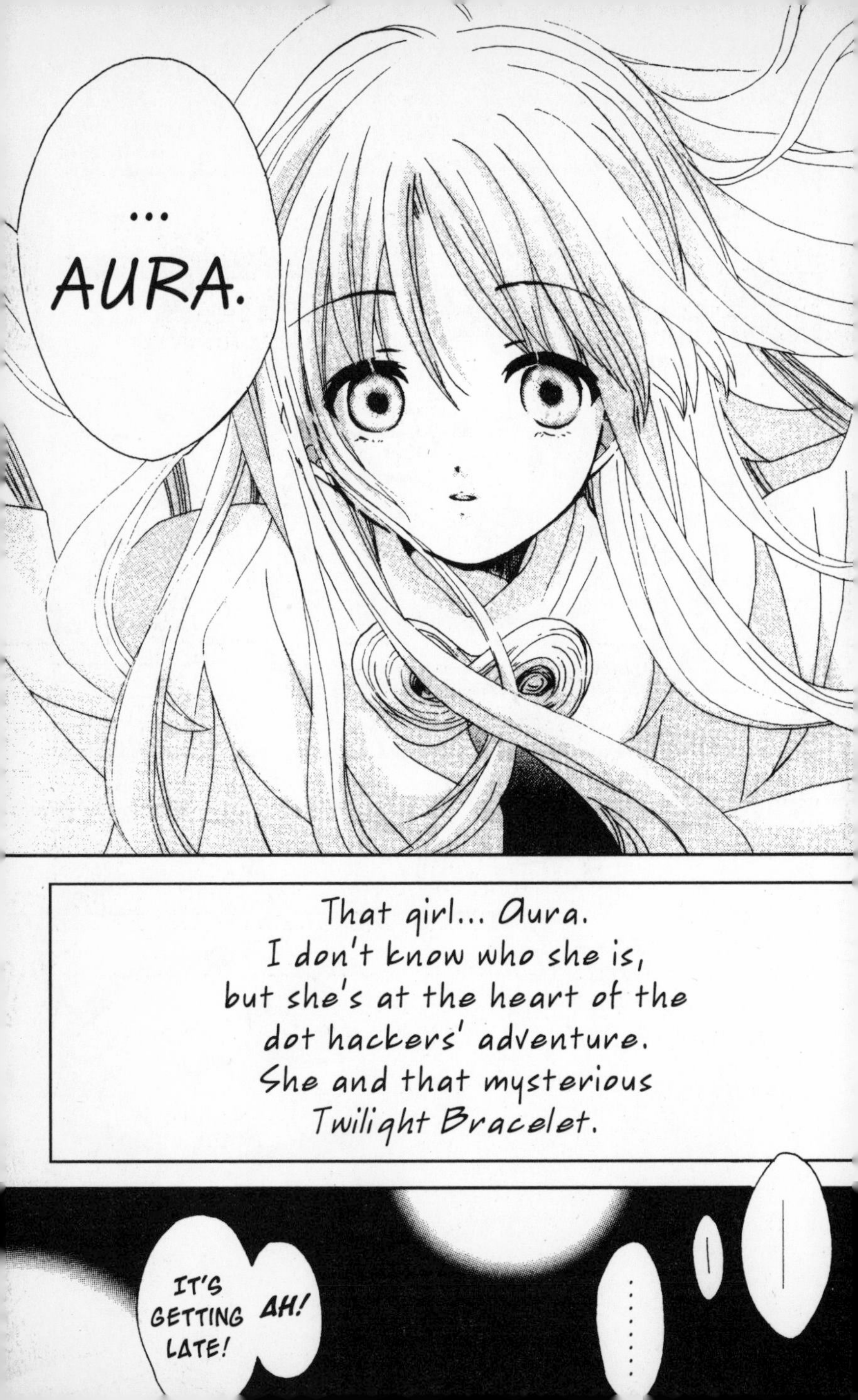

... AURA.
That girl... Aura. I don't know who she is, but she's at the heart of the dot hackers' adventure. She and that mysterious Twilight Bracelet.
......
AH!
IT'S GETTING LATE!

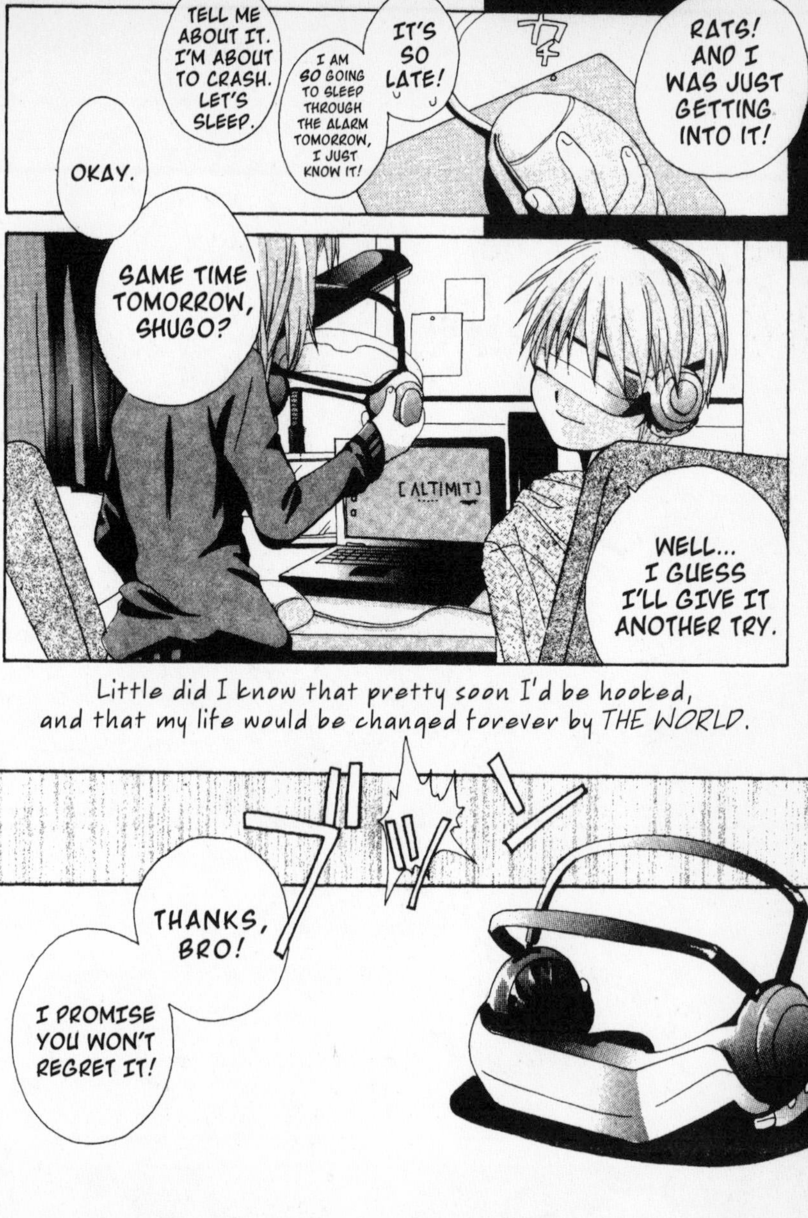
RATS! AND I WAS JUST GETTING INTO IT!
IT'S SO LATE!
I AM SO GOING TO SLEEP THROUGH THE ALARM TOMORROW, I JUST KNOW IT!
TELL ME ABOUT IT. I'M ABOUT TO CRASH. LET'S SLEEP.
OKAY.
SAME TIME TOMORROW, SHUGO?
[ALTIMIT]
WELL... I GUESS I'LL GIVE IT ANOTHER TRY.
Little did I know that pretty soon I'd be hooked, and that my life would be changed forever by THE WORLD.
THANKS, BRO!
I PROMISE YOU WON'T REGRET IT!

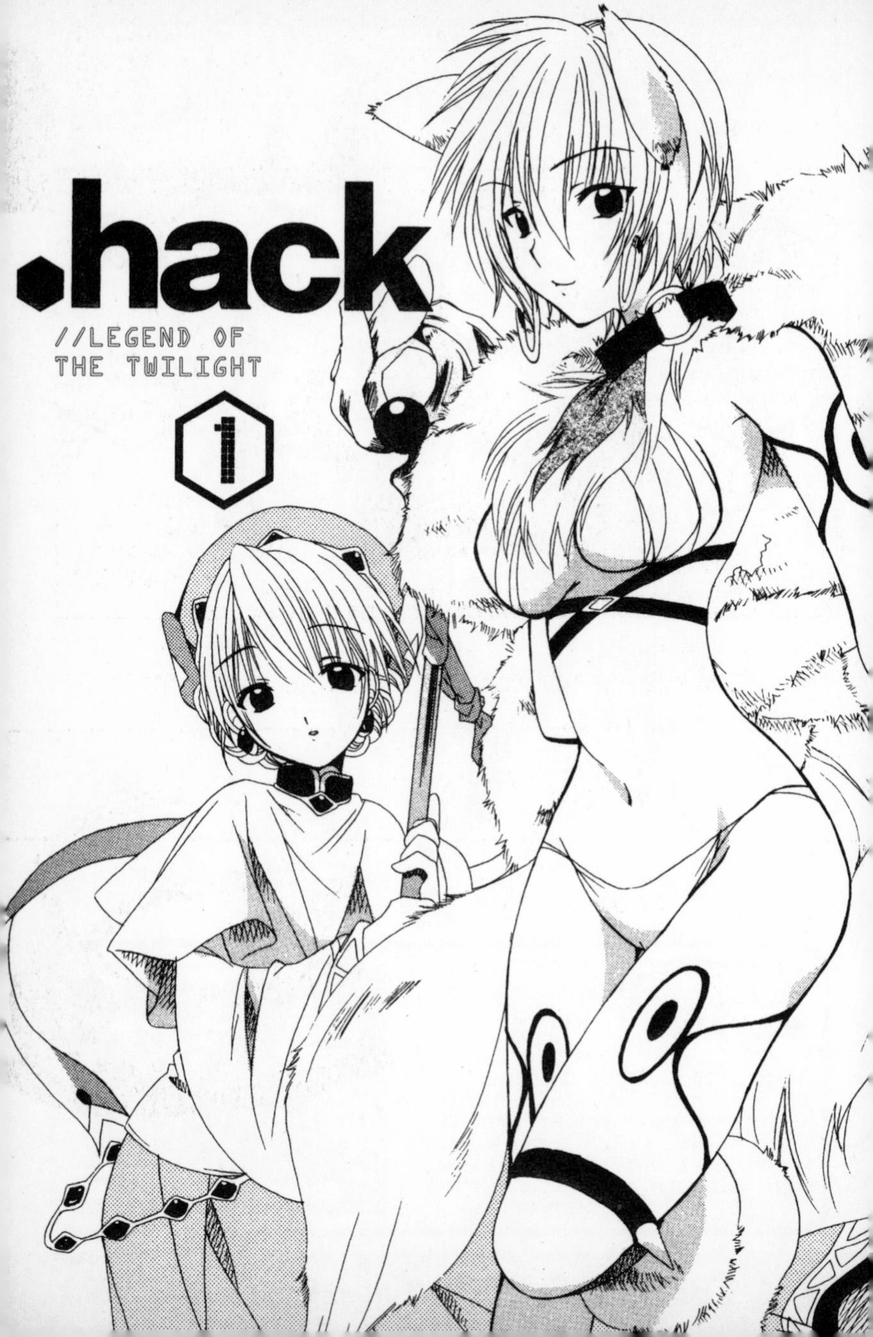
.hack
//LEGEND OF
THE TWILIGHT
1

キャラクター紹介

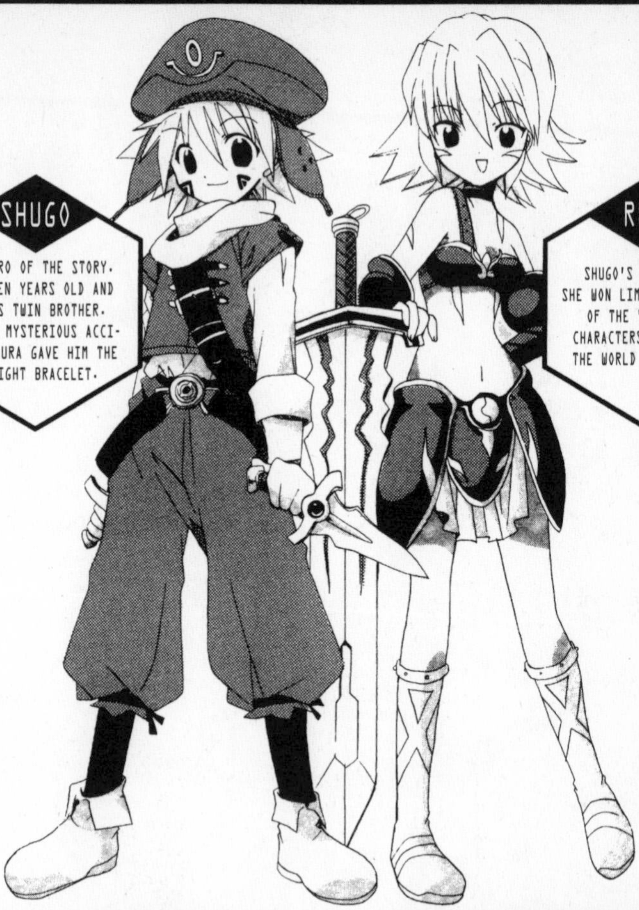

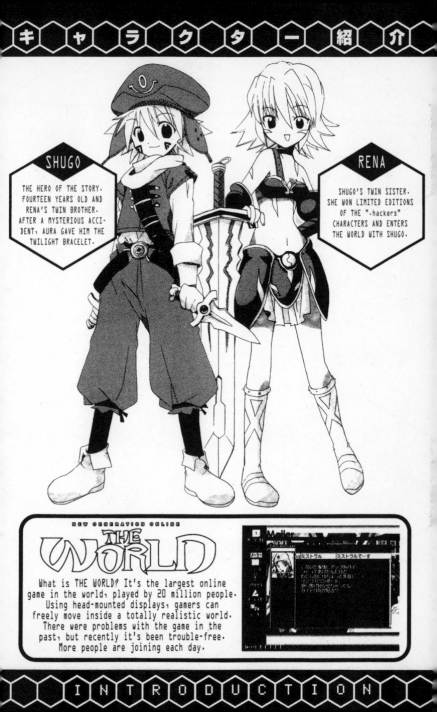

SHUGO

THE HERO OF THE STORY. FOURTEEN YEARS OLD AND RENA'S TWIN BROTHER. AFTER A MYSTERIOUS ACCIDENT, AURA GAVE HIM THE TWILIGHT BRACELET.

RENA

SHUGO'S TWIN SISTER. SHE WON LIMITED EDITIONS OF THE ".hackers" CHARACTERS AND ENTERS THE WORLD WITH SHUGO.

NEW GENERATION ONLINE

THE WORLD

What is THE WORLD? It's the largest online game in the world, played by 20 million people. Using head-mounted displays, gamers can freely move inside a totally realistic world. There were problems with the game in the past, but recently it's been trouble-free. More people are joining each day.

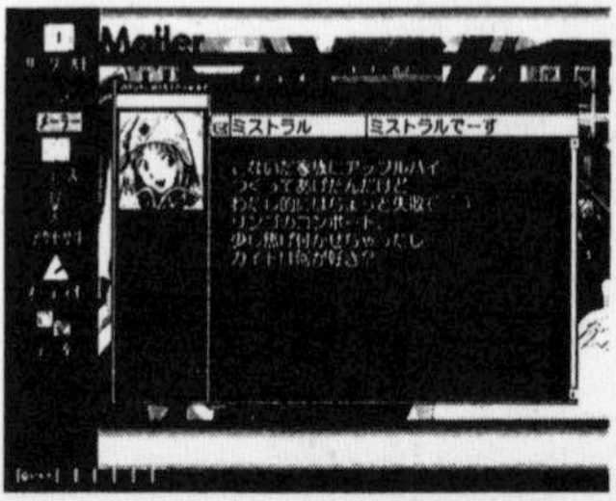
Mailer
ミストラル
ミストラルでーす

INTRODUCTION

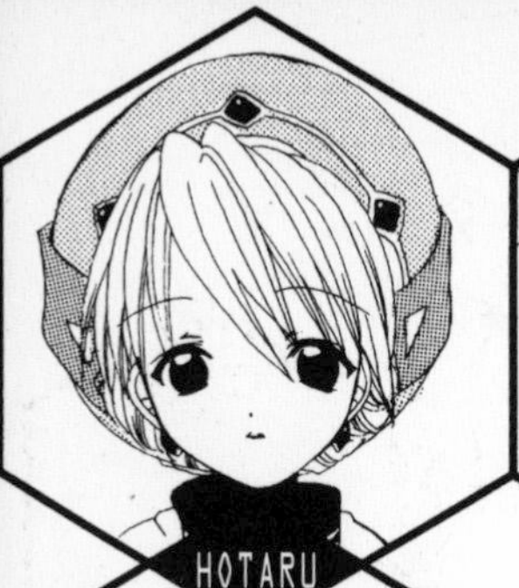

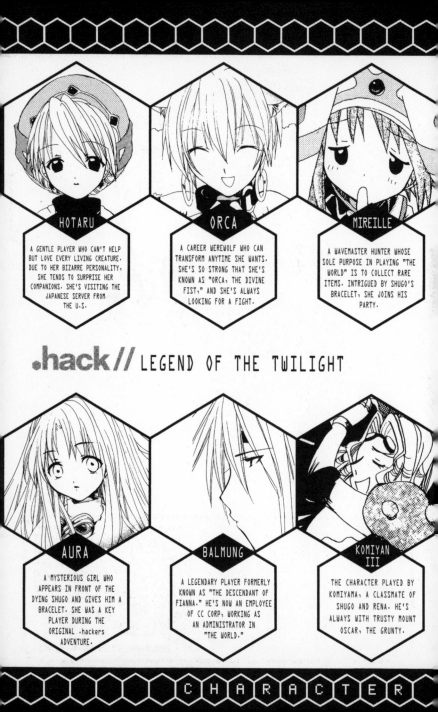

HOTARU

A GENTLE PLAYER WHO CAN'T HELP BUT LOVE EVERY LIVING CREATURE. DUE TO HER BIZARRE PERSONALITY, SHE TENDS TO SURPRISE HER COMPANIONS. SHE'S VISITING THE JAPANESE SERVER FROM THE U.S.

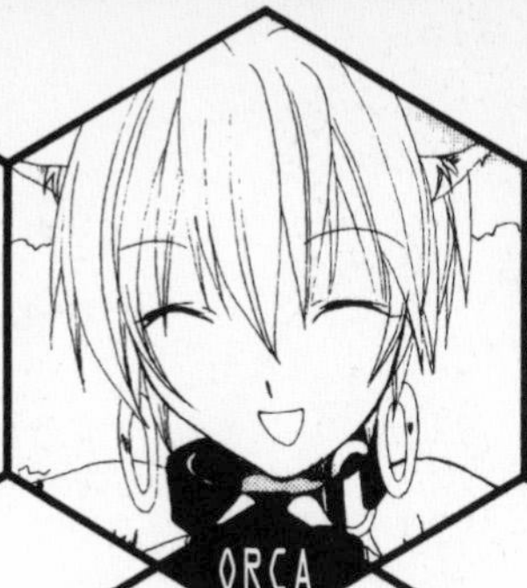

ORCA

A CAREER WEREWOLF WHO CAN TRANSFORM ANYTIME SHE WANTS. SHE'S SO STRONG THAT SHE'S KNOWN AS "ORCA, THE DIVINE FIST," AND SHE'S ALWAYS LOOKING FOR A FIGHT.

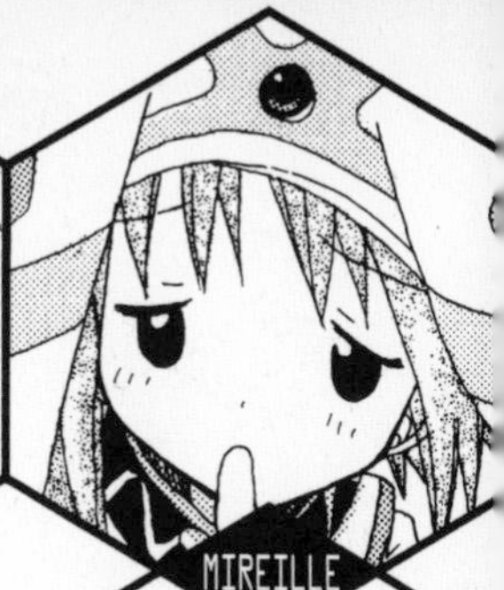

MIREILLE

A WAVEMASTER HUNTER WHOSE SOLE PURPOSE IN PLAYING "THE WORLD" IS TO COLLECT RARE ITEMS. INTRIGUED BY SHUGO'S BRACELET, SHE JOINS HIS PARTY.

.hack// LEGEND OF THE TWILIGHT

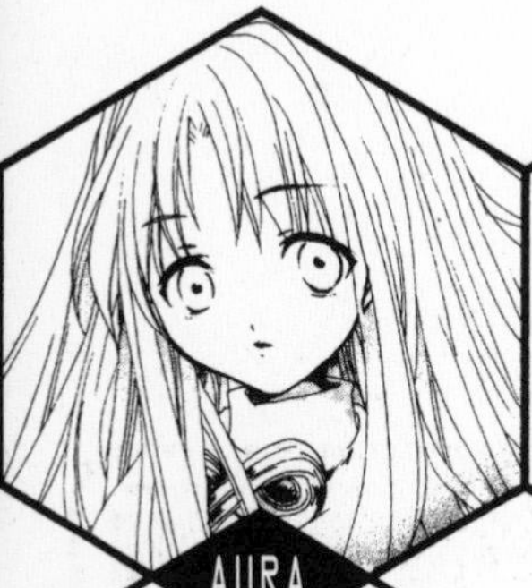

AURA

A MYSTERIOUS GIRL WHO APPEARS IN FRONT OF THE DYING SHUGO AND GIVES HIM A BRACELET. SHE WAS A KEY PLAYER DURING THE ORIGINAL .hackers ADVENTURE.

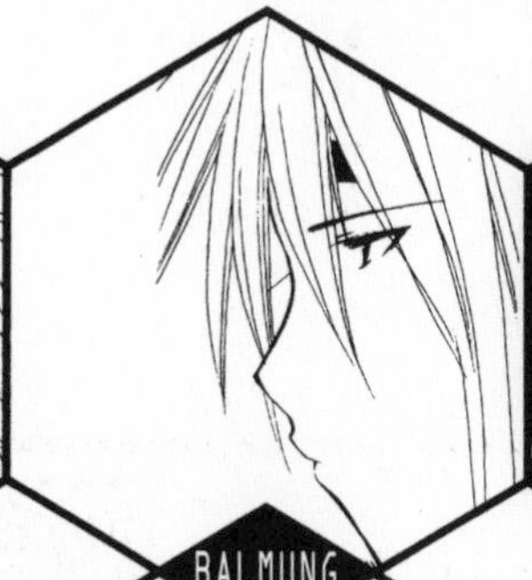

BALMUNG

A LEGENDARY PLAYER FORMERLY KNOWN AS "THE DESCENDANT OF FIANNA." HE'S NOW AN EMPLOYEE OF CC CORP, WORKING AS AN ADMINISTRATOR IN "THE WORLD."

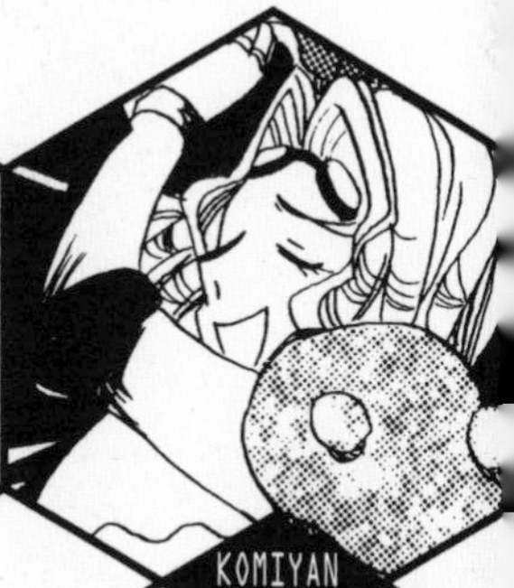

KOMIYAN III

THE CHARACTER PLAYED BY KOMIYAMA, A CLASSMATE OF SHUGO AND RENA. HE'S ALWAYS WITH TRUSTY MOUNT OSCAR, THE GRUNTY.

CHARACTER

NEW GENERATION ONLINE
THE WORLD™

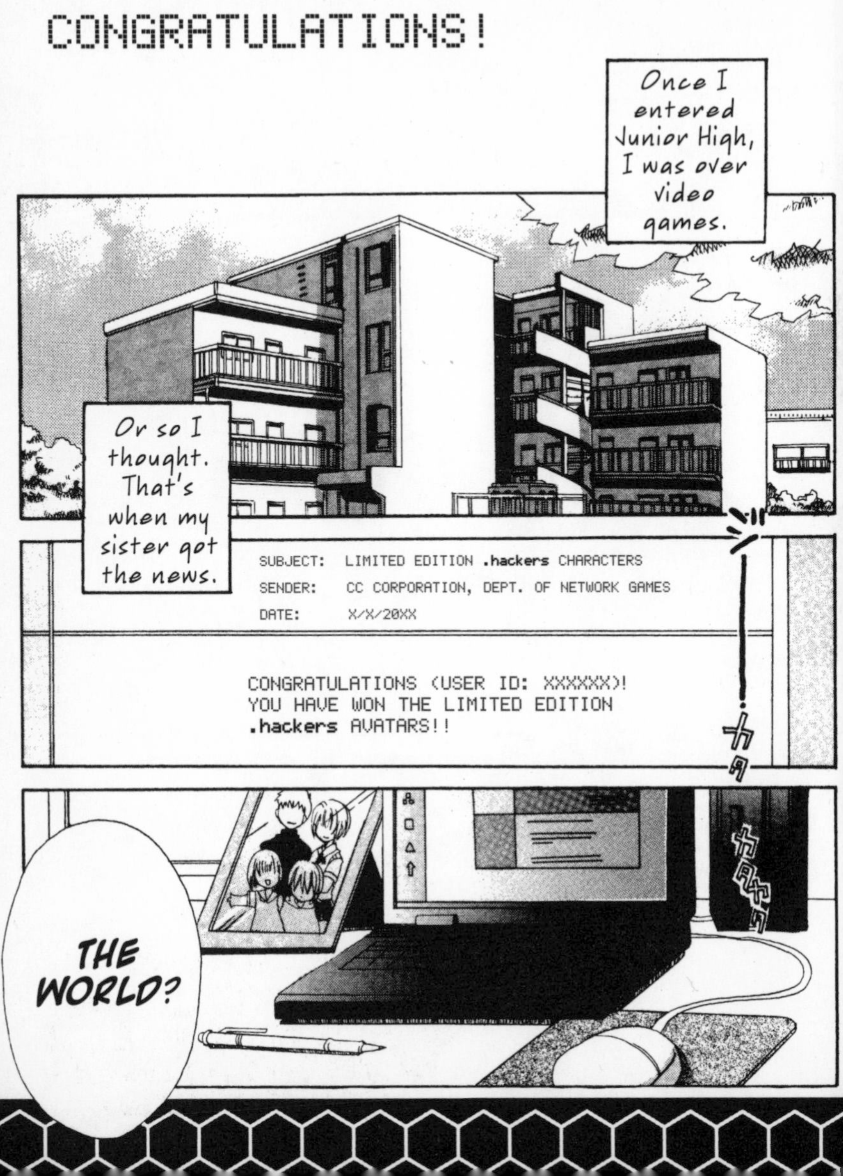
CONGRATULATIONS!
Once I entered Junior High, I was over video games.
Or so I thought. That's when my sister got the news.
SUBJECT: LIMITED EDITION .hackers CHARACTERS
SENDER: CC CORPORATION, DEPT. OF NETWORK GAMES
DATE: X/X/20XX
CONGRATULATIONS (USER ID: XXXXXX)! YOU HAVE WON THE LIMITED EDITION .hackers AVATARS!!
THE WORLD?

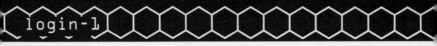

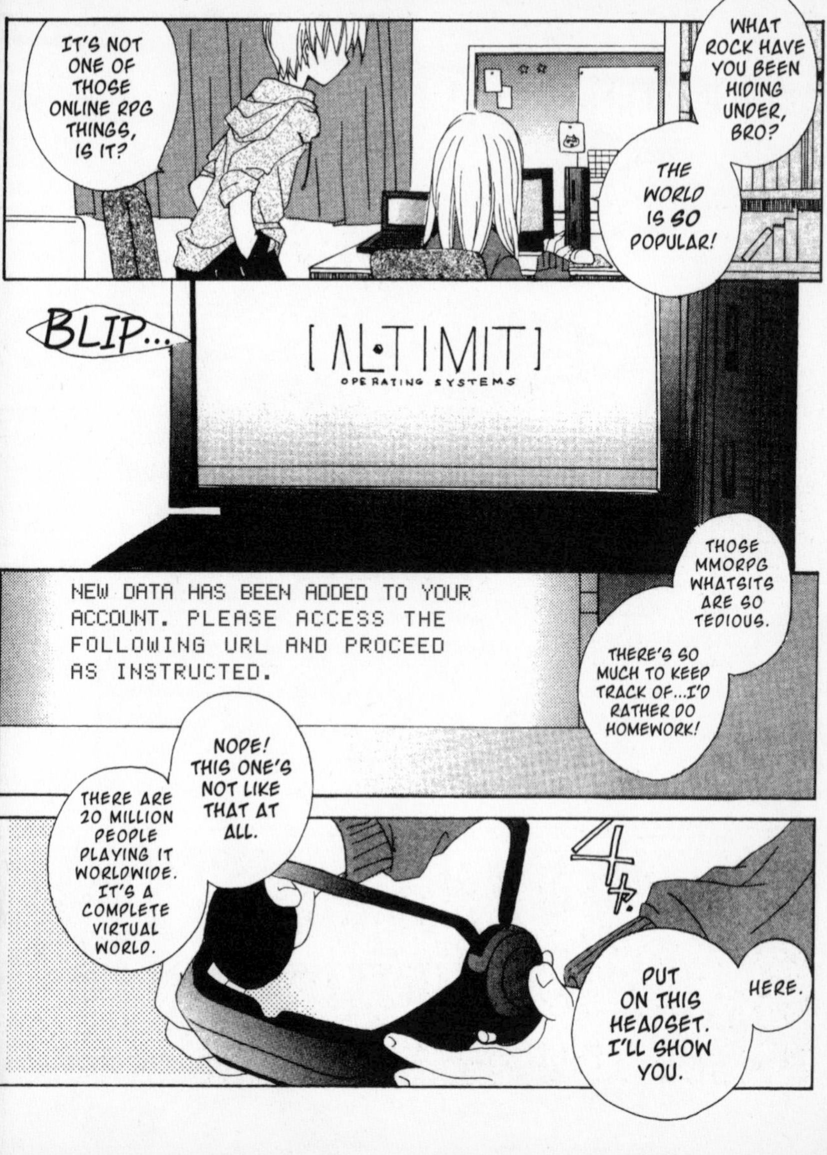
WHAT ROCK HAVE YOU BEEN HIDING UNDER, BRO?
THE WORLD IS SO POPULAR!
IT'S NOT ONE OF THOSE ONLINE RPG THINGS, IS IT?
BLIP...
[ALTIMIT]
OPERATING SYSTEMS
THOSE MMORPG WHATSITS ARE SO TEDIOUS.
THERE'S SO MUCH TO KEEP TRACK OF...I'D RATHER DO HOMEWORK!
NEW DATA HAS BEEN ADDED TO YOUR ACCOUNT. PLEASE ACCESS THE FOLLOWING URL AND PROCEED AS INSTRUCTED.
NOPE! THIS ONE'S NOT LIKE THAT AT ALL.
THERE ARE 20 MILLION PEOPLE PLAYING IT WORLDWIDE. IT'S A COMPLETE VIRTUAL WORLD.
HERE.
PUT ON THIS HEADSET. I'LL SHOW YOU.

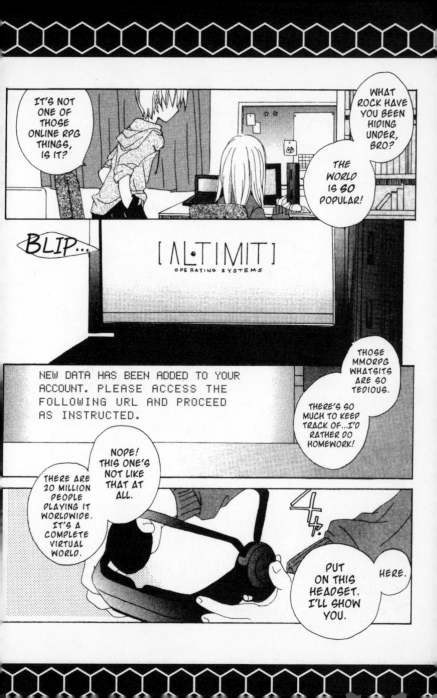

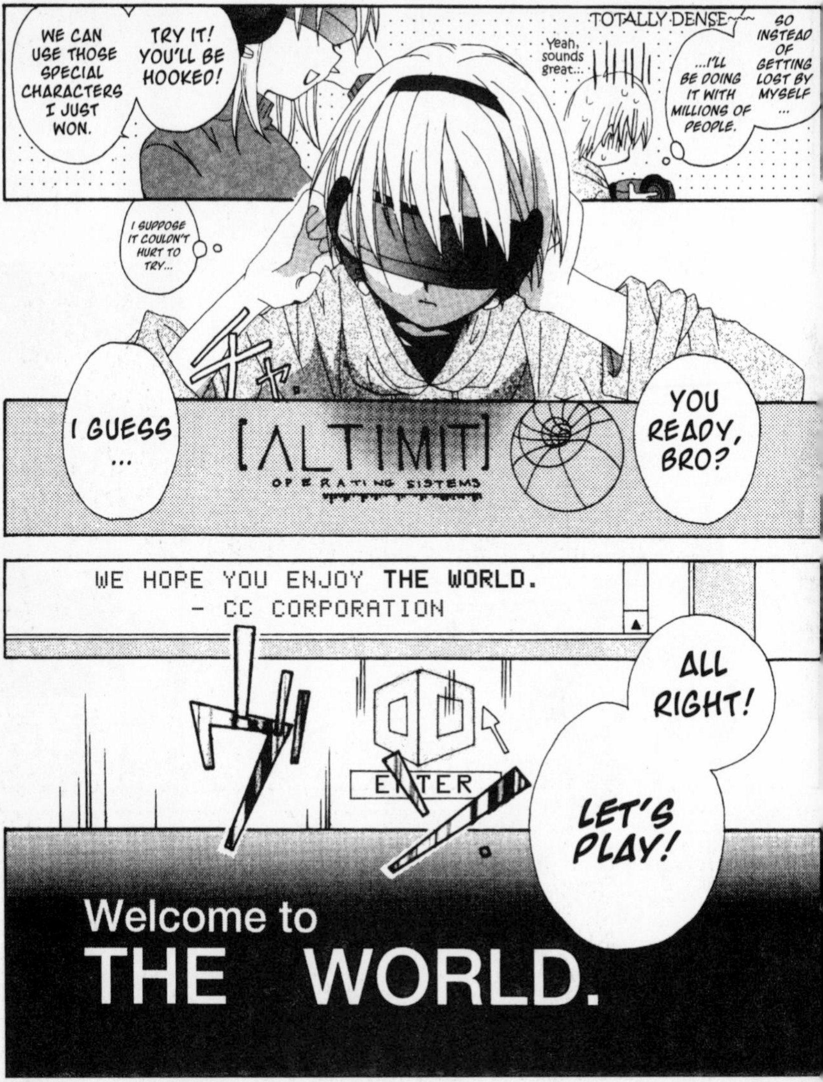
TOTALLY DENSE~~~
SO INSTEAD OF GETTING LOST BY MYSELF ...
...I'LL BE DOING IT WITH MILLIONS OF PEOPLE.
Yeah, sounds great...
TRY IT! YOU'LL BE HOOKED!
WE CAN USE THOSE SPECIAL CHARACTERS I JUST WON.
I SUPPOSE IT COULDN'T HURT TO TRY...
YOU READY, BRO?
[ALTIMIT]
OPERATING SISTEMS
I GUESS ...
WE HOPE YOU ENJOY THE WORLD.
- CC CORPORATION
ALL RIGHT!
LET'S PLAY!
ENTER
Welcome to
THE WORLD.

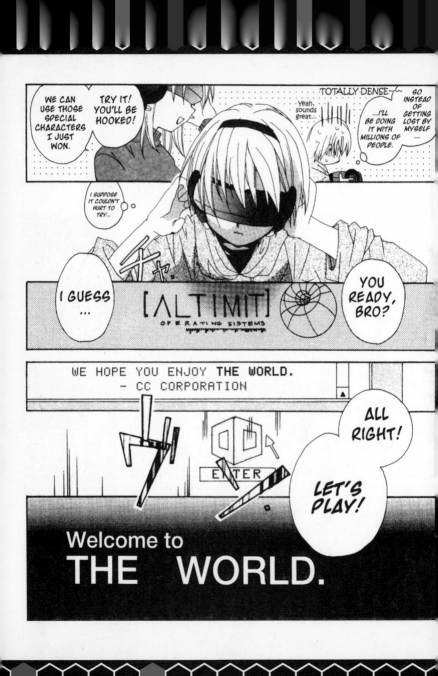

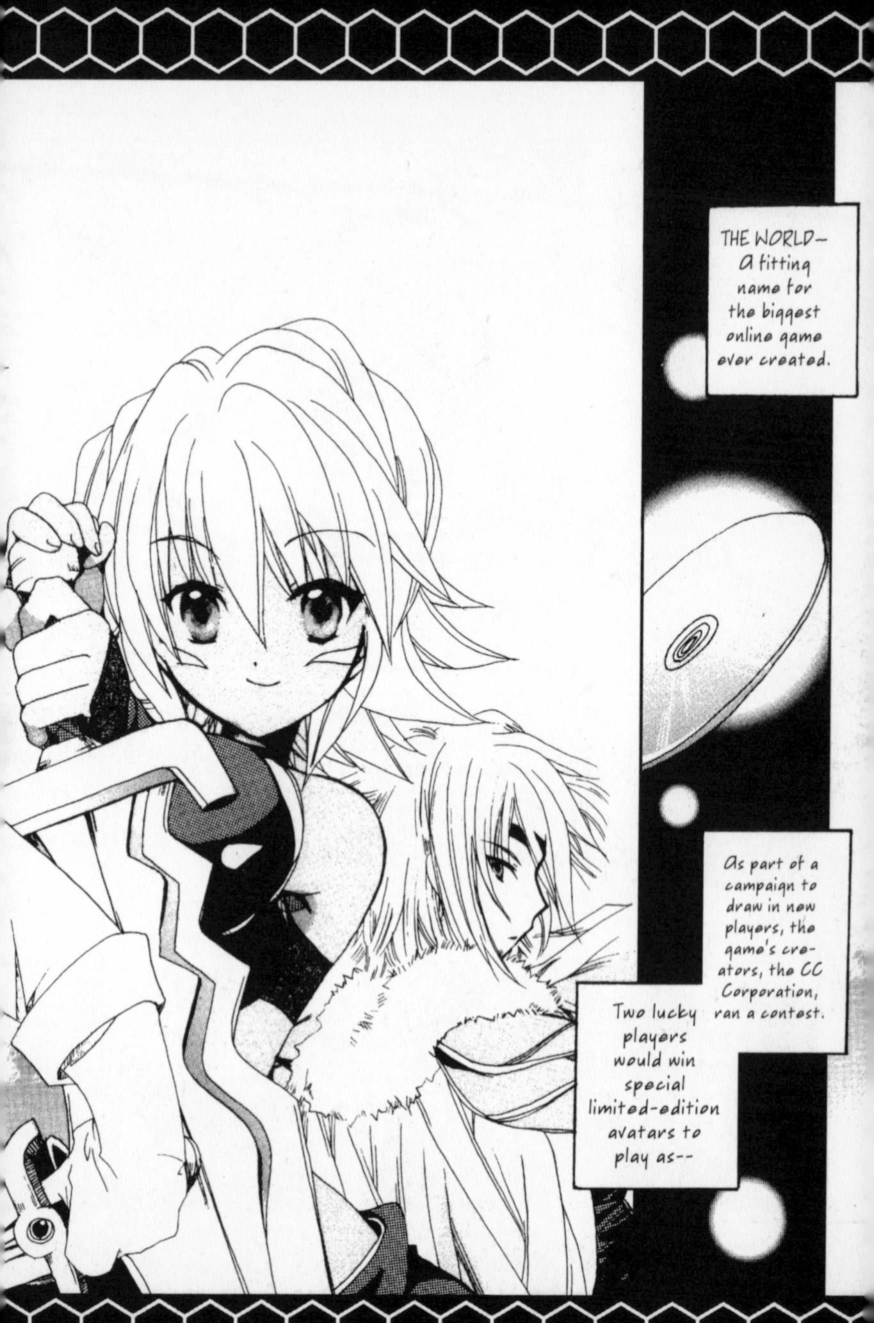
THE WORLD— a fitting name for the biggest online game ever created.
As part of a campaign to draw in new players, the game's creators, the CC Corporation, ran a contest.
Two lucky players would win special limited-edition avatars to play as--

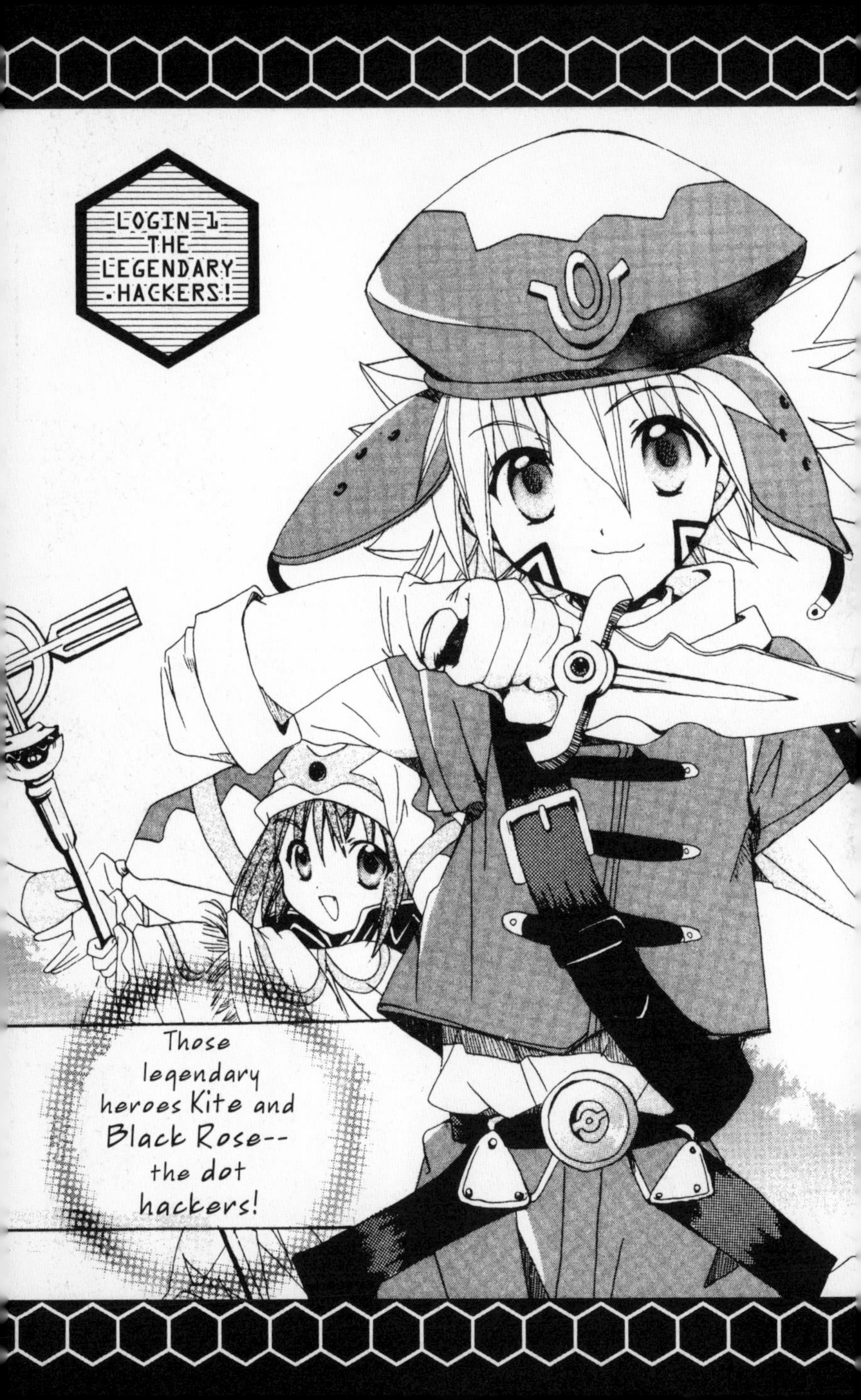
LOGIN 1 THE LEGENDARY HACKERS!
Those legendary heroes Kite and Black Rose-- the dot hackers!

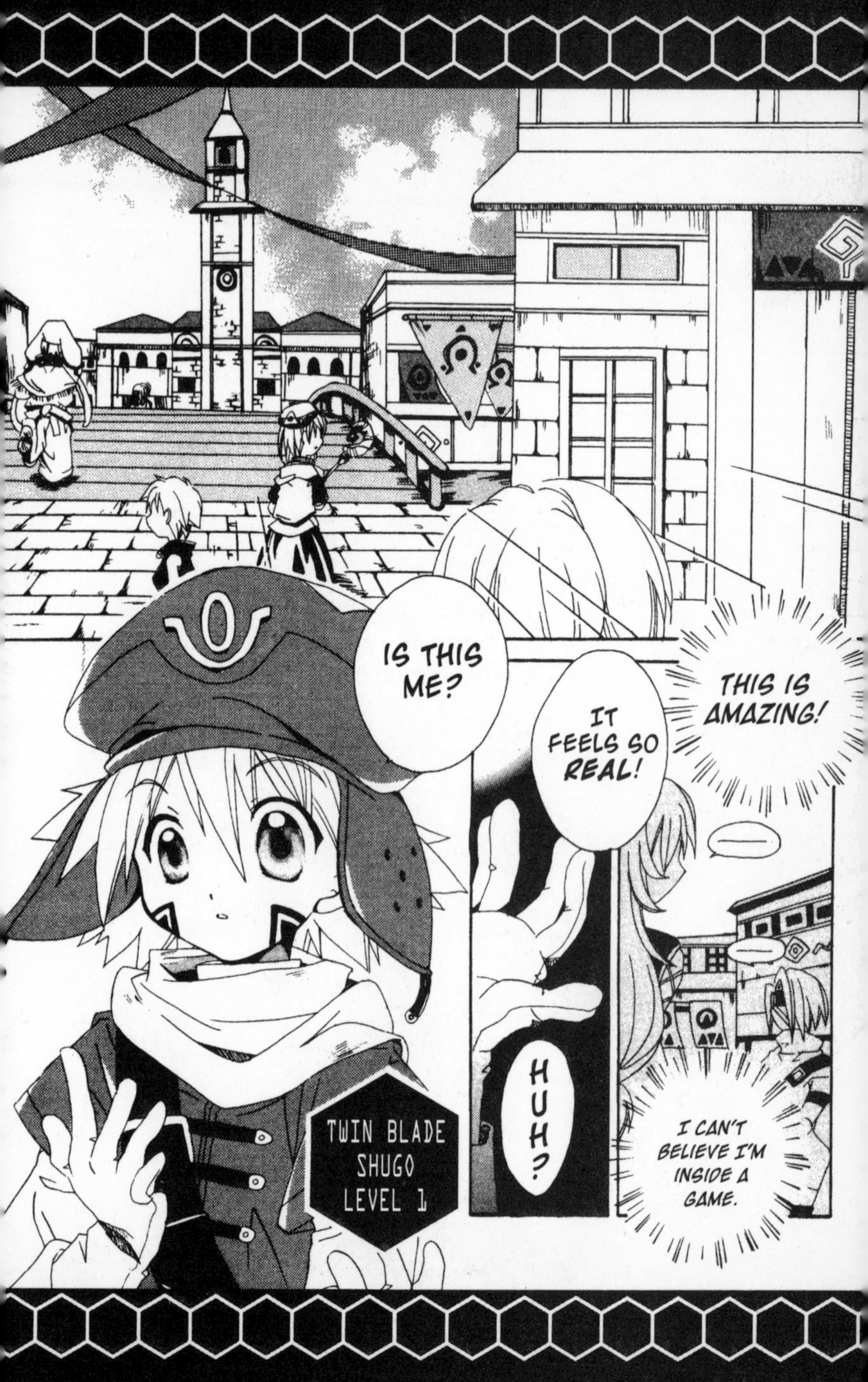
THIS IS AMAZING!
IT FEELS SO REAL!
IS THIS ME?
TWIN BLADE SHUGO LEVEL 1
—
—
I CAN'T BELIEVE I'M INSIDE A GAME.
HUH?

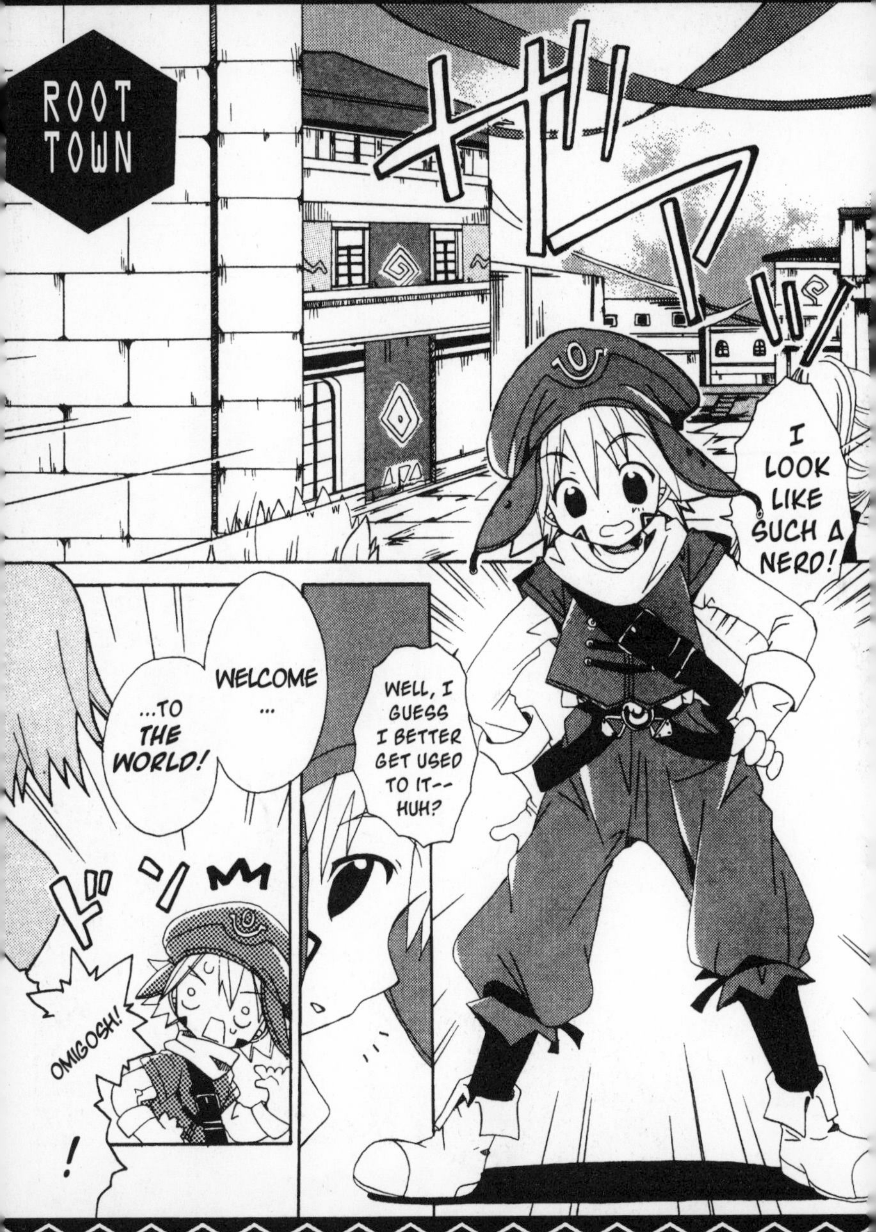
ROOT TOWN
I LOOK LIKE SUCH A NERD!
WELL, I GUESS I BETTER GET USED TO IT--HUH?
WELCOME...
...TO THE WORLD!
OMIGOSH!
!

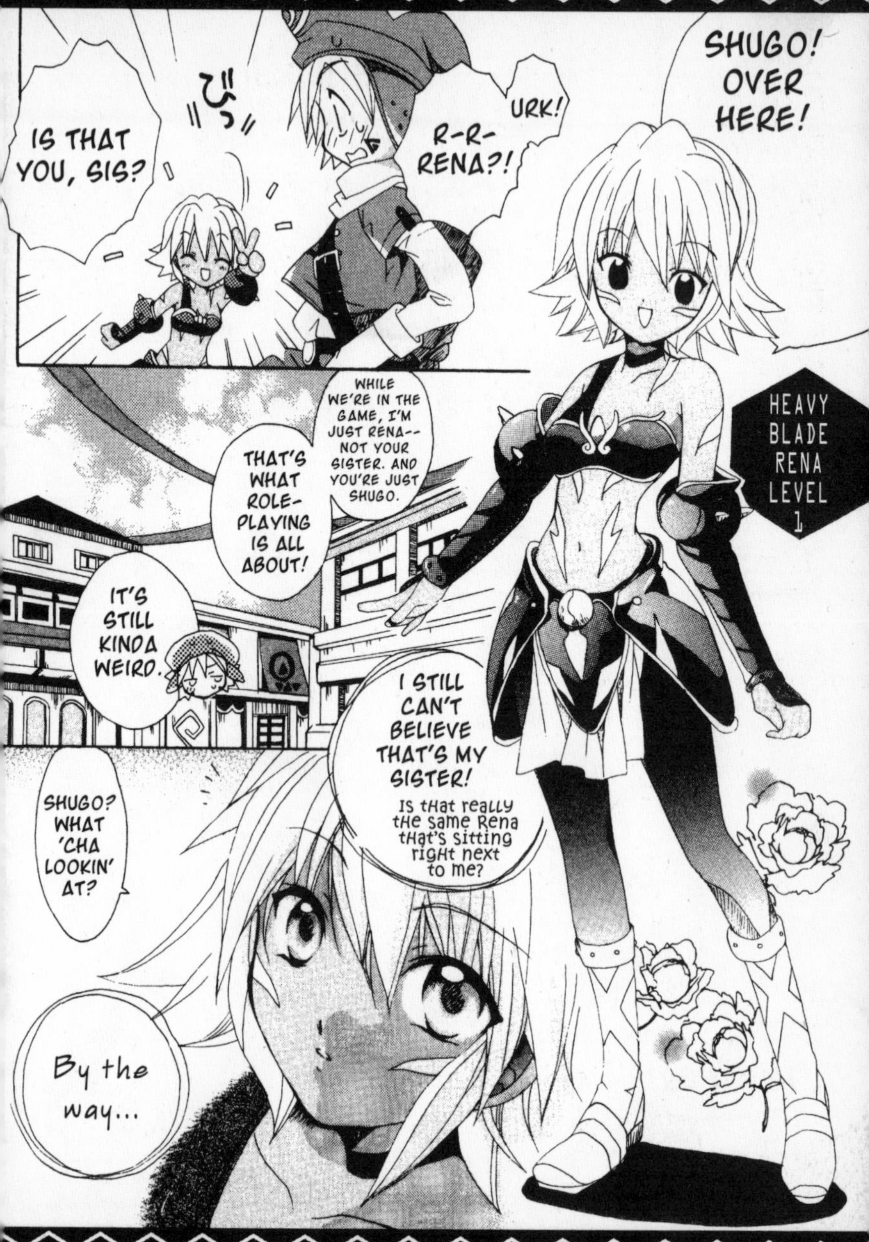
SHUGO! OVER HERE!
HEAVY BLADE RENA LEVEL 1
URK!
R-R-RENA?!
びっ
IS THAT YOU, SIS?
WHILE WE'RE IN THE GAME, I'M JUST RENA-- NOT YOUR SISTER. AND YOU'RE JUST SHUGO.
THAT'S WHAT ROLE-PLAYING IS ALL ABOUT!
IT'S STILL KINDA WEIRD.
I STILL CAN'T BELIEVE THAT'S MY SISTER!
Is that really the same Rena that's sitting right next to me?
SHUGO? WHAT 'CHA LOOKIN' AT?
By the way...

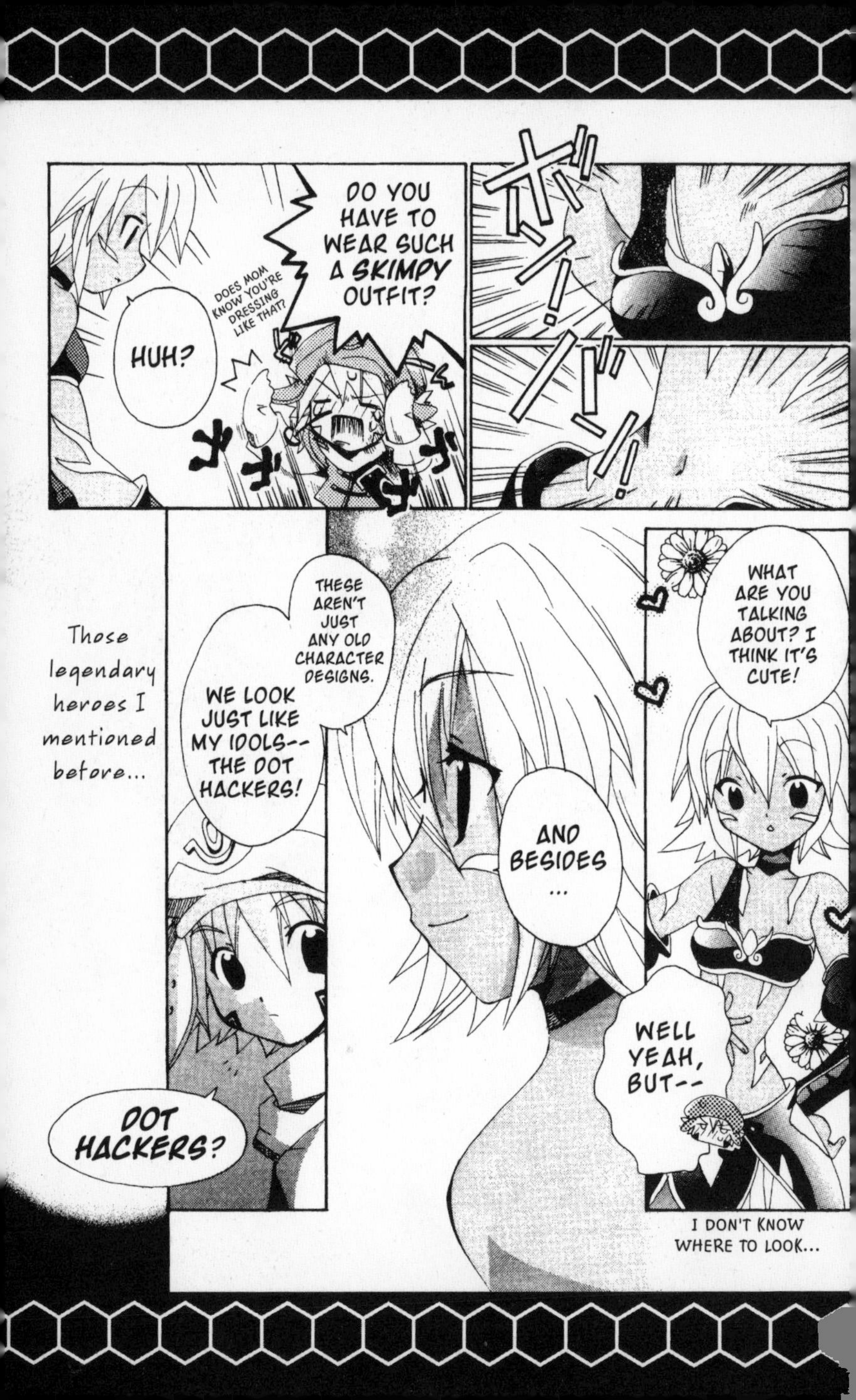
DO YOU HAVE TO WEAR SUCH A SKIMPY OUTFIT?
DOES MOM KNOW YOU'RE DRESSING LIKE THAT?
HUH?
WHAT ARE YOU TALKING ABOUT? I THINK IT'S CUTE!
WELL YEAH, BUT--
I DON'T KNOW WHERE TO LOOK...
AND BESIDES...
THESE AREN'T JUST ANY OLD CHARACTER DESIGNS.
WE LOOK JUST LIKE MY IDOLS--THE DOT HACKERS!
Those legendary heroes I mentioned before...
DOT HACKERS?

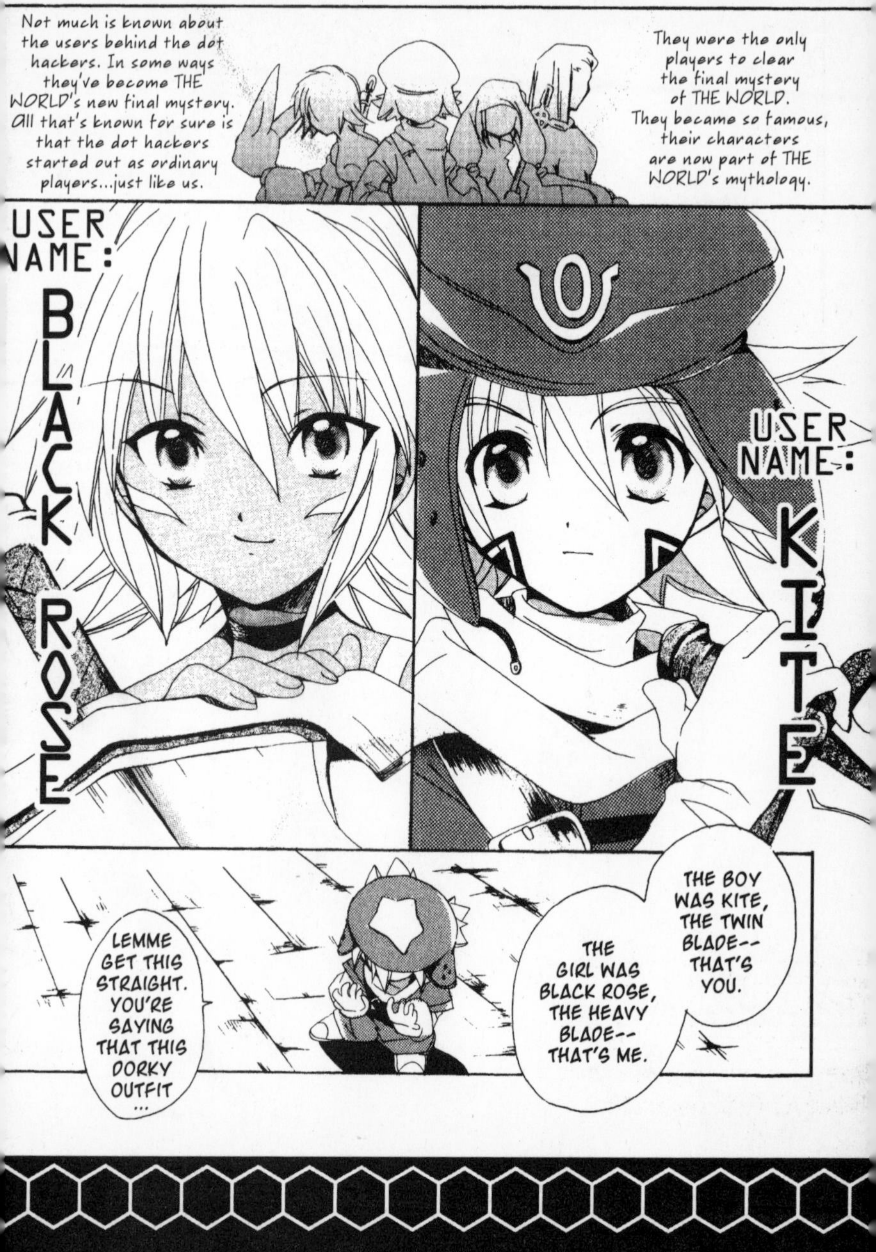
They were the only players to clear the final mystery of THE WORLD. They became so famous, their characters are now part of THE WORLD's mythology.
Not much is known about the users behind the dot hackers. In some ways they've become THE WORLD's new final mystery. All that's known for sure is that the dot hackers started out as ordinary players...just like us.
USER NAME: KITE
USER NAME: BLACK ROSE
THE BOY WAS KITE, THE TWIN BLADE--THAT'S YOU.
THE GIRL WAS BLACK ROSE, THE HEAVY BLADE--THAT'S ME.
LEMME GET THIS STRAIGHT. YOU'RE SAYING THAT THIS DORKY OUTFIT ...

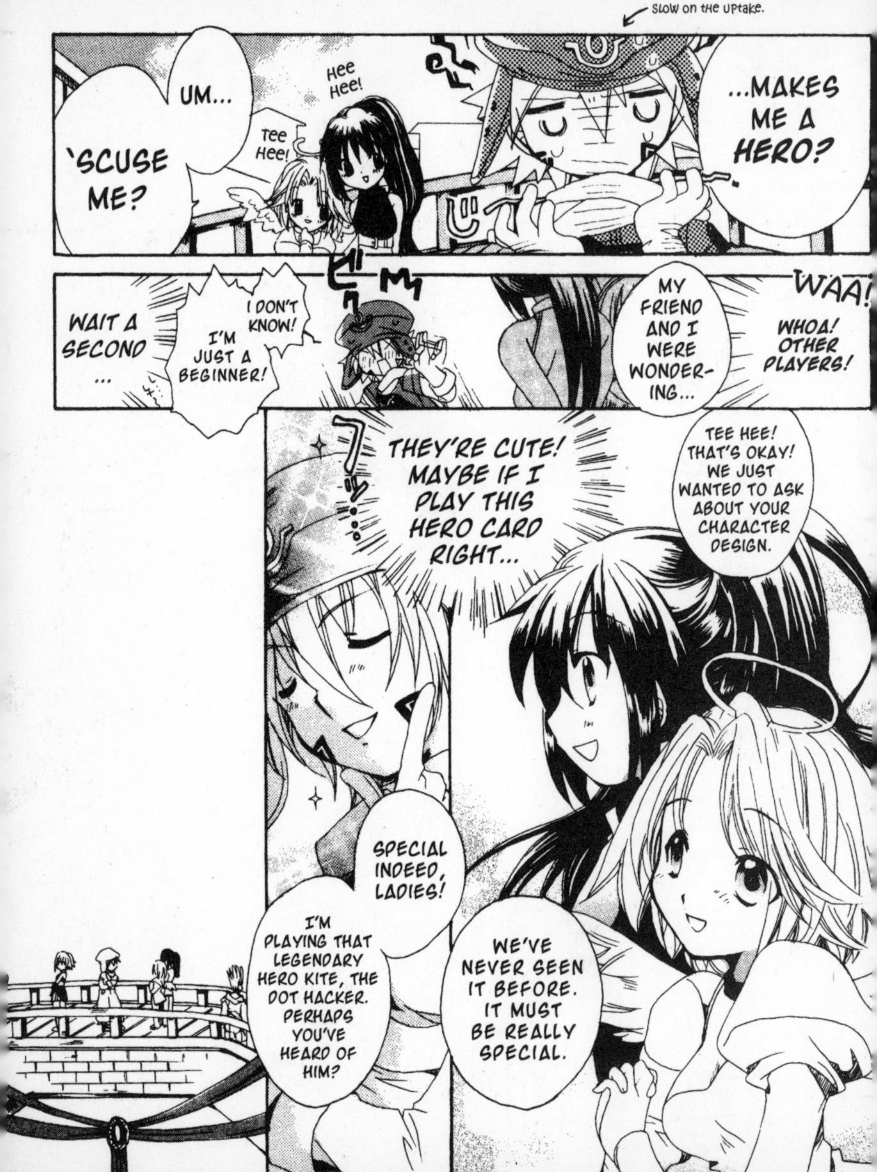
SLOW ON THE UPTAKE.
...MAKES ME A HERO?
HEE HEE!
TEE HEE!
UM...
'SCUSE ME?
WAA!
WHOA! OTHER PLAYERS!
MY FRIEND AND I WERE WONDERING...
I DON'T KNOW!
I'M JUST A BEGINNER!
WAIT A SECOND ...
TEE HEE! THAT'S OKAY! WE JUST WANTED TO ASK ABOUT YOUR CHARACTER DESIGN.
WE'VE NEVER SEEN IT BEFORE. IT MUST BE REALLY SPECIAL.
THEY'RE CUTE! MAYBE IF I PLAY THIS HERO CARD RIGHT...
SPECIAL INDEED, LADIES!
I'M PLAYING THAT LEGENDARY HERO KITE, THE DOT HACKER. PERHAPS YOU'VE HEARD OF HIM?

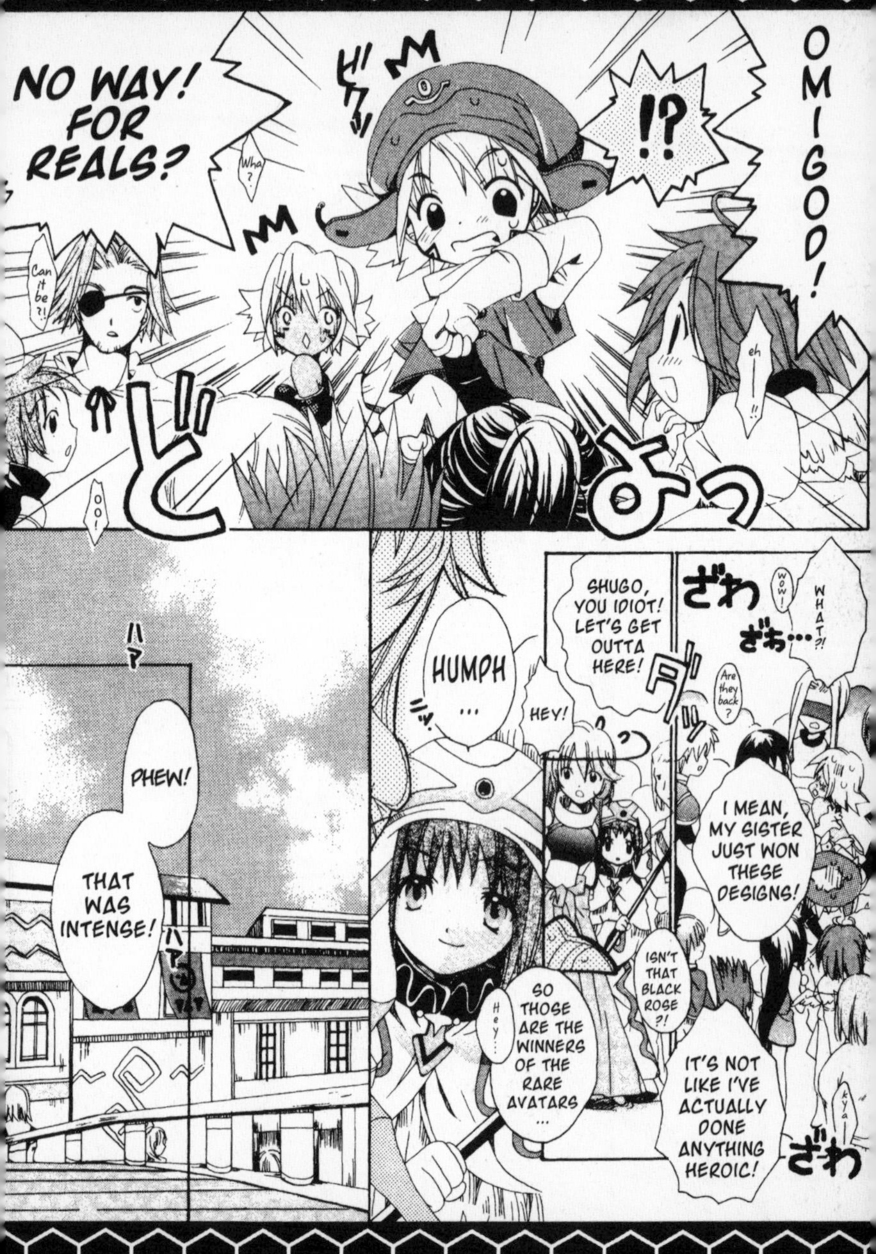
OMIGOOD!
!?
eh—!!
Wha?
NO WAY! FOR REALS?
Can it be?!
oo!
どよっ
WHAT?!
wow!
ざわ
ざわ…
SHUGO, YOU IDIOT! LET'S GET OUTTA HERE!
ダッ
Are they back?
HEY!
HUMPH ...
I MEAN, MY SISTER JUST WON THESE DESIGNS!
ISN'T THAT BLACK ROSE?!
SO THOSE ARE THE WINNERS OF THE RARE AVATARS ...
Hey...
kya!
IT'S NOT LIKE I'VE ACTUALLY DONE ANYTHING HEROIC!
ざわ
ハア
PHEW!
THAT WAS INTENSE!
ハア

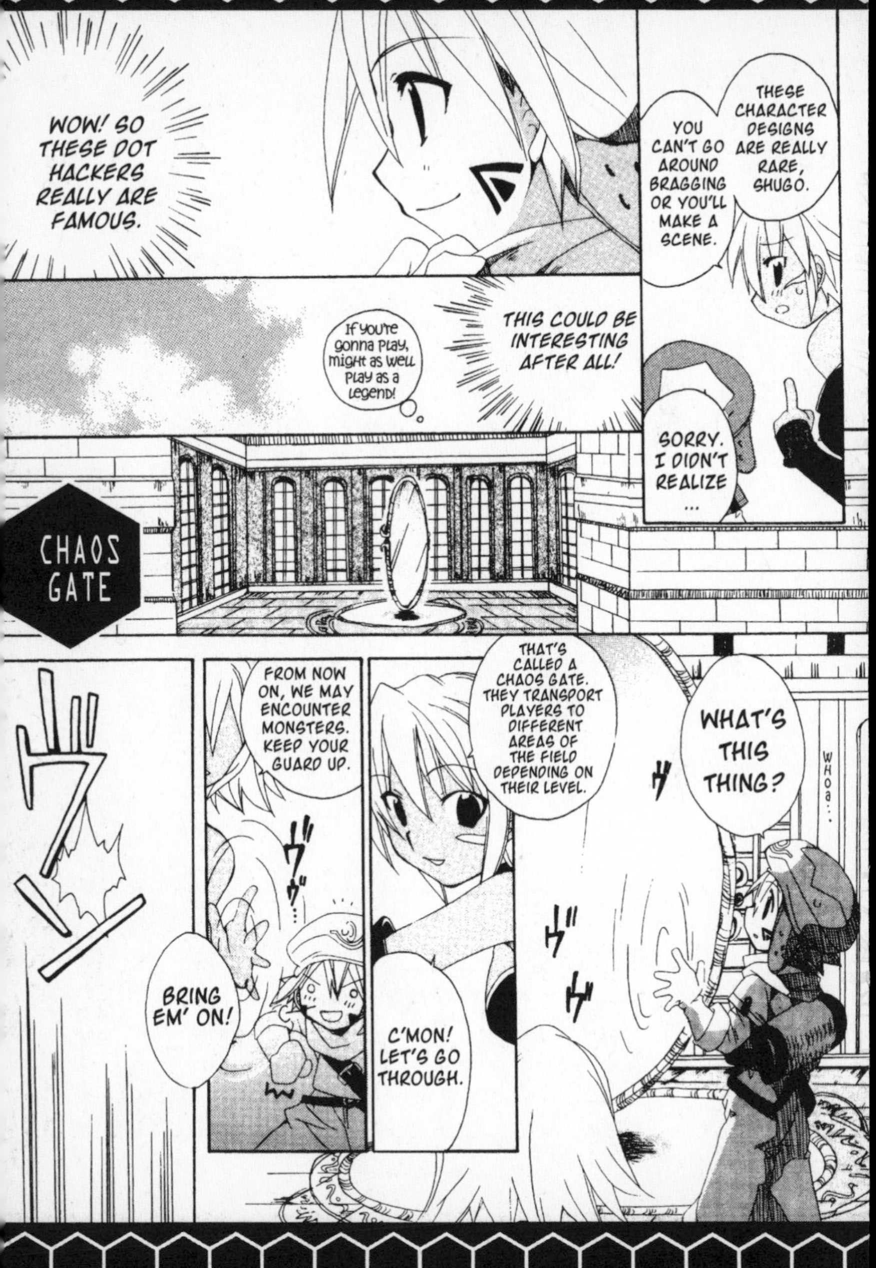
THESE CHARACTER DESIGNS ARE REALLY RARE, SHUGO.
YOU CAN'T GO AROUND BRAGGING OR YOU'LL MAKE A SCENE.
SORRY. I DIDN'T REALIZE ...
WOW! SO THESE DOT HACKERS REALLY ARE FAMOUS.
THIS COULD BE INTERESTING AFTER ALL!
If you're gonna play, might as well play as a legend!
CHAOS GATE
WHAT'S THIS THING?
Whoa...
THAT'S CALLED A CHAOS GATE. THEY TRANSPORT PLAYERS TO DIFFERENT AREAS OF THE FIELD DEPENDING ON THEIR LEVEL.
C'MON! LET'S GO THROUGH.
FROM NOW ON, WE MAY ENCOUNTER MONSTERS. KEEP YOUR GUARD UP.
BRING EM' ON!

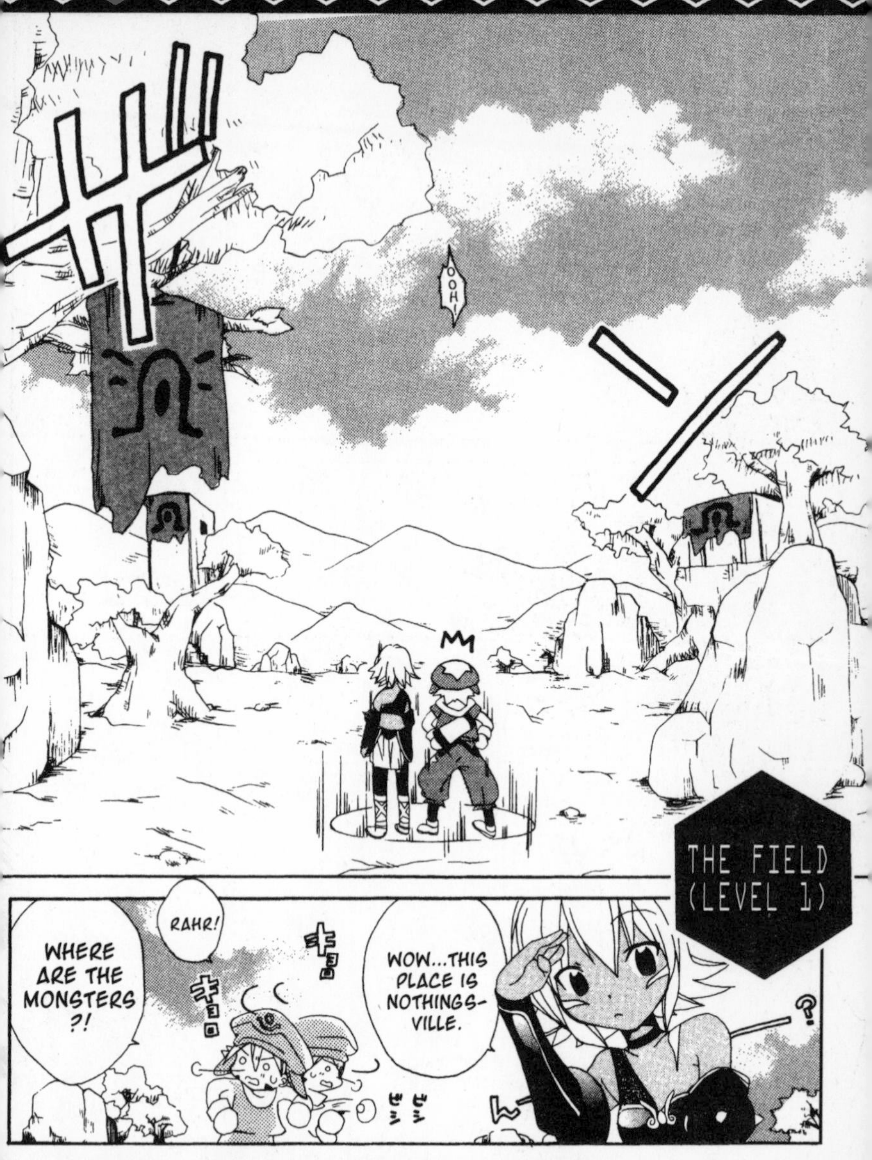
OOH!
THE FIELD (LEVEL 1)
WOW...THIS PLACE IS NOTHINGS-VILLE.
RAHR!
WHERE ARE THE MONSTERS?!

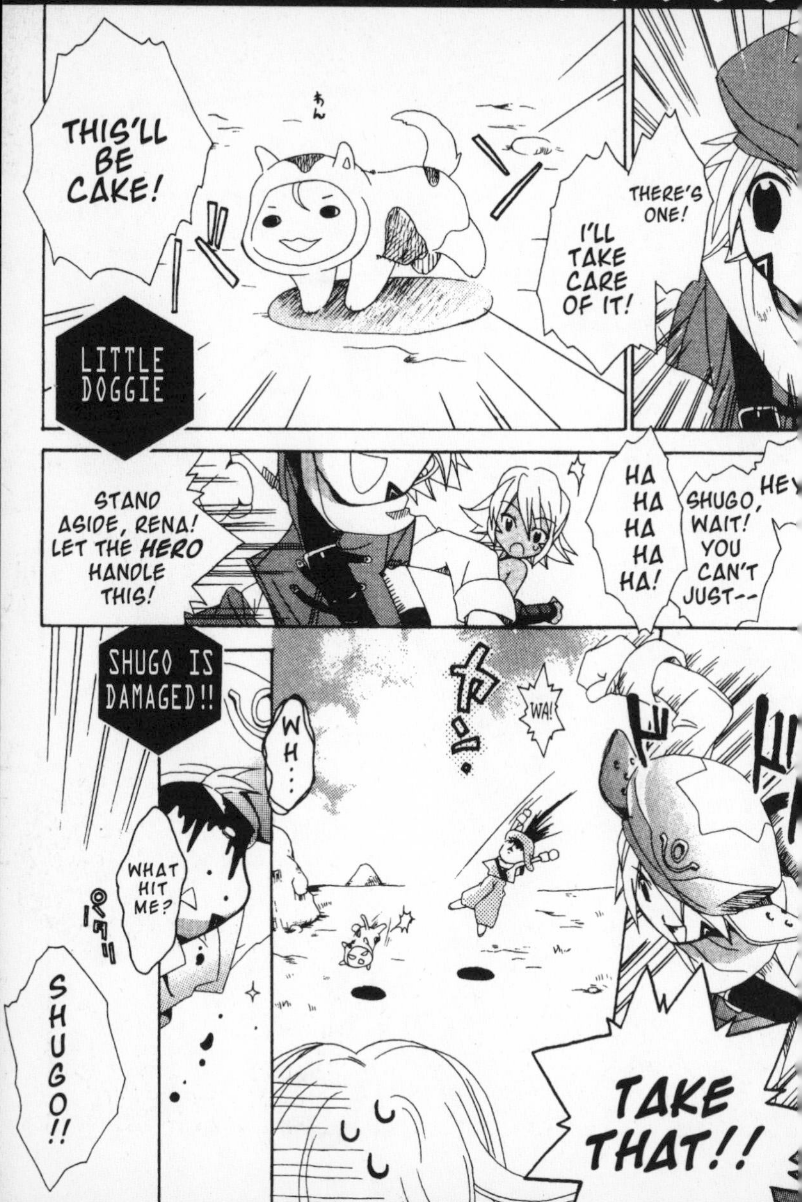
THERE'S ONE!
I'LL TAKE CARE OF IT!
THIS'LL BE CAKE!
LITTLE DOGGIE
HEY
SHUGO, WAIT! YOU CAN'T JUST--
HA HA HA HA HA!
STAND ASIDE, RENA! LET THE HERO HANDLE THIS!
TAKE THAT!!
WA!
SHUGO IS DAMAGED!!
WH...
WHAT HIT ME?
SHUGO!!

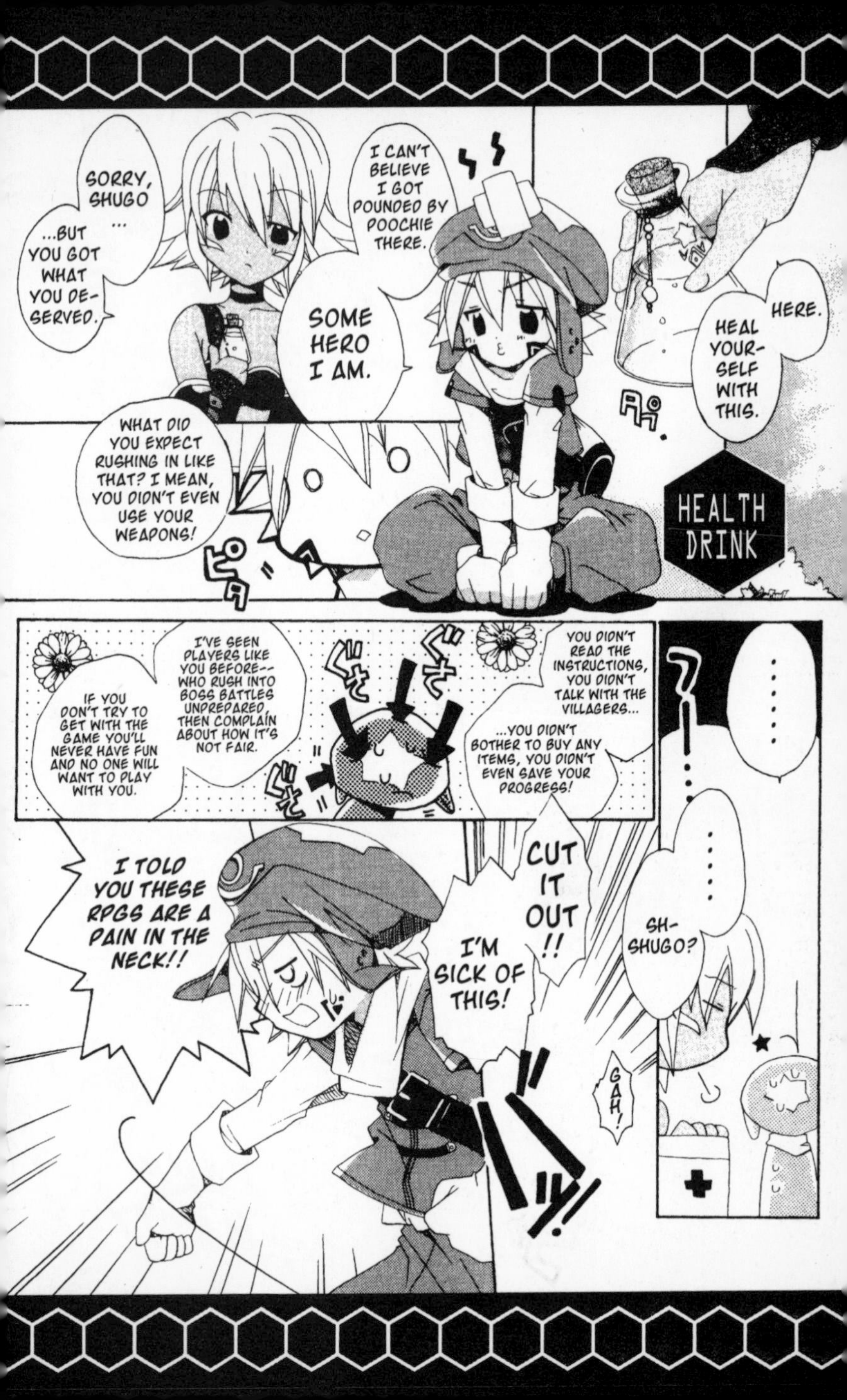
HERE.
HEAL YOURSELF WITH THIS.
HEALTH DRINK
I CAN'T BELIEVE I GOT POUNDED BY POOCHIE THERE.
SOME HERO I AM.
SORRY, SHUGO ...
...BUT YOU GOT WHAT YOU DESERVED.
WHAT DID YOU EXPECT RUSHING IN LIKE THAT? I MEAN, YOU DIDN'T EVEN USE YOUR WEAPONS!
......
?!
YOU DIDN'T READ THE INSTRUCTIONS, YOU DIDN'T TALK WITH THE VILLAGERS...
...YOU DIDN'T BOTHER TO BUY ANY ITEMS, YOU DIDN'T EVEN SAVE YOUR PROGRESS!
ぐさ
I'VE SEEN PLAYERS LIKE YOU BEFORE--WHO RUSH INTO BOSS BATTLES UNPREPARED, THEN COMPLAIN ABOUT HOW IT'S NOT FAIR.
IF YOU DON'T TRY TO GET WITH THE GAME YOU'LL NEVER HAVE FUN AND NO ONE WILL WANT TO PLAY WITH YOU.
......
SH-SHUGO?
GAH!
CUT IT OUT!!
I'M SICK OF THIS!
I TOLD YOU THESE RPGS ARE A PAIN IN THE NECK!!

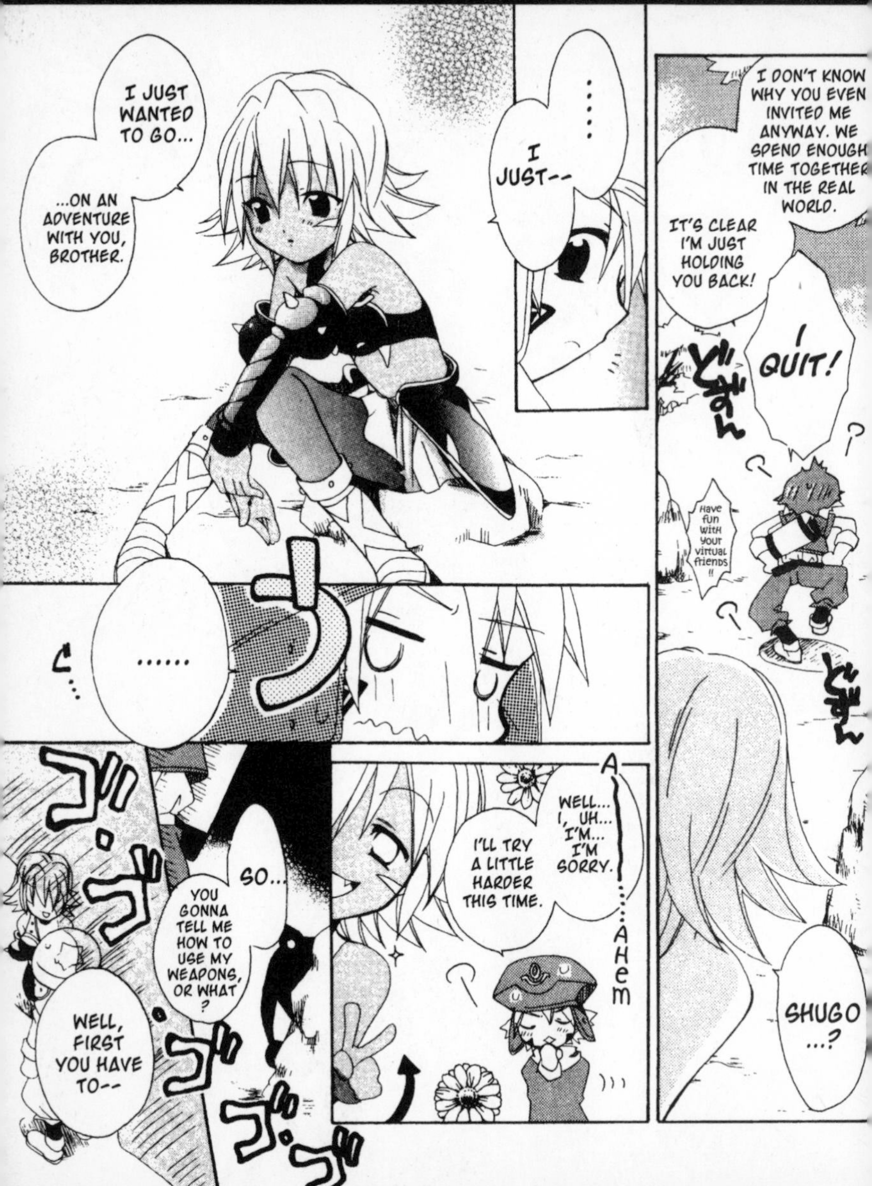

I DON'T KNOW WHY YOU EVEN INVITED ME ANYWAY. WE SPEND ENOUGH TIME TOGETHER IN THE REAL WORLD.
IT'S CLEAR I'M JUST HOLDING YOU BACK!
I QUIT!
どずん
Have fun with your virtual friends!!
どずん
SHUGO ...?
.....
I JUST--
I JUST WANTED TO GO...
...ON AN ADVENTURE WITH YOU, BROTHER.
......
く...
A--------...AHem
WELL... I, UH... I'M... I'M SORRY.
I'LL TRY A LITTLE HARDER THIS TIME.
SO...
YOU GONNA TELL ME HOW TO USE MY WEAPONS, OR WHAT?
WELL, FIRST YOU HAVE TO--

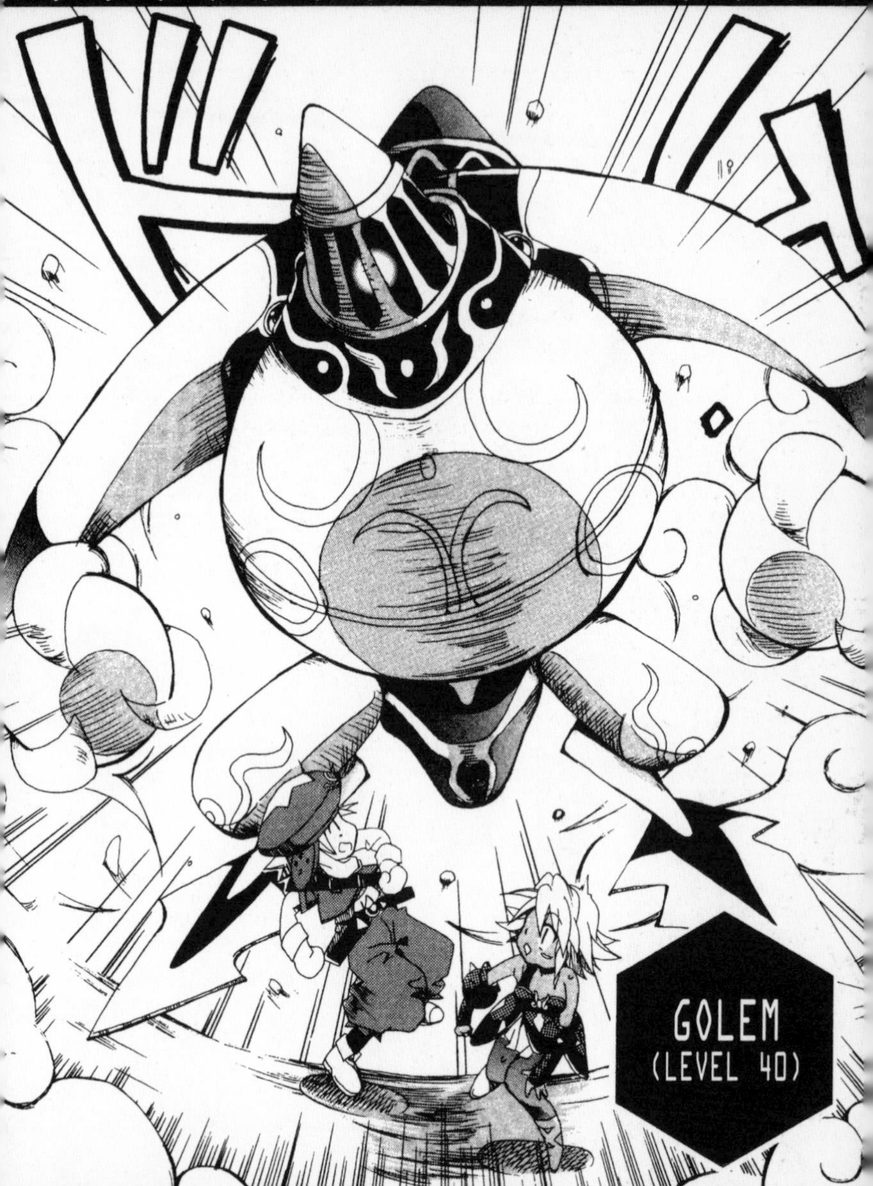
GOLEM
(LEVEL 40)

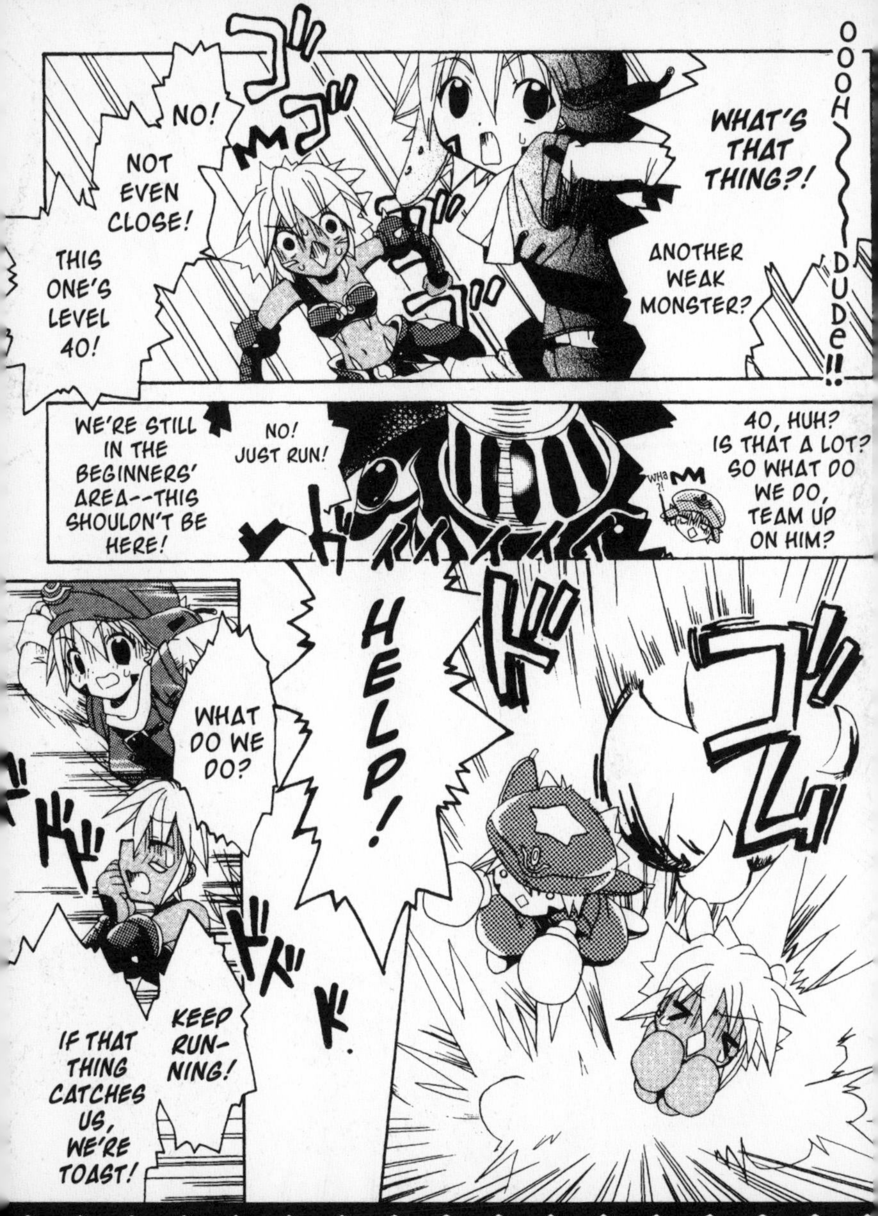
OOOH~~~DUDE!!
WHAT'S THAT THING?!
ANOTHER WEAK MONSTER?
NO!
NOT EVEN CLOSE!
THIS ONE'S LEVEL 40!
40, HUH? IS THAT A LOT? SO WHAT DO WE DO, TEAM UP ON HIM?
WHA ?!
NO! JUST RUN!
WE'RE STILL IN THE BEGINNERS' AREA--THIS SHOULDN'T BE HERE!
HELP!
WHAT DO WE DO?
KEEP RUN-NING!
IF THAT THING CATCHES US, WE'RE TOAST!

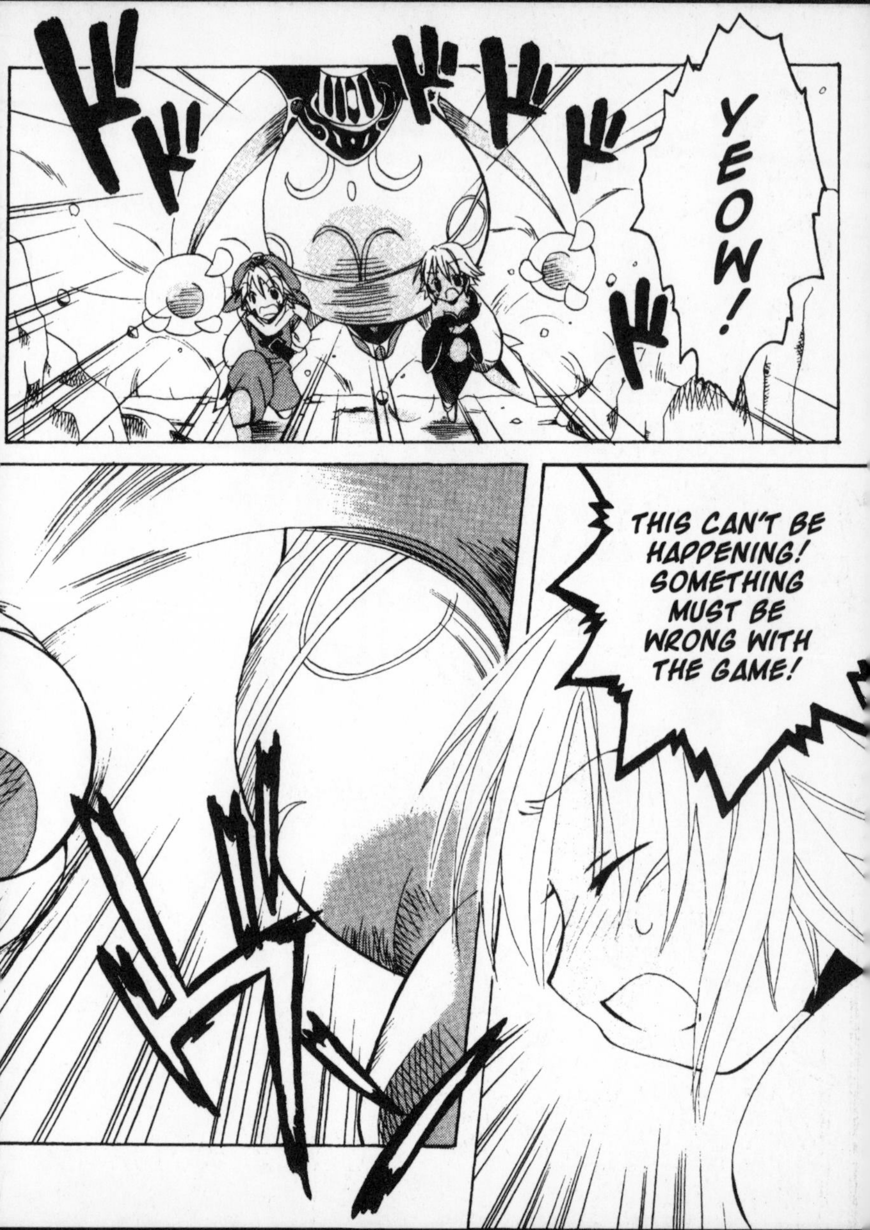
YEOW!
THIS CAN'T BE HAPPENING! SOMETHING MUST BE WRONG WITH THE GAME!

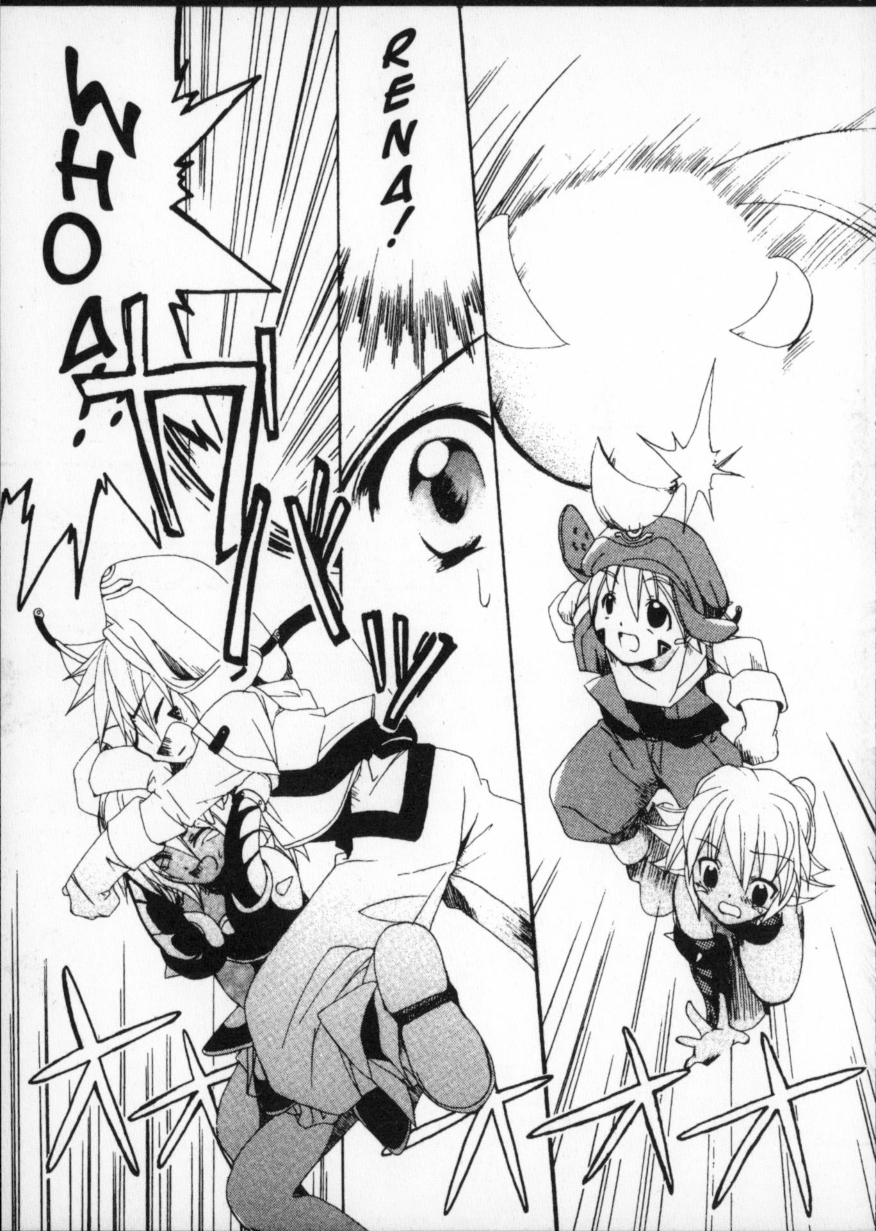
RENA!
WHOA!

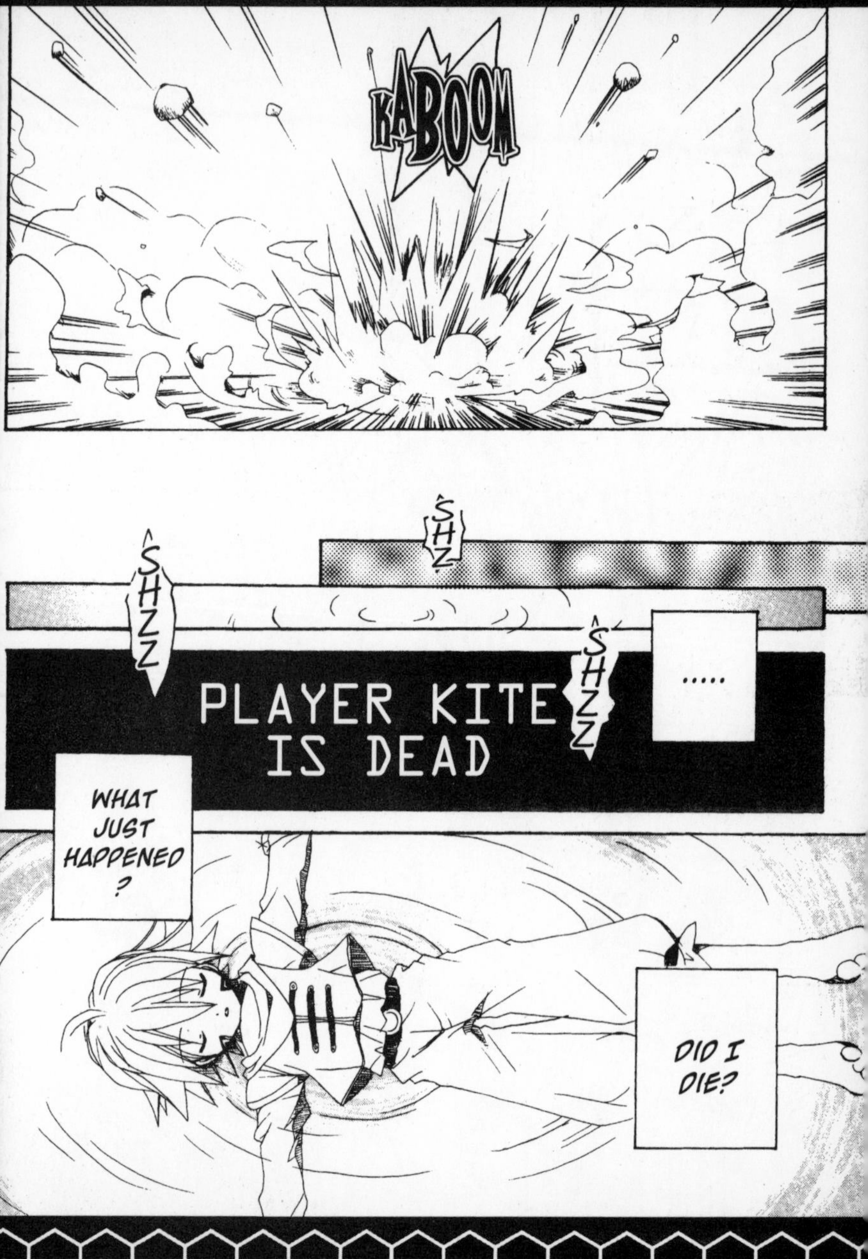
KABOOM
SHZ
SHZZ
.....
SHZZ
PLAYER KITE IS DEAD
WHAT JUST HAPPENED?
DID I DIE?

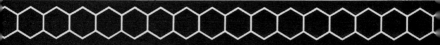

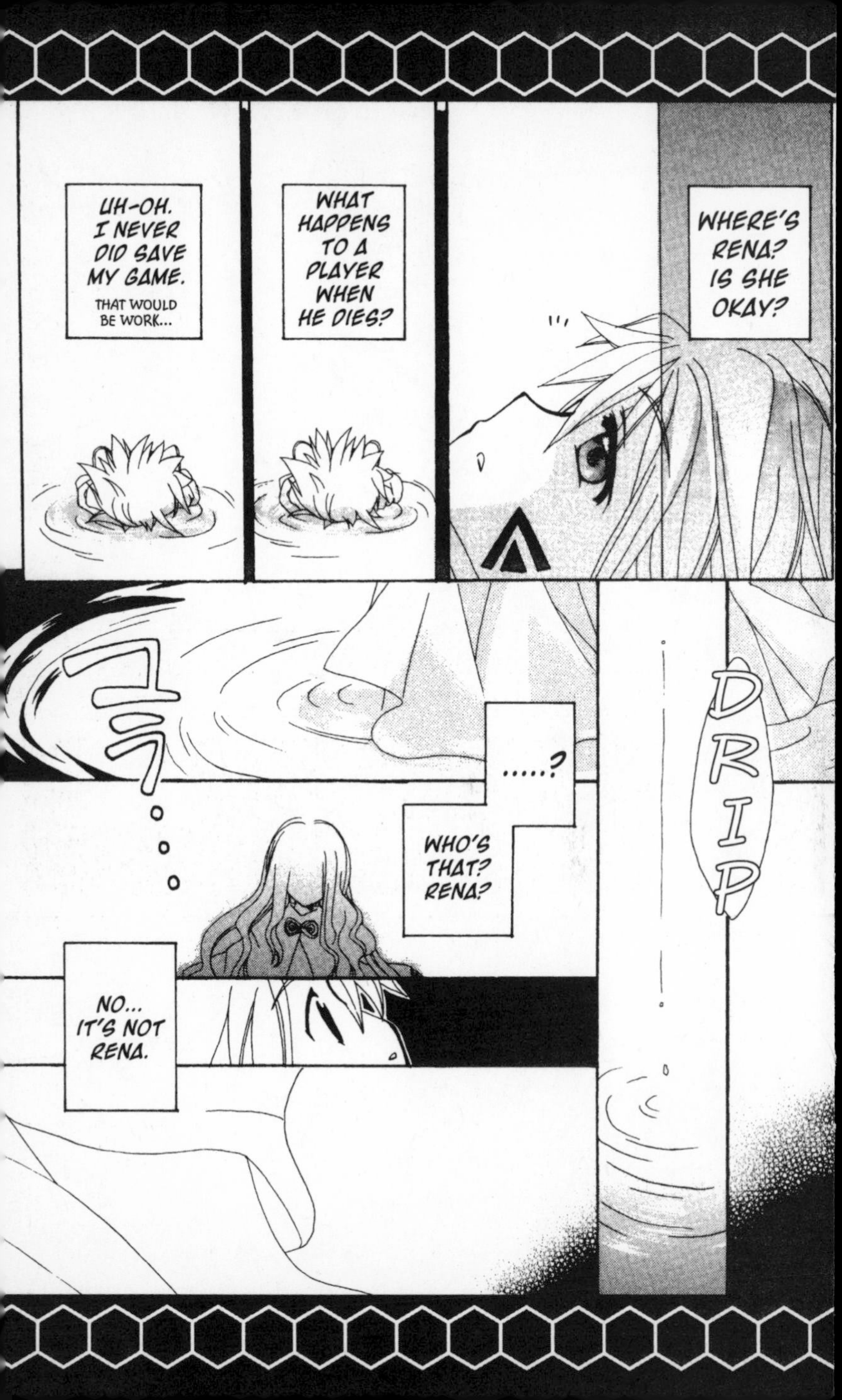
WHERE'S RENA? IS SHE OKAY?
WHAT HAPPENS TO A PLAYER WHEN HE DIES?
UH-OH. I NEVER DID SAVE MY GAME.
THAT WOULD BE WORK...
DRIP
.....?
WHO'S THAT? RENA?
ユラ
NO... IT'S NOT RENA.

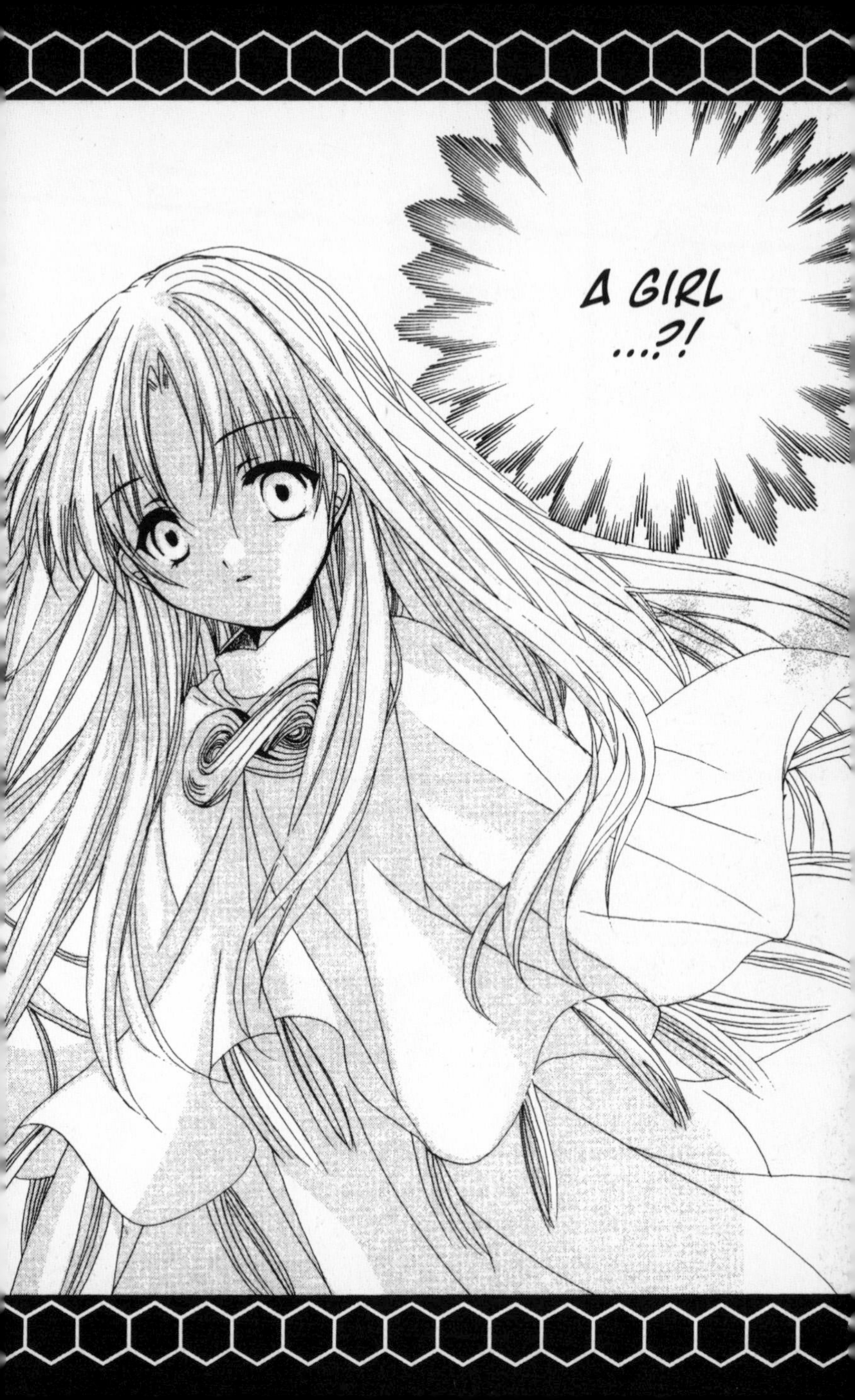
A GIRL ...?!

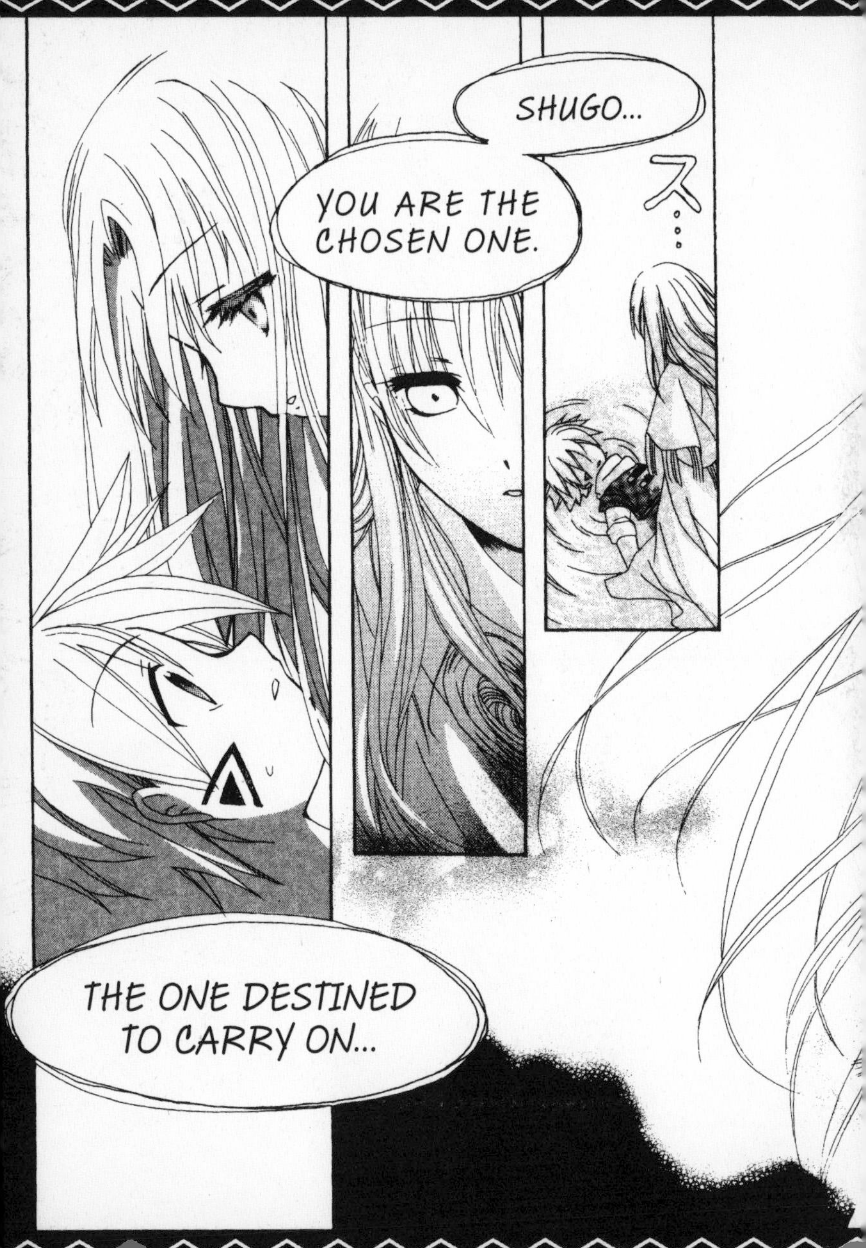
SHUGO...
ス…
YOU ARE THE CHOSEN ONE.
THE ONE DESTINED TO CARRY ON...

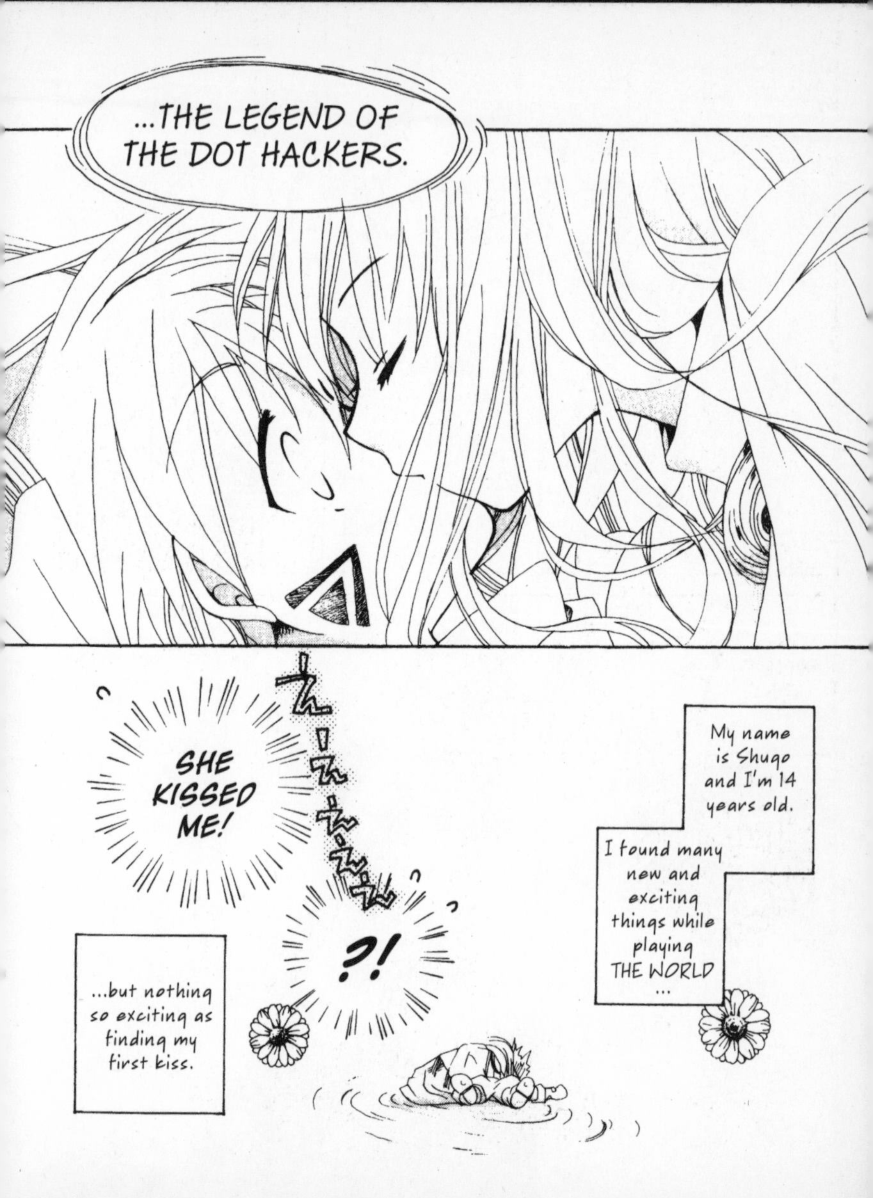
...THE LEGEND OF THE DOT HACKERS.
My name is Shugo and I'm 14 years old.
I found many new and exciting things while playing THE WORLD ...
SHE KISSED ME!
?!
...but nothing so exciting as finding my first kiss.

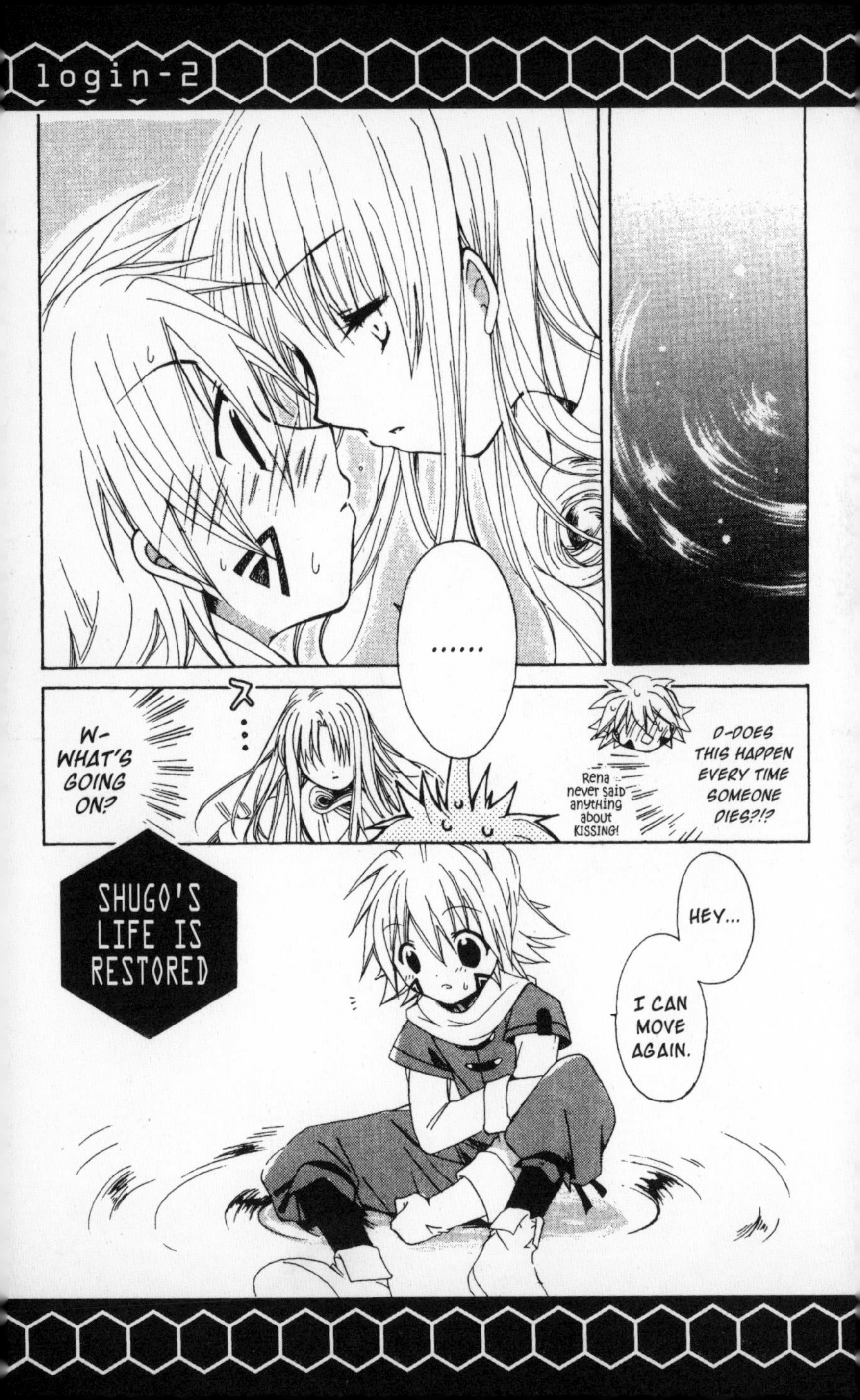
......
D-DOES THIS HAPPEN EVERY TIME SOMEONE DIES?!?
Rena never said anything about KISSING!
ス...
W-WHAT'S GOING ON?
HEY...
I CAN MOVE AGAIN.
SHUGO'S LIFE IS RESTORED

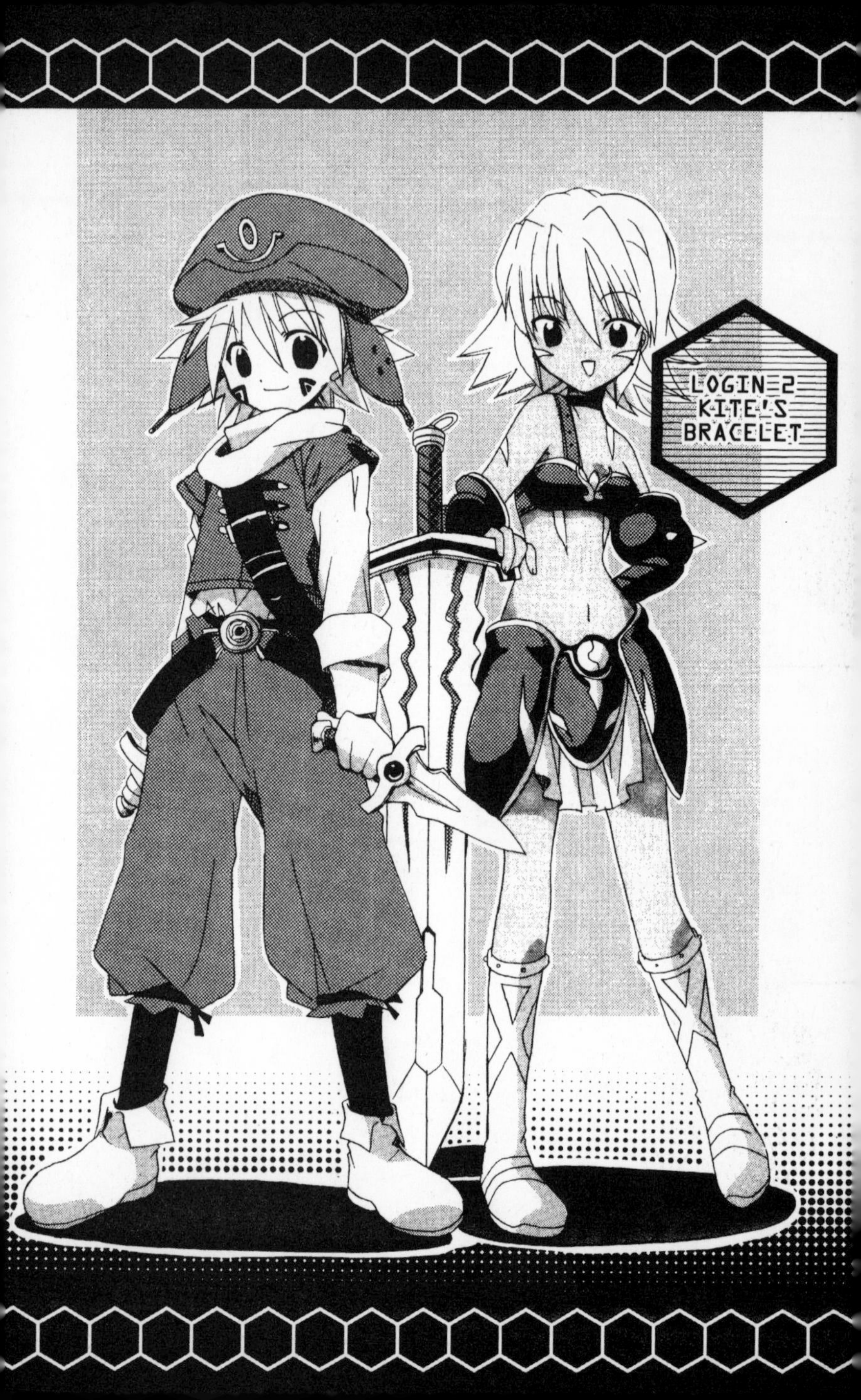
LOGIN 2
KITE'S
BRACELET

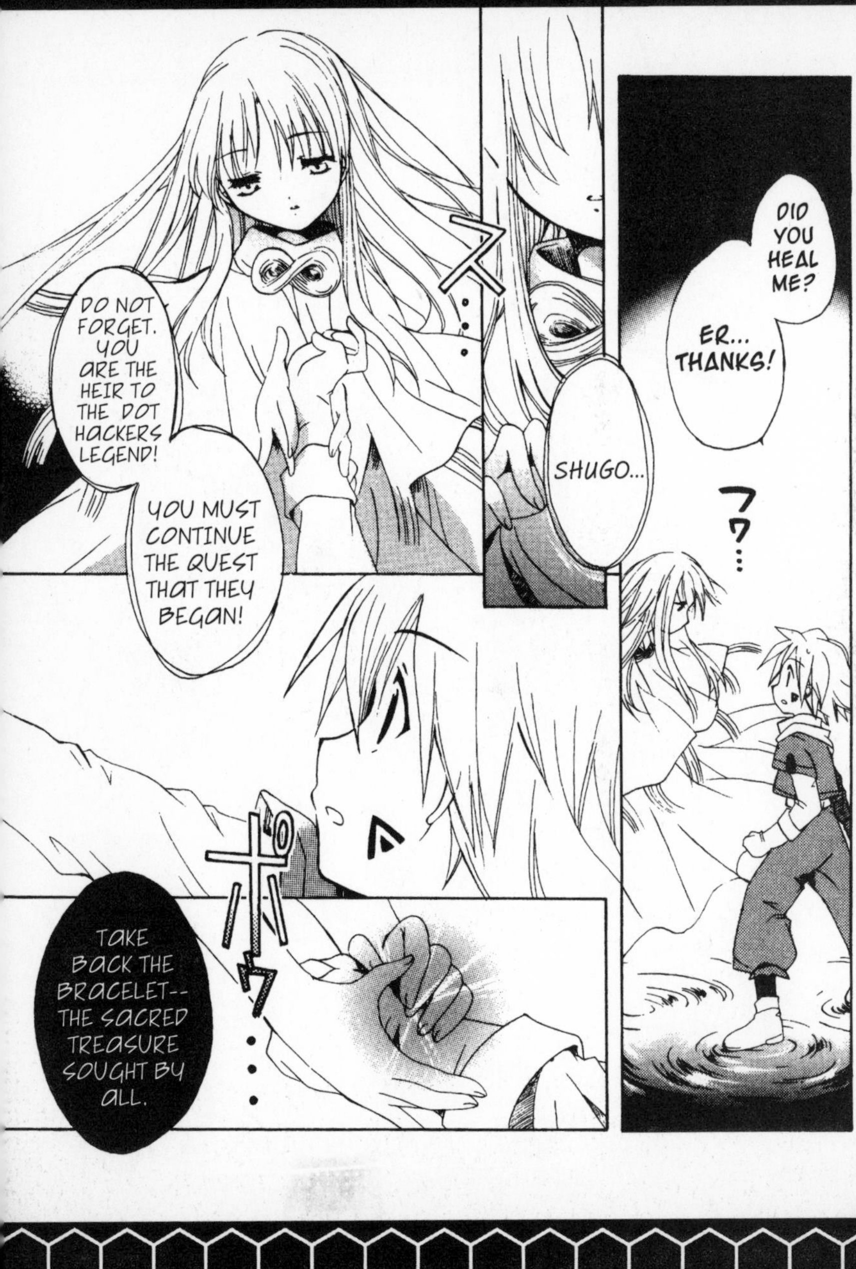
DID YOU HEAL ME?
ER... THANKS!
フワ…
ス…
SHUGO...
DO NOT FORGET. YOU ARE THE HEIR TO THE DOT HACKERS LEGEND!
YOU MUST CONTINUE THE QUEST THAT THEY BEGAN!
ホロ…
TAKE BACK THE BRACELET-- THE SACRED TREASURE SOUGHT BY ALL.

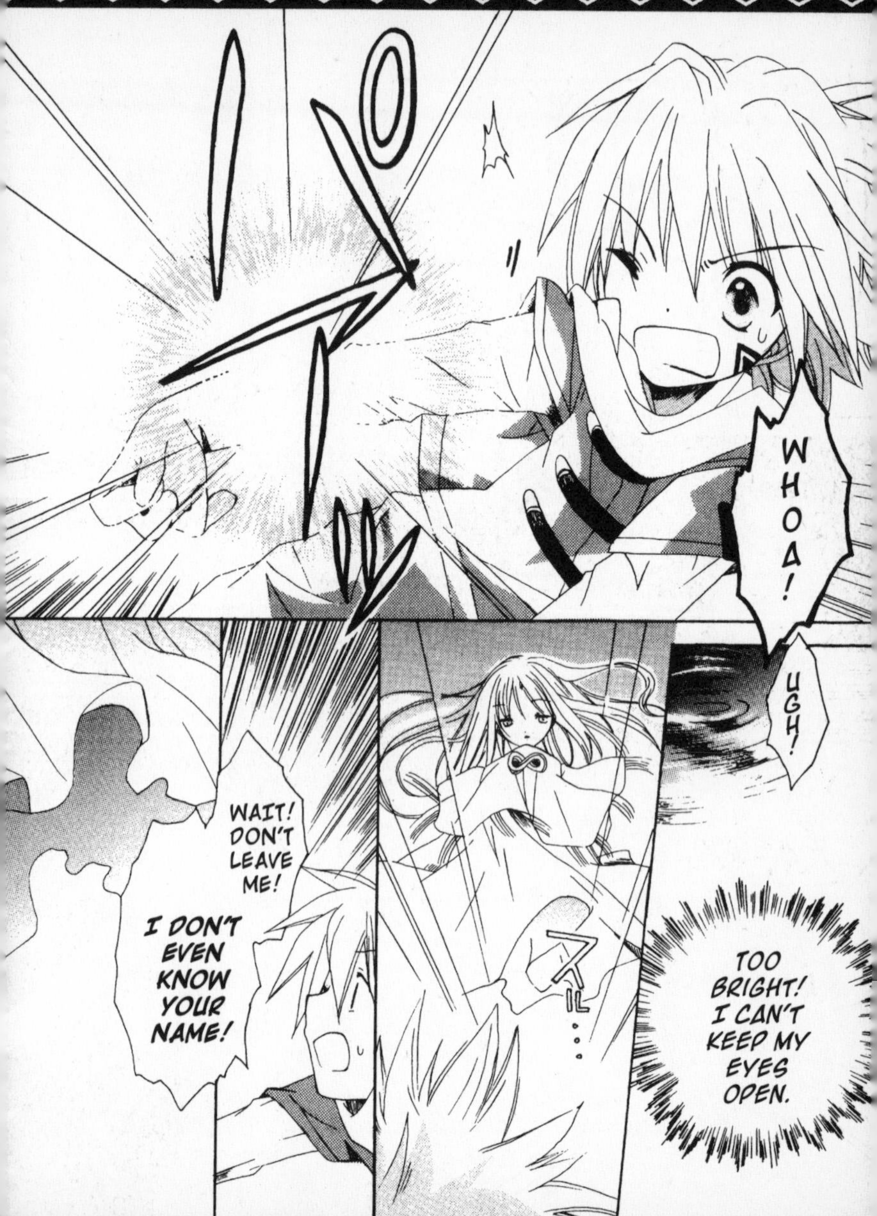
WHOA!
UGH!
TOO BRIGHT! I CAN'T KEEP MY EYES OPEN.
WAIT! DON'T LEAVE ME!
I DON'T EVEN KNOW YOUR NAME!

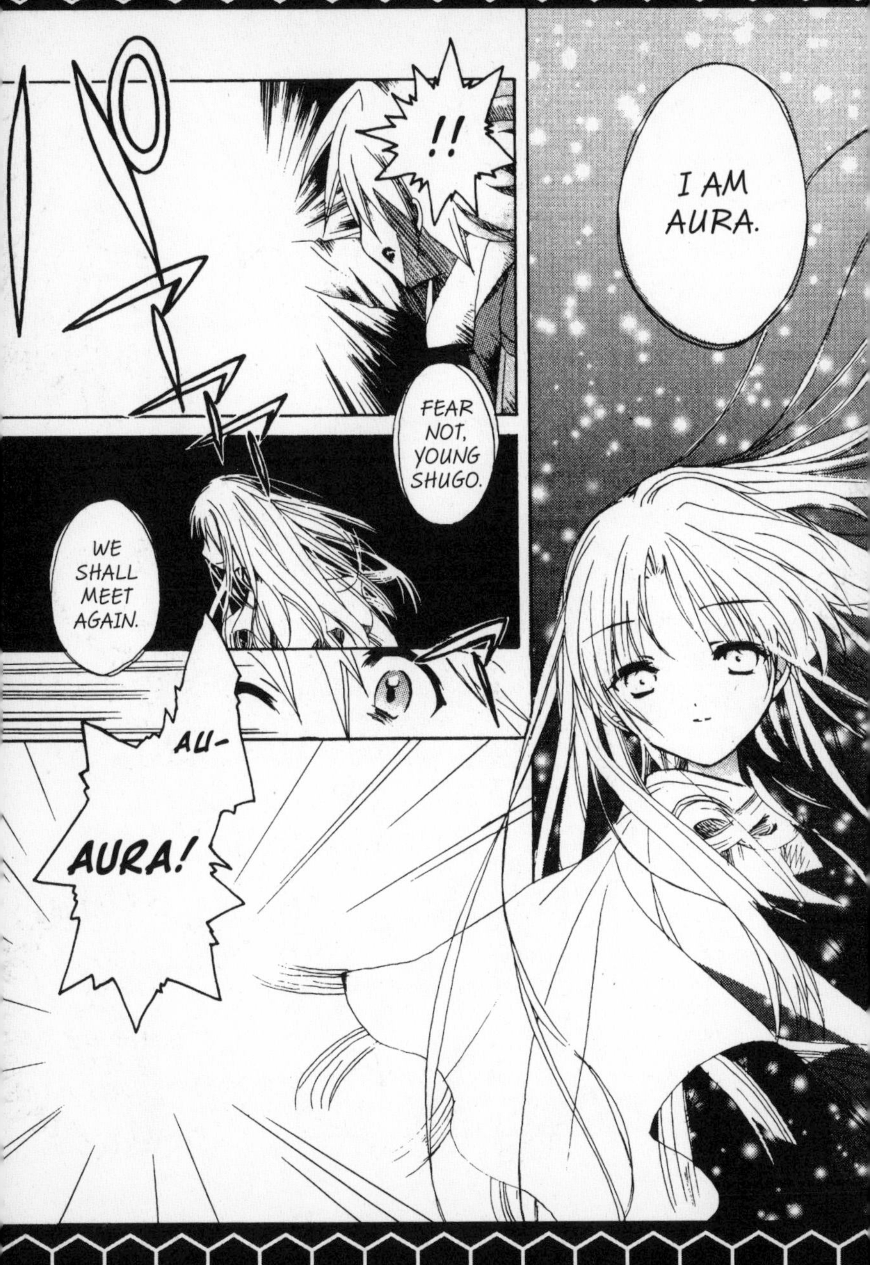

I AM AURA.
!!
FEAR NOT, YOUNG SHUGO.
WE SHALL MEET AGAIN.
AU-
AURA!

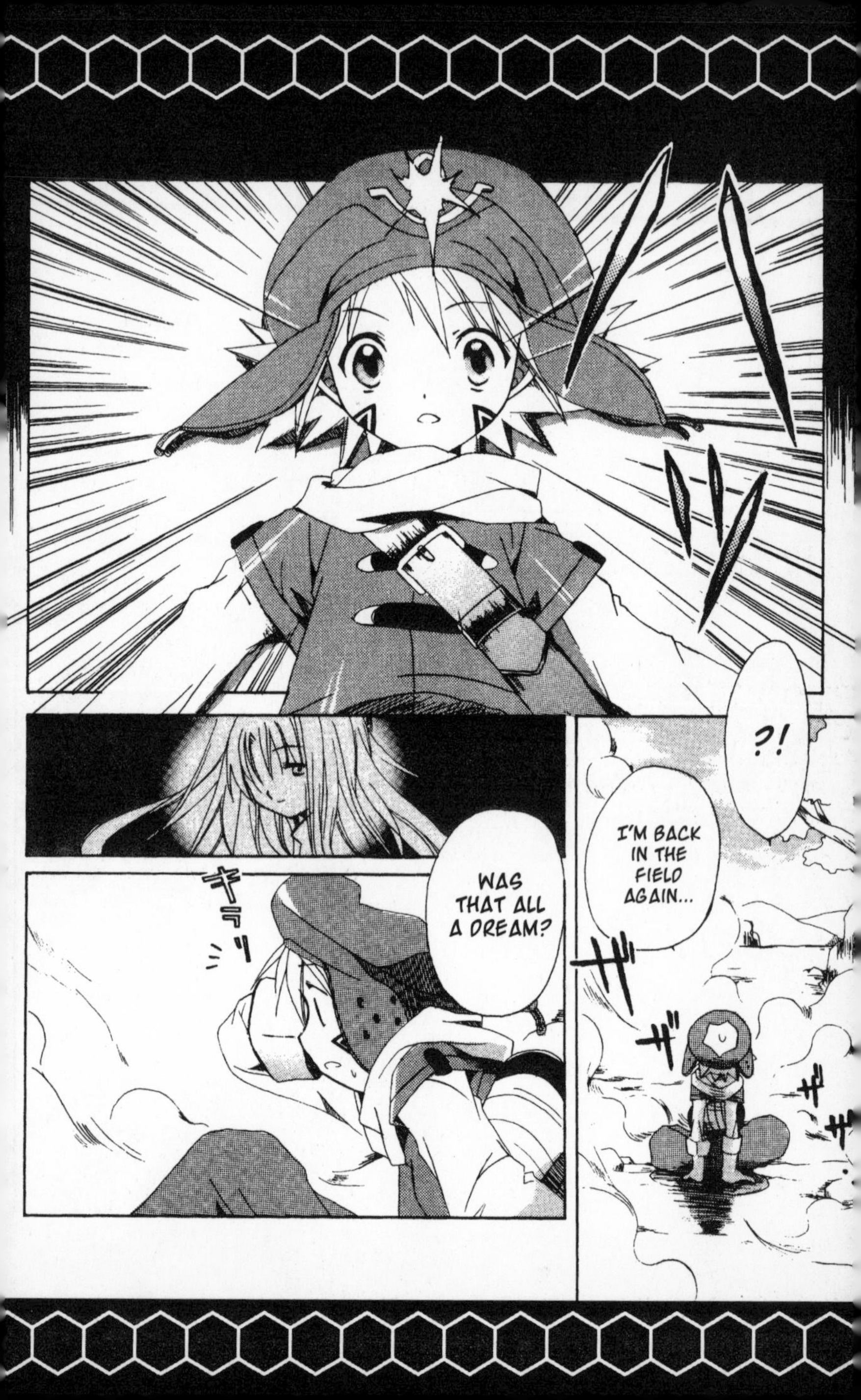
?!
I'M BACK IN THE FIELD AGAIN...
ザ
ザ
ザ
ザ
WAS THAT ALL A DREAM?
キラッ

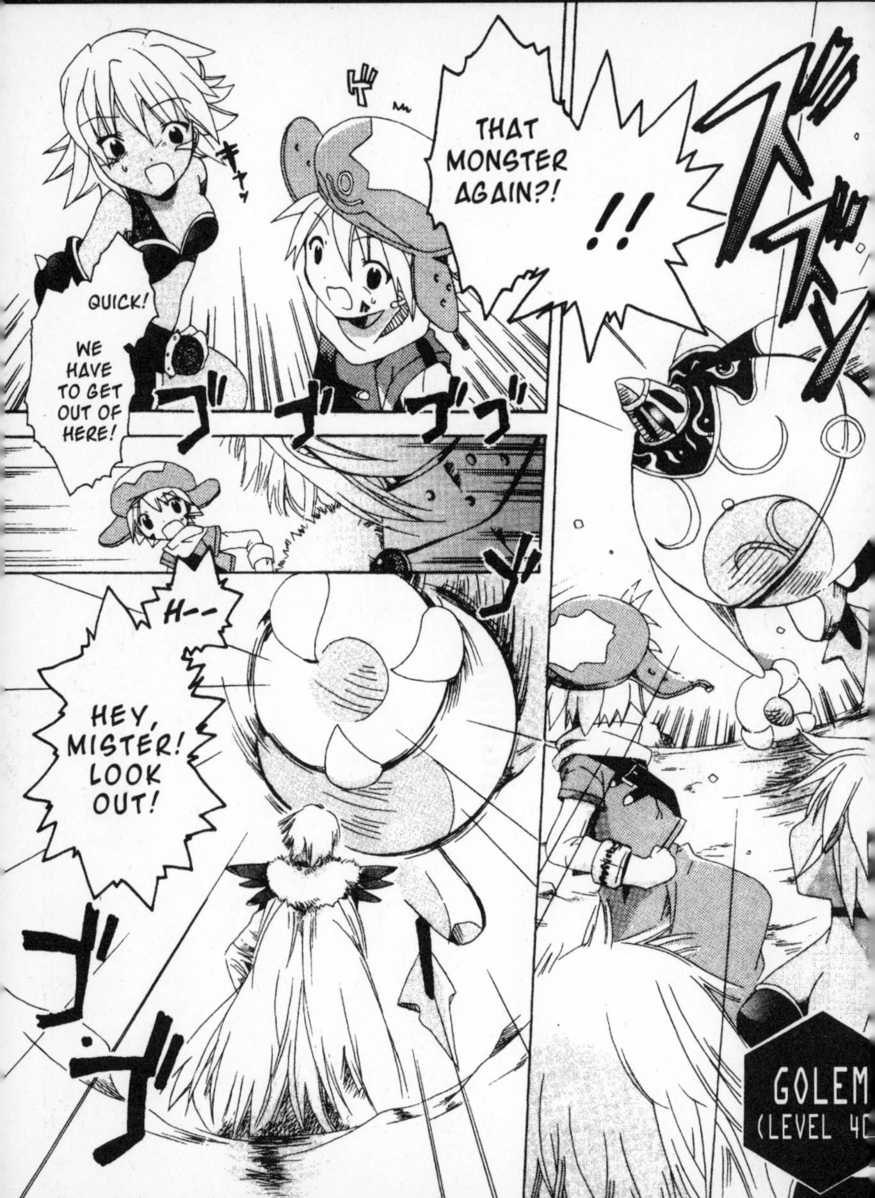
!!
GOLEM (LEVEL 4
THAT MONSTER AGAIN?!
QUICK! WE HAVE TO GET OUT OF HERE!
H--
HEY, MISTER! LOOK OUT!

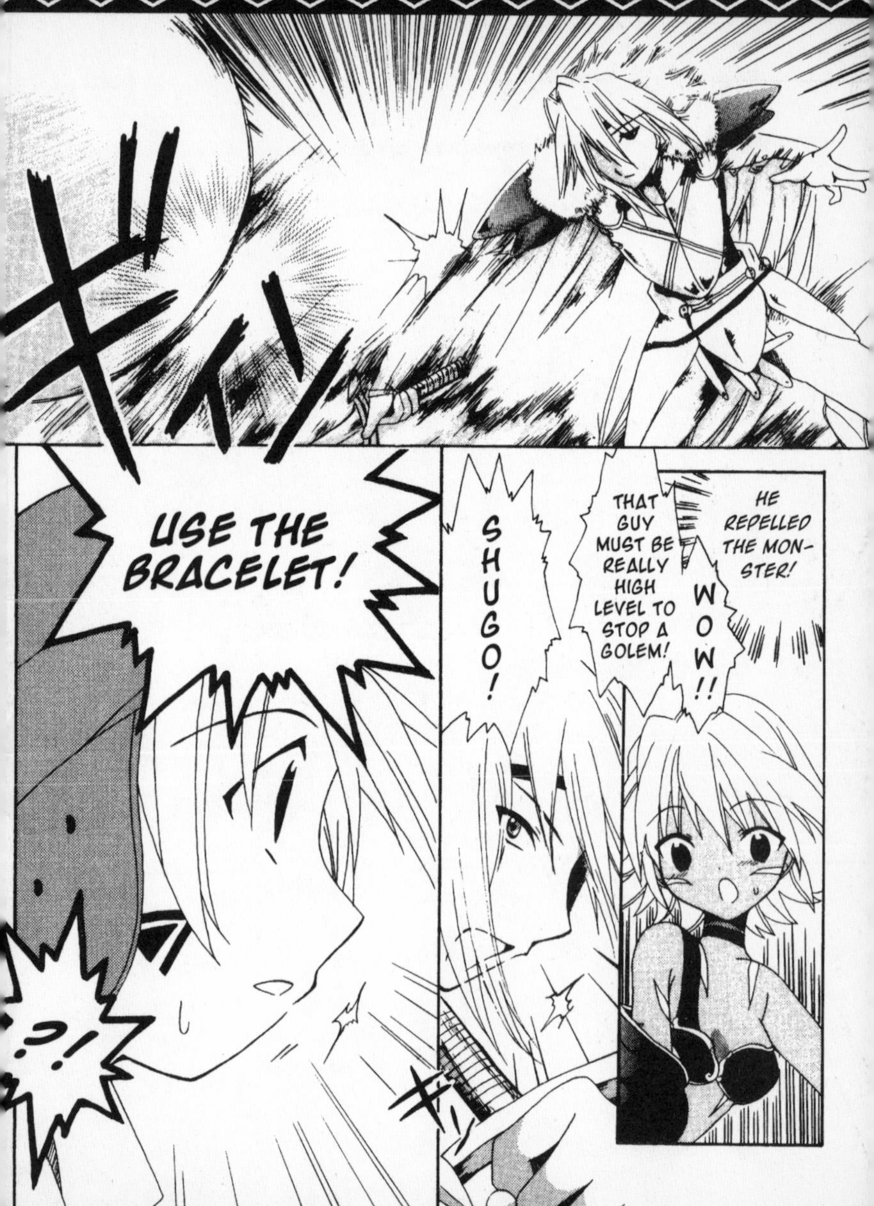
ギィン
HE REPELLED THE MON-STER!
WOW!!
THAT GUY MUST BE REALLY HIGH LEVEL TO STOP A GOLEM!
SHUGO!
USE THE BRACELET!
?!

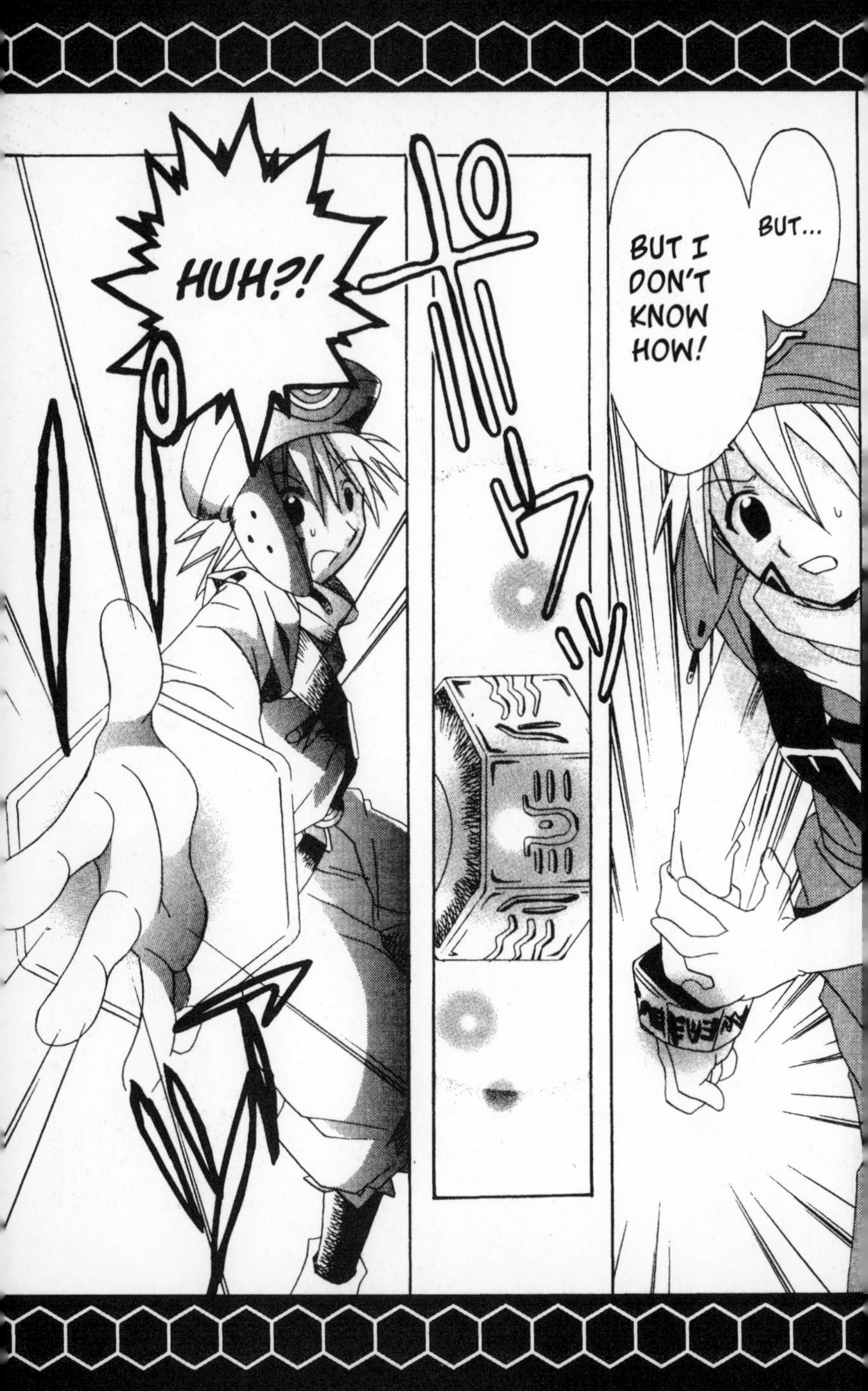
BUT...
BUT I DON'T KNOW HOW!
HUH?!

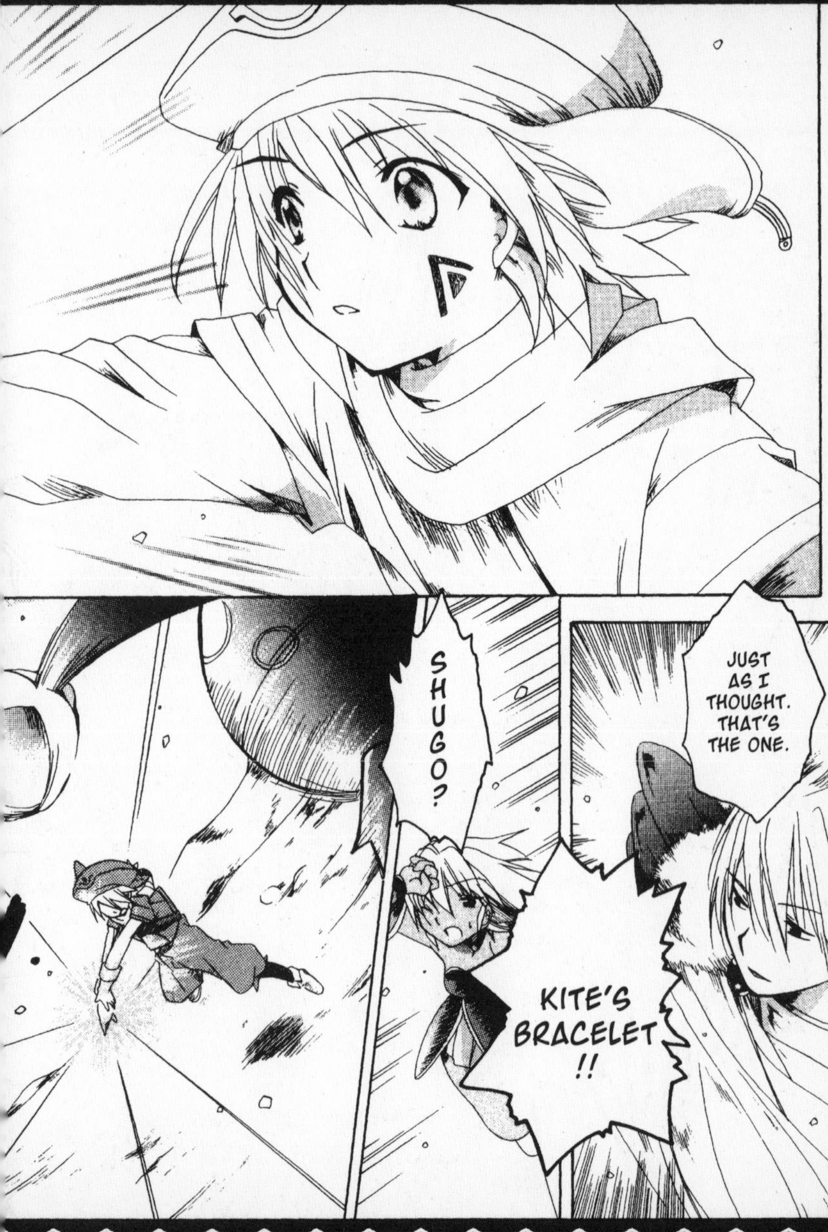
JUST AS I THOUGHT. THAT'S THE ONE.
KITE'S BRACELET!!
SHUGO?

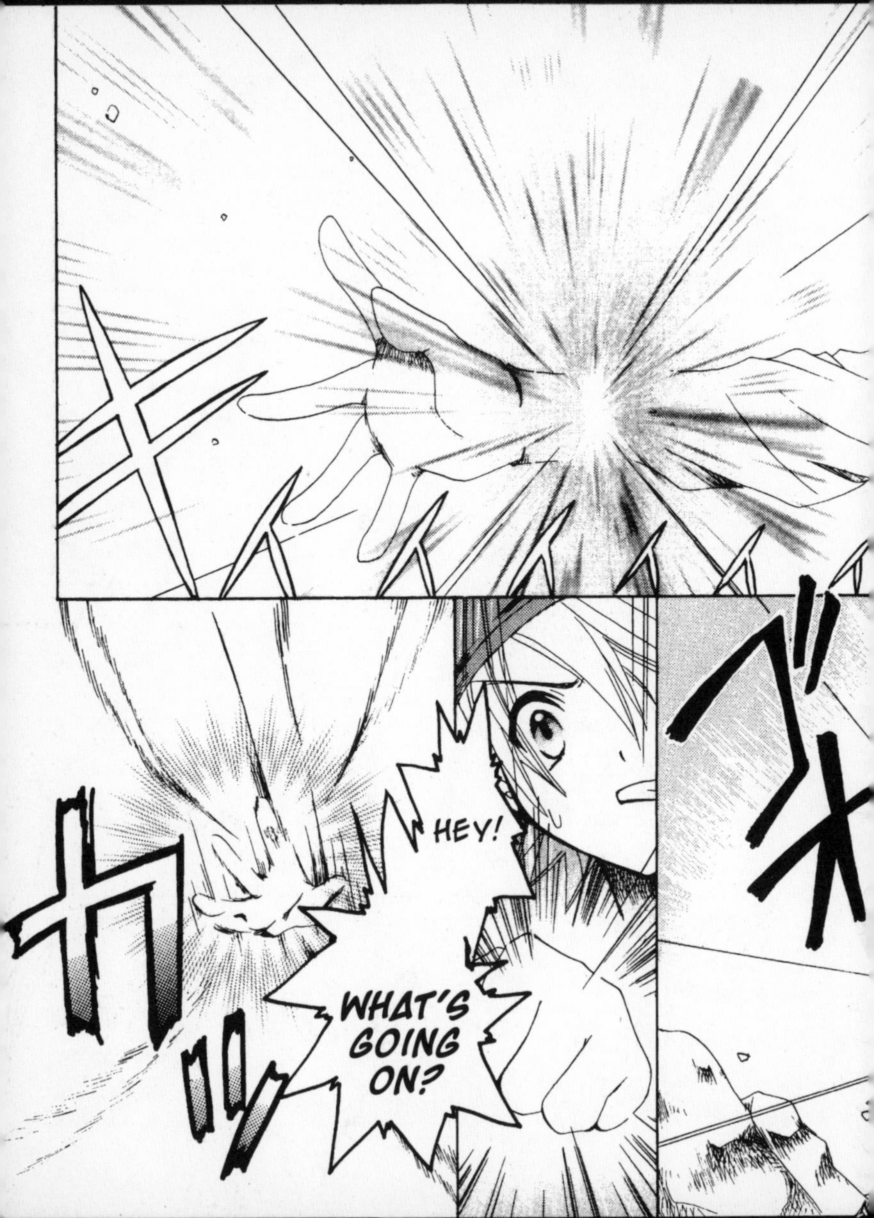
HEY!
WHAT'S GOING ON?

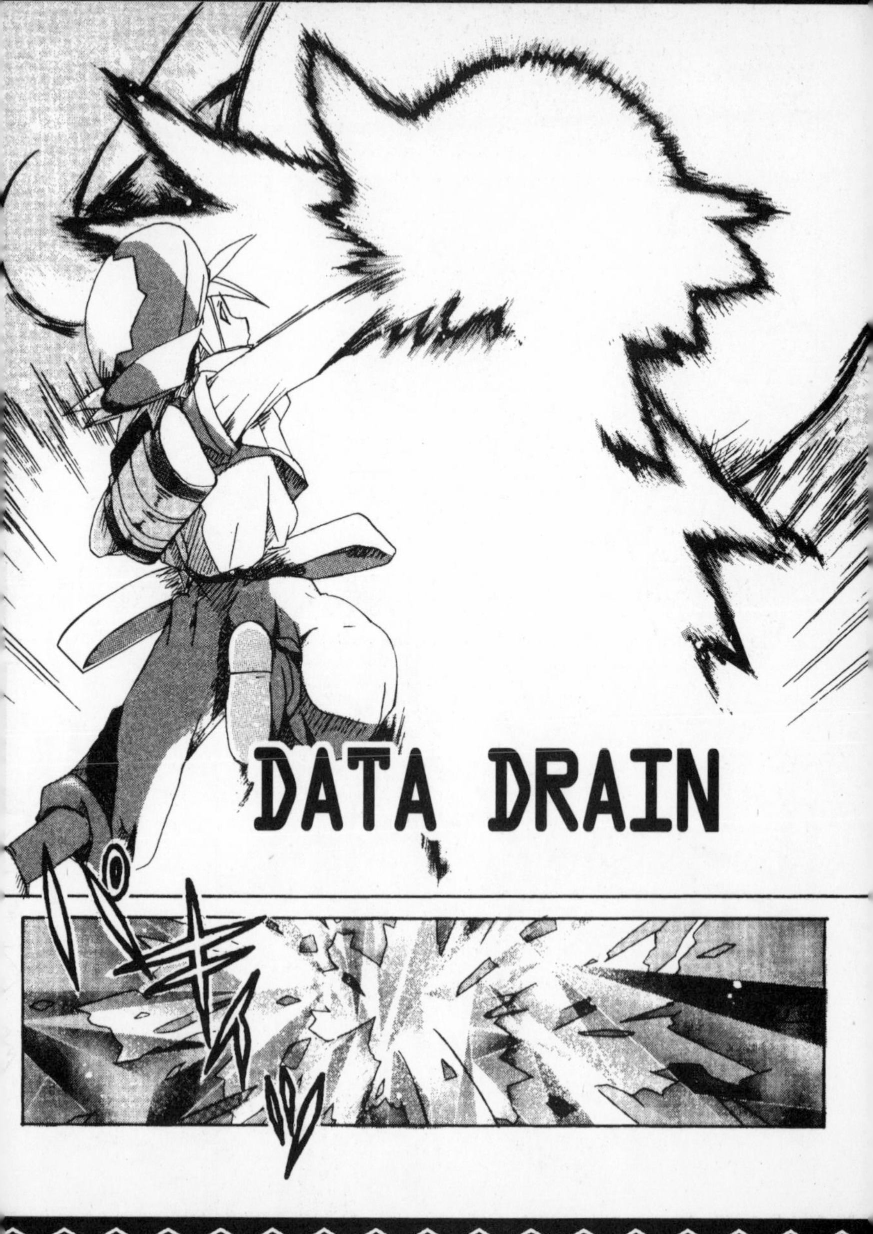
DATA DRAIN

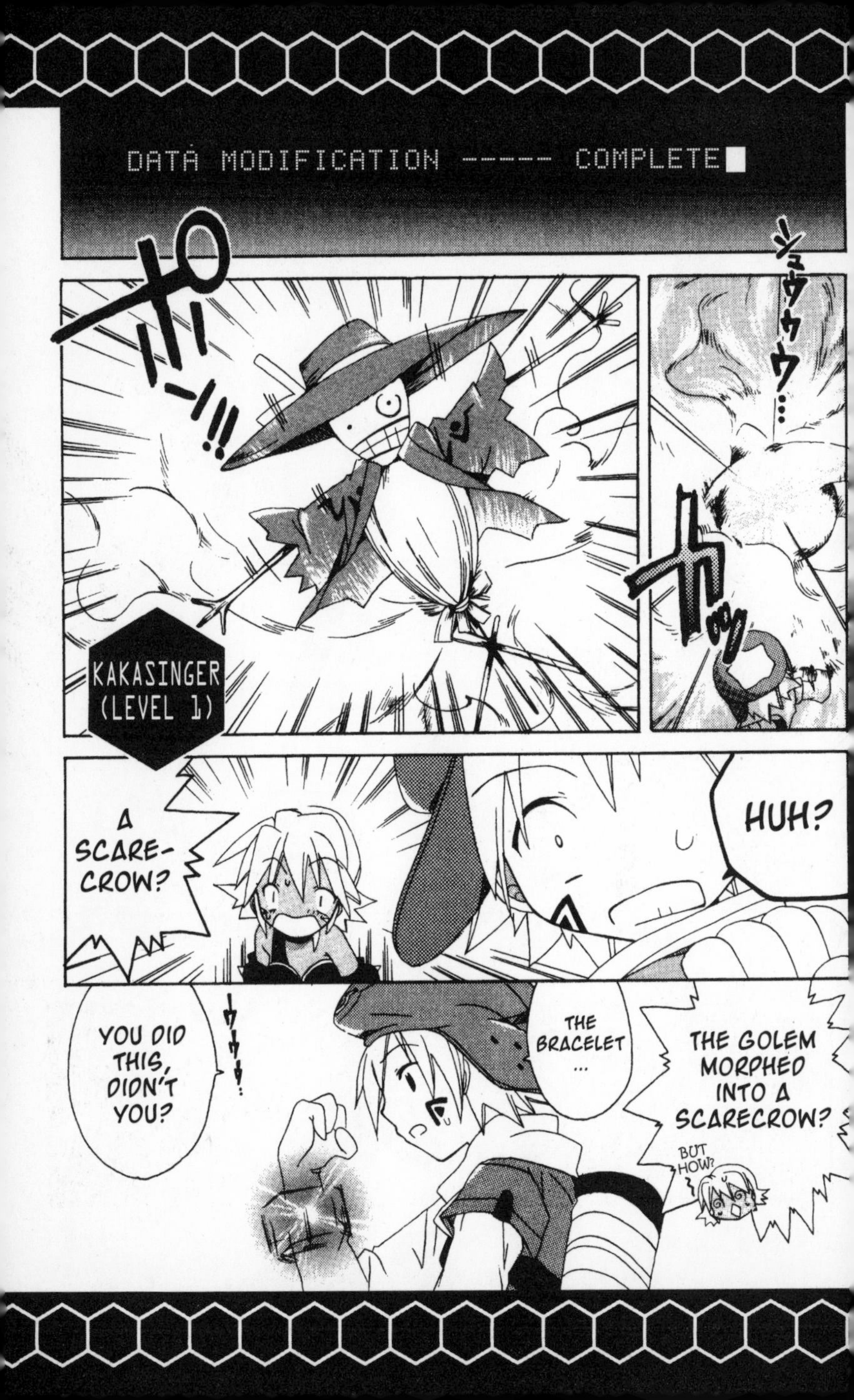
DATA MODIFICATION ----- COMPLETE
シュウウウ…
カッ
ポーン!!!
KAKASINGER (LEVEL 1)
HUH?
A SCARE-CROW?
THE GOLEM MORPHED INTO A SCARECROW?
BUT HOW?
THE BRACELET ...
ウゥゥ…
YOU DID THIS, DIDN'T YOU?

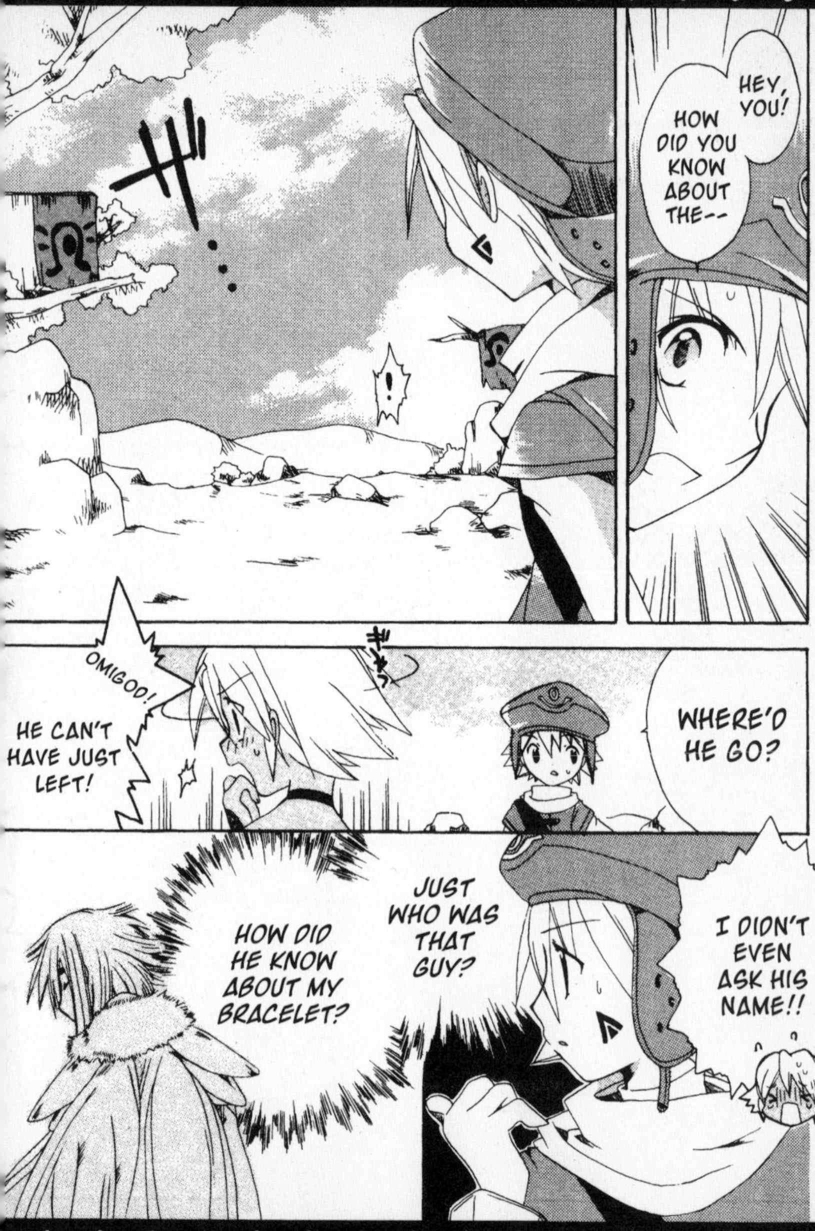
HEY, YOU!
HOW DID YOU KNOW ABOUT THE--
!
WHERE'D HE GO?
OMIGOD!
HE CAN'T HAVE JUST LEFT!
I DIDN'T EVEN ASK HIS NAME!!
JUST WHO WAS THAT GUY?
HOW DID HE KNOW ABOUT MY BRACELET?

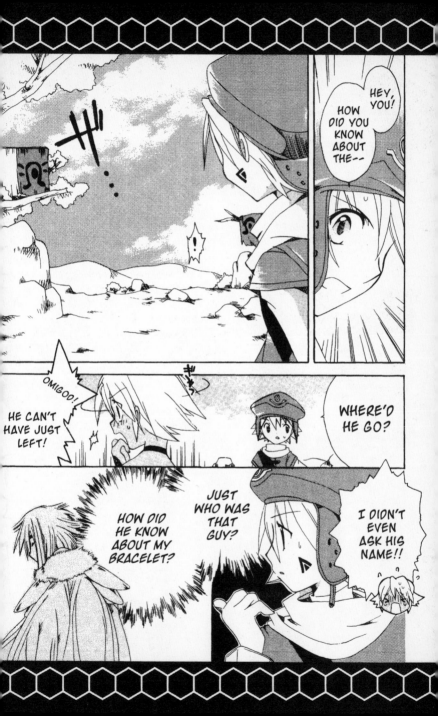

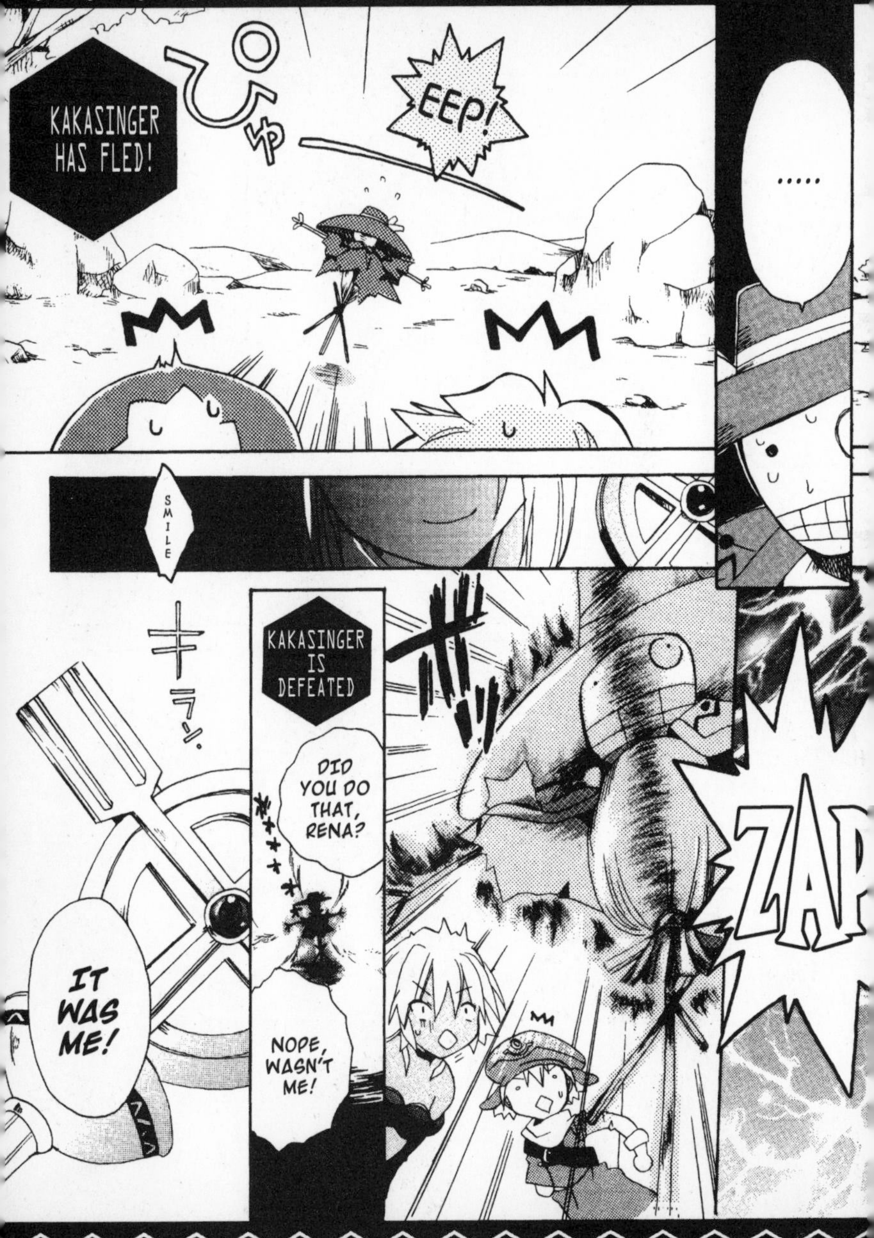
.....
EEP!
ぴゅ
KAKASINGER HAS FLED!
SMILE
ZAP
KAKASINGER IS DEFEATED
DID YOU DO THAT, RENA?
NOPE, WASN'T ME!
キラン
IT WAS ME!

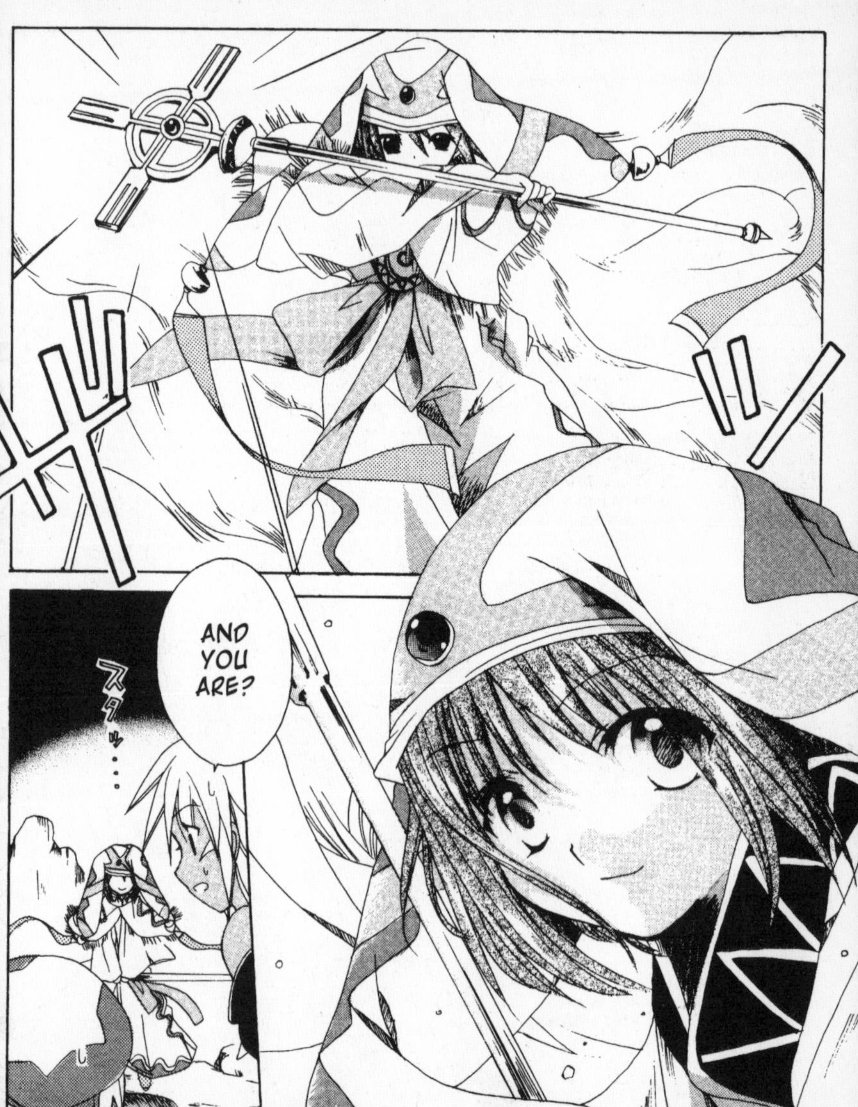
AND YOU ARE?
スタッ…

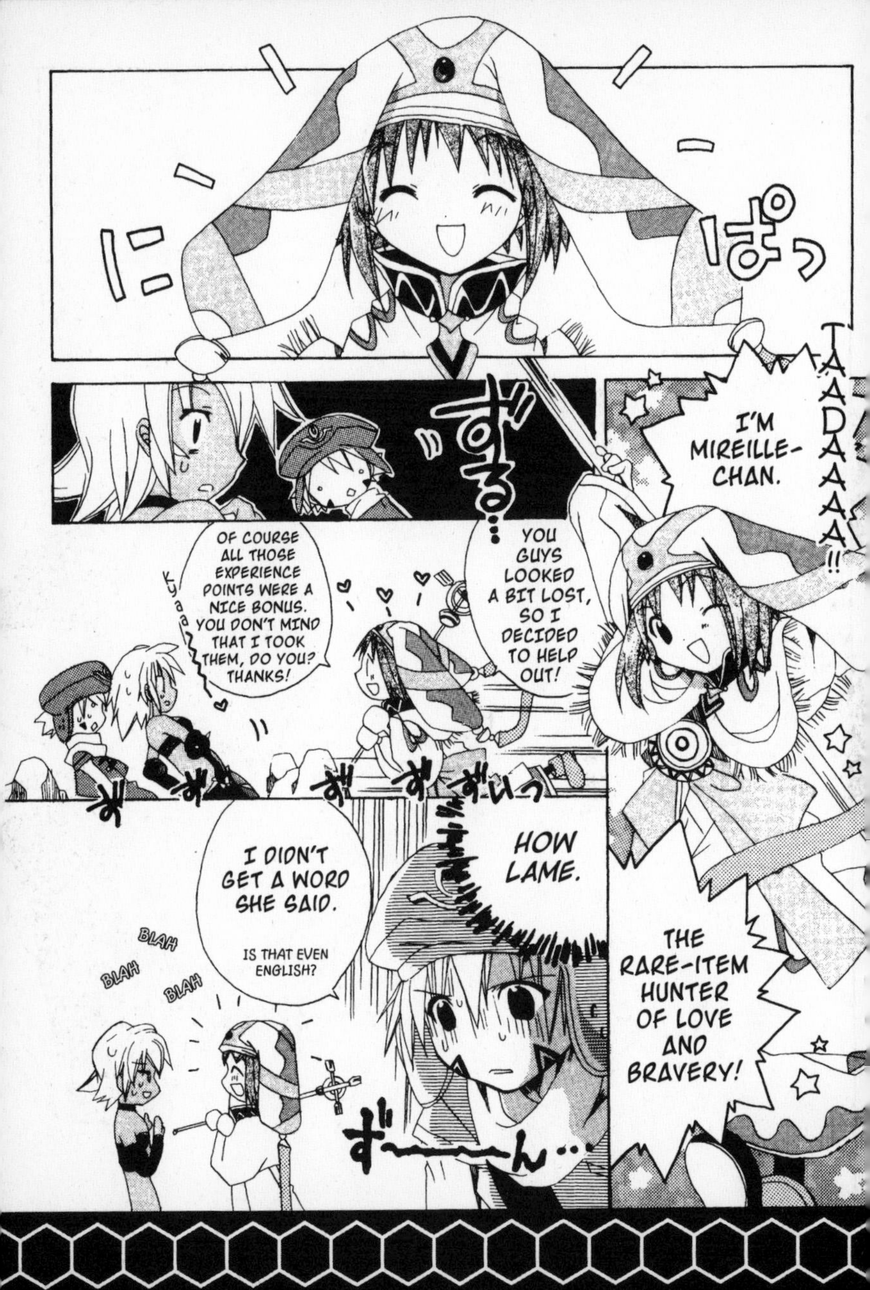
ぱっ
にー
TAADAAAAA!!
I'M MIREILLE-CHAN.
ずる…
YOU GUYS LOOKED A BIT LOST, SO I DECIDED TO HELP OUT!
OF COURSE ALL THOSE EXPERIENCE POINTS WERE A NICE BONUS. YOU DON'T MIND THAT I TOOK THEM, DO YOU? THANKS!
Kyaa
ずずずいっ
THE RARE-ITEM HUNTER OF LOVE AND BRAVERY!
HOW LAME.
I DIDN'T GET A WORD SHE SAID.
IS THAT EVEN ENGLISH?
BLAH
BLAH
BLAH
ず~~ん…

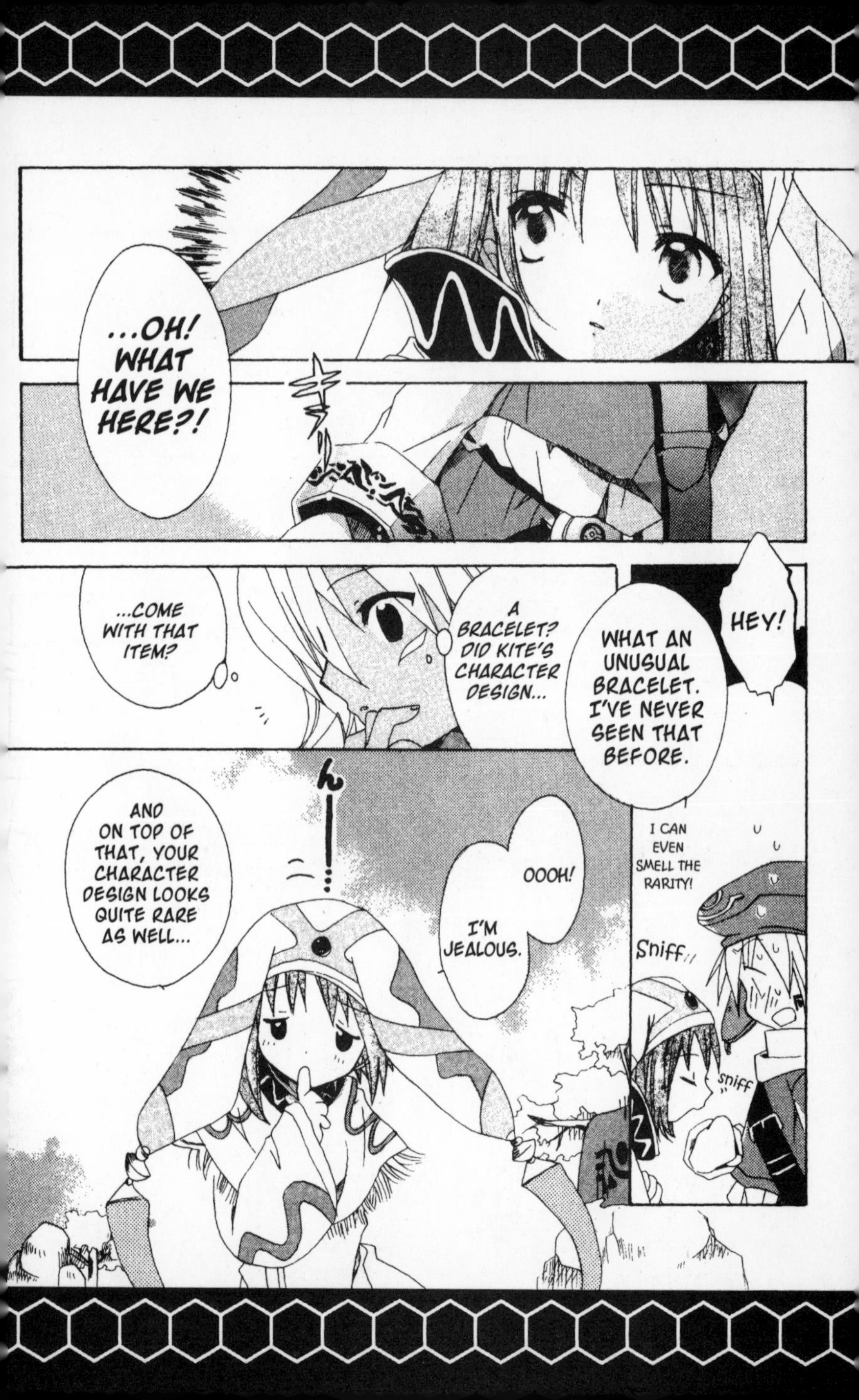
...OH! WHAT HAVE WE HERE?!
HEY!
WHAT AN UNUSUAL BRACELET. I'VE NEVER SEEN THAT BEFORE.
A BRACELET? DID KITE'S CHARACTER DESIGN...
...COME WITH THAT ITEM?
I CAN EVEN SMELL THE RARITY!
Sniff
sniff
AND ON TOP OF THAT, YOUR CHARACTER DESIGN LOOKS QUITE RARE AS WELL...
OOOH!
I'M JEALOUS.

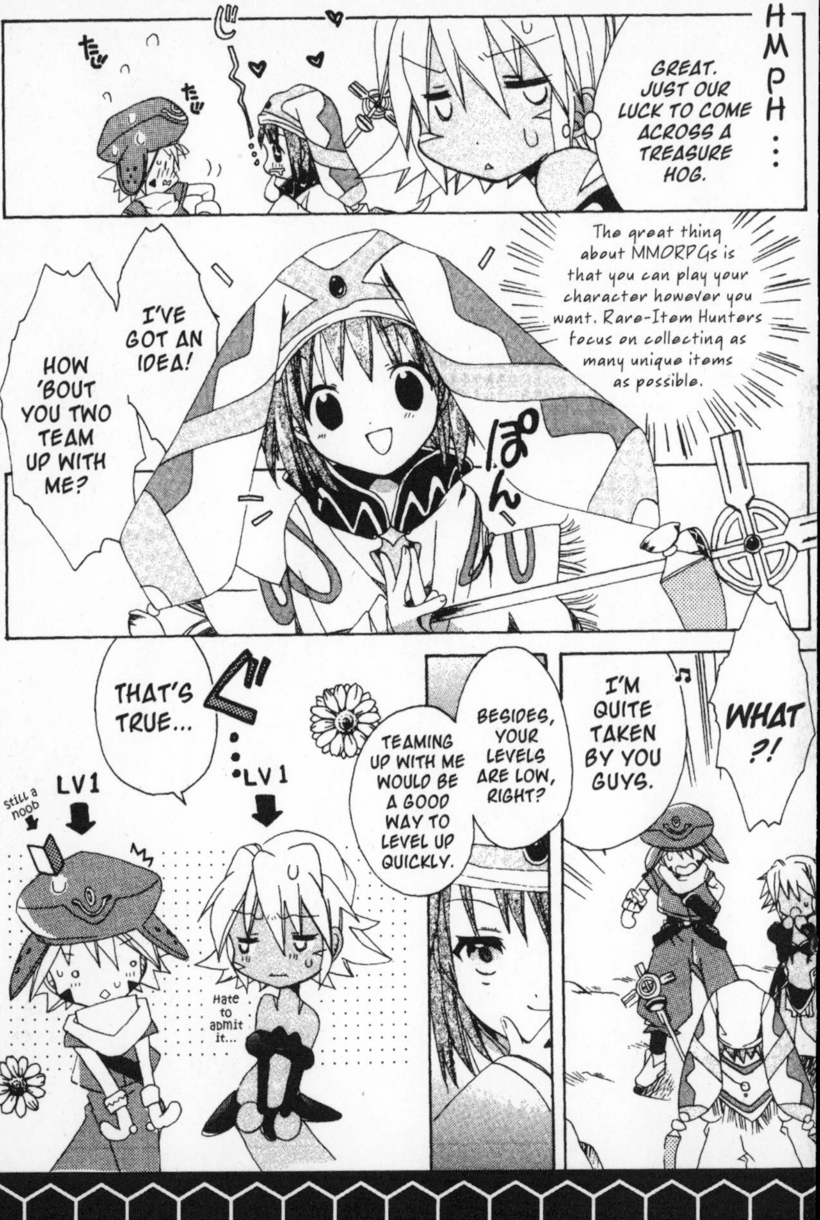
HMPH...
GREAT. JUST OUR LUCK TO COME ACROSS A TREASURE HOG.
The great thing about MMORPGs is that you can play your character however you want. Rare-Item Hunters focus on collecting as many unique items as possible.
I'VE GOT AN IDEA!
HOW 'BOUT YOU TWO TEAM UP WITH ME?
ぽん
WHAT?!
I'M QUITE TAKEN BY YOU GUYS.
BESIDES, YOUR LEVELS ARE LOW, RIGHT?
TEAMING UP WITH ME WOULD BE A GOOD WAY TO LEVEL UP QUICKLY.
THAT'S TRUE...
LV1
LV1
Still a noob
Hate to admit it...

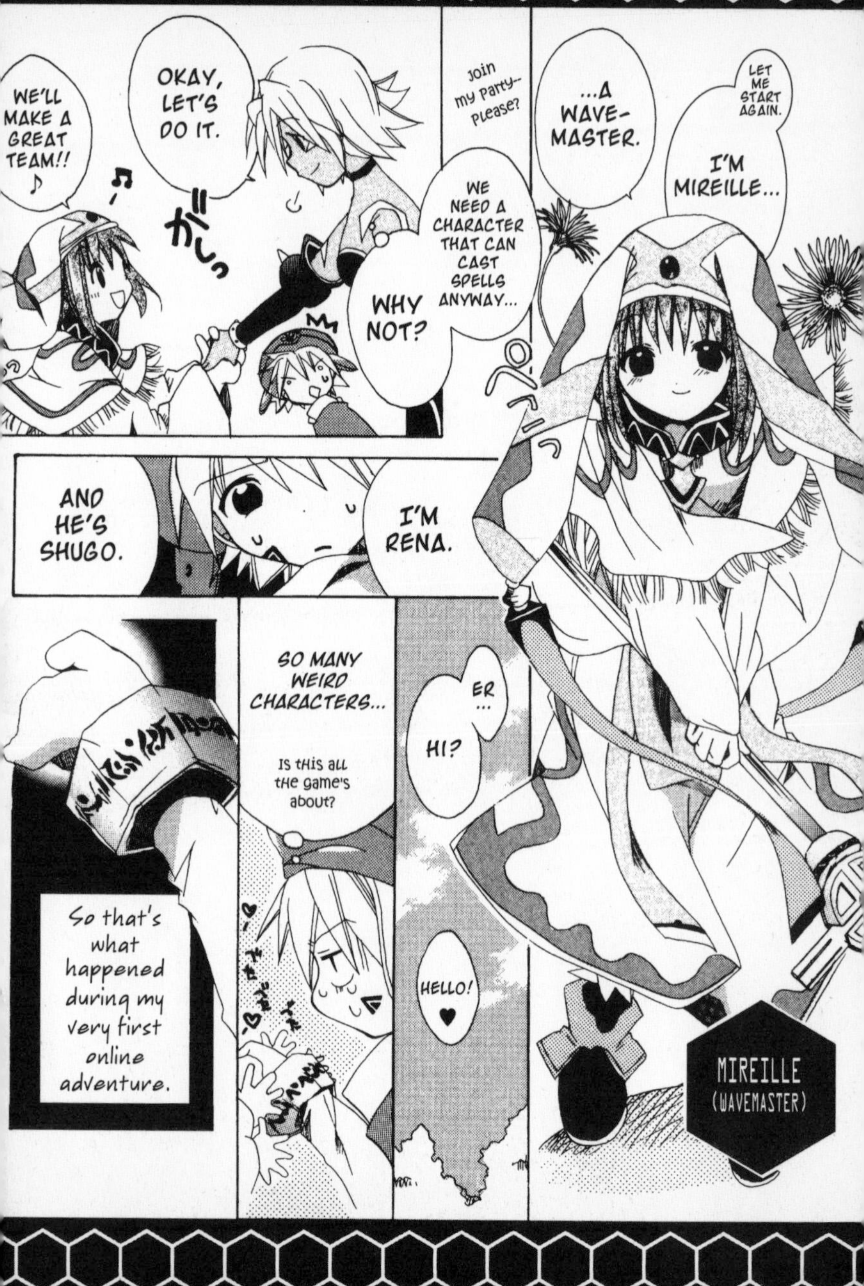
LET ME START AGAIN.
I'M MIREILLE...
...A WAVE-MASTER.
MIREILLE (WAVEMASTER)
Join my party—please?
WE NEED A CHARACTER THAT CAN CAST SPELLS ANYWAY...
WHY NOT?
OKAY, LET'S DO IT.
がしっ
WE'LL MAKE A GREAT TEAM!! ♪
I'M RENA.
AND HE'S SHUGO.
ER...
HI?
HELLO! ♥
SO MANY WEIRD CHARACTERS...
Is this all the game's about?
So that's what happened during my very first online adventure.

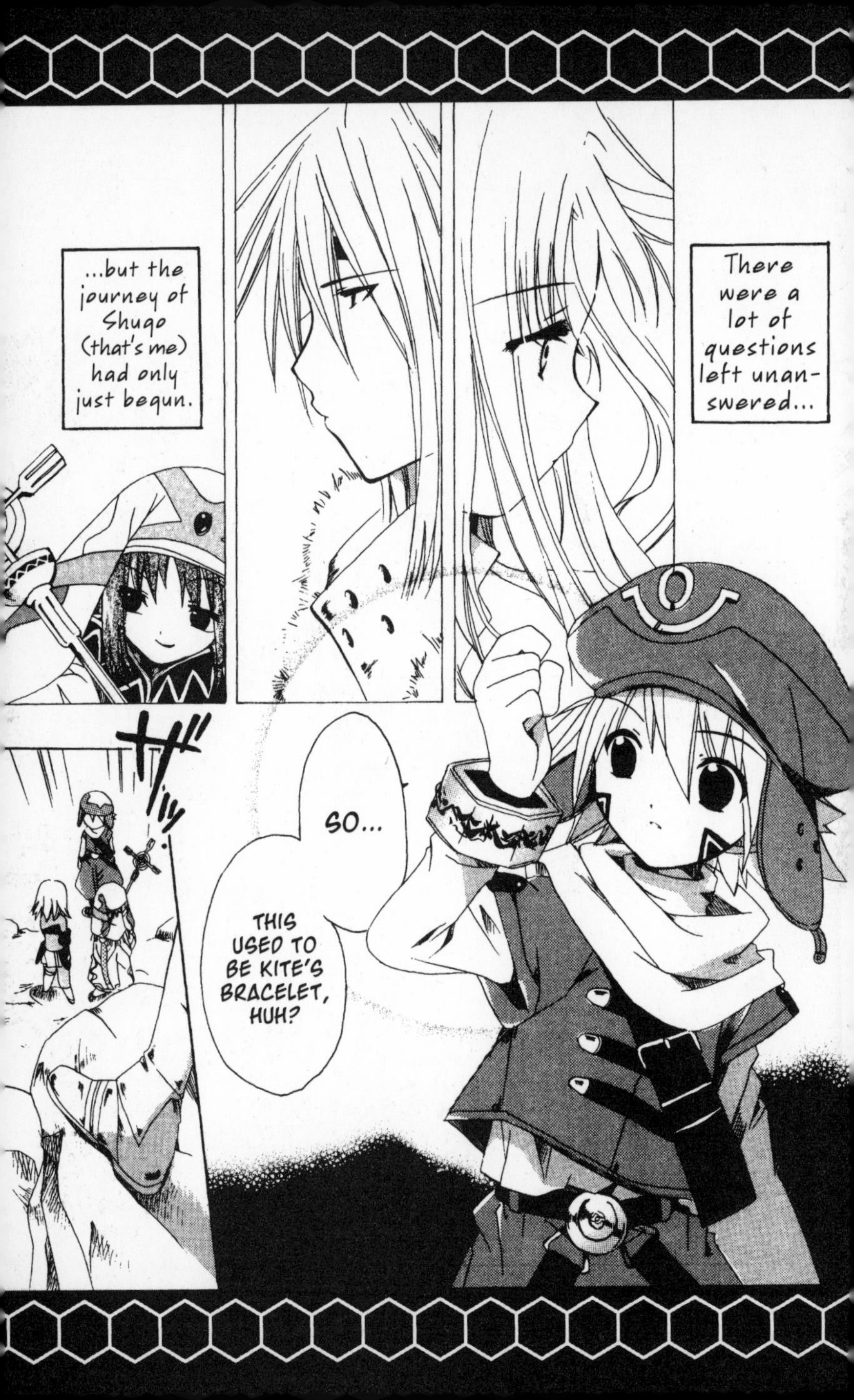
There were a lot of questions left unanswered...
...but the journey of Shugo (that's me) had only just begun.
SO...
THIS USED TO BE KITE'S BRACELET, HUH?

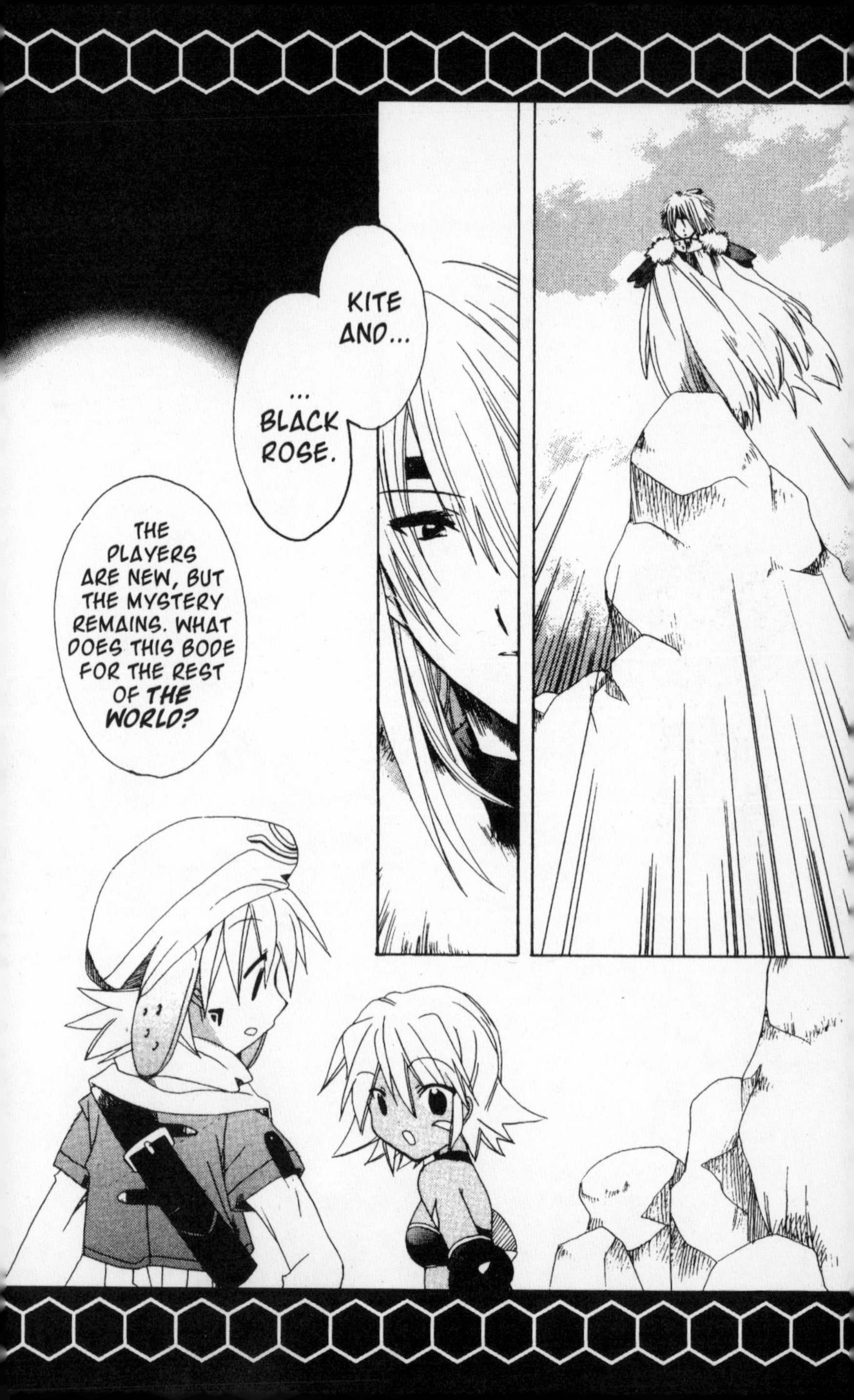
KITE AND... ...BLACK ROSE.
THE PLAYERS ARE NEW, BUT THE MYSTERY REMAINS. WHAT DOES THIS BODE FOR THE REST OF THE WORLD?

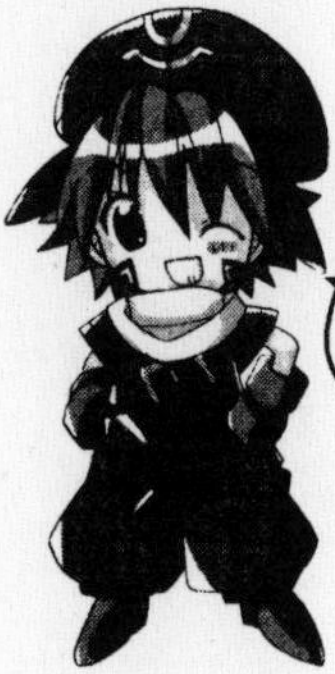

NEW GENERATION ONLINE
THE WORLD

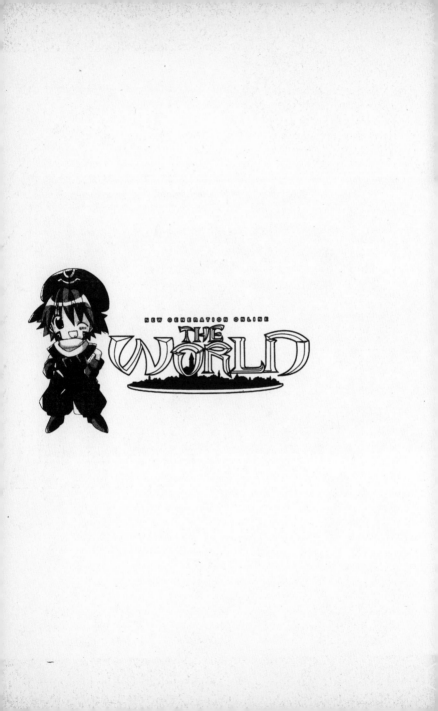

SUBJECT: YAHOO! WELCOME =) | **FROM: MIREILLE**

HELLO, SHUGO!
AREN'T YOU LUCKY TO GET YOUR VERY FIRST EMAIL FROM
ME, MIREILLE-CHAN! (>_<)
I DIDN'T WIN THE LIMITED CHARACTER EDITIONS, BUT
I'M GLAD I COULD GET A HOLD OF THIS EXTREMELY RARE
INFORMATION--YOUR E-MAIL ADDRESS! (*_*)
LET'S GO ON LOTS AND LOTS OF ADVENTURES TOGETHER,
'KAY? (^_^)

BTW, AS A SPECIAL TOKEN OF OUR FIRST MEETING,
I'D LIKE TO INVITE YOU TO MY SECRET HIDEOUT--
HEE HEE HEE!! (>_<)
BESIDES, I WANNA LEARN MORE ABOUT YOU.
I'LL BE WAITING!! (@_@)

JA NE!
MIREILLE-CHAN

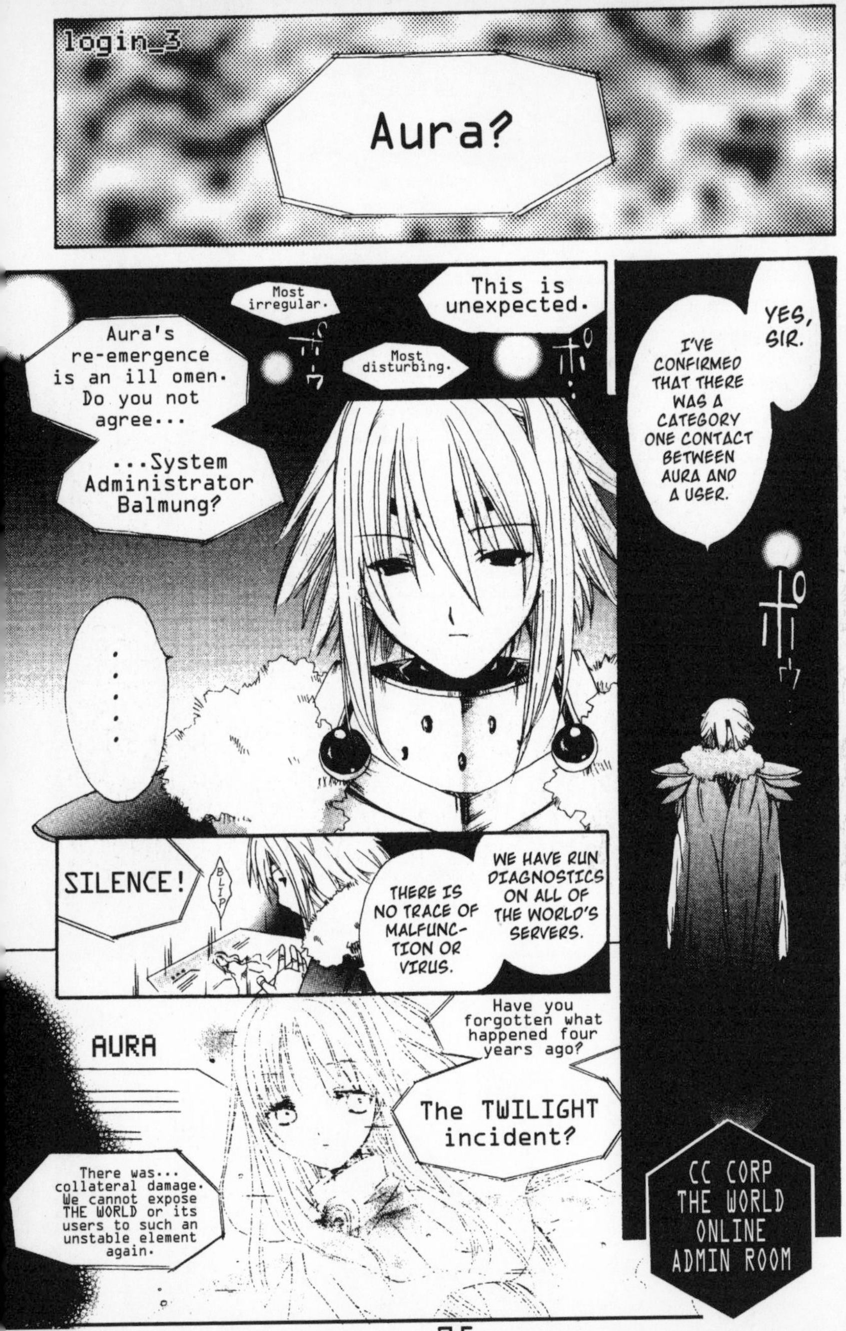
login_3
Aura?
YES, SIR.
I'VE CONFIRMED THAT THERE WAS A CATEGORY ONE CONTACT BETWEEN AURA AND A USER.
CC CORP THE WORLD ONLINE ADMIN ROOM
This is unexpected.
Most irregular.
Most disturbing.
Aura's re-emergence is an ill omen. Do you not agree...
...System Administrator Balmung?
......
WE HAVE RUN DIAGNOSTICS ON ALL OF THE WORLD'S SERVERS.
THERE IS NO TRACE OF MALFUNCTION OR VIRUS.
BLIP
SILENCE!
Have you forgotten what happened four years ago?
The TWILIGHT incident?
AURA
There was... collateral damage. We cannot expose THE WORLD or its users to such an unstable element again.

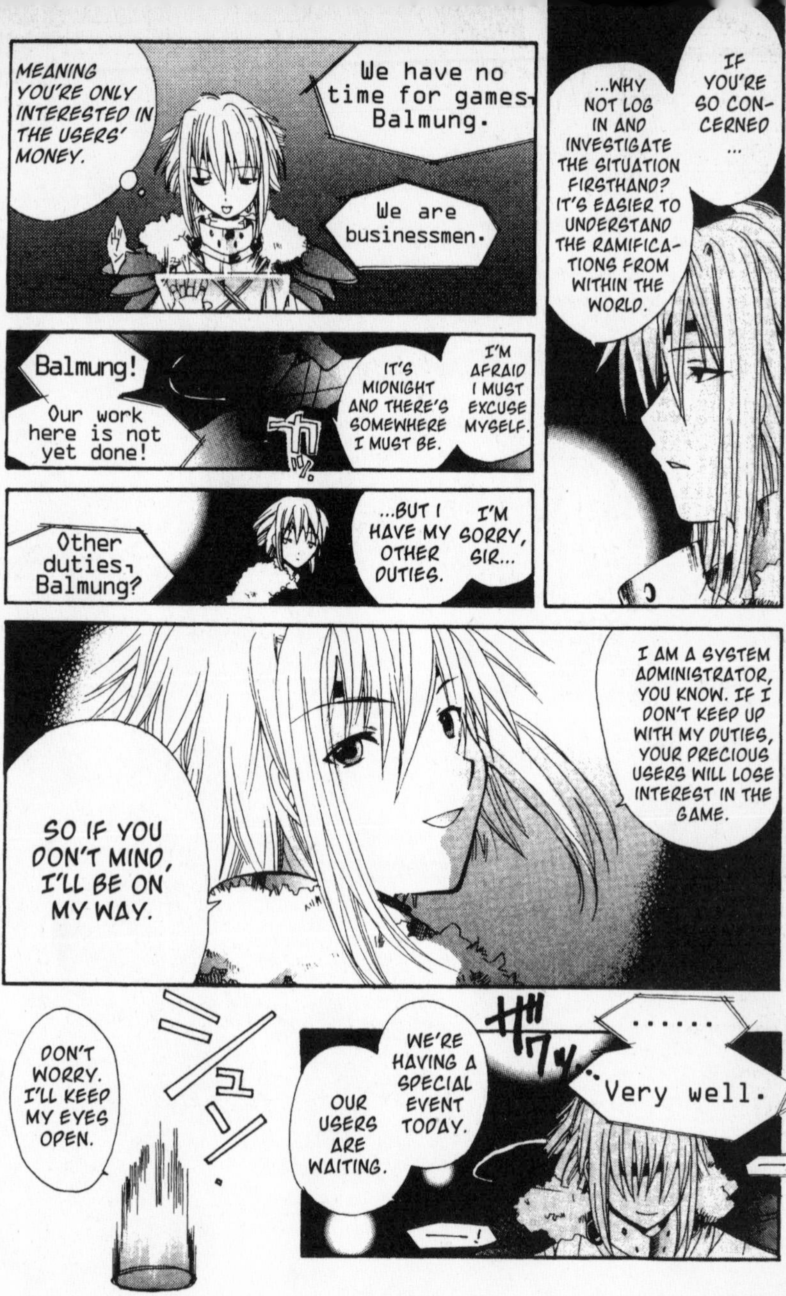
IF YOU'RE SO CONCERNED...
...WHY NOT LOG IN AND INVESTIGATE THE SITUATION FIRSTHAND? IT'S EASIER TO UNDERSTAND THE RAMIFICATIONS FROM WITHIN THE WORLD.
We have no time for games, Balmung.
MEANING YOU'RE ONLY INTERESTED IN THE USERS' MONEY.
We are businessmen.
I'M AFRAID I MUST EXCUSE MYSELF.
IT'S MIDNIGHT AND THERE'S SOMEWHERE I MUST BE.
Balmung!
Our work here is not yet done!
I'M SORRY, SIR...
...BUT I HAVE MY OTHER DUTIES.
Other duties, Balmung?
I AM A SYSTEM ADMINISTRATOR, YOU KNOW. IF I DON'T KEEP UP WITH MY DUTIES, YOUR PRECIOUS USERS WILL LOSE INTEREST IN THE GAME.
SO IF YOU DON'T MIND, I'LL BE ON MY WAY.
......
...Very well.
—!
WE'RE HAVING A SPECIAL EVENT TODAY.
OUR USERS ARE WAITING.
—!
DON'T WORRY. I'LL KEEP MY EYES OPEN.

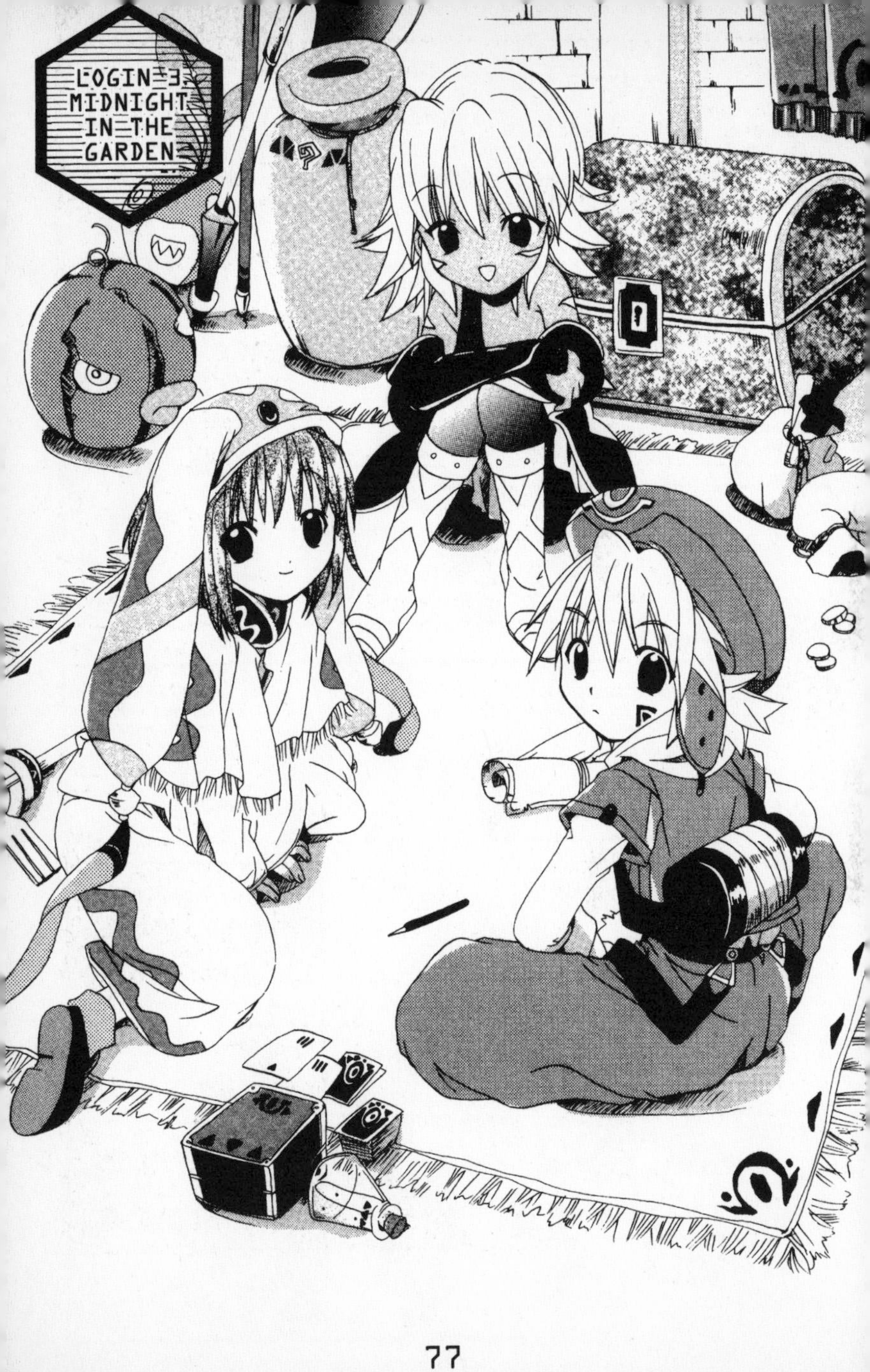
LOGIN 3: MIDNIGHT IN THE GARDEN

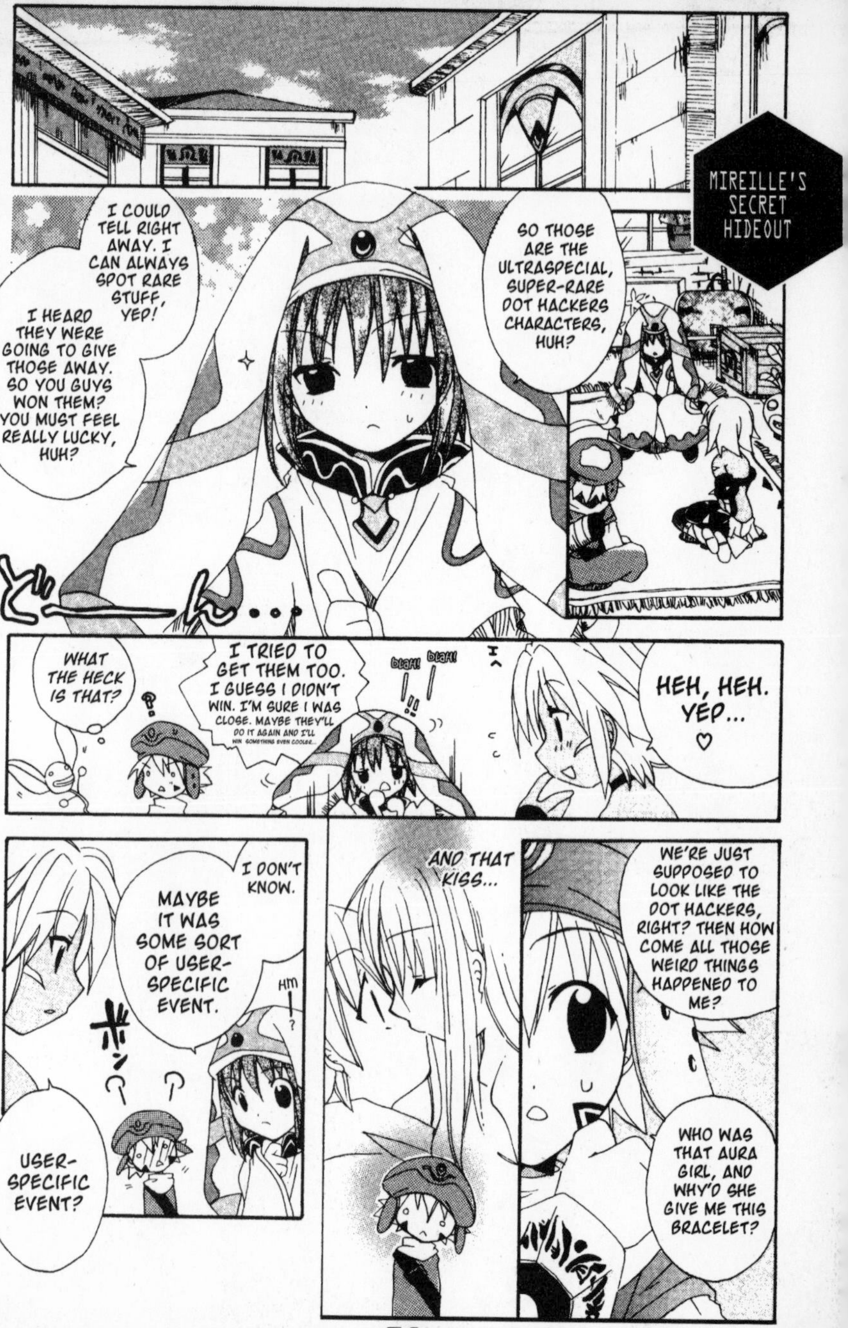
MIREILLE'S SECRET HIDEOUT
SO THOSE ARE THE ULTRASPECIAL, SUPER-RARE DOT HACKERS CHARACTERS, HUH?
I COULD TELL RIGHT AWAY. I CAN ALWAYS SPOT RARE STUFF, YEP!
I HEARD THEY WERE GOING TO GIVE THOSE AWAY. SO YOU GUYS WON THEM? YOU MUST FEEL REALLY LUCKY, HUH?
どーん…
HEH, HEH. YEP... ♡
blah! blah!
I TRIED TO GET THEM TOO. I GUESS I DIDN'T WIN. I'M SURE I WAS CLOSE. MAYBE THEY'LL DO IT AGAIN AND I'LL WIN SOMETHING EVEN COOLER...
WHAT THE HECK IS THAT?
WE'RE JUST SUPPOSED TO LOOK LIKE THE DOT HACKERS, RIGHT? THEN HOW COME ALL THOSE WEIRD THINGS HAPPENED TO ME?
WHO WAS THAT AURA GIRL, AND WHY'D SHE GIVE ME THIS BRACELET?
AND THAT KISS...
I DON'T KNOW.
MAYBE IT WAS SOME SORT OF USER-SPECIFIC EVENT.
HM!?
ボン
USER-SPECIFIC EVENT?

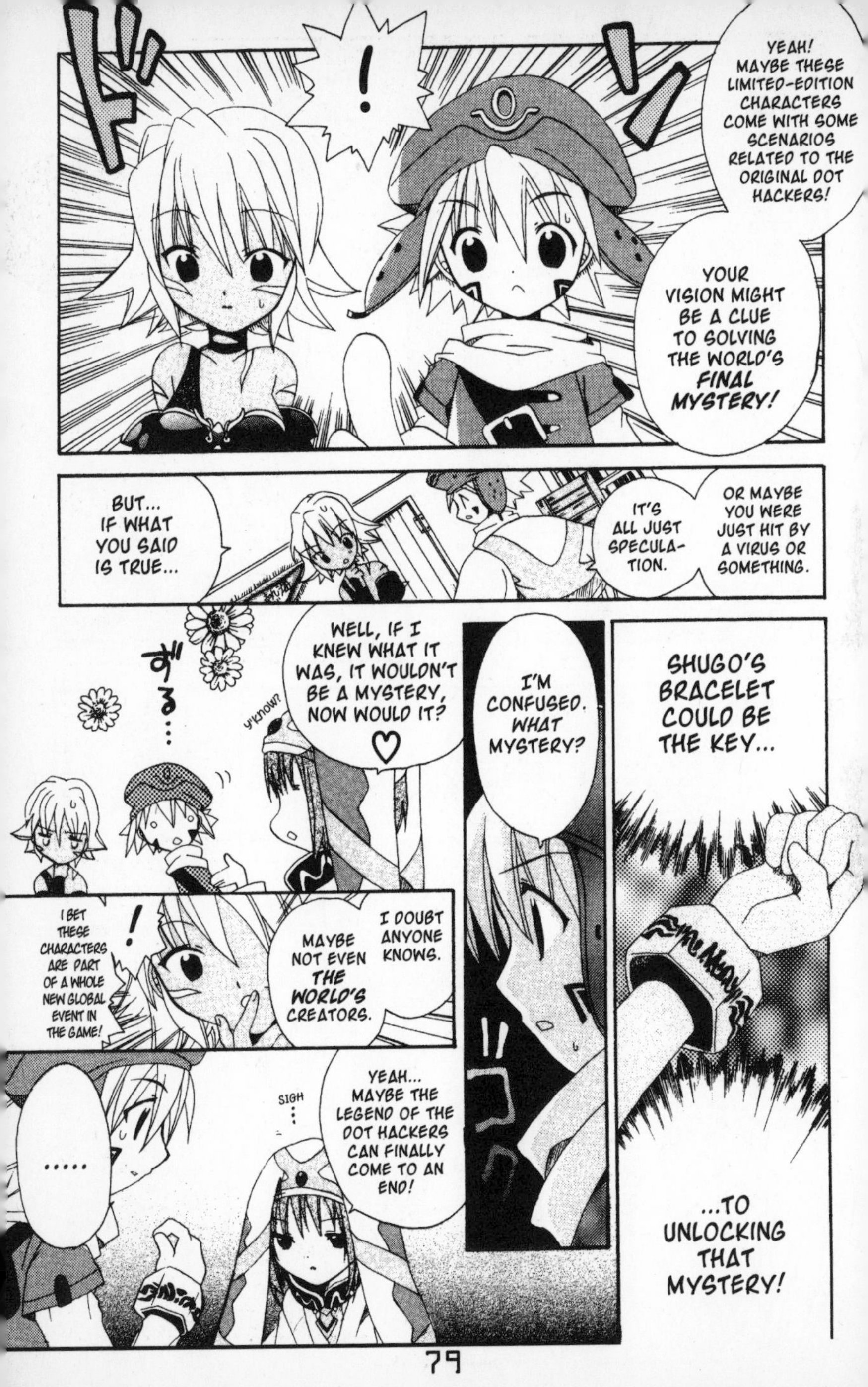
YEAH! MAYBE THESE LIMITED-EDITION CHARACTERS COME WITH SOME SCENARIOS RELATED TO THE ORIGINAL DOT HACKERS!
YOUR VISION MIGHT BE A CLUE TO SOLVING THE WORLD'S FINAL MYSTERY!
!
ド
OR MAYBE YOU WERE JUST HIT BY A VIRUS OR SOMETHING.
IT'S ALL JUST SPECULA-TION.
BUT... IF WHAT YOU SAID IS TRUE...
SHUGO'S BRACELET COULD BE THE KEY...
...TO UNLOCKING THAT MYSTERY!
I'M CONFUSED. WHAT MYSTERY?
WELL, IF I KNEW WHAT IT WAS, IT WOULDN'T BE A MYSTERY, NOW WOULD IT? ♡
Y'KNOW?
ずる…
I DOUBT ANYONE KNOWS.
MAYBE NOT EVEN THE WORLD'S CREATORS.
!
I BET THESE CHARACTERS ARE PART OF A WHOLE NEW GLOBAL EVENT IN THE GAME!
YEAH... MAYBE THE LEGEND OF THE DOT HACKERS CAN FINALLY COME TO AN END!
SIGH
...
.....

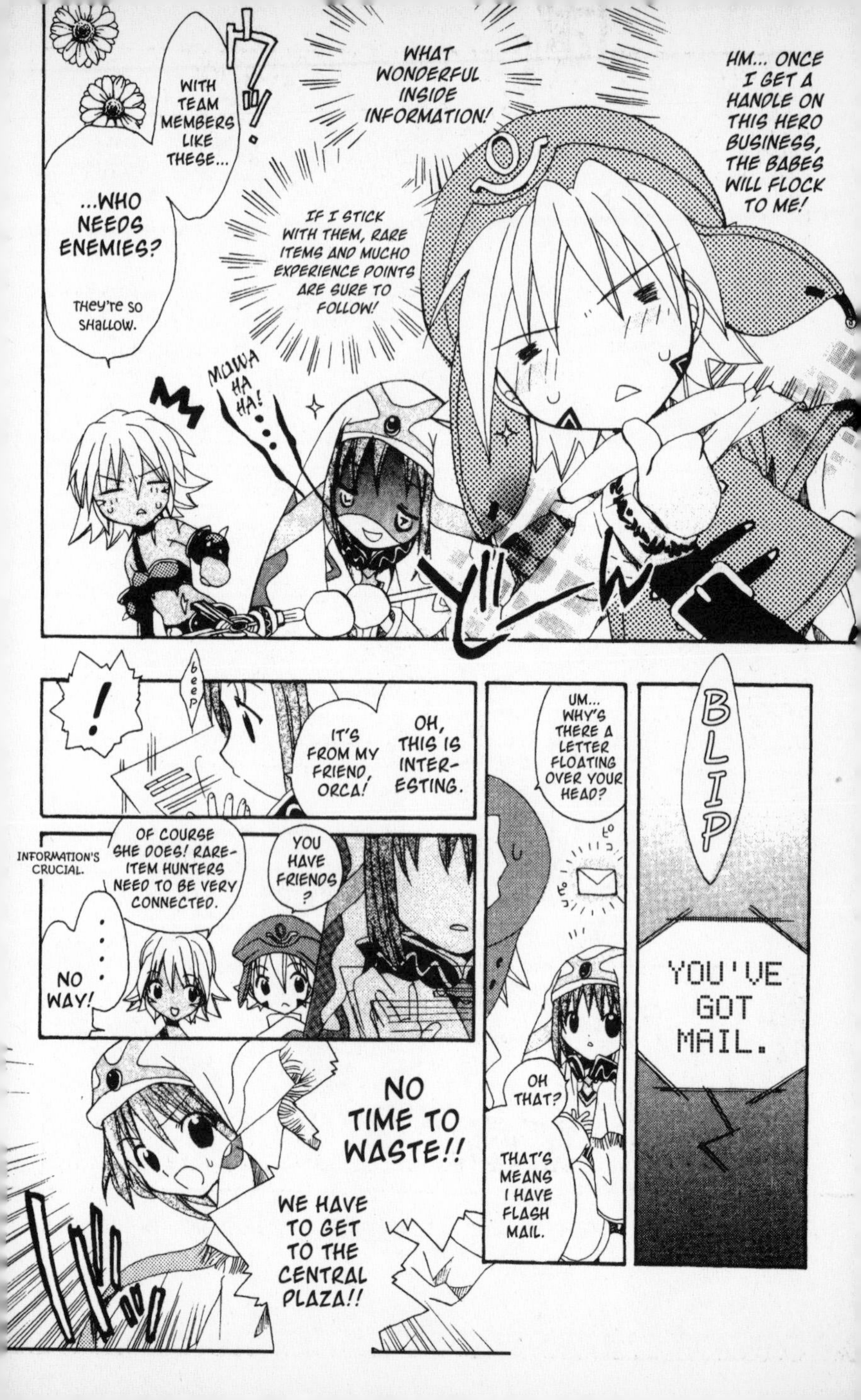
HM... ONCE I GET A HANDLE ON THIS HERO BUSINESS, THE BABES WILL FLOCK TO ME!
WHAT WONDERFUL INSIDE INFORMATION!
IF I STICK WITH THEM, RARE ITEMS AND MUCHO EXPERIENCE POINTS ARE SURE TO FOLLOW!
WITH TEAM MEMBERS LIKE THESE...
...WHO NEEDS ENEMIES?
They're so shallow.
MUWA HA HA!
BLIP
YOU'VE GOT MAIL.
UM... WHY'S THERE A LETTER FLOATING OVER YOUR HEAD?
OH THAT?
THAT'S MEANS I HAVE FLASH MAIL.
OH, THIS IS INTERESTING.
IT'S FROM MY FRIEND, ORCA!
beep
!
YOU HAVE FRIENDS?
OF COURSE SHE DOES! RARE-ITEM HUNTERS NEED TO BE VERY CONNECTED.
INFORMATION'S CRUCIAL.
... NO WAY!
NO TIME TO WASTE!!
WE HAVE TO GET TO THE CENTRAL PLAZA!!

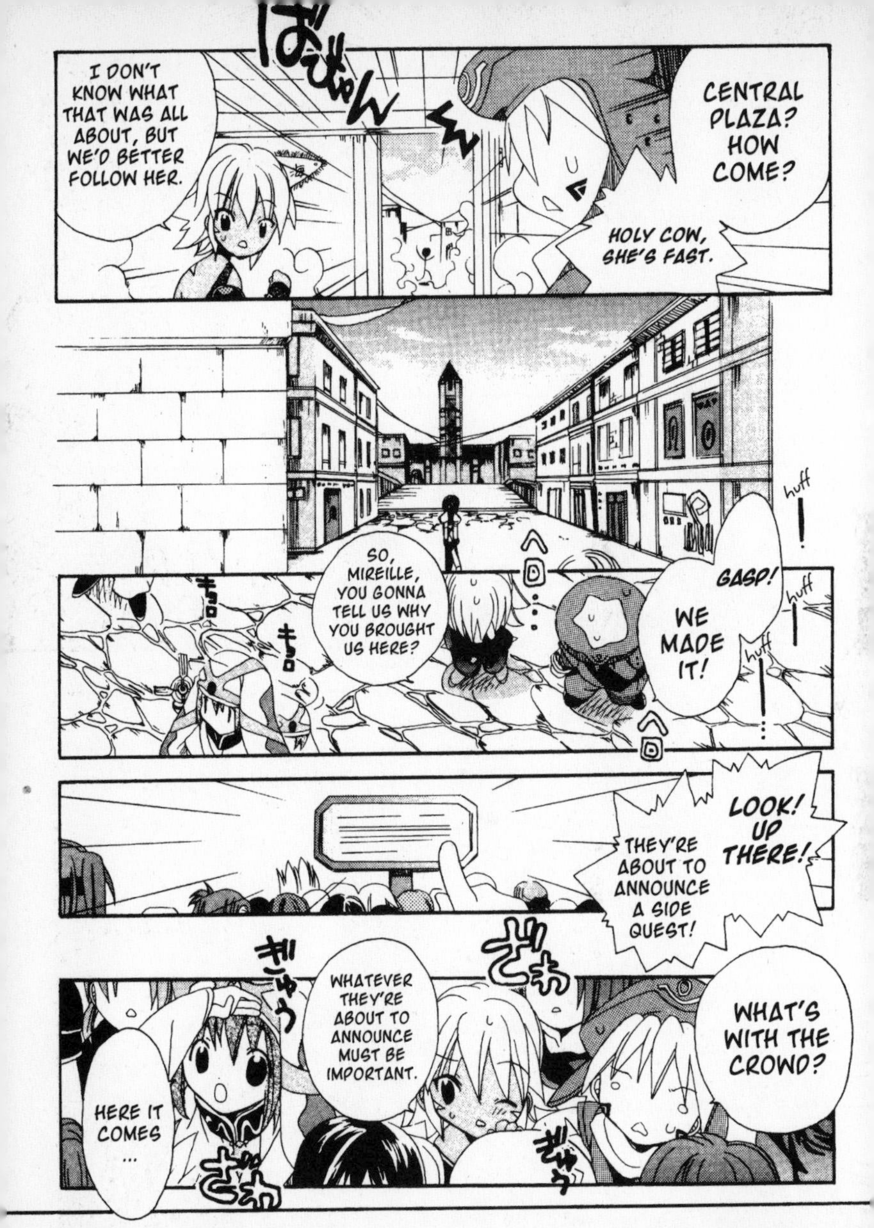
CENTRAL PLAZA? HOW COME?
HOLY COW, SHE'S FAST.
I DON'T KNOW WHAT THAT WAS ALL ABOUT, BUT WE'D BETTER FOLLOW HER.
huff
GASP!
WE MADE IT!
huff
huff
SO, MIREILLE, YOU GONNA TELL US WHY YOU BROUGHT US HERE?
LOOK! UP THERE!
THEY'RE ABOUT TO ANNOUNCE A SIDE QUEST!
WHAT'S WITH THE CROWD?
WHATEVER THEY'RE ABOUT TO ANNOUNCE MUST BE IMPORTANT.
HERE IT COMES ...

SUBJECT: VALENTINE'S DAY EVENT SENDER: BALMUNG

201X / X / X 0:15
SUBJECT: VALENTINE'S DAY EVENT SENDER: BALMUNG
TO: ALL

COME ONE AND ALL TO THE ABUNDANT GARDEN OF GAIA IN CELEBRATION OF THE DAY OF LOVE! THE FIRST 100 PLAYERS TO SOLVE MY CHALLENGE WILL RECEIVE AN ULTRA-RARE ARTIFACT, GUARANTEED TO ENHANCE ONE'S LOVE LIFE. THIS SPECIAL SIDE QUEST LASTS TODAY ONLY!

AND REMEMBER, A BEET IS NEAT, BUT A GOURD IS ADORED!

LORD BALMUNG
SYSTEM ADMINISTRATOR

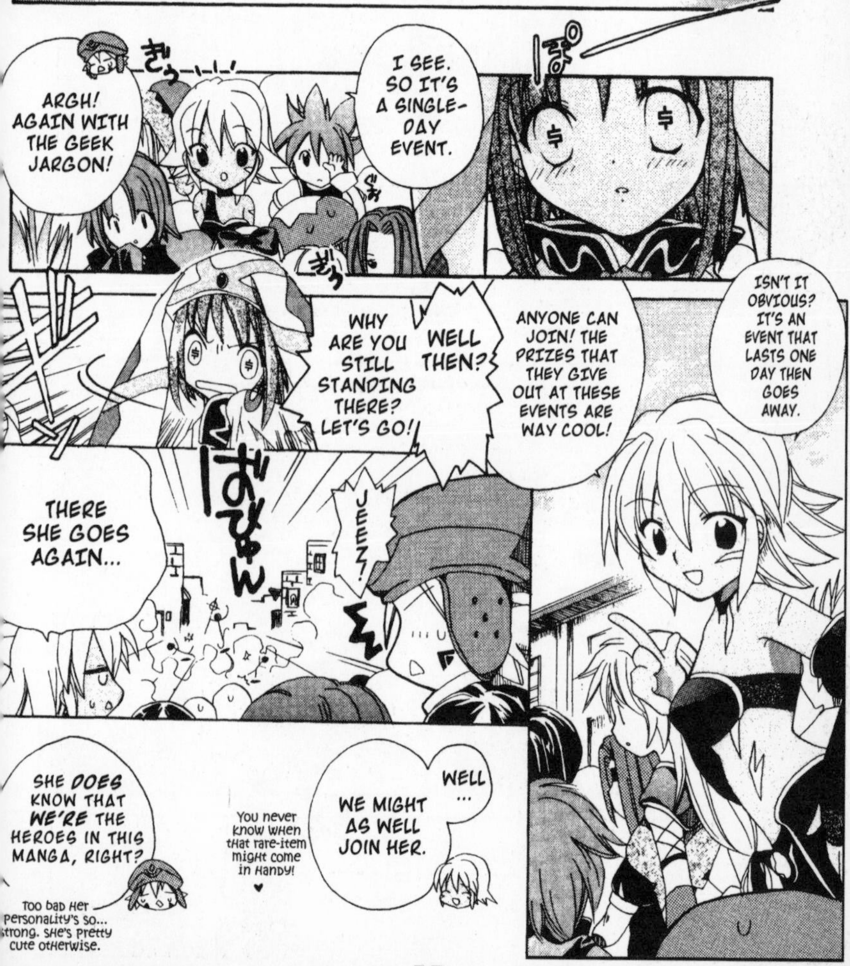
ぽ
I SEE. SO IT'S A SINGLE-DAY EVENT.
ぎゅ
ARGH! AGAIN WITH THE GEEK JARGON!
ISN'T IT OBVIOUS? IT'S AN EVENT THAT LASTS ONE DAY THEN GOES AWAY.
ANYONE CAN JOIN! THE PRIZES THAT THEY GIVE OUT AT THESE EVENTS ARE WAY COOL!
WELL THEN?
WHY ARE YOU STILL STANDING THERE? LET'S GO!
ぼびゅん
JEEZ!
THERE SHE GOES AGAIN...
WELL...
WE MIGHT AS WELL JOIN HER.
You never know when that rare-item might come in handy! ♥
SHE DOES KNOW THAT WE'RE THE HEROES IN THIS MANGA, RIGHT?
Too bad her personality's so... strong. She's pretty cute otherwise.

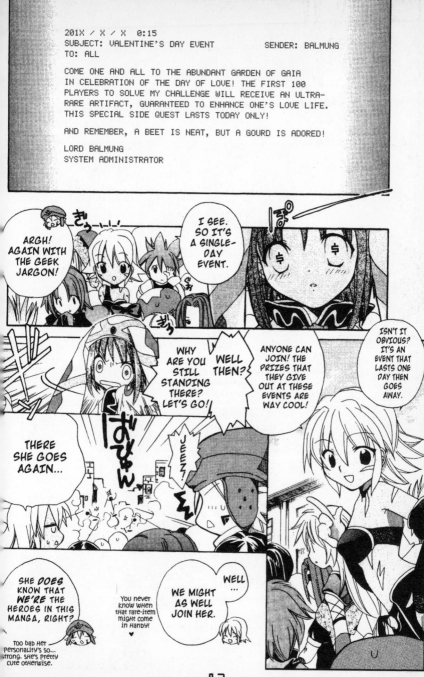

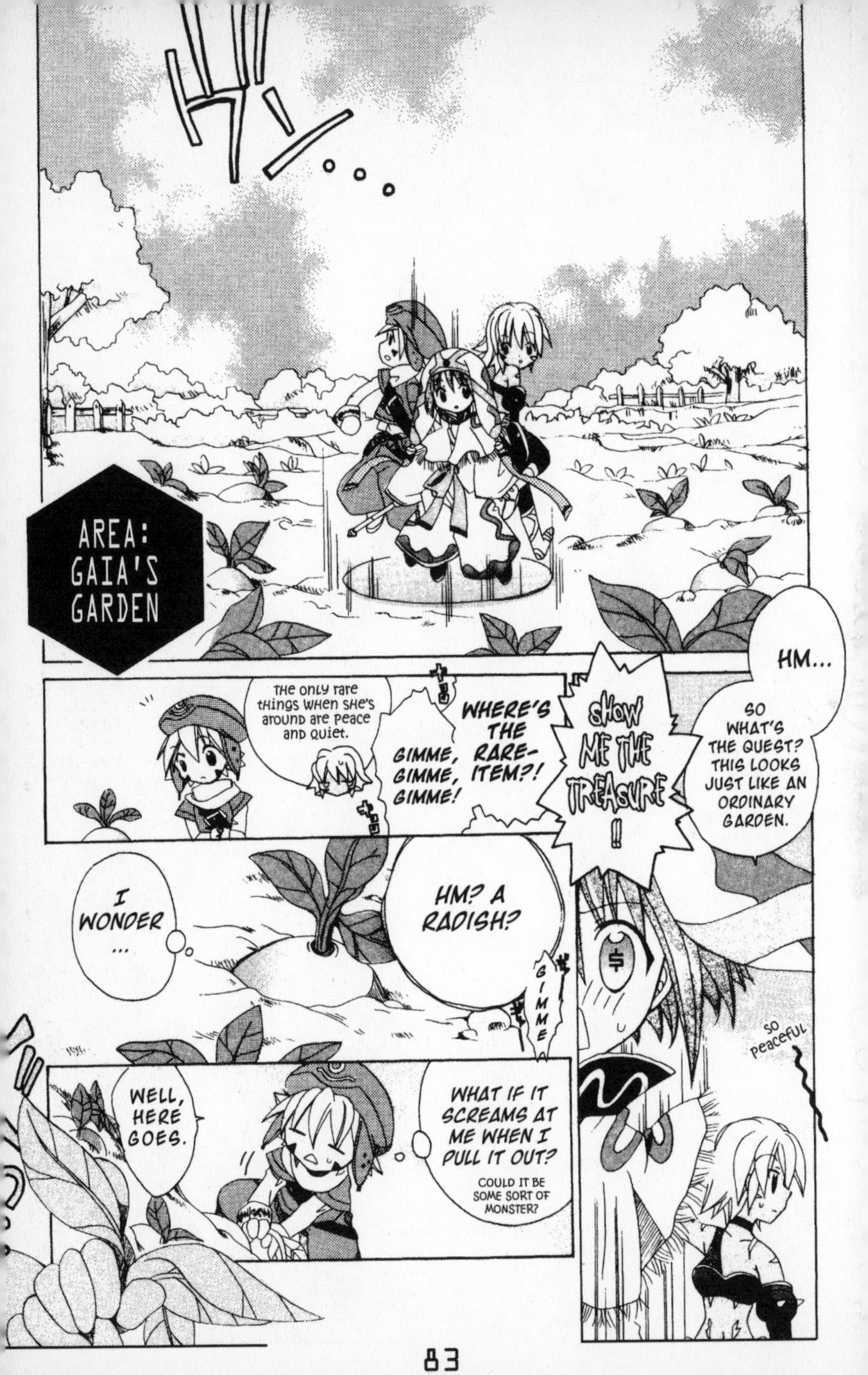
AREA: GAIA'S GARDEN
HM...
SO WHAT'S THE QUEST? THIS LOOKS JUST LIKE AN ORDINARY GARDEN.
SHOW ME THE TREASURE !!
WHERE'S THE RARE-ITEM?!
GIMME, GIMME, GIMME!
The only rare things when she's around are peace and quiet.
HM? A RADISH?
GIMME GIMME
I WONDER ...
SO peaceful
WHAT IF IT SCREAMS AT ME WHEN I PULL IT OUT?
COULD IT BE SOME SORT OF MONSTER?
WELL, HERE GOES.

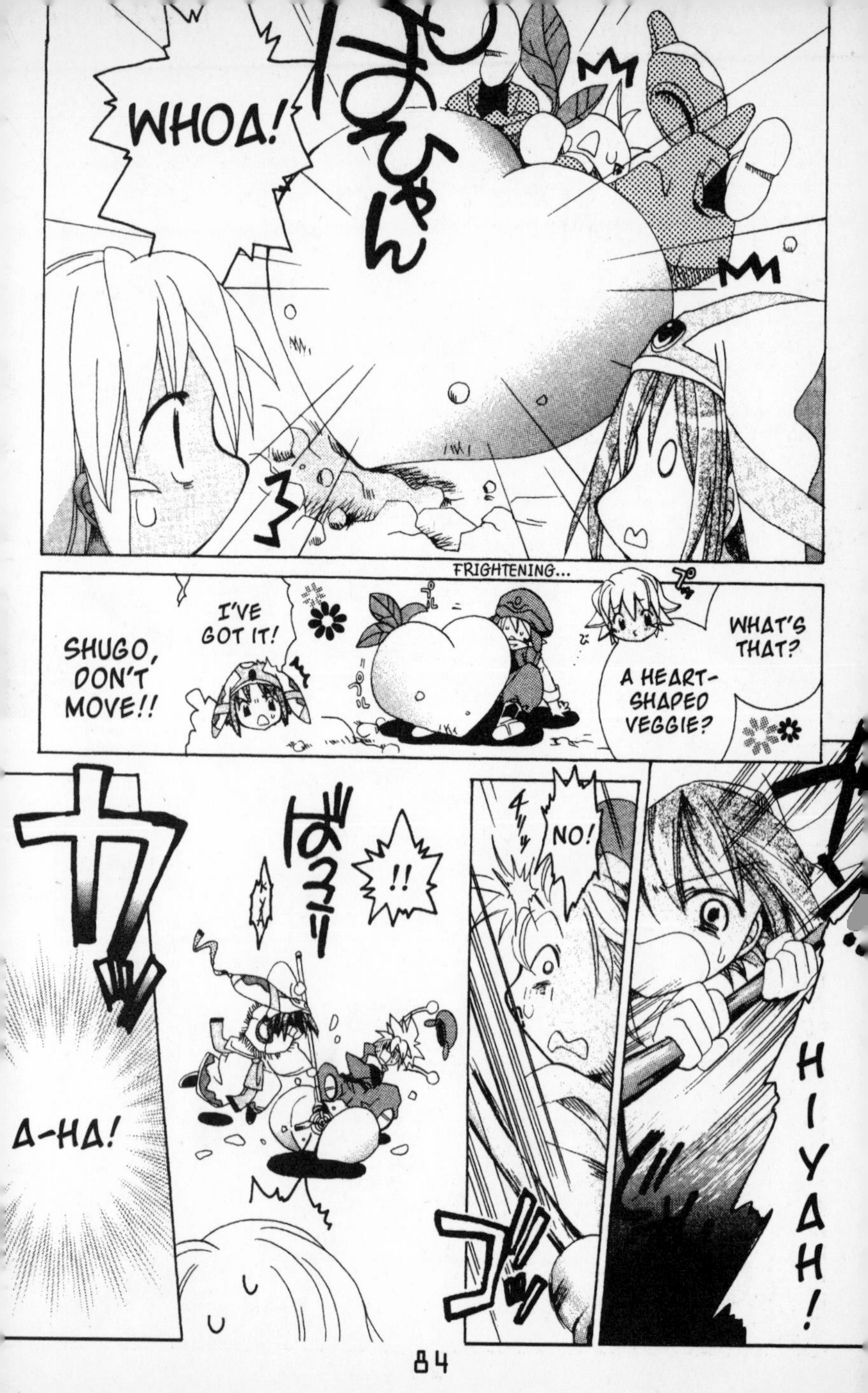
WHOA!
FRIGHTENING...
WHAT'S THAT?
A HEART-SHAPED VEGGIE?
I'VE GOT IT!
SHUGO, DON'T MOVE!!
HIYAH!
NO!
!!
A-HA!

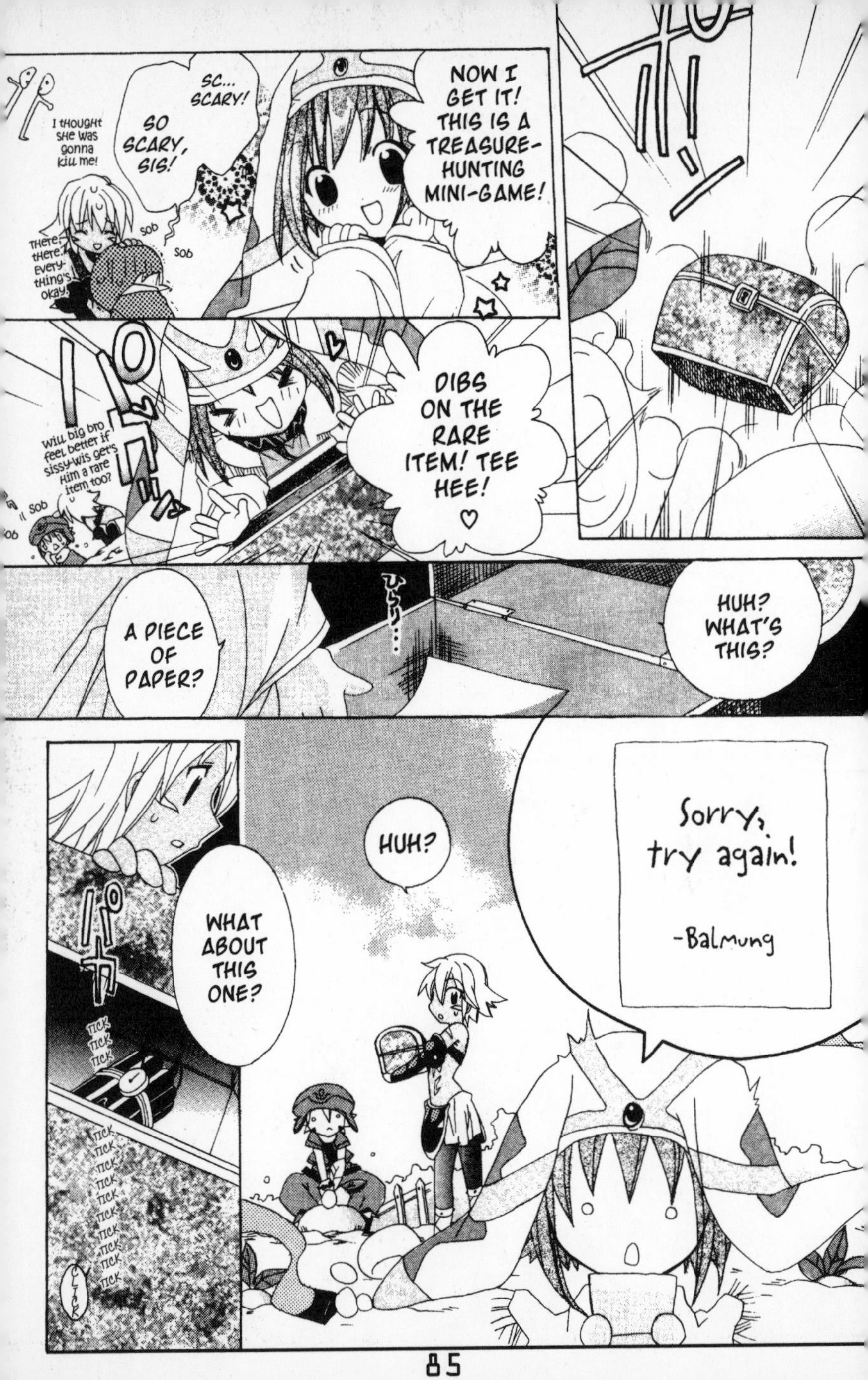
NOW I GET IT! THIS IS A TREASURE-HUNTING MINI-GAME!
SC... SCARY!
SO SCARY, SIS!
I THOUGHT SHE WAS GONNA KILL ME!
SOB
SOB
THERE, THERE. EVERYTHING'S OKAY.
DIBS ON THE RARE ITEM! TEE HEE! ♡
WILL BIG BRO FEEL BETTER IF SISSY-WIS GET'S HIM A RARE ITEM TOO?
SOB
HUH? WHAT'S THIS?
A PIECE OF PAPER?
Sorry, try again!
-Balmung
HUH?
WHAT ABOUT THIS ONE?
TICK TICK TICK
TICK TICK TICK TICK TICK TICK TICK TICK TICK TICK
CLICK

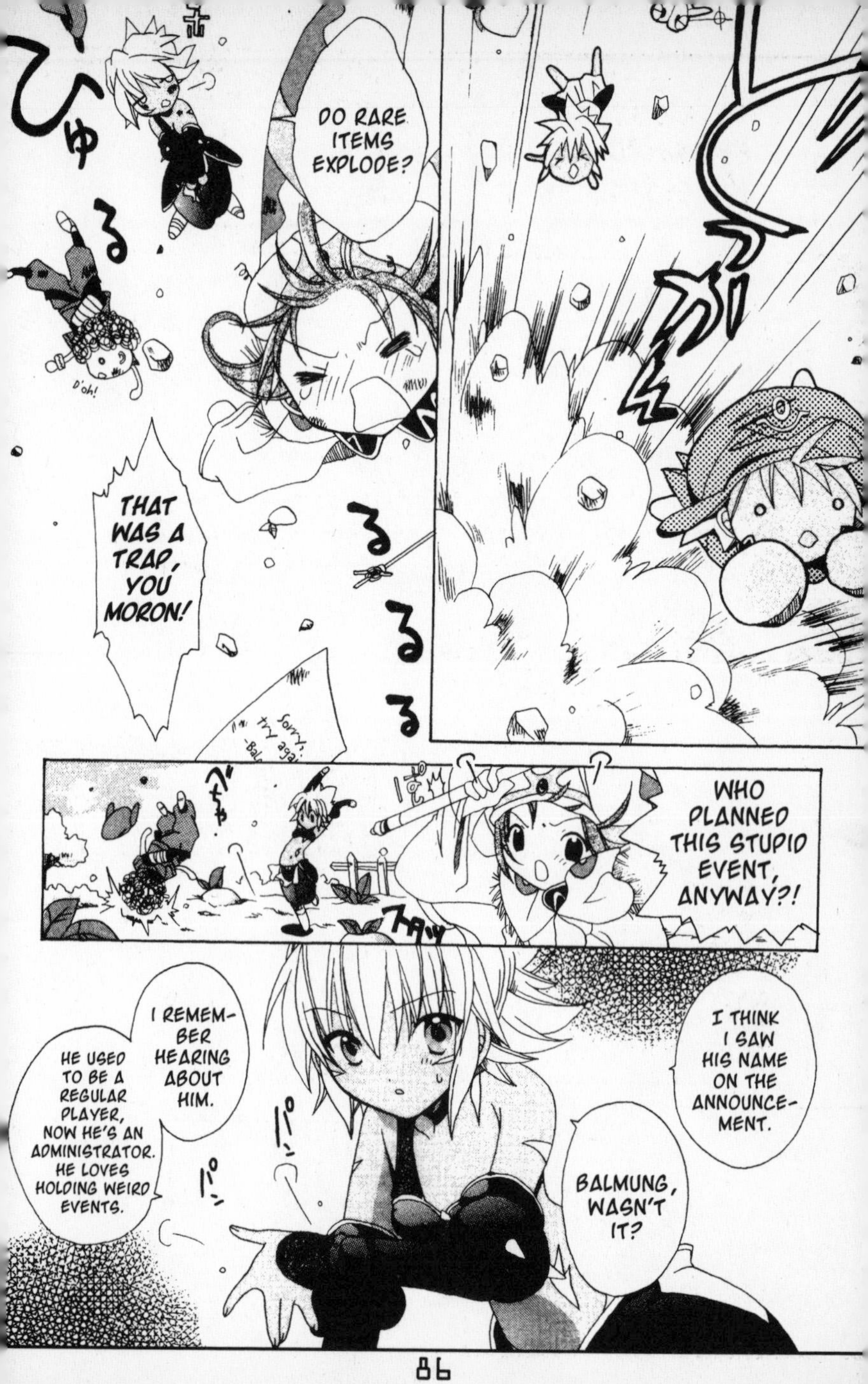

ひゅるるるる
DO RARE ITEMS EXPLODE?
D'oh!
THAT WAS A TRAP, YOU MORON!
WHO PLANNED THIS STUPID EVENT, ANYWAY?!
I THINK I SAW HIS NAME ON THE ANNOUNCEMENT.
BALMUNG, WASN'T IT?
I REMEMBER HEARING ABOUT HIM.
HE USED TO BE A REGULAR PLAYER, NOW HE'S AN ADMINISTRATOR. HE LOVES HOLDING WEIRD EVENTS.

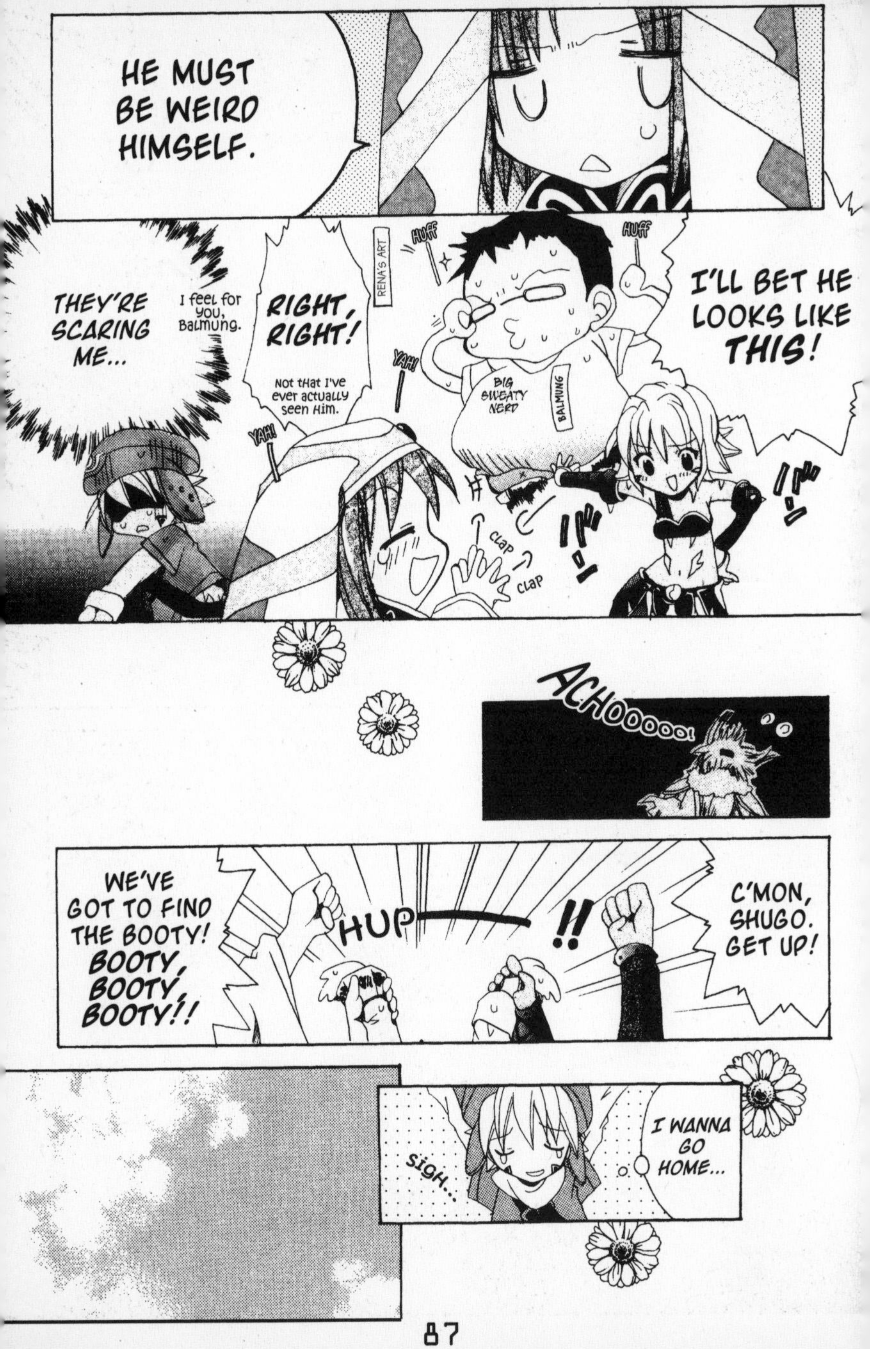
HE MUST BE WEIRD HIMSELF.
I'LL BET HE LOOKS LIKE THIS!
HUFF
HUFF
BIG SWEATY NERD
BALMUNG
RENA'S ART
YAH!
RIGHT, RIGHT!
Not that I've ever actually seen him.
YAH!
Clap
Clap
I feel for you, Balmung.
THEY'RE SCARING ME...
ACHOOOOOO!
C'MON, SHUGO. GET UP!
HUP——!!
WE'VE GOT TO FIND THE BOOTY! BOOTY, BOOTY, BOOTY!!
I WANNA GO HOME...
Sigh...

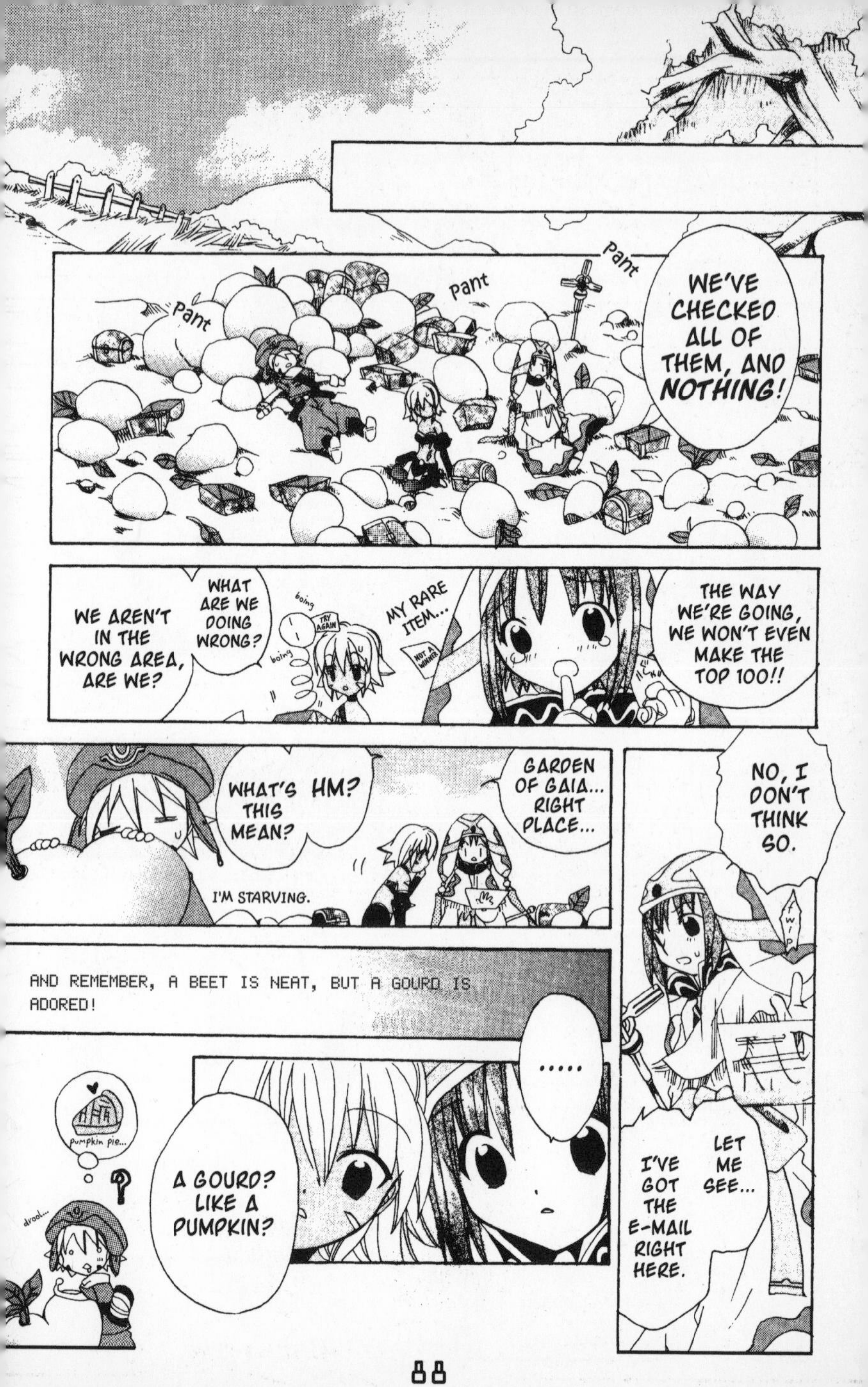
Pant
Pant
Pant
WE'VE CHECKED ALL OF THEM, AND NOTHING!
THE WAY WE'RE GOING, WE WON'T EVEN MAKE THE TOP 100!!
MY RARE ITEM...
NOT A WINNER
TRY AGAIN
boing
boing
WHAT ARE WE DOING WRONG?
WE AREN'T IN THE WRONG AREA, ARE WE?
NO, I DON'T THINK SO.
TWIP
LET ME SEE...
I'VE GOT THE E-MAIL RIGHT HERE.
GARDEN OF GAIA... RIGHT PLACE...
HM?
WHAT'S THIS MEAN?
I'M STARVING.
AND REMEMBER, A BEET IS NEAT, BUT A GOURD IS ADORED!
.....
A GOURD? LIKE A PUMPKIN?
pumpkin pie...
drool...

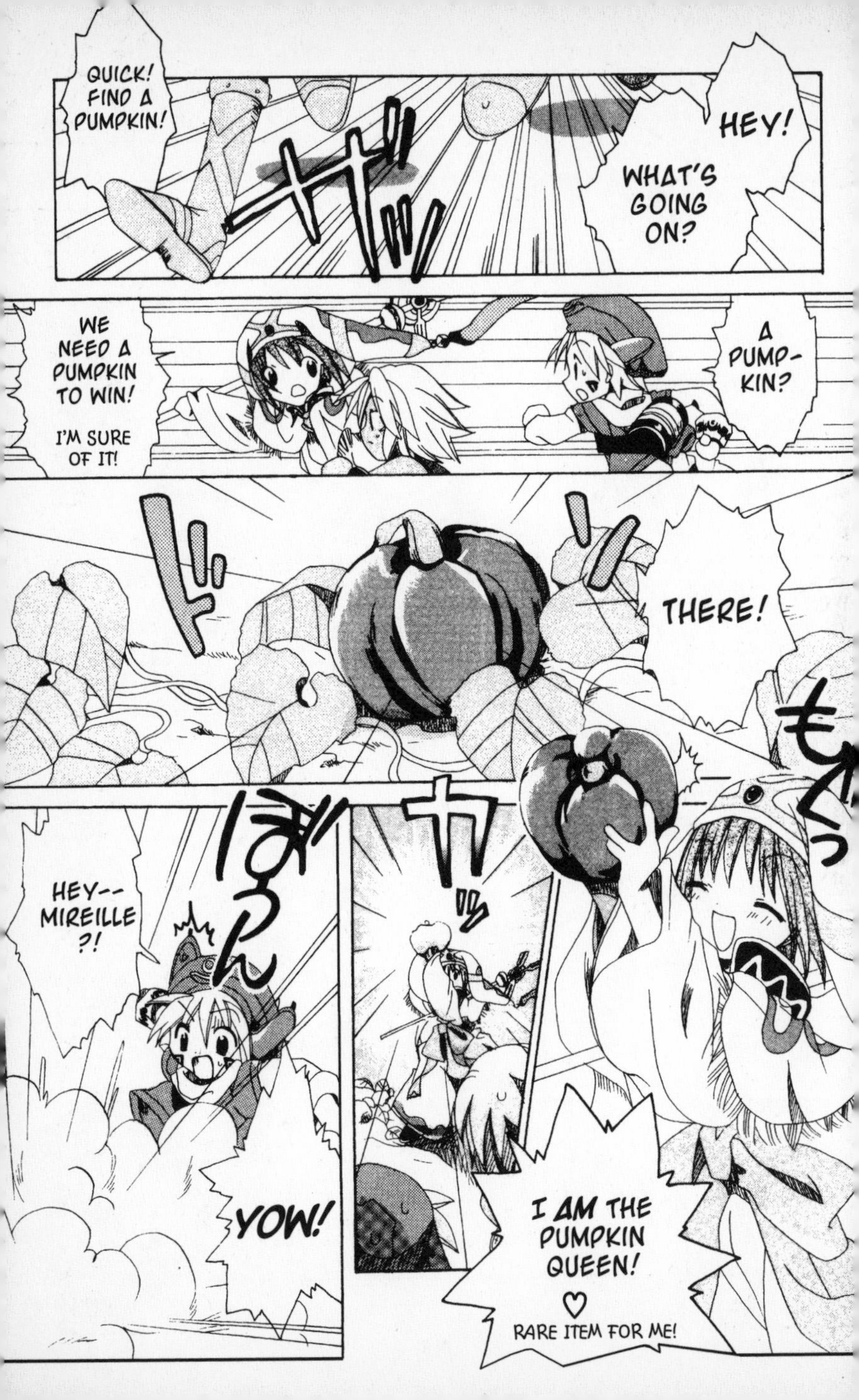
HEY!
WHAT'S GOING ON?
QUICK! FIND A PUMPKIN!
A PUMP-KIN?
WE NEED A PUMPKIN TO WIN!
I'M SURE OF IT!
THERE!
I AM THE PUMPKIN QUEEN! ♡
RARE ITEM FOR ME!
HEY-- MIREILLE?!
YOW!

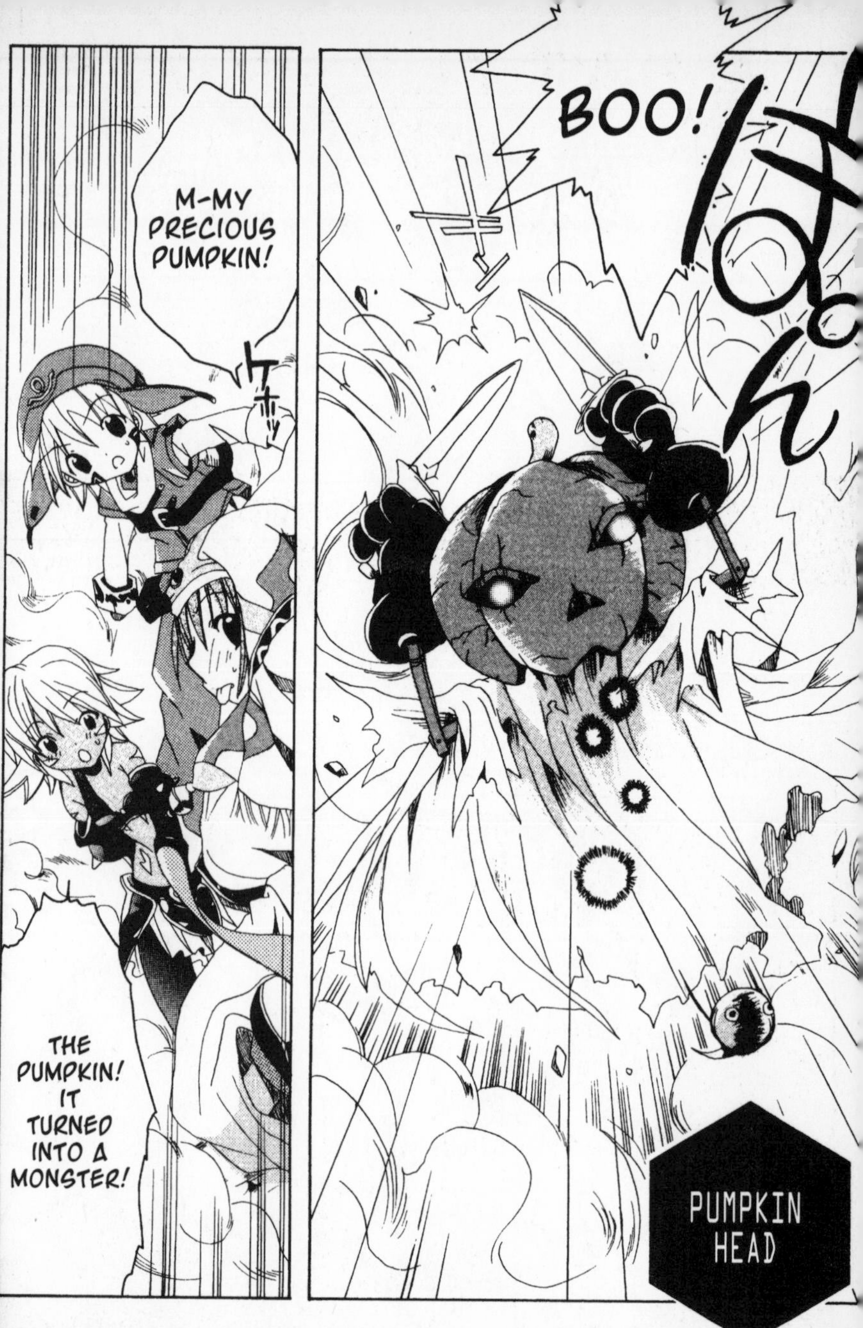
BOO!
PUMPKIN HEAD
M-MY PRECIOUS PUMPKIN!
THE PUMPKIN! IT TURNED INTO A MONSTER!

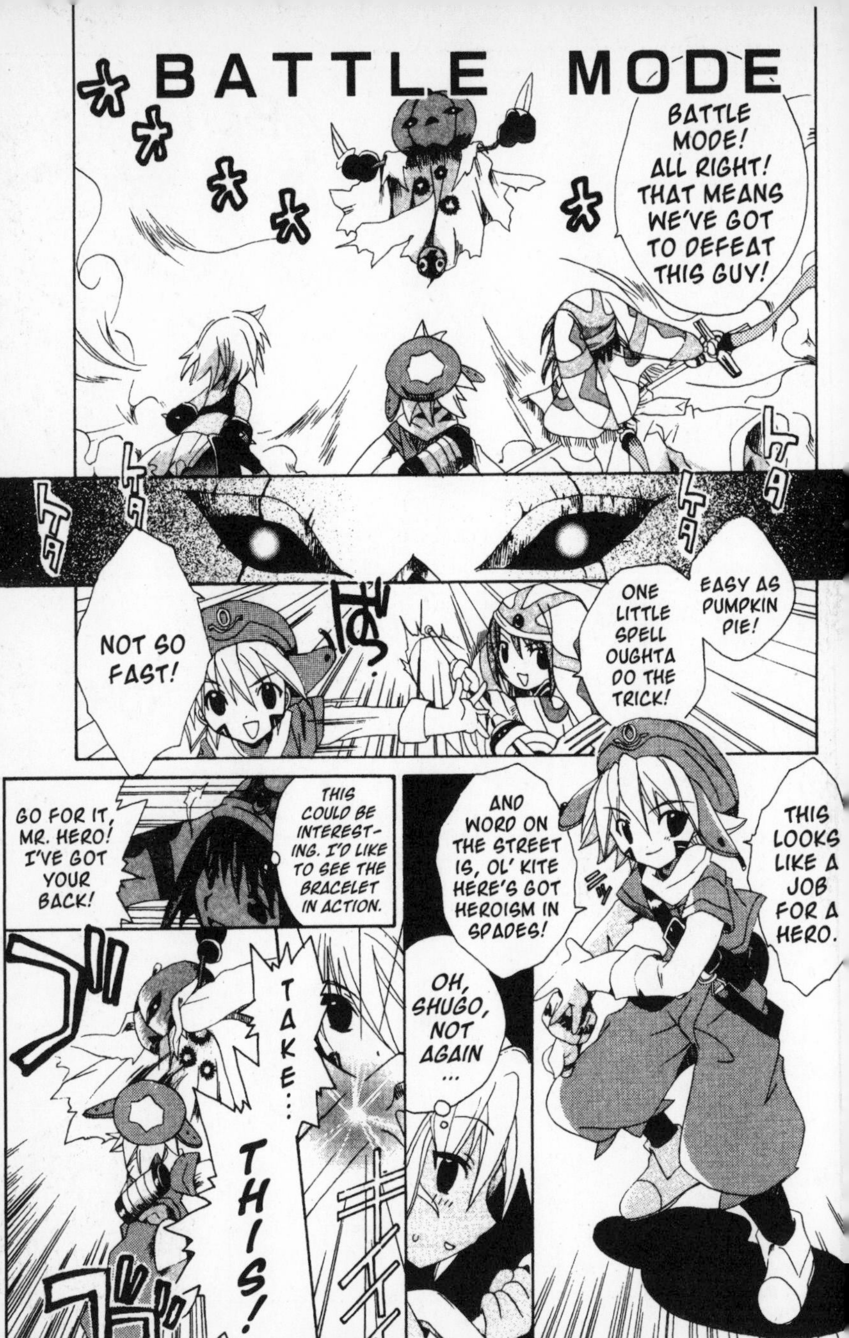
BATTLE MODE
BATTLE MODE! ALL RIGHT! THAT MEANS WE'VE GOT TO DEFEAT THIS GUY!
EASY AS PUMPKIN PIE!
ONE LITTLE SPELL OUGHTA DO THE TRICK!
NOT SO FAST!
THIS LOOKS LIKE A JOB FOR A HERO.
AND WORD ON THE STREET IS, OL' KITE HERE'S GOT HEROISM IN SPADES!
OH, SHUGO, NOT AGAIN...
THIS COULD BE INTERESTING. I'D LIKE TO SEE THE BRACELET IN ACTION.
GO FOR IT, MR. HERO! I'VE GOT YOUR BACK!
TAKE... THIS!

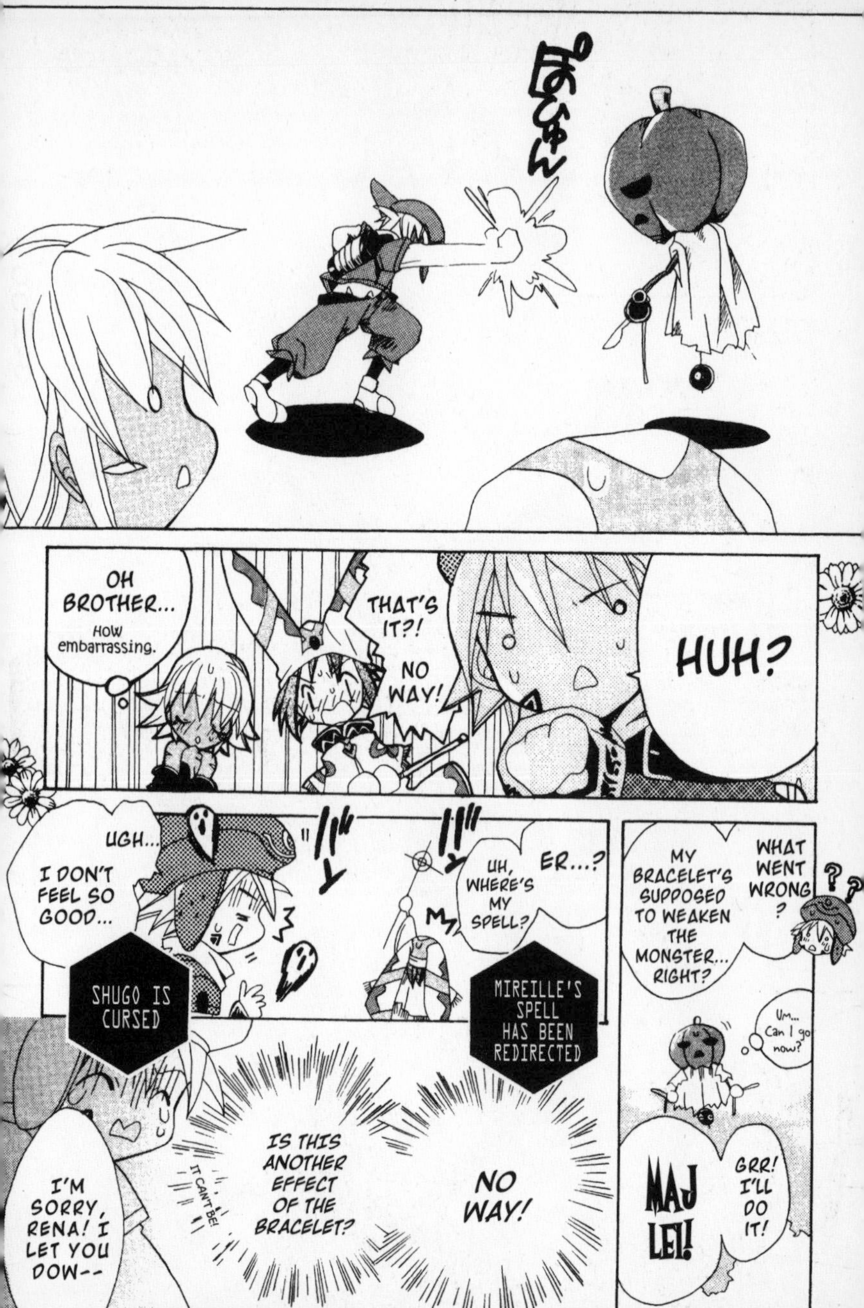
ぽひゅん
HUH?
THAT'S IT?! NO WAY!
OH BROTHER... HOW embarrassing.
WHAT WENT WRONG?
MY BRACELET'S SUPPOSED TO WEAKEN THE MONSTER... RIGHT?
Um... Can I go now?
GRR! I'LL DO IT!
MAJ LEI!
ER...?
UH, WHERE'S MY SPELL?
UGH... I DON'T FEEL SO GOOD...
MIREILLE'S SPELL HAS BEEN REDIRECTED
SHUGO IS CURSED
NO WAY!
IS THIS ANOTHER EFFECT OF THE BRACELET?
IT CAN'T BE!
I'M SORRY, RENA! I LET YOU DOW--

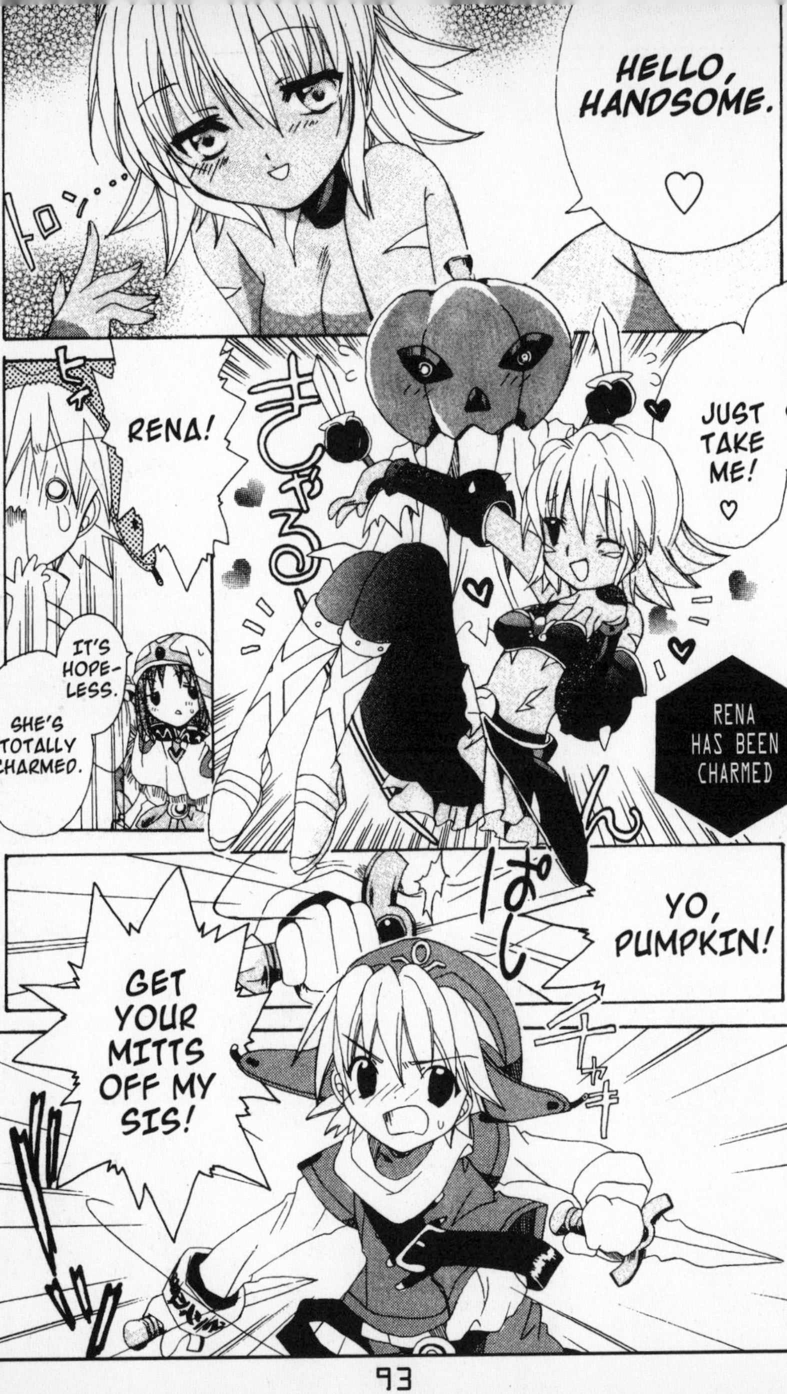
HELLO, HANDSOME. ♡
OOH! ♡
JUST TAKE ME! ♡
RENA HAS BEEN CHARMED
RENA!
IT'S HOPELESS.
SHE'S TOTALLY CHARMED.
YO, PUMPKIN!
GET YOUR MITTS OFF MY SIS!

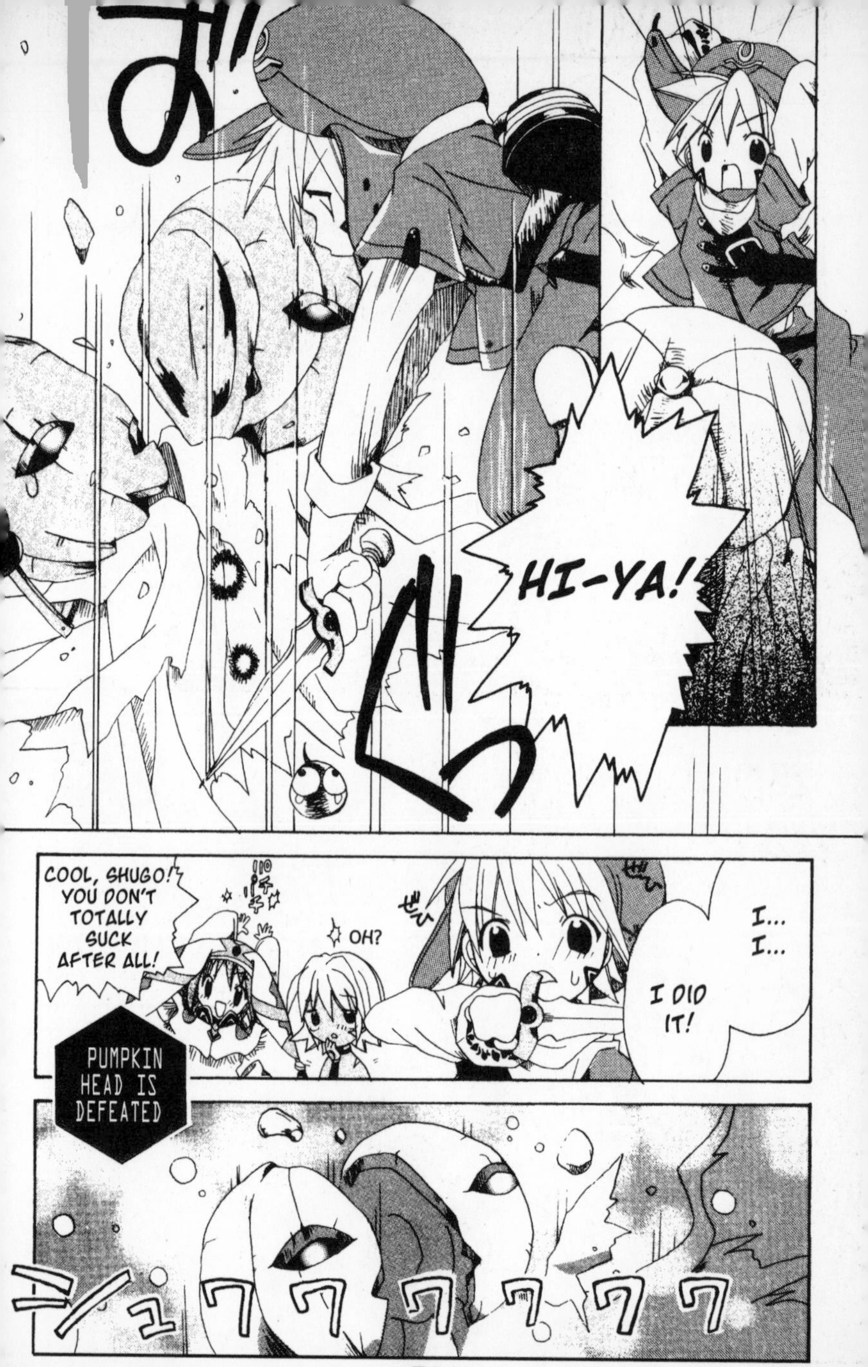
HI-YA!
I...
I...
I DID IT!
OH?
COOL, SHUGO! YOU DON'T TOTALLY SUCK AFTER ALL!
PUMPKIN HEAD IS DEFEATED

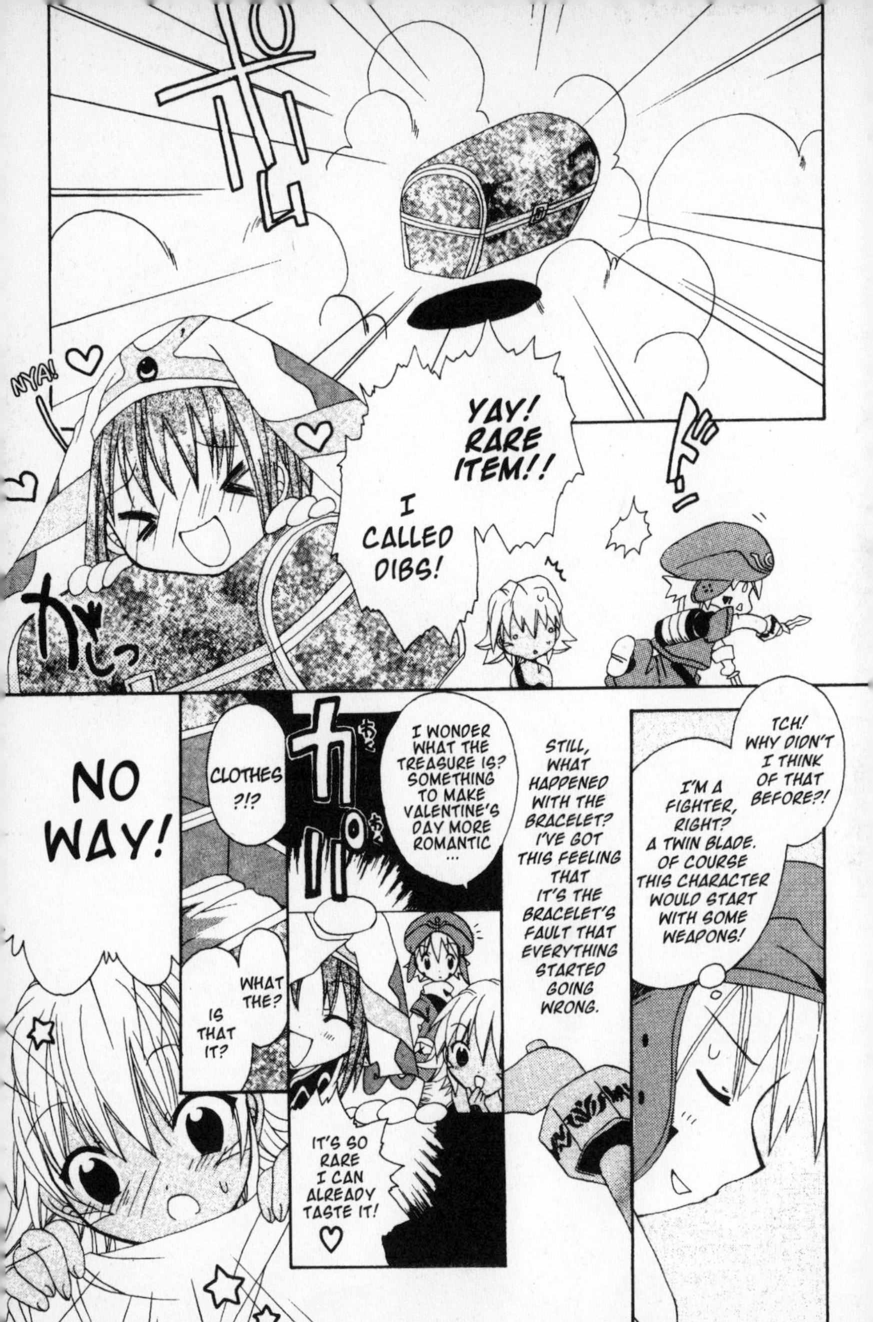
YAY! RARE ITEM!!
I CALLED DIBS!
NYA!
TCH! WHY DIDN'T I THINK OF THAT BEFORE?!
I'M A FIGHTER, RIGHT? A TWIN BLADE. OF COURSE THIS CHARACTER WOULD START WITH SOME WEAPONS!
STILL, WHAT HAPPENED WITH THE BRACELET? I'VE GOT THIS FEELING THAT IT'S THE BRACELET'S FAULT THAT EVERYTHING STARTED GOING WRONG.
I WONDER WHAT THE TREASURE IS? SOMETHING TO MAKE VALENTINE'S DAY MORE ROMANTIC ...
CLOTHES ?!?
WHAT THE?
IS THAT IT?
IT'S SO RARE I CAN ALREADY TASTE IT! ♡
NO WAY!

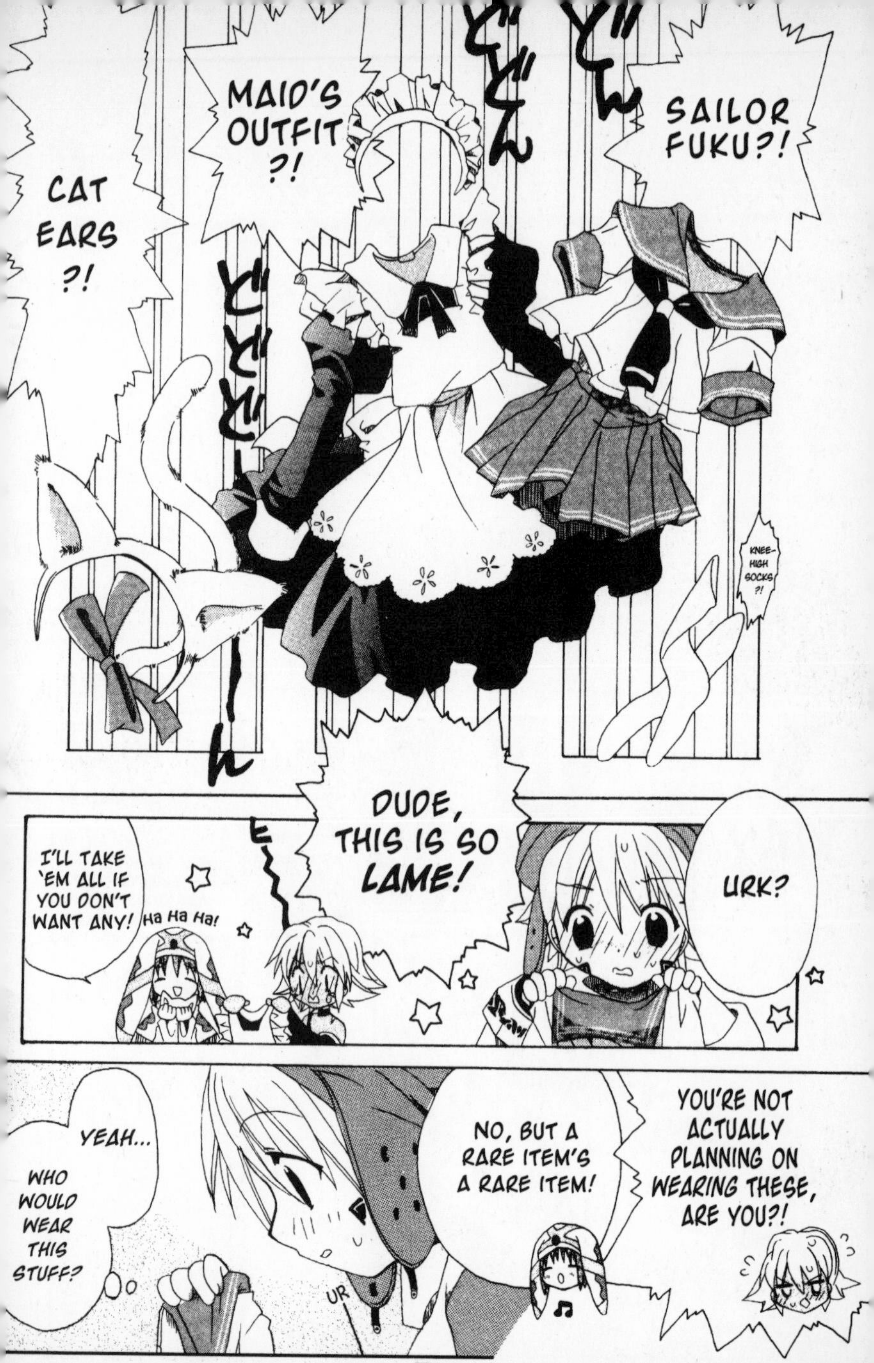
SAILOR FUKU?!
MAID'S OUTFIT ?!
CAT EARS ?!
KNEE-HIGH SOCKS ?!
URK?
DUDE, THIS IS SO LAME!
I'LL TAKE 'EM ALL IF YOU DON'T WANT ANY!
Ha Ha Ha!
YOU'RE NOT ACTUALLY PLANNING ON WEARING THESE, ARE YOU?!
NO, BUT A RARE ITEM'S A RARE ITEM!
UR
YEAH...
WHO WOULD WEAR THIS STUFF?

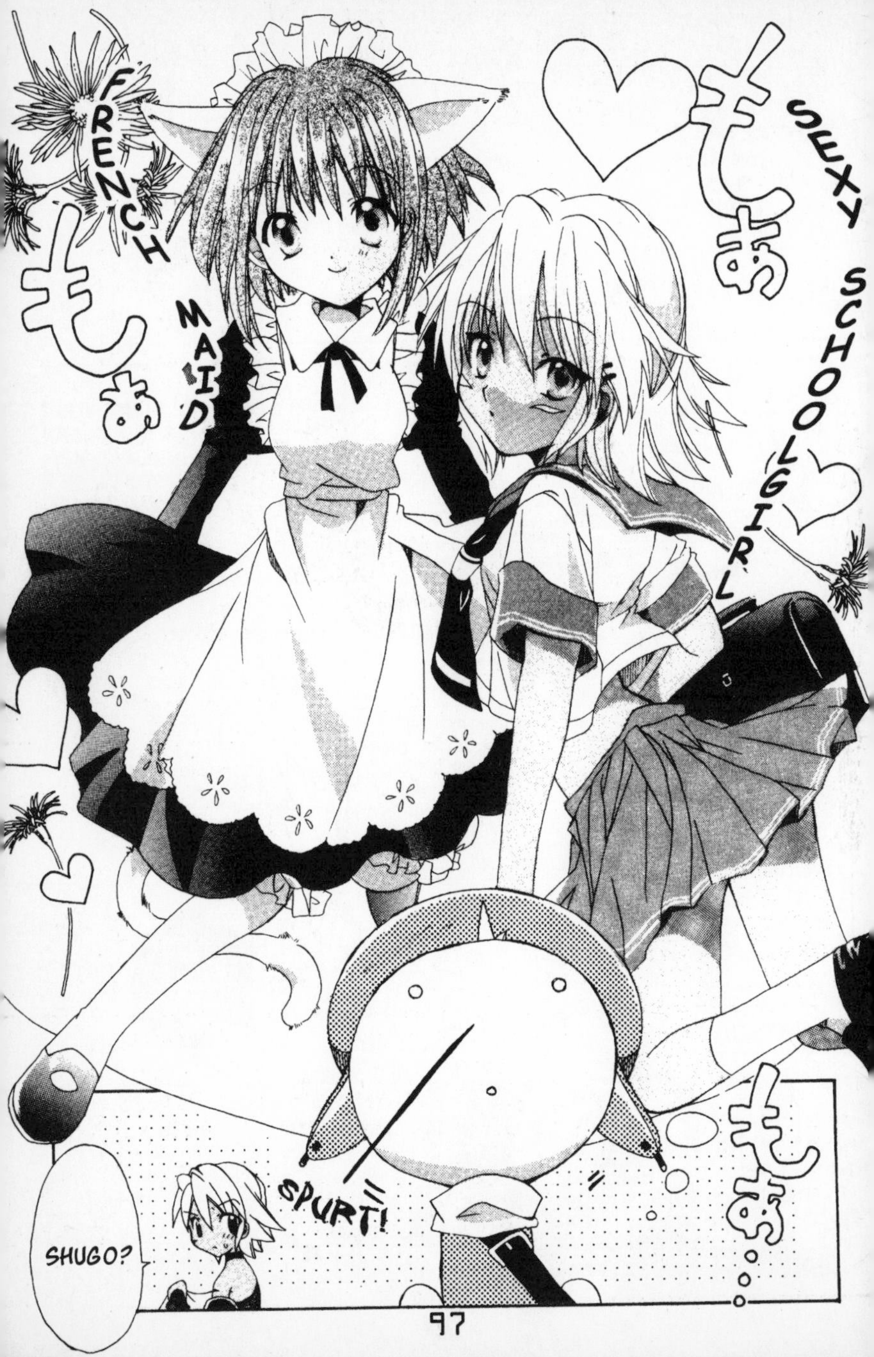
もあ
SEXY SCHOOLGIRL
FRENCH MAID
もあ
もあ…
SPURT!
SHUGO?

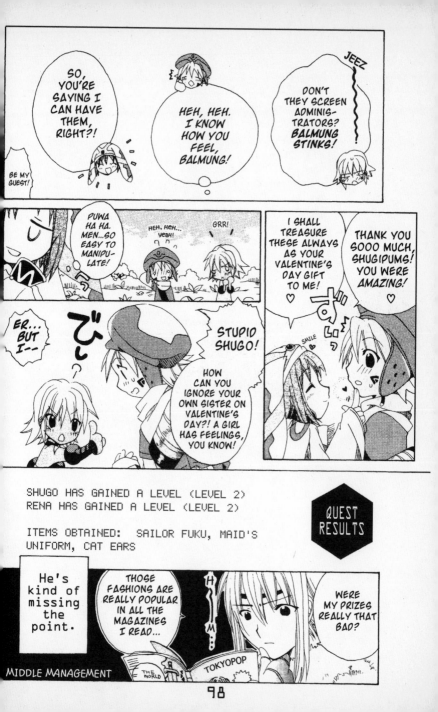

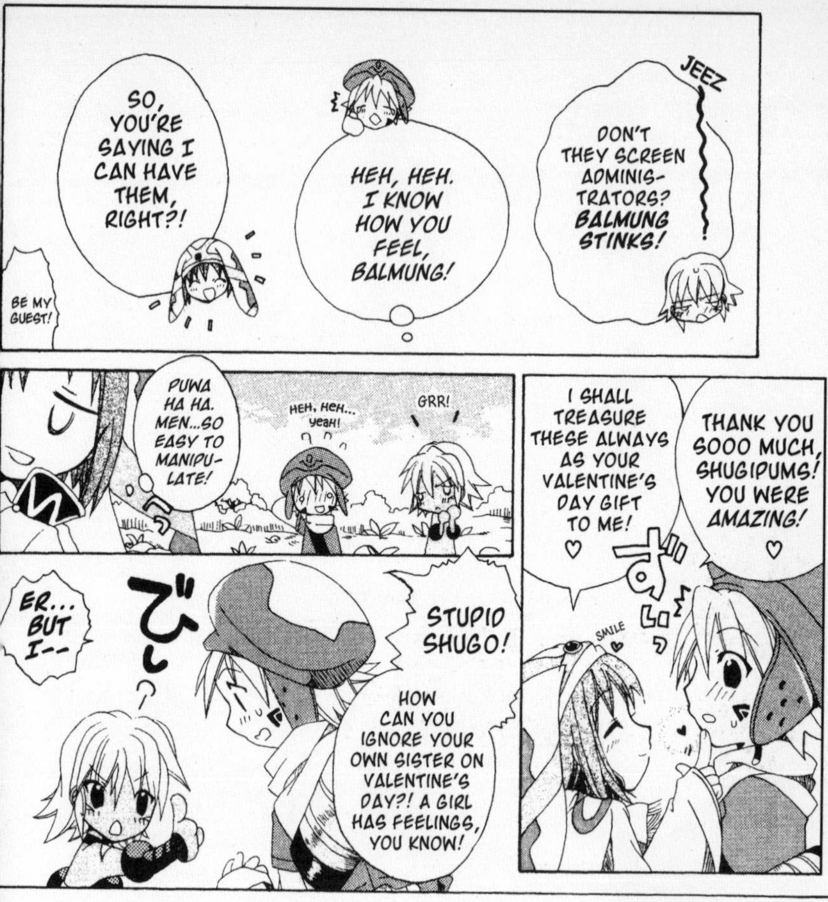
JEEZ
DON'T THEY SCREEN ADMINIS-TRATORS? BALMUNG STINKS!
HEH, HEH. I KNOW HOW YOU FEEL, BALMUNG!
SO, YOU'RE SAYING I CAN HAVE THEM, RIGHT?!
BE MY GUEST!
THANK YOU SOOO MUCH, SHUGIPUMS! YOU WERE AMAZING! ♡
I SHALL TREASURE THESE ALWAYS AS YOUR VALENTINE'S DAY GIFT TO ME! ♡
SMILE ♡
GRR!
HEH, HEH... yeah!
PUWA HA HA. MEN...SO EASY TO MANIPU-LATE!
STUPID SHUGO!
HOW CAN YOU IGNORE YOUR OWN SISTER ON VALENTINE'S DAY?! A GIRL HAS FEELINGS, YOU KNOW!
ER... BUT I--

QUEST RESULTS

SHUGO HAS GAINED A LEVEL (LEVEL 2)
RENA HAS GAINED A LEVEL (LEVEL 2)

ITEMS OBTAINED: SAILOR FUKU, MAID'S UNIFORM, CAT EARS

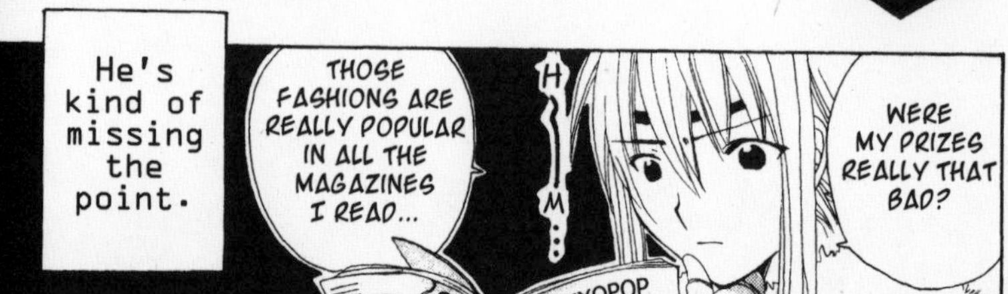
WERE MY PRIZES REALLY THAT BAD?
HMM...
THOSE FASHIONS ARE REALLY POPULAR IN ALL THE MAGAZINES I READ...
He's kind of missing the point.
TOKYOPOP
THE WORLD
MIDDLE MANAGEMENT

NEW GENERATION ONLINE

THE WORLD

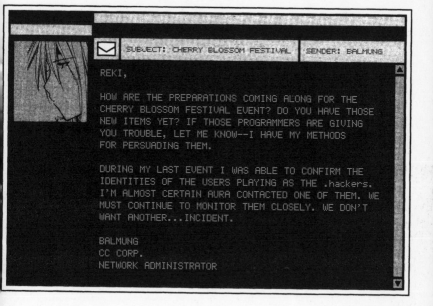

SUBJECT: CHERRY BLOSSOM FESTIVAL   SENDER: BALMUNG

REKI,

HOW ARE THE PREPARATIONS COMING ALONG FOR THE
CHERRY BLOSSOM FESTIVAL EVENT? DO YOU HAVE THOSE
NEW ITEMS YET? IF THOSE PROGRAMMERS ARE GIVING
YOU TROUBLE, LET ME KNOW--I HAVE MY METHODS
FOR PERSUADING THEM.

DURING MY LAST EVENT I WAS ABLE TO CONFIRM THE
IDENTITIES OF THE USERS PLAYING AS THE .hackers.
I'M ALMOST CERTAIN AURA CONTACTED ONE OF THEM. WE
MUST CONTINUE TO MONITOR THEM CLOSELY. WE DON'T
WANT ANOTHER...INCIDENT.

BALMUNG
CC CORP.
NETWORK ADMINISTRATOR

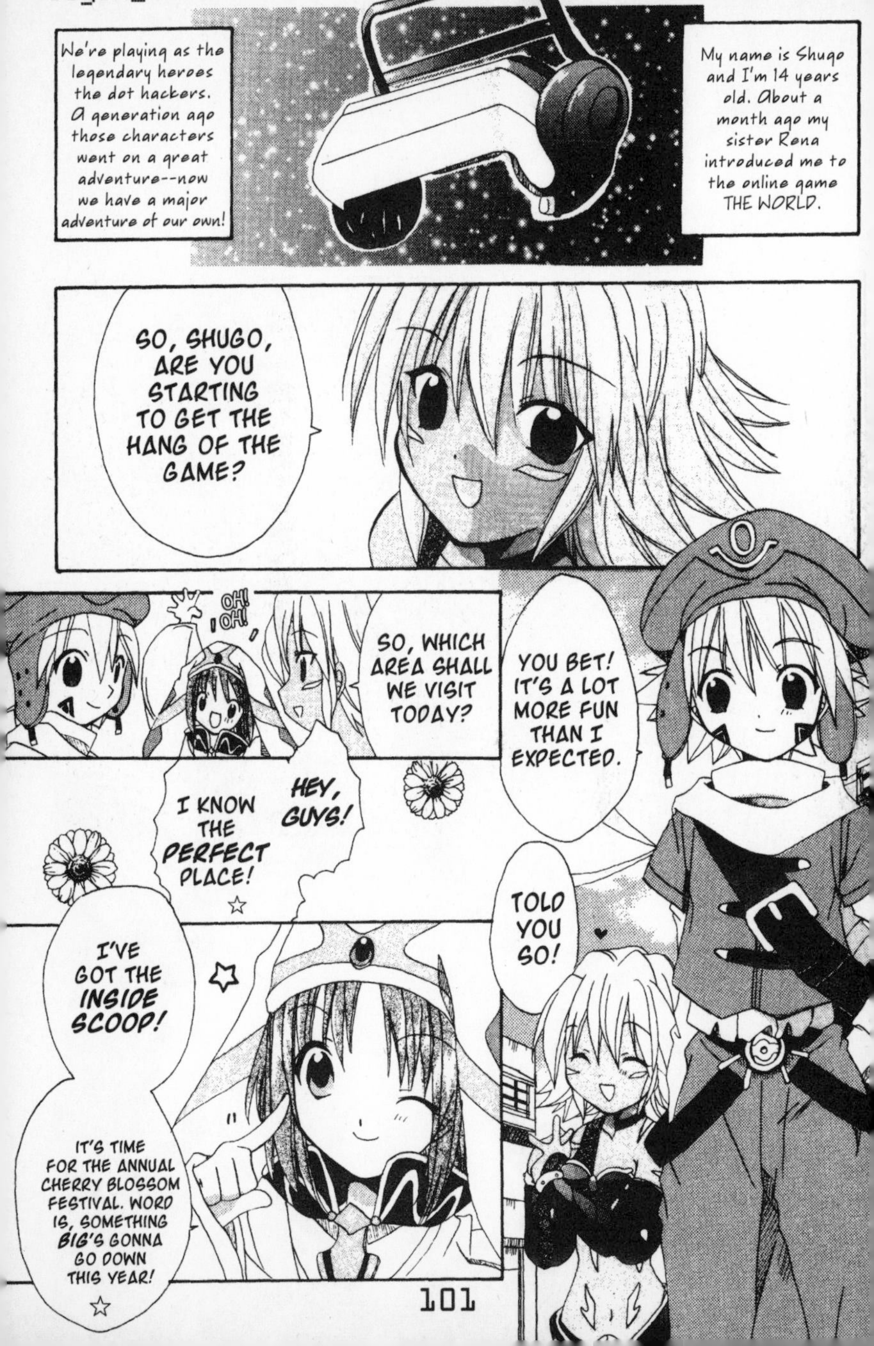
My name is Shugo and I'm 14 years old. About a month ago my sister Rena introduced me to the online game THE WORLD.
We're playing as the legendary heroes the dot hackers. A generation ago those characters went on a great adventure--now we have a major adventure of our own!
SO, SHUGO, ARE YOU STARTING TO GET THE HANG OF THE GAME?
YOU BET! IT'S A LOT MORE FUN THAN I EXPECTED.
TOLD YOU SO!
SO, WHICH AREA SHALL WE VISIT TODAY?
OH! OH!
HEY, GUYS!
I KNOW THE PERFECT PLACE!
I'VE GOT THE INSIDE SCOOP!
IT'S TIME FOR THE ANNUAL CHERRY BLOSSOM FESTIVAL. WORD IS, SOMETHING BIG'S GONNA GO DOWN THIS YEAR!

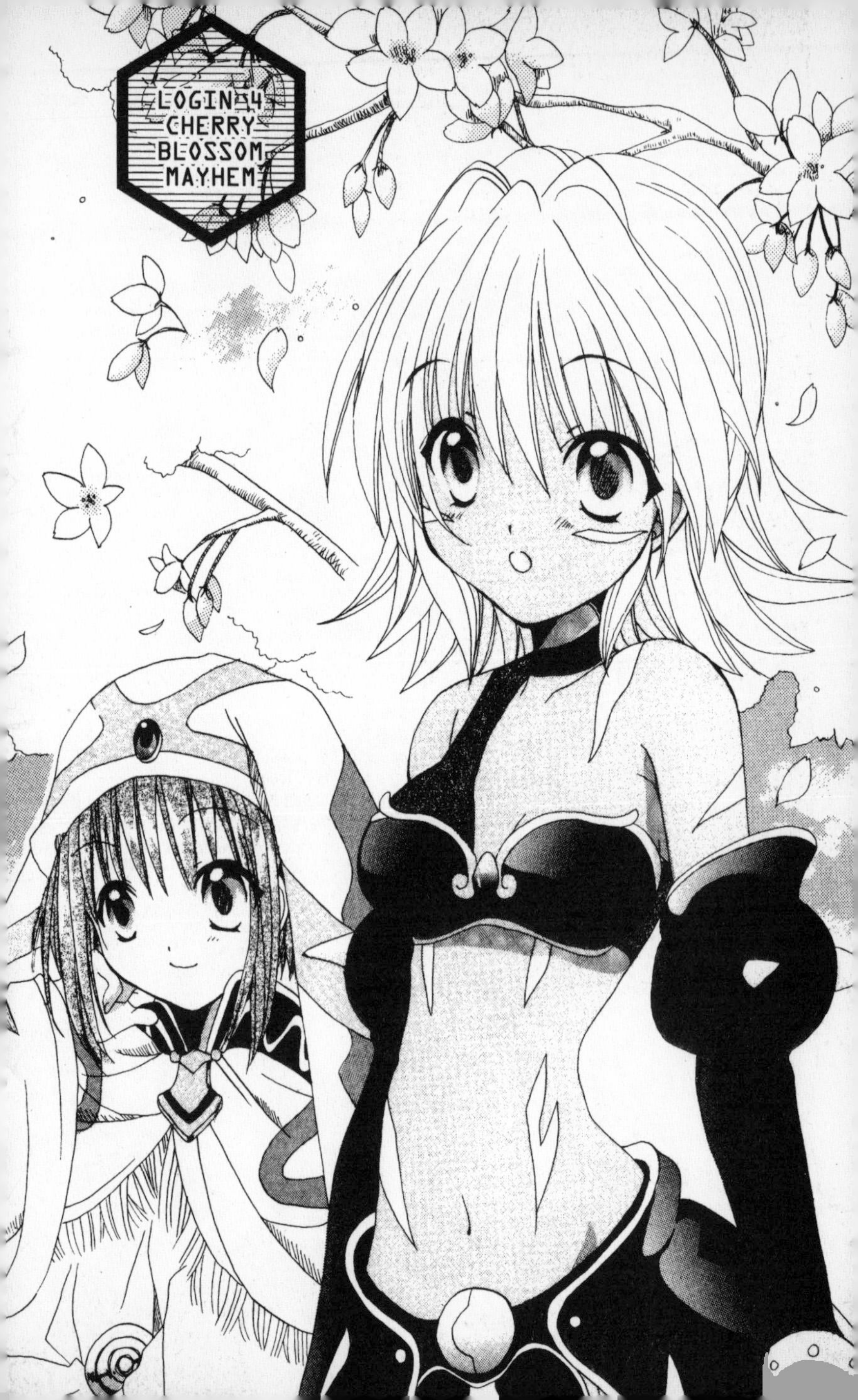
LOGIN 4
CHERRY
BLOSSOM
MAYHEM

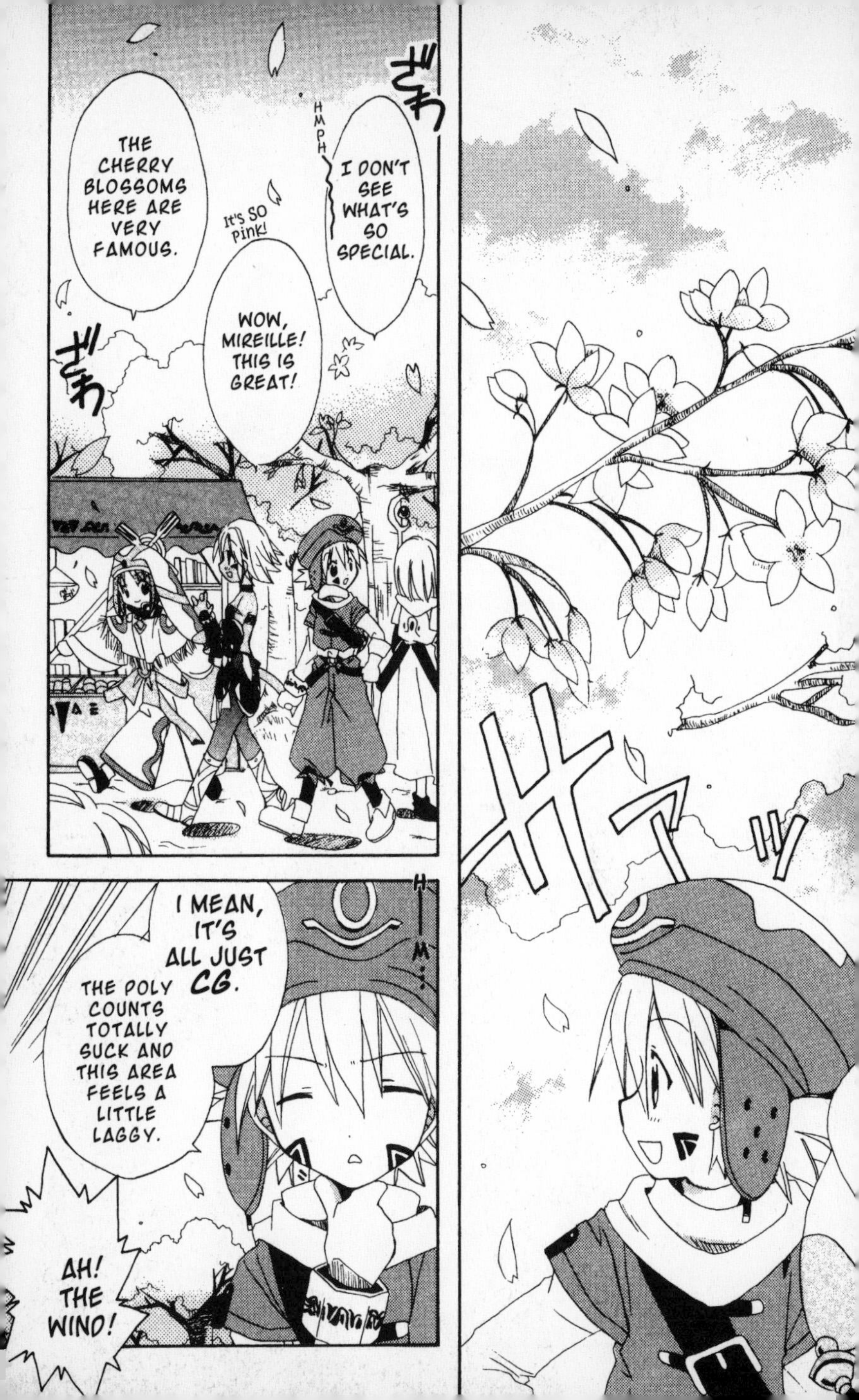

ザァッ
ざわ
HMPH
I DON'T SEE WHAT'S SO SPECIAL.
THE CHERRY BLOSSOMS HERE ARE VERY FAMOUS.
It's SO Pink!
WOW, MIREILLE! THIS IS GREAT!
ざわ
H-M...
I MEAN, IT'S ALL JUST CG.
THE POLY COUNTS TOTALLY SUCK AND THIS AREA FEELS A LITTLE LAGGY.
AH! THE WIND!

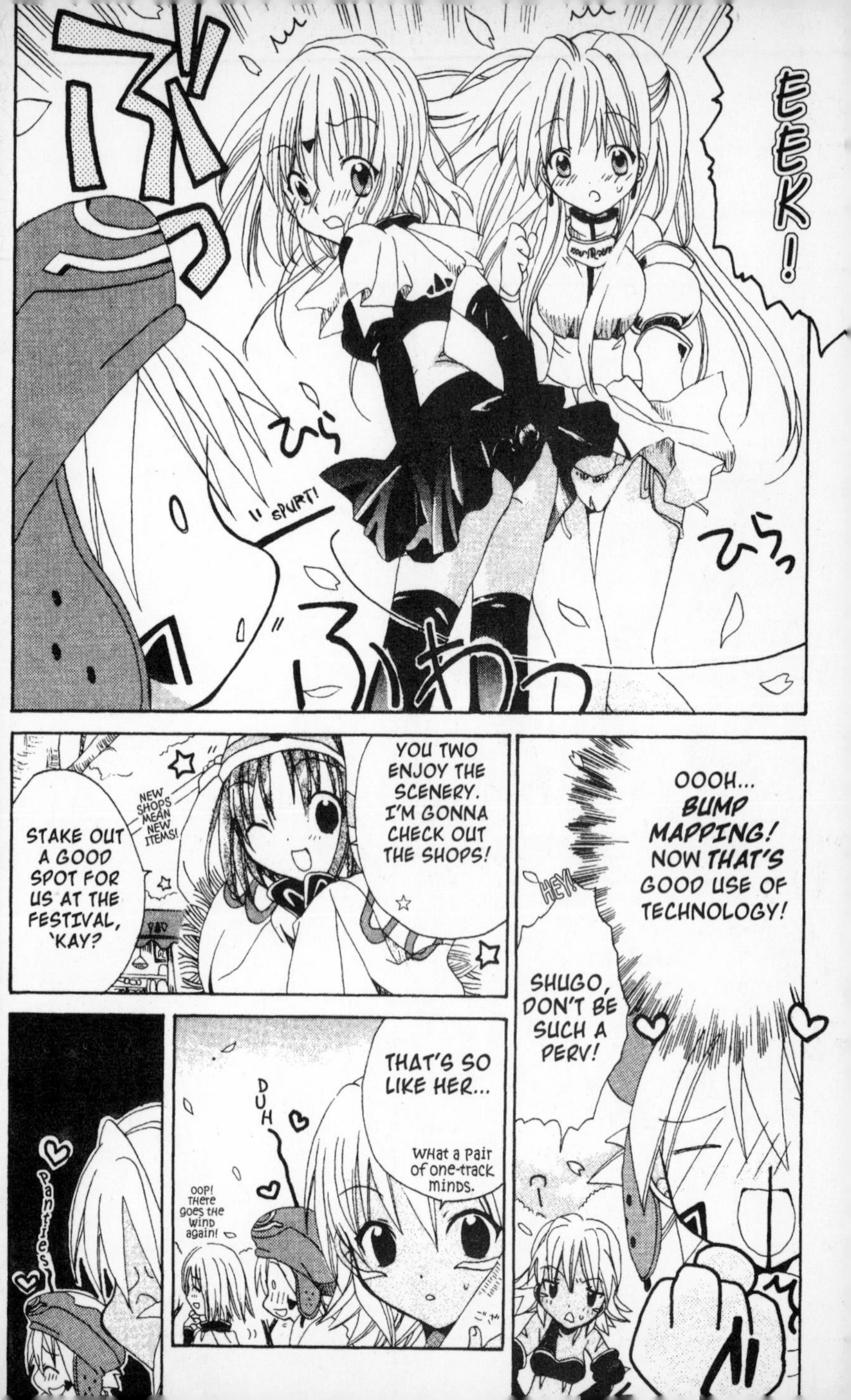
EEEK!
ぶっ
ひら
SPURT!
ひらっ
ふわっ
OOOH... BUMP MAPPING! NOW THAT'S GOOD USE OF TECHNOLOGY!
HEY!
SHUGO, DON'T BE SUCH A PERV!
YOU TWO ENJOY THE SCENERY. I'M GONNA CHECK OUT THE SHOPS!
NEW SHOPS MEAN NEW ITEMS!
STAKE OUT A GOOD SPOT FOR US AT THE FESTIVAL, 'KAY?
THAT'S SO LIKE HER...
DUH
What a pair of one-track minds.
OOP! There goes the wind again!
Panties

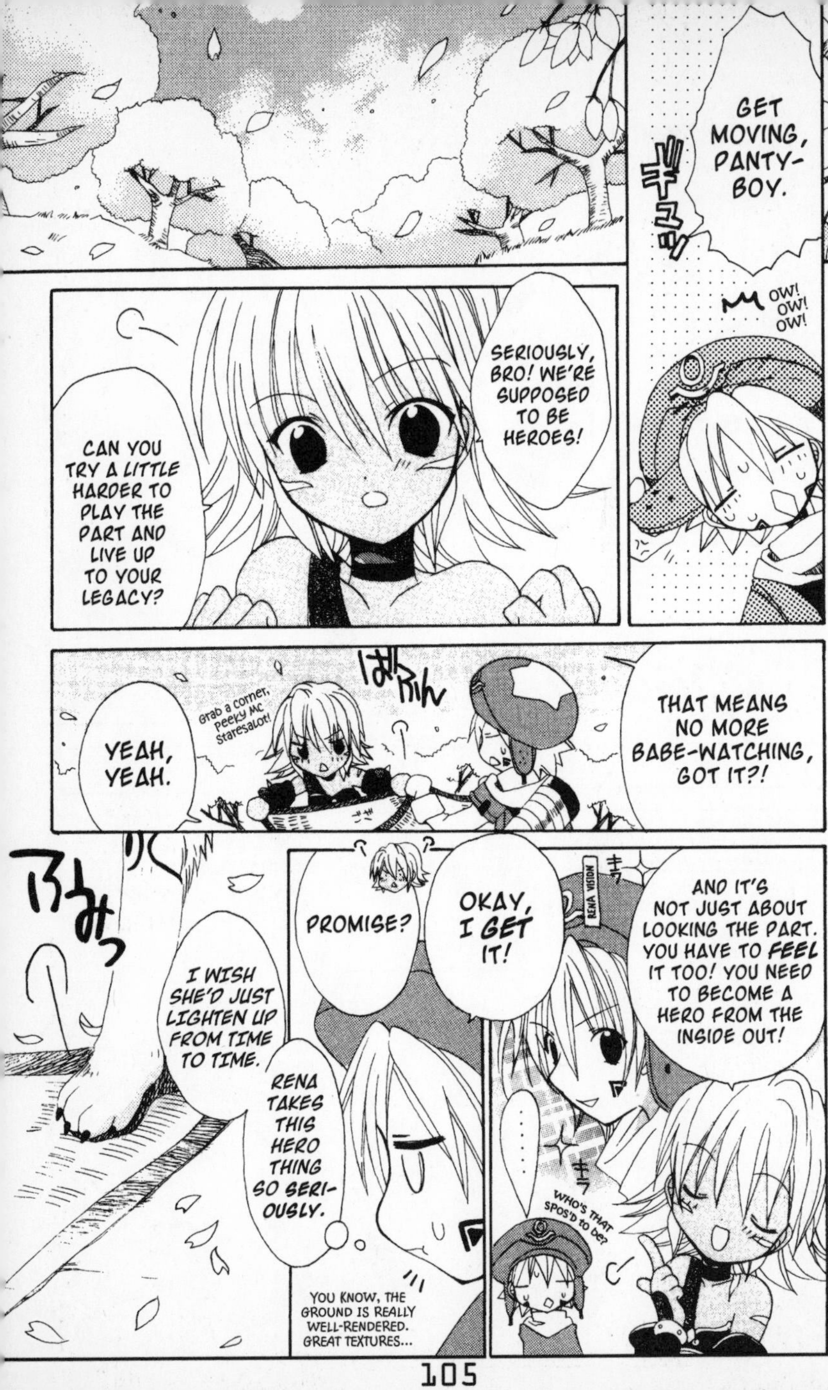
GET MOVING, PANTY-BOY.
OW! OW! OW!
SERIOUSLY, BRO! WE'RE SUPPOSED TO BE HEROES!
CAN YOU TRY A LITTLE HARDER TO PLAY THE PART AND LIVE UP TO YOUR LEGACY?
THAT MEANS NO MORE BABE-WATCHING, GOT IT?!
Grab a corner, Peeky Mc Staresalot!
YEAH, YEAH.
AND IT'S NOT JUST ABOUT LOOKING THE PART. YOU HAVE TO *FEEL* IT TOO! YOU NEED TO BECOME A HERO FROM THE INSIDE OUT!
RENA VISION
WHO'S THAT SPOS'D to be?
OKAY, I *GET* IT!
PROMISE?
RENA TAKES THIS HERO THING SO SERIOUSLY.
I WISH SHE'D JUST LIGHTEN UP FROM TIME TO TIME.
YOU KNOW, THE GROUND IS REALLY WELL-RENDERED. GREAT TEXTURES...
ふみっ

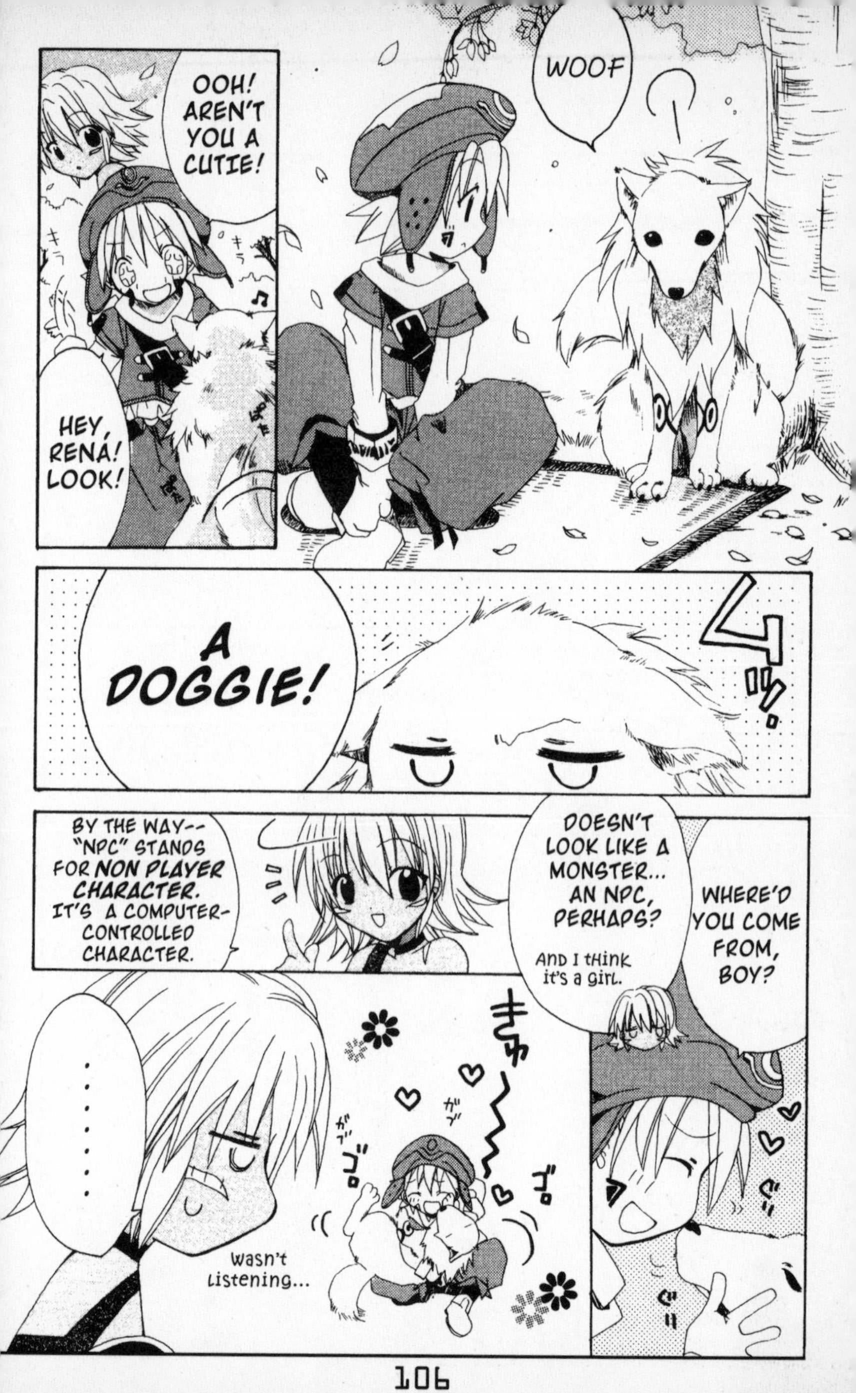
WOOF
OOH! AREN'T YOU A CUTIE!
HEY, RENA! LOOK!
A DOGGIE!
WHERE'D YOU COME FROM, BOY?
DOESN'T LOOK LIKE A MONSTER... AN NPC, PERHAPS?
And I think it's a girl.
BY THE WAY-- "NPC" STANDS FOR NON PLAYER CHARACTER. IT'S A COMPUTER-CONTROLLED CHARACTER.
Wasn't listening...
......

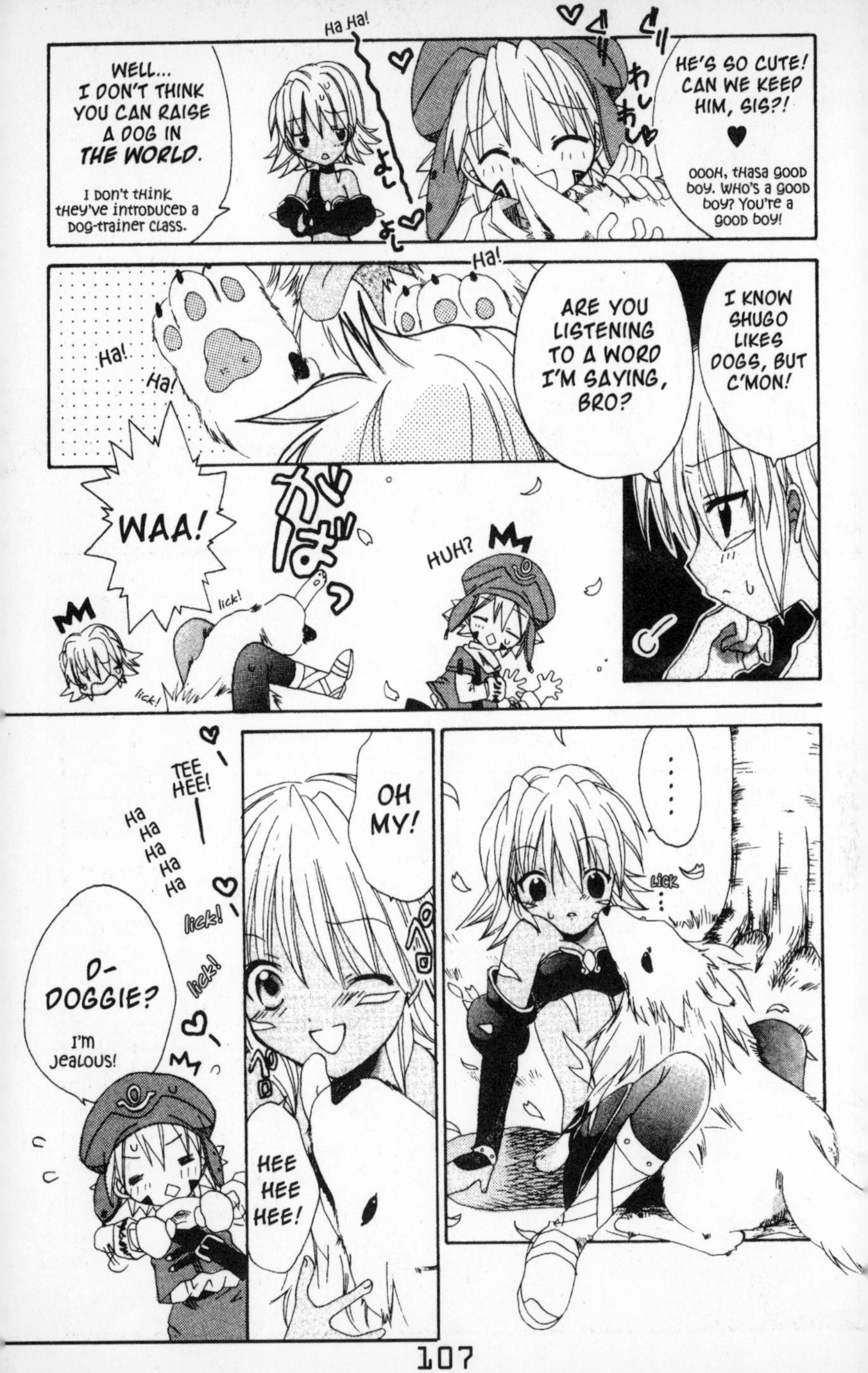
HE'S SO CUTE! CAN WE KEEP HIM, SIS?! ♥
OOOH, thasa good boy. WHO'S a good boy? You're a good boy!
わしわし
Ha Ha!
よしよし
WELL... I DON'T THINK YOU CAN RAISE A DOG IN **THE WORLD**.
I DON'T tHINK tHey've introduced a Dog-trainer class.
I KNOW SHUGO LIKES DOGS, BUT C'MON!
ARE YOU LISTENING TO A WORD I'M SAYING, BRO?
Ha!
Ha!
Ha!
かぱっ
HUH?
WAA!
lick!
lick!
......
Lick ...
OH MY!
HEE HEE HEE!
TEE HEE!
Ha Ha Ha Ha Ha
lick!
lick!
D-DOGGIE?
I'M JEALOUS!

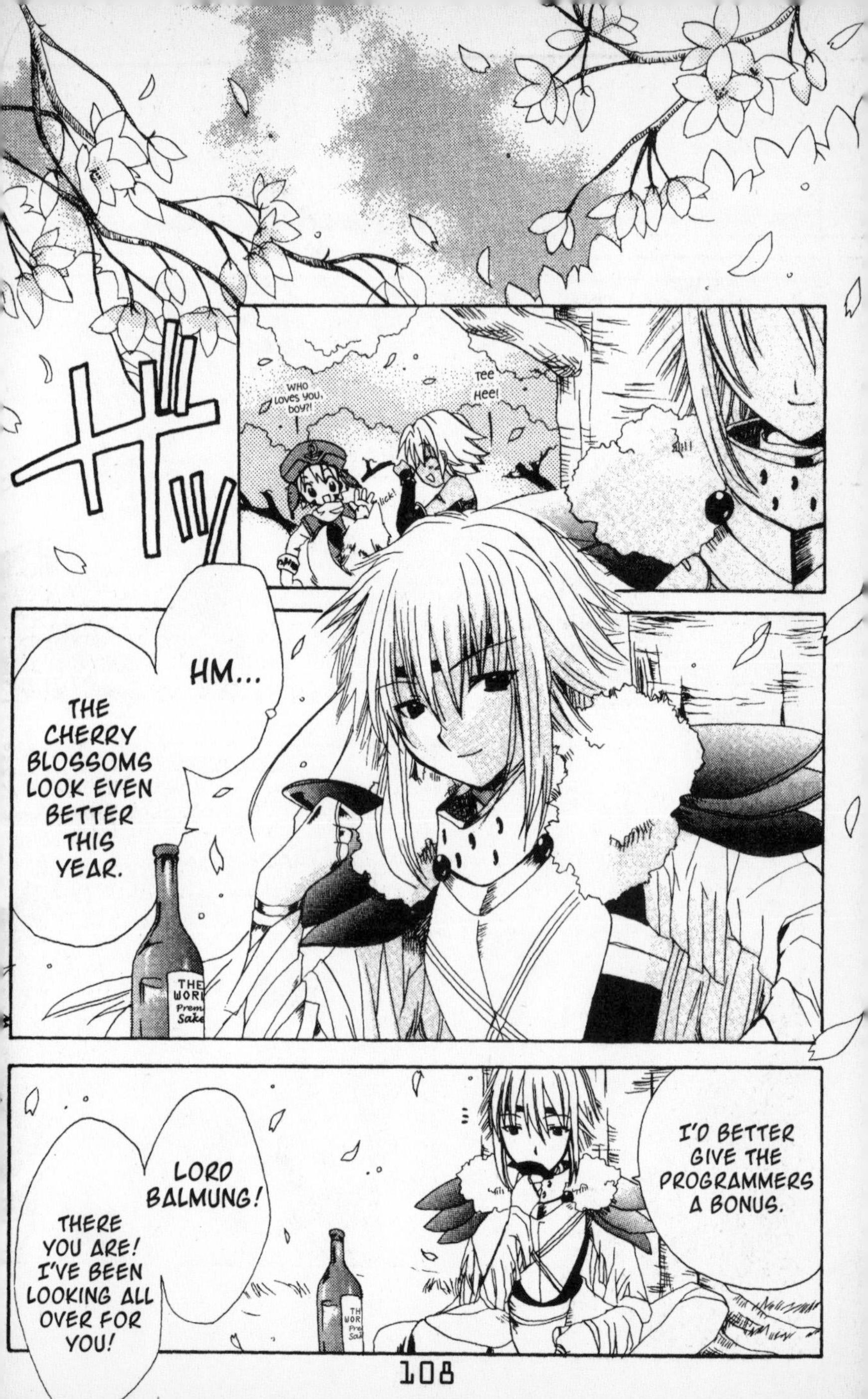
TEE HEE!
WHO LOVES YOU, BOY?!
lick!
HM...
THE CHERRY BLOSSOMS LOOK EVEN BETTER THIS YEAR.
I'D BETTER GIVE THE PROGRAMMERS A BONUS.
LORD BALMUNG!
THERE YOU ARE! I'VE BEEN LOOKING ALL OVER FOR YOU!

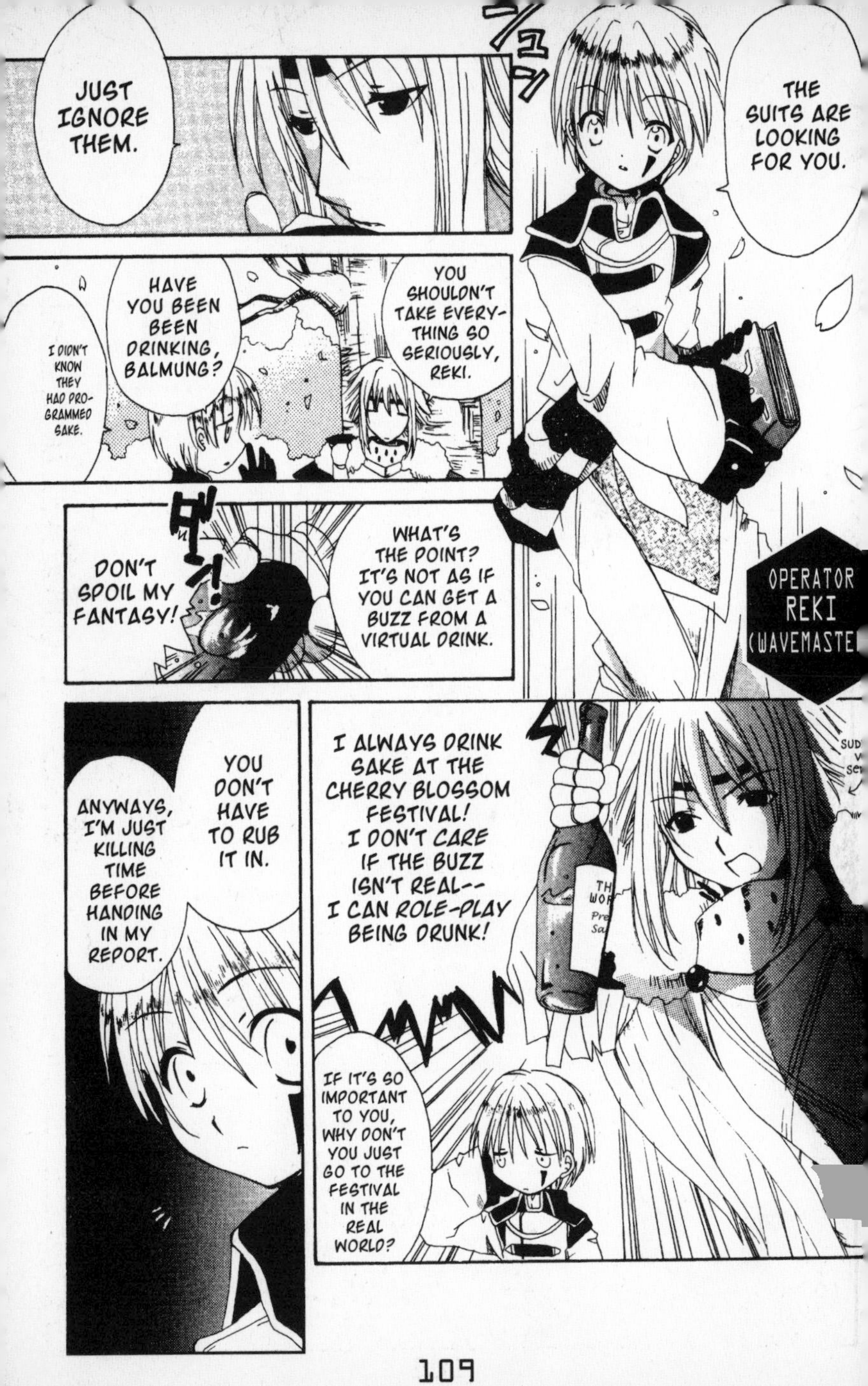
THE SUITS ARE LOOKING FOR YOU.
OPERATOR REKI (WAVEMASTE
JUST IGNORE THEM.
YOU SHOULDN'T TAKE EVERY-THING SO SERIOUSLY, REKI.
HAVE YOU BEEN BEEN DRINKING, BALMUNG?
I DIDN'T KNOW THEY HAD PRO-GRAMMED SAKE.
WHAT'S THE POINT? IT'S NOT AS IF YOU CAN GET A BUZZ FROM A VIRTUAL DRINK.
DON'T SPOIL MY FANTASY!
I ALWAYS DRINK SAKE AT THE CHERRY BLOSSOM FESTIVAL! I DON'T CARE IF THE BUZZ ISN'T REAL-- I CAN ROLE-PLAY BEING DRUNK!
IF IT'S SO IMPORTANT TO YOU, WHY DON'T YOU JUST GO TO THE FESTIVAL IN THE REAL WORLD?
YOU DON'T HAVE TO RUB IT IN.
ANYWAYS, I'M JUST KILLING TIME BEFORE HANDING IN MY REPORT.

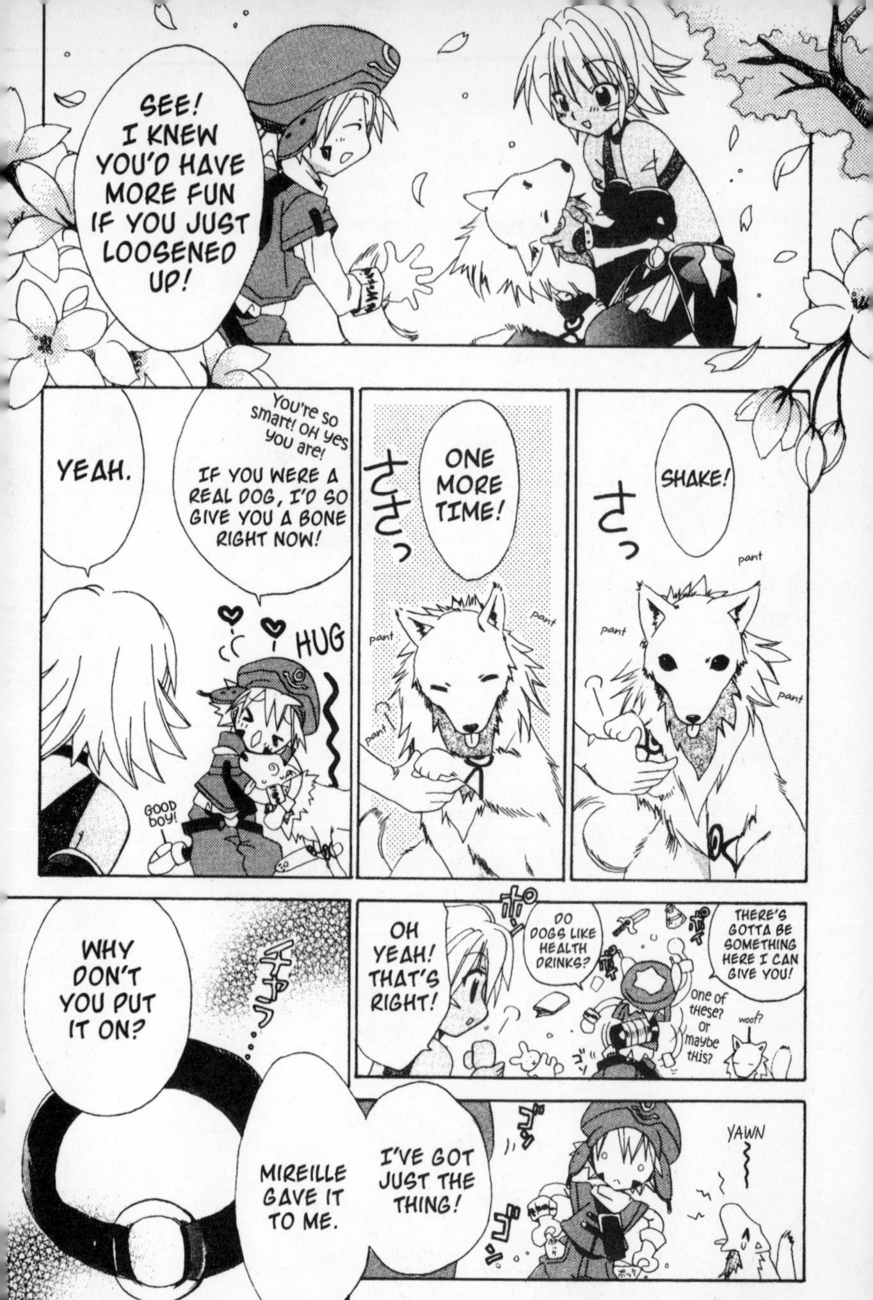

SEE! I KNEW YOU'D HAVE MORE FUN IF YOU JUST LOOSENED UP!
SHAKE!
さっ
pant
pant
pant
ONE MORE TIME!
ささっ
pant
pant
pant
You're so smart! OH yes you are!
IF YOU WERE A REAL DOG, I'D SO GIVE YOU A BONE RIGHT NOW!
HUG
GOOD BOY!
YEAH.
THERE'S GOTTA BE SOMETHING HERE I CAN GIVE YOU!
DO DOGS LIKE HEALTH DRINKS?
One of these? Or maybe this?
woof?
OH YEAH! THAT'S RIGHT!
YAWN
I'VE GOT JUST THE THING!
MIREILLE GAVE IT TO ME.
WHY DON'T YOU PUT IT ON?

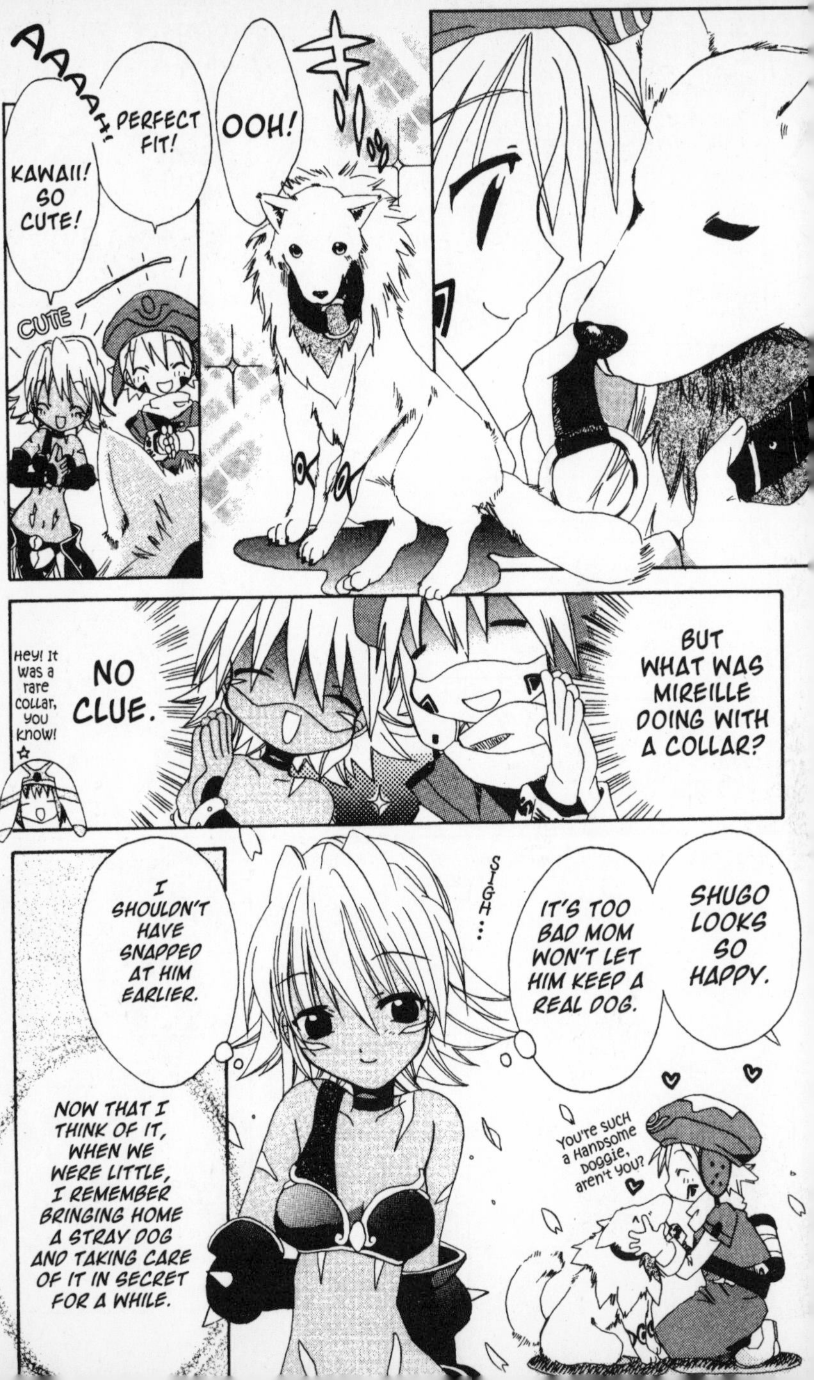
OOH!
PERFECT FIT!
AAAAH!
KAWAII! SO CUTE!
CUTE
BUT WHAT WAS MIREILLE DOING WITH A COLLAR?
NO CLUE.
Hey! It was a rare collar, you know! ☆
SHUGO LOOKS SO HAPPY.
IT'S TOO BAD MOM WON'T LET HIM KEEP A REAL DOG.
SIGH...
I SHOULDN'T HAVE SNAPPED AT HIM EARLIER.
You're SUCH a Handsome Doggie, aren't you?
NOW THAT I THINK OF IT, WHEN WE WERE LITTLE, I REMEMBER BRINGING HOME A STRAY DOG AND TAKING CARE OF IT IN SECRET FOR A WHILE.

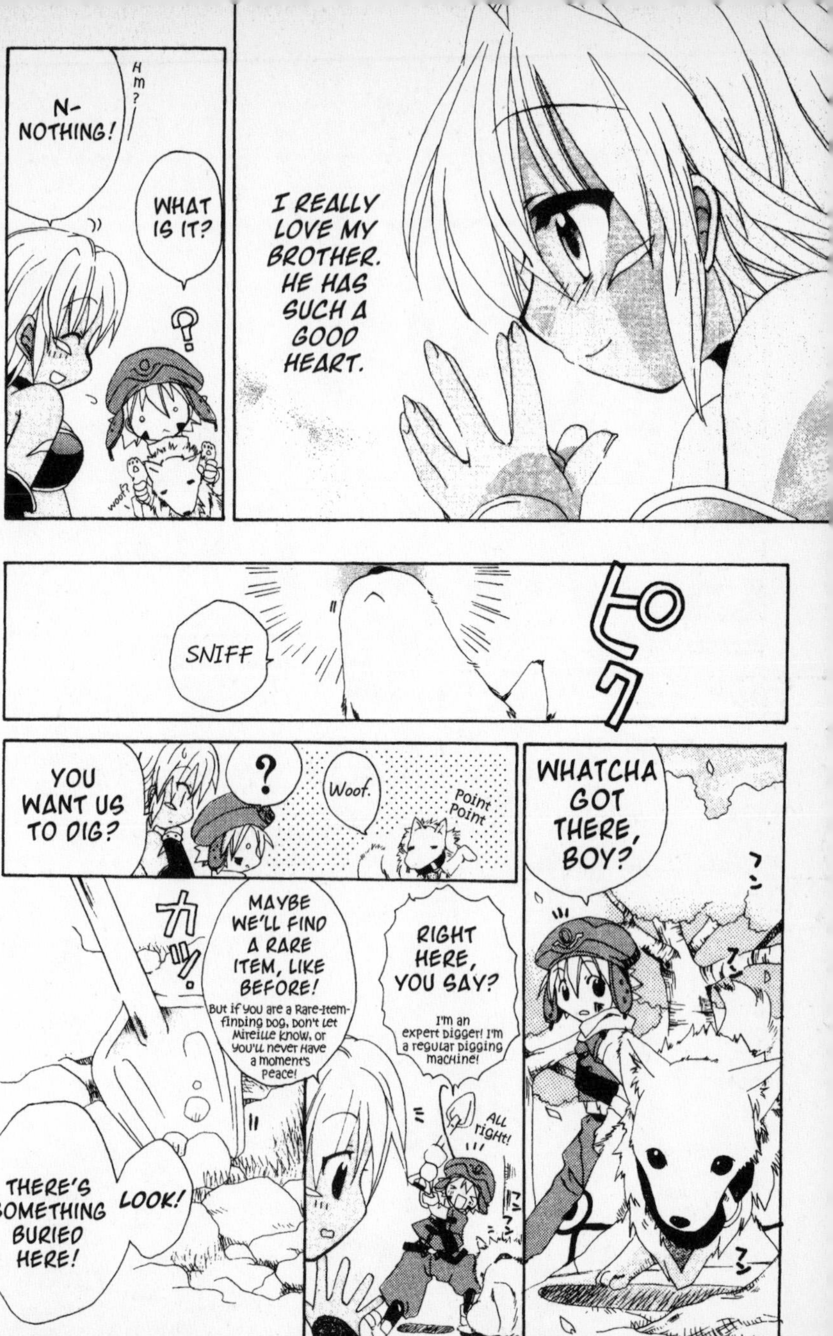
I REALLY LOVE MY BROTHER. HE HAS SUCH A GOOD HEART.
Hm?
N- NOTHING!
WHAT IS IT?
?
woof?
ピク
SNIFF
WHATCHA GOT THERE, BOY?
フン
フン
フン
Point Point
Woof.
?
YOU WANT US TO DIG?
RIGHT HERE, YOU SAY?
I'm an expert digger! I'm a regular digging machine!
All right!
MAYBE WE'LL FIND A RARE ITEM, LIKE BEFORE!
But if you are a Rare-Item-finding dog, don't let Mireille know, or you'll never have a moment's peace!
カッ
LOOK!
THERE'S SOMETHING BURIED HERE!

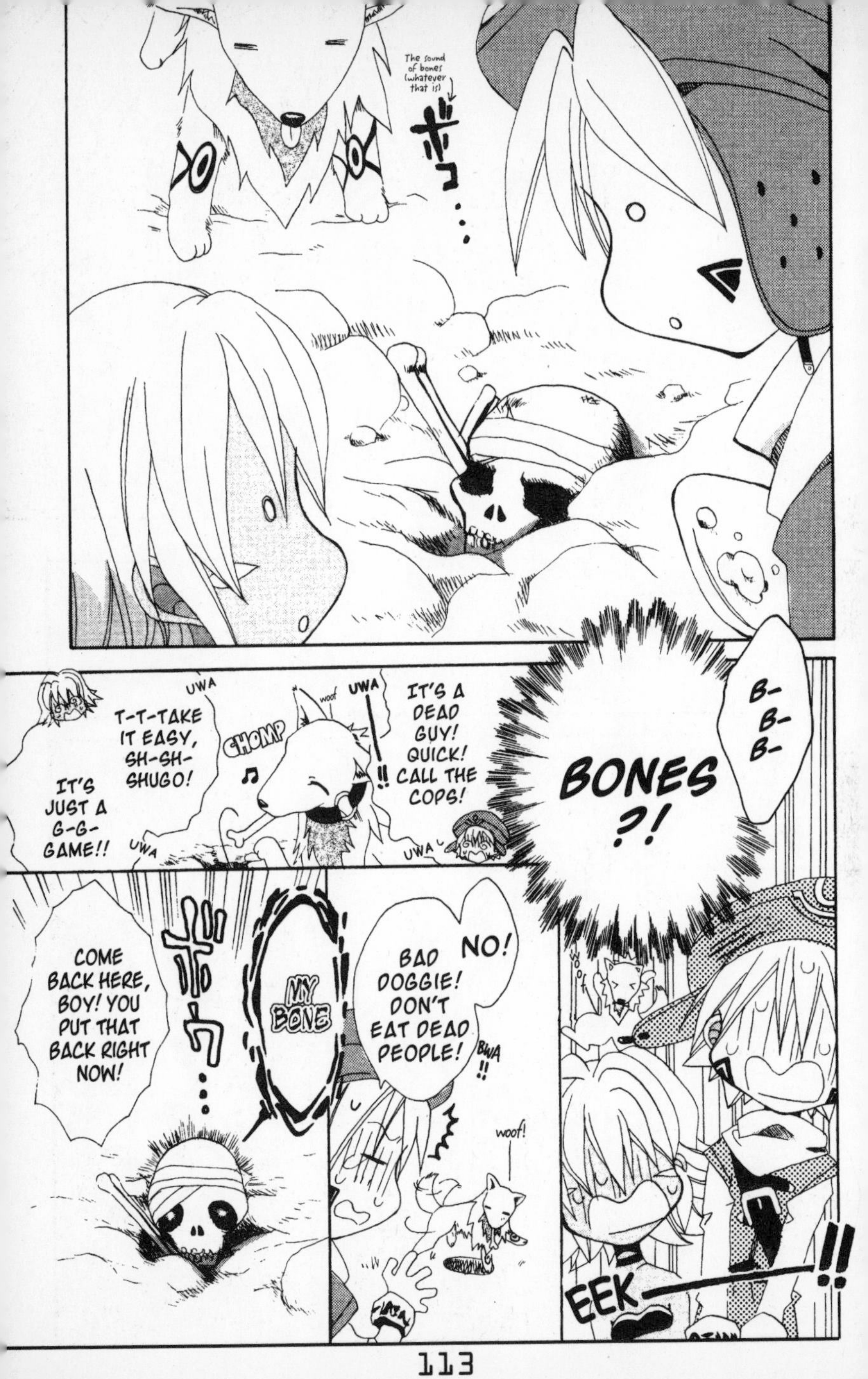

The sound of bones (whatever that is)
B-B-B-
BONES?!
IT'S A DEAD GUY! QUICK! CALL THE COPS!
UWA
UWA
woof
CHOMP
UWA
T-T-TAKE IT EASY, SH-SH-SHUGO!
IT'S JUST A G-G-GAME!!
UWA
EEK!!
woof
NO!
BAD DOGGIE! DON'T EAT DEAD PEOPLE!
BWA!!
woof!
MY BONE
COME BACK HERE, BOY! YOU PUT THAT BACK RIGHT NOW!

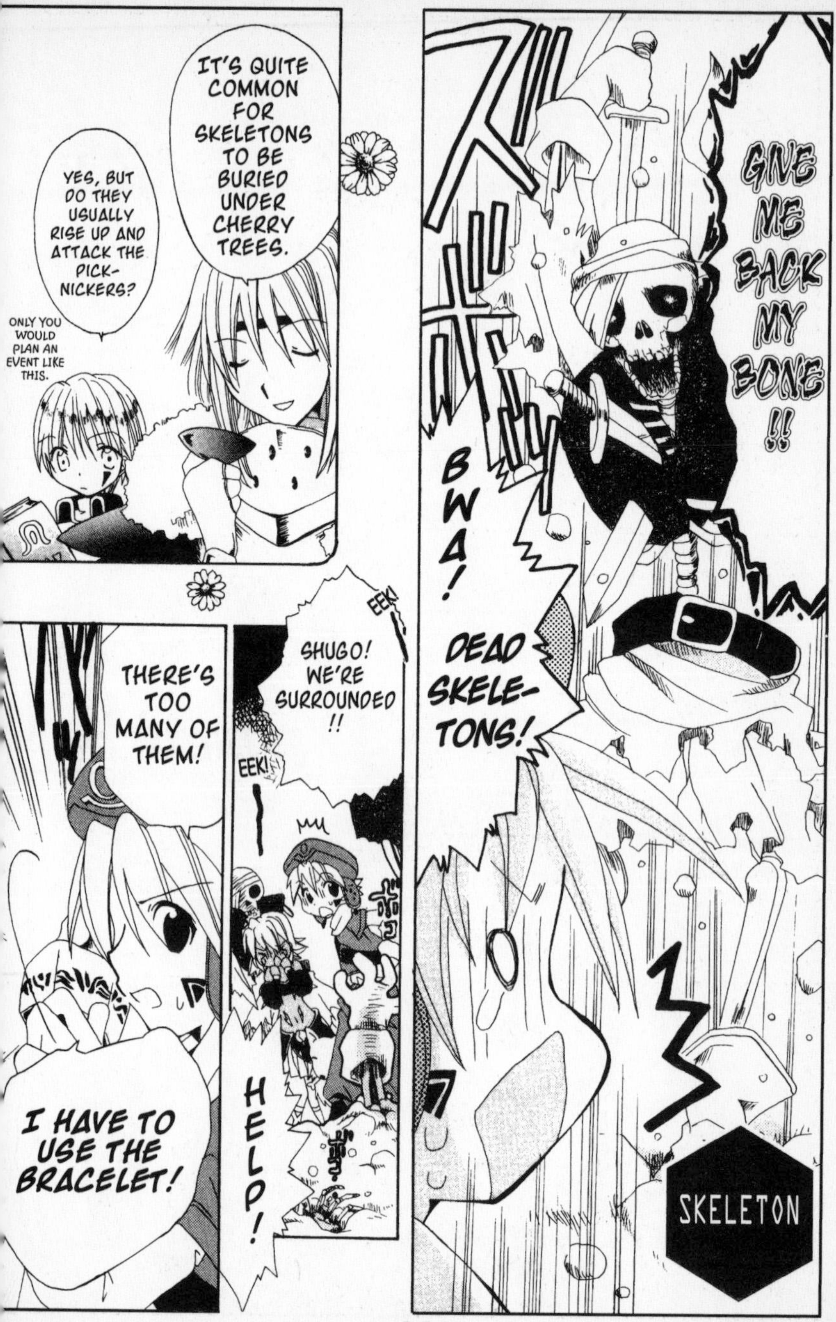
GIVE ME BACK MY BONE!!
BWA!
DEAD SKELE-TONS!
SKELETON
IT'S QUITE COMMON FOR SKELETONS TO BE BURIED UNDER CHERRY TREES.
YES, BUT DO THEY USUALLY RISE UP AND ATTACK THE PICK-NICKERS?
ONLY YOU WOULD PLAN AN EVENT LIKE THIS.
EEK!
SHUGO! WE'RE SURROUNDED!!
EEK!
HELP!
THERE'S TOO MANY OF THEM!
I HAVE TO USE THE BRACELET!

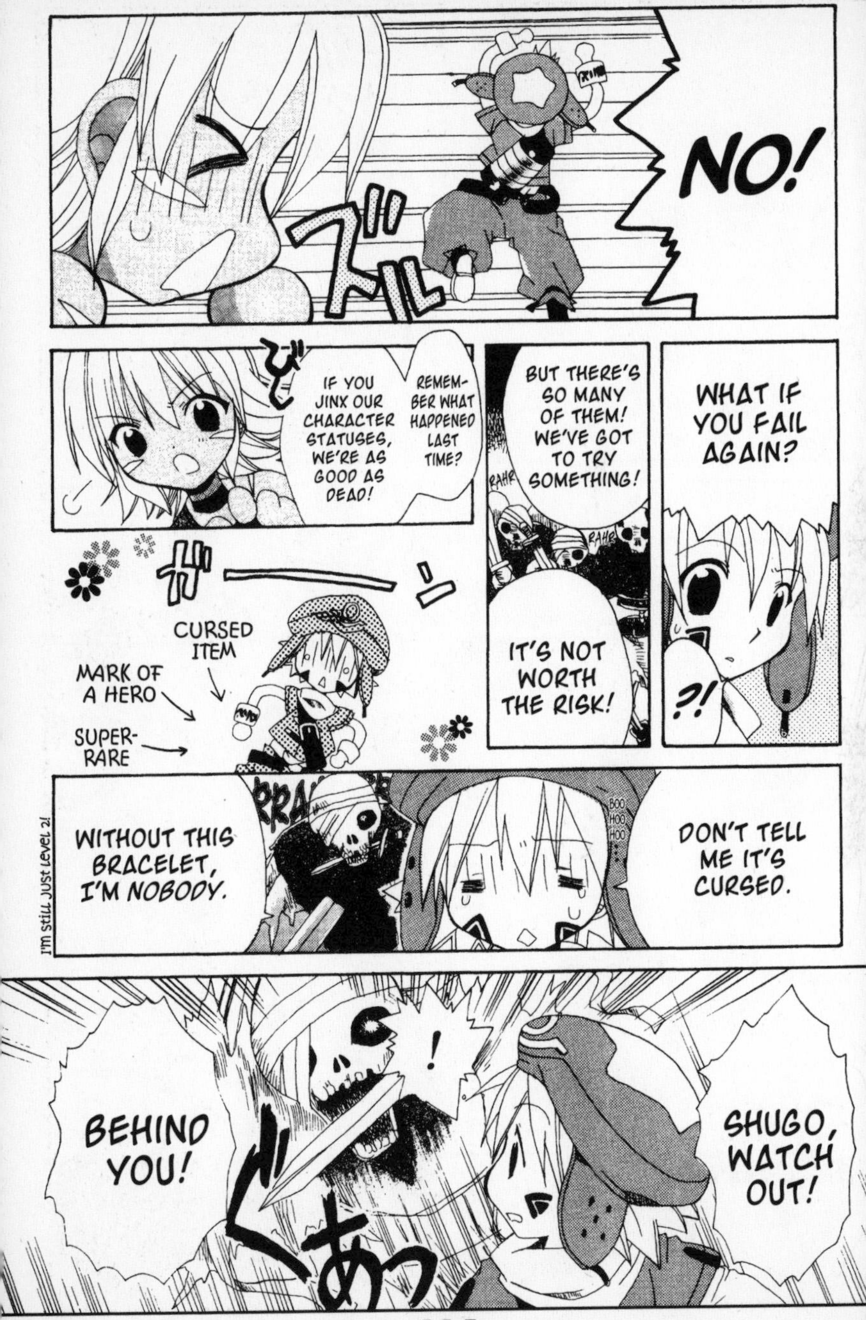
NO!
WHAT IF YOU FAIL AGAIN?
?!
BUT THERE'S SO MANY OF THEM! WE'VE GOT TO TRY SOMETHING!
RAHR
RAHR
IT'S NOT WORTH THE RISK!
REMEMBER WHAT HAPPENED LAST TIME?
IF YOU JINX OUR CHARACTER STATUSES, WE'RE AS GOOD AS DEAD!
CURSED ITEM
MARK OF A HERO
SUPER-RARE
DON'T TELL ME IT'S CURSED.
BOO HOO HOO
WITHOUT THIS BRACELET, I'M NOBODY.
I'm still just level 2!
SHUGO, WATCH OUT!
!
BEHIND YOU!

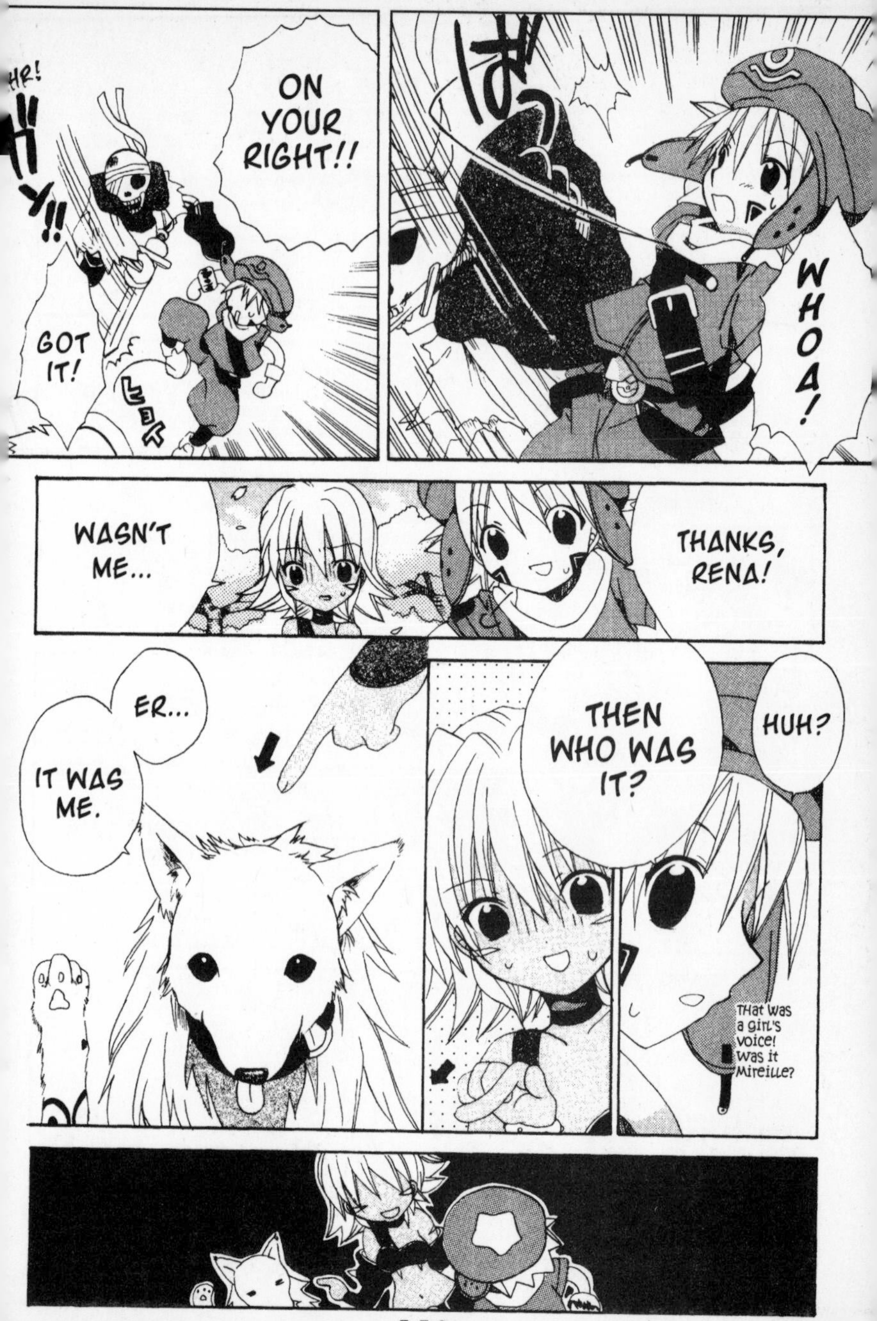
WHOA!
ON YOUR RIGHT!!
GOT IT!
THANKS, RENA!
WASN'T ME...
HUH?
THEN WHO WAS IT?
That was a girl's voice! Was it Mireille?
ER...
IT WAS ME.

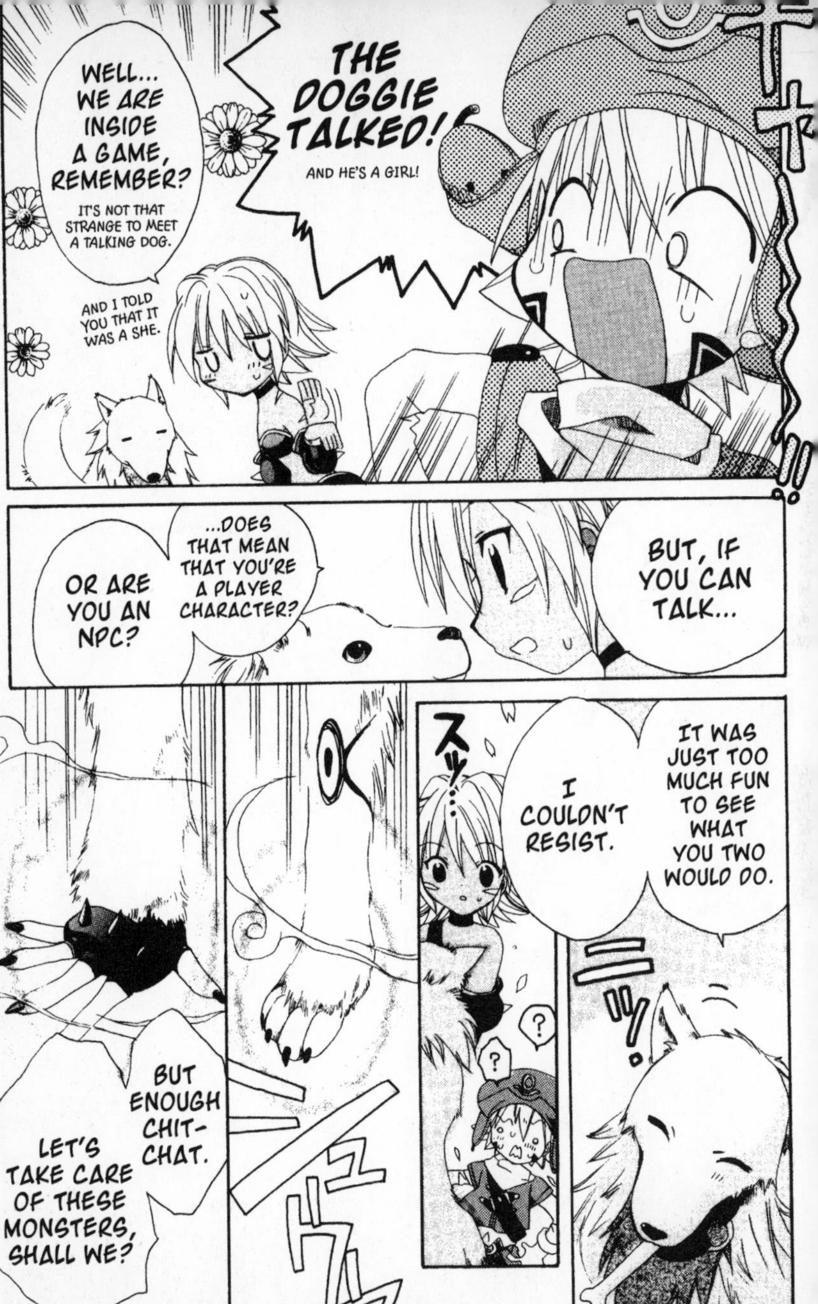
THE DOGGIE TALKED!
AND HE'S A GIRL!
WELL... WE ARE INSIDE A GAME, REMEMBER?
IT'S NOT THAT STRANGE TO MEET A TALKING DOG.
AND I TOLD YOU THAT IT WAS A SHE.
BUT, IF YOU CAN TALK...
...DOES THAT MEAN THAT YOU'RE A PLAYER CHARACTER?
OR ARE YOU AN NPC?
IT WAS JUST TOO MUCH FUN TO SEE WHAT YOU TWO WOULD DO.
I COULDN'T RESIST.
BUT ENOUGH CHIT-CHAT.
LET'S TAKE CARE OF THESE MONSTERS, SHALL WE?

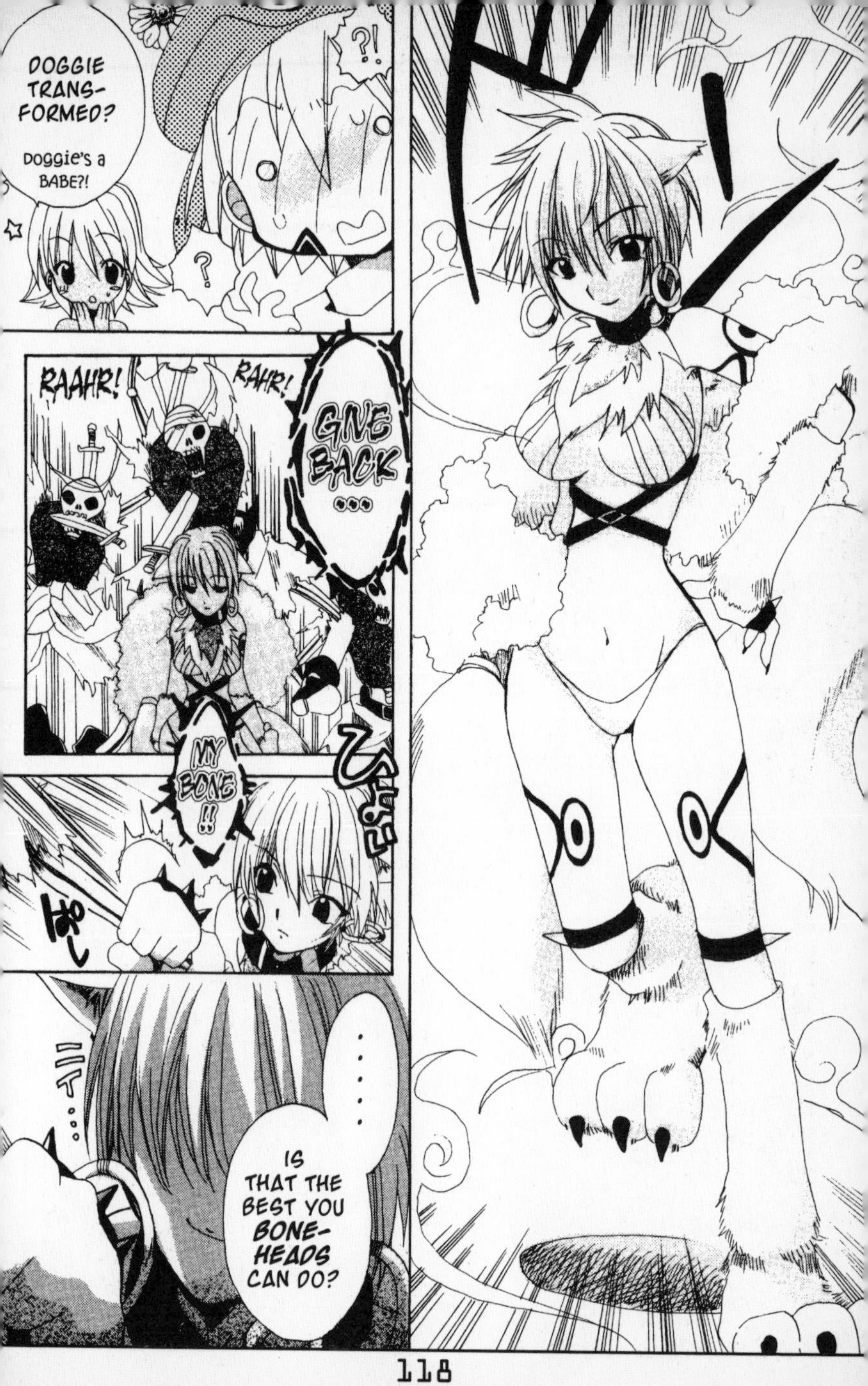
?!
DOGGIE TRANSFORMED?
Doggie's a BABE?!
?
GIVE BACK...
RAHR!
RAAHR!
MY BONE!!
ぱし
ニィ...
.....
IS THAT THE BEST YOU BONE-HEADS CAN DO?

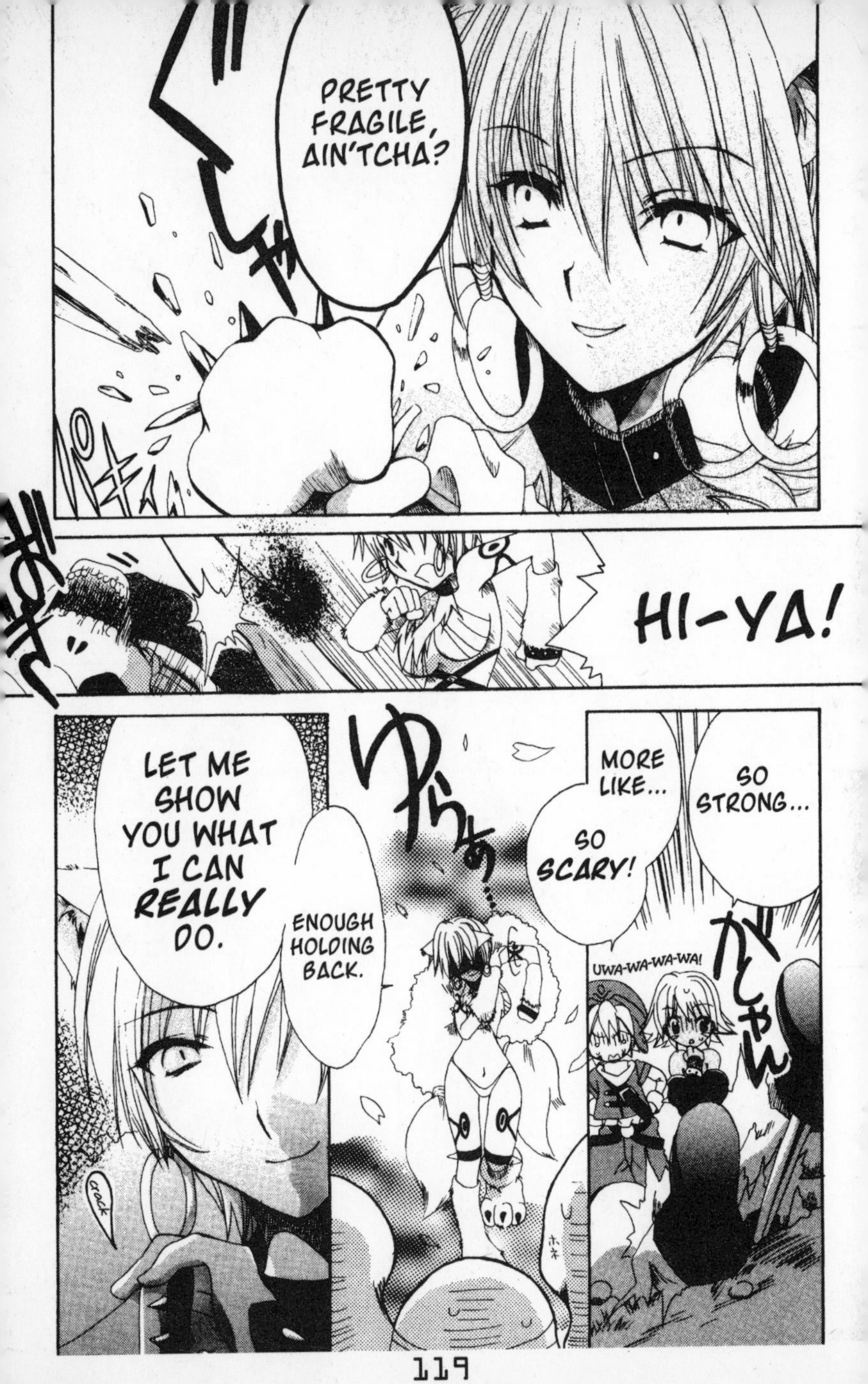
PRETTY FRAGILE, AIN'TCHA?
HI-YA!
SO STRONG...
MORE LIKE... SO SCARY!
UWA-WA-WA-WA!
がしゃん
ゆらぁ
ENOUGH HOLDING BACK.
LET ME SHOW YOU WHAT I CAN REALLY DO.
crack

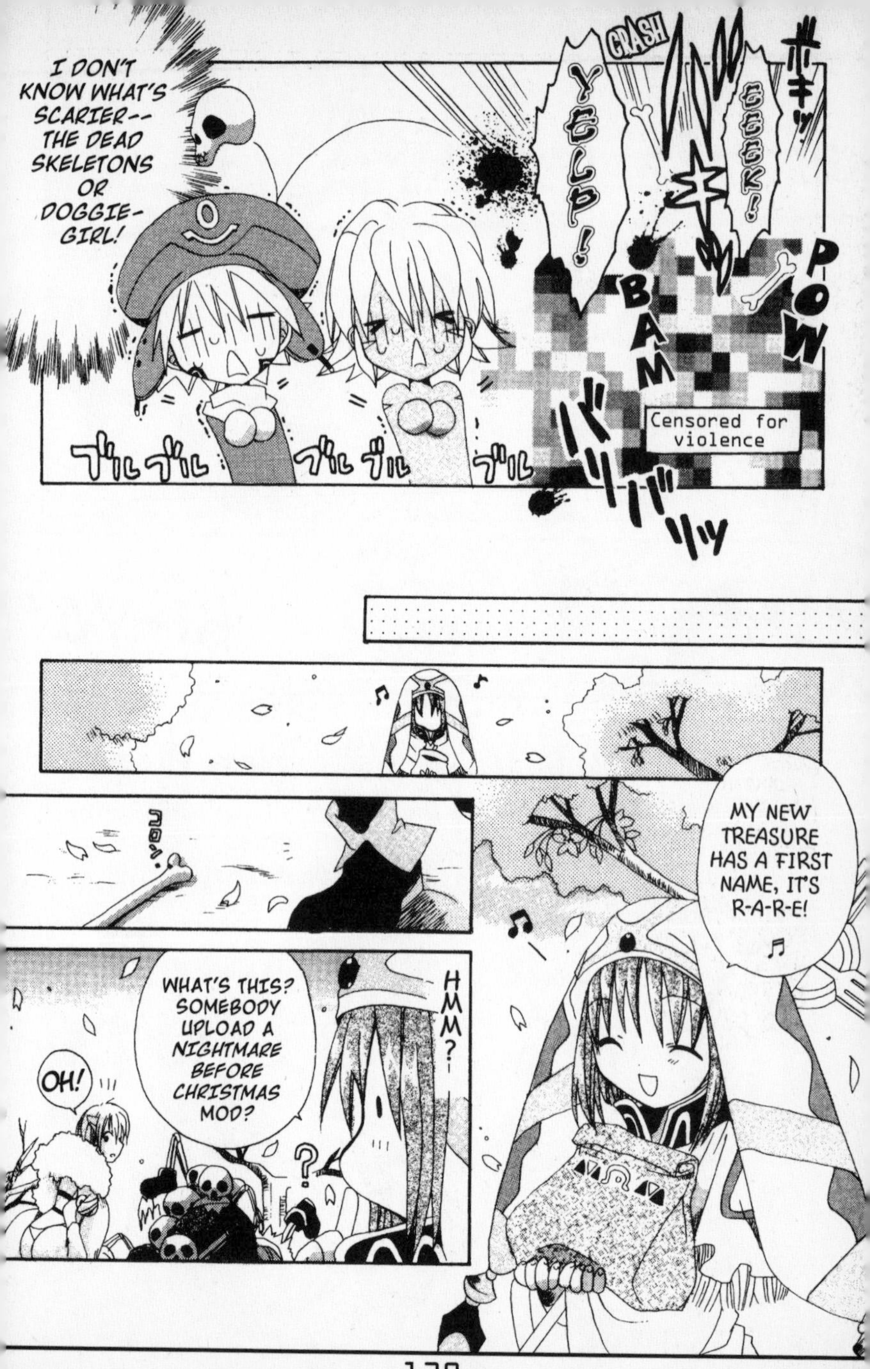

ボキッ
CRASH
EEEEK!
YELP!
POW
BAM
Censored for violence
バリバリッ
ブルブル ブルブル ブル
I DON'T KNOW WHAT'S SCARIER-- THE DEAD SKELETONS OR DOGGIE-GIRL!
MY NEW TREASURE HAS A FIRST NAME, IT'S R-A-R-E! ♫
コロン
HMM?
WHAT'S THIS? SOMEBODY UPLOAD A NIGHTMARE BEFORE CHRISTMAS MOD?
OH!

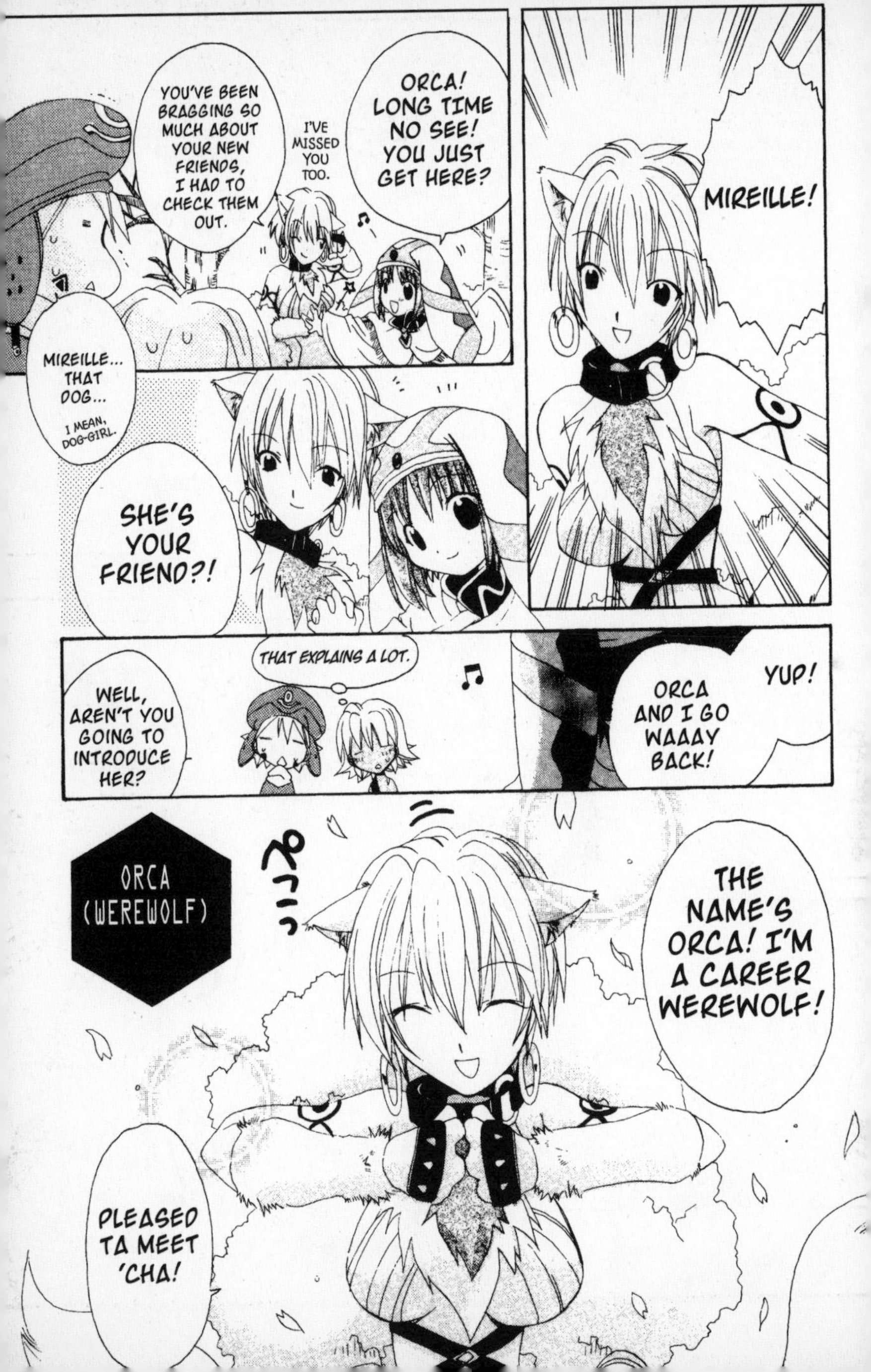
MIREILLE!
ORCA! LONG TIME NO SEE! YOU JUST GET HERE?
I'VE MISSED YOU TOO.
YOU'VE BEEN BRAGGING SO MUCH ABOUT YOUR NEW FRIENDS, I HAD TO CHECK THEM OUT.
MIREILLE... THAT DOG...
I MEAN, DOG-GIRL.
SHE'S YOUR FRIEND?!
YUP!
ORCA AND I GO WAAAY BACK!
THAT EXPLAINS A LOT.
WELL, AREN'T YOU GOING TO INTRODUCE HER?
THE NAME'S ORCA! I'M A CAREER WEREWOLF!
ぺこっ
ORCA (WEREWOLF)
PLEASED TA MEET 'CHA!

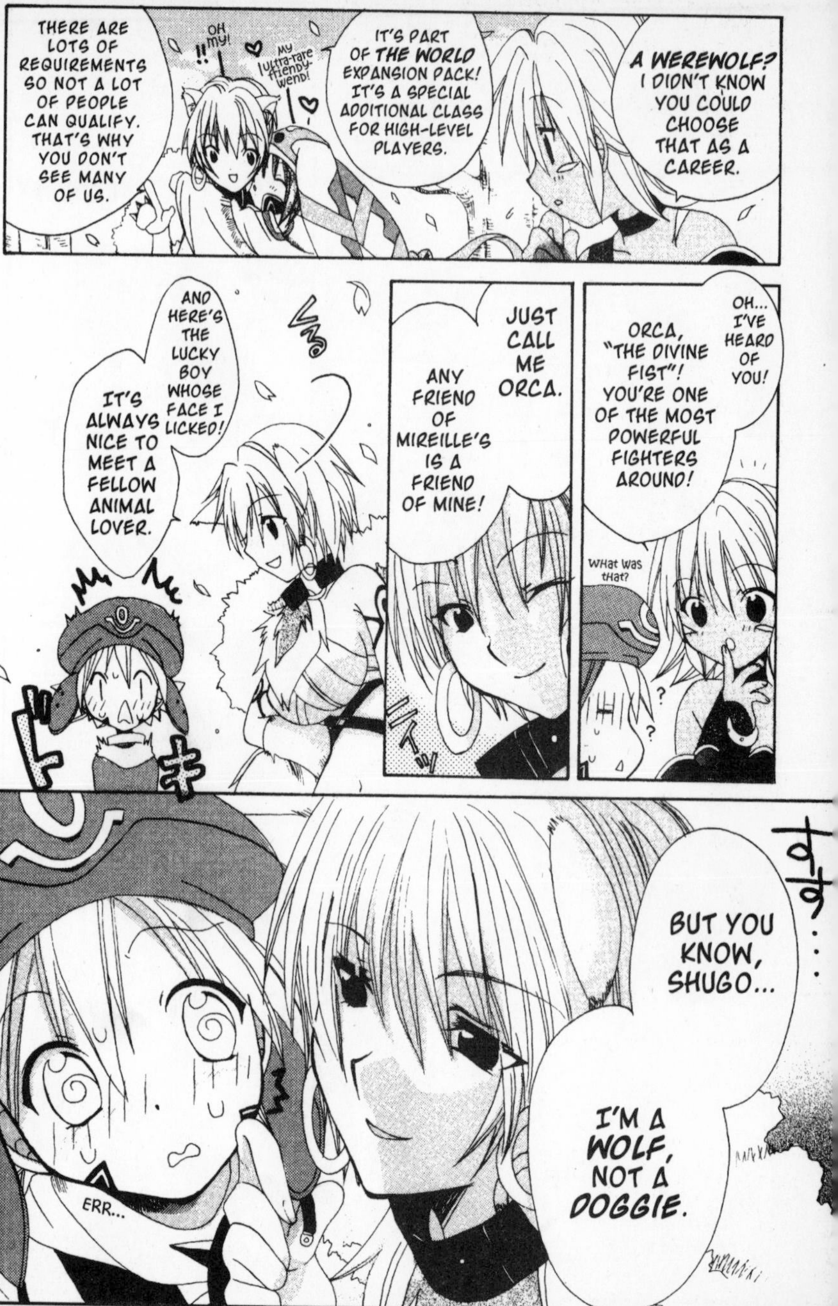
A WEREWOLF? I DIDN'T KNOW YOU COULD CHOOSE THAT AS A CAREER.
IT'S PART OF THE WORLD EXPANSION PACK! IT'S A SPECIAL ADDITIONAL CLASS FOR HIGH-LEVEL PLAYERS.
My ultra-rare friendy-wend!
OH my!
!!
THERE ARE LOTS OF REQUIREMENTS SO NOT A LOT OF PEOPLE CAN QUALIFY. THAT'S WHY YOU DON'T SEE MANY OF US.
OH... I'VE HEARD OF YOU!
ORCA, "THE DIVINE FIST"! YOU'RE ONE OF THE MOST POWERFUL FIGHTERS AROUND!
What was that?
?
?
JUST CALL ME ORCA.
ANY FRIEND OF MIREILLE'S IS A FRIEND OF MINE!
AND HERE'S THE LUCKY BOY WHOSE FACE I LICKED!
IT'S ALWAYS NICE TO MEET A FELLOW ANIMAL LOVER.
BUT YOU KNOW, SHUGO...
I'M A WOLF, NOT A DOGGIE.
ERR...

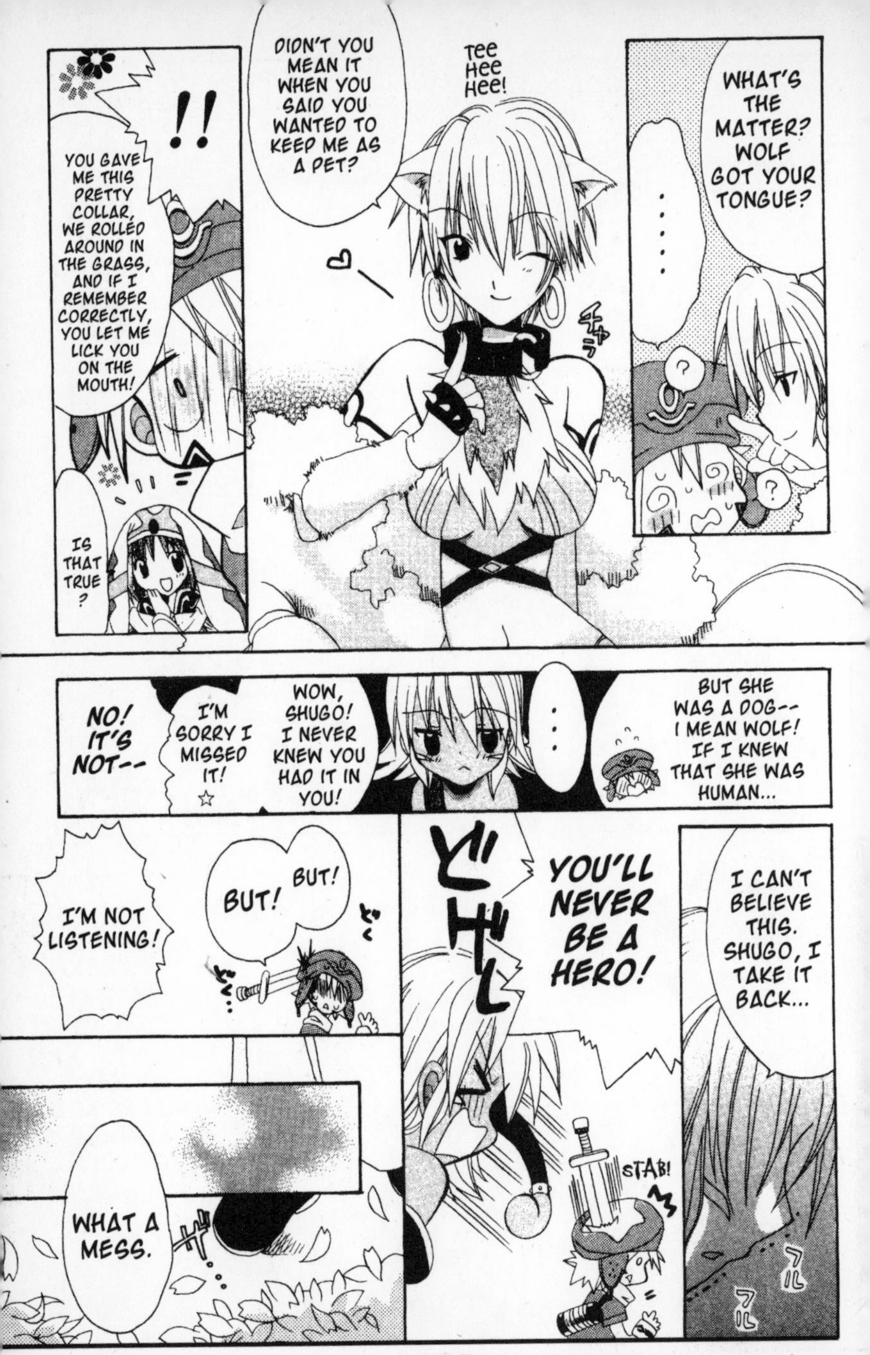
WHAT'S THE MATTER? WOLF GOT YOUR TONGUE?
......
TEE HEE HEE!
DIDN'T YOU MEAN IT WHEN YOU SAID YOU WANTED TO KEEP ME AS A PET?
!!
YOU GAVE ME THIS PRETTY COLLAR, WE ROLLED AROUND IN THE GRASS, AND IF I REMEMBER CORRECTLY, YOU LET ME LICK YOU ON THE MOUTH!
IS THAT TRUE?
BUT SHE WAS A DOG-- I MEAN WOLF! IF I KNEW THAT SHE WAS HUMAN...
...
WOW, SHUGO! I NEVER KNEW YOU HAD IT IN YOU!
I'M SORRY I MISSED IT! ☆
NO! IT'S NOT--
I CAN'T BELIEVE THIS. SHUGO, I TAKE IT BACK...
YOU'LL NEVER BE A HERO!
STAB!
BUT! BUT!
I'M NOT LISTENING!
WHAT A MESS.

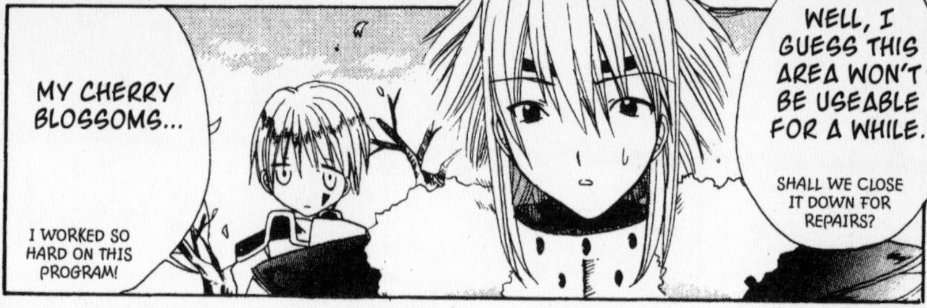
WELL, I GUESS THIS AREA WON'T BE USEABLE FOR A WHILE.
SHALL WE CLOSE IT DOWN FOR REPAIRS?
MY CHERRY BLOSSOMS...
I WORKED SO HARD ON THIS PROGRAM!

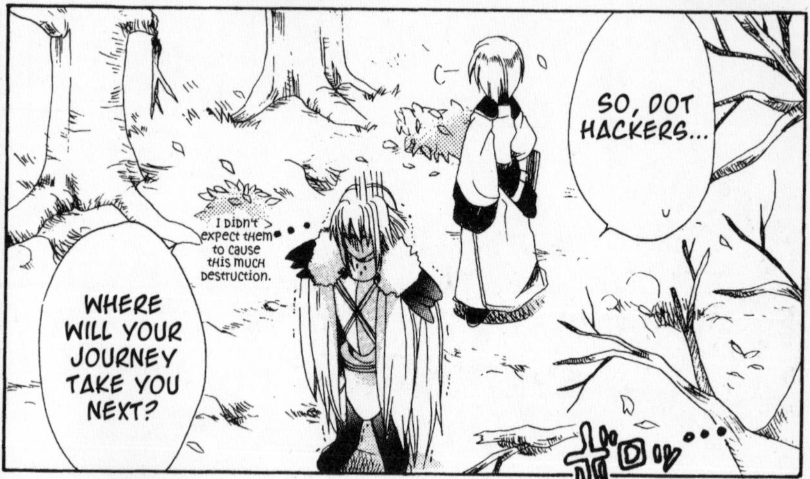
SO, DOT HACKERS...
I DIDN'T EXPECT THEM TO CAUSE THIS MUCH DESTRUCTION.
WHERE WILL YOUR JOURNEY TAKE YOU NEXT?

TODAY'S ADVENTURE

ORCA'S EXPERIENCE POINTS ARE UP!
ORCA OBTAINED THE "COLLAR"!
SHUGO'S REPUTATION WENT DOWN.

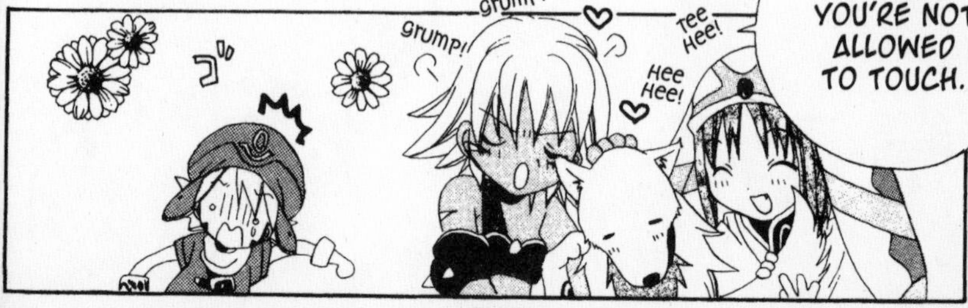
SHUGO, YOU'RE NOT ALLOWED TO TOUCH.
Tee Hee!
Hee Hee!
grump!
grump!

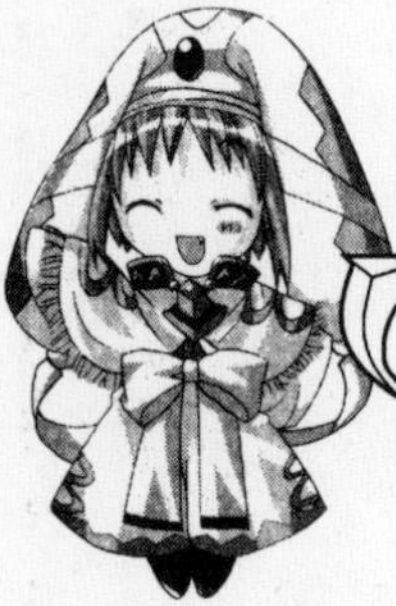

NEW GENERATION ONLINE

THE WORLD

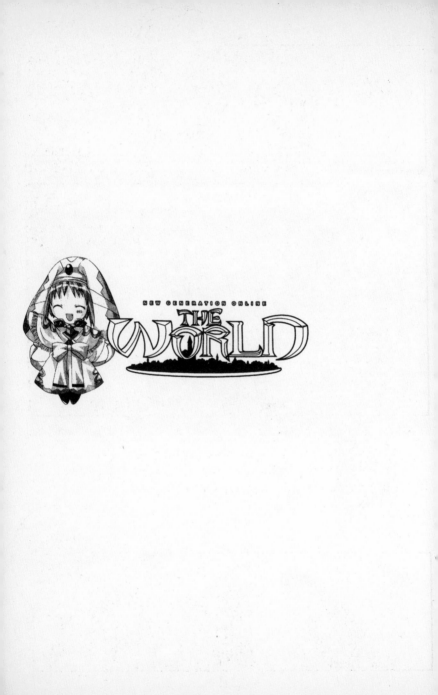

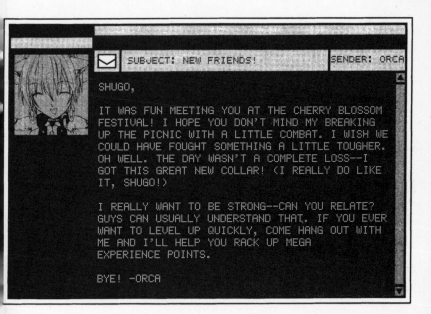

SUBJECT: NEW FRIENDS!　　　　　SENDER: ORCA

SHUGO,

IT WAS FUN MEETING YOU AT THE CHERRY BLOSSOM
FESTIVAL! I HOPE YOU DON'T MIND MY BREAKING
UP THE PICNIC WITH A LITTLE COMBAT. I WISH WE
COULD HAVE FOUGHT SOMETHING A LITTLE TOUGHER.
OH WELL. THE DAY WASN'T A COMPLETE LOSS--I
GOT THIS GREAT NEW COLLAR! (I REALLY DO LIKE
IT, SHUGO!)

I REALLY WANT TO BE STRONG--CAN YOU RELATE?
GUYS CAN USUALLY UNDERSTAND THAT. IF YOU EVER
WANT TO LEVEL UP QUICKLY, COME HANG OUT WITH
ME AND I'LL HELP YOU RACK UP MEGA
EXPERIENCE POINTS.

BYE! -ORCA

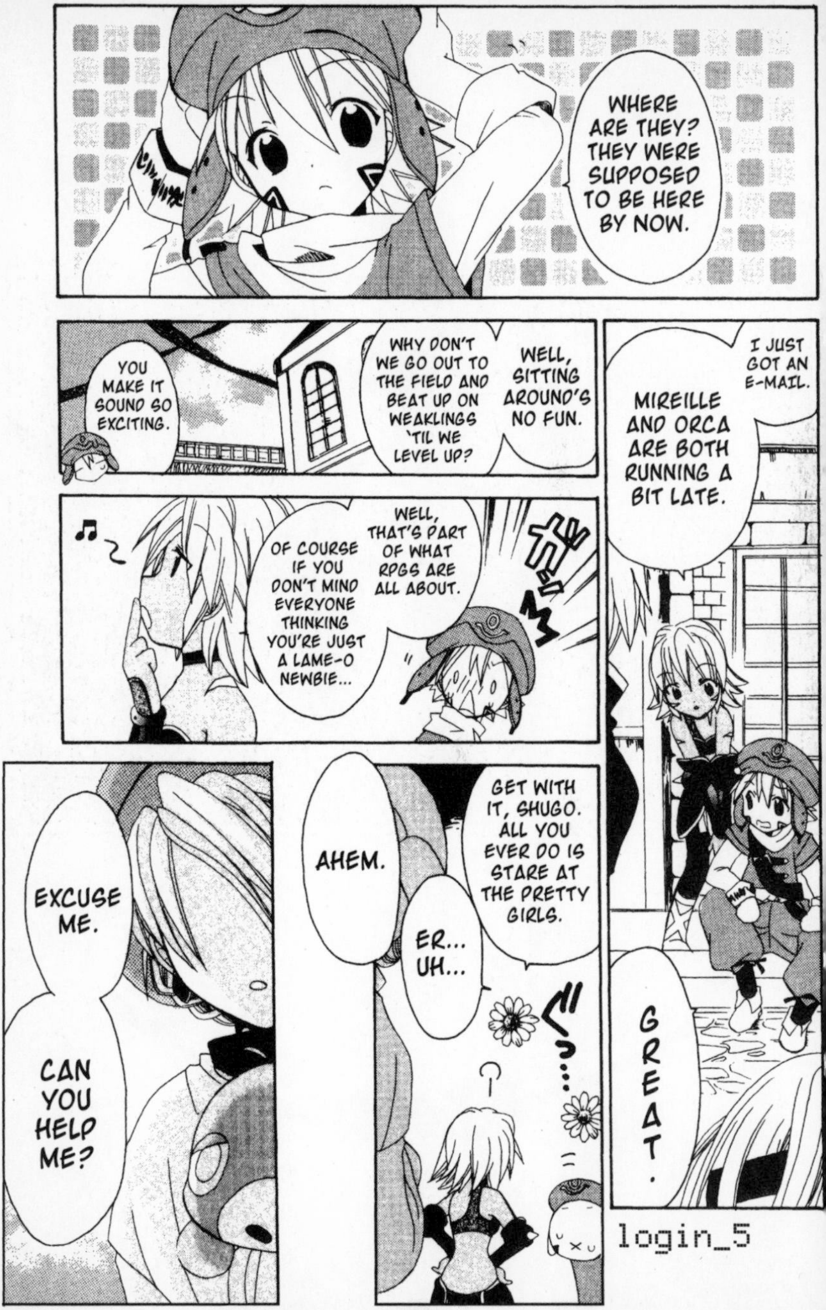
WHERE ARE THEY? THEY WERE SUPPOSED TO BE HERE BY NOW.
I JUST GOT AN E-MAIL.
MIREILLE AND ORCA ARE BOTH RUNNING A BIT LATE.
GREAT.
WELL, SITTING AROUND'S NO FUN.
WHY DON'T WE GO OUT TO THE FIELD AND BEAT UP ON WEAKLINGS 'TIL WE LEVEL UP?
YOU MAKE IT SOUND SO EXCITING.
WELL, THAT'S PART OF WHAT RPGS ARE ALL ABOUT.
OF COURSE IF YOU DON'T MIND EVERYONE THINKING YOU'RE JUST A LAME-O NEWBIE...
GET WITH IT, SHUGO. ALL YOU EVER DO IS STARE AT THE PRETTY GIRLS.
AHEM.
ER... UH...
EXCUSE ME.
CAN YOU HELP ME?
login_5

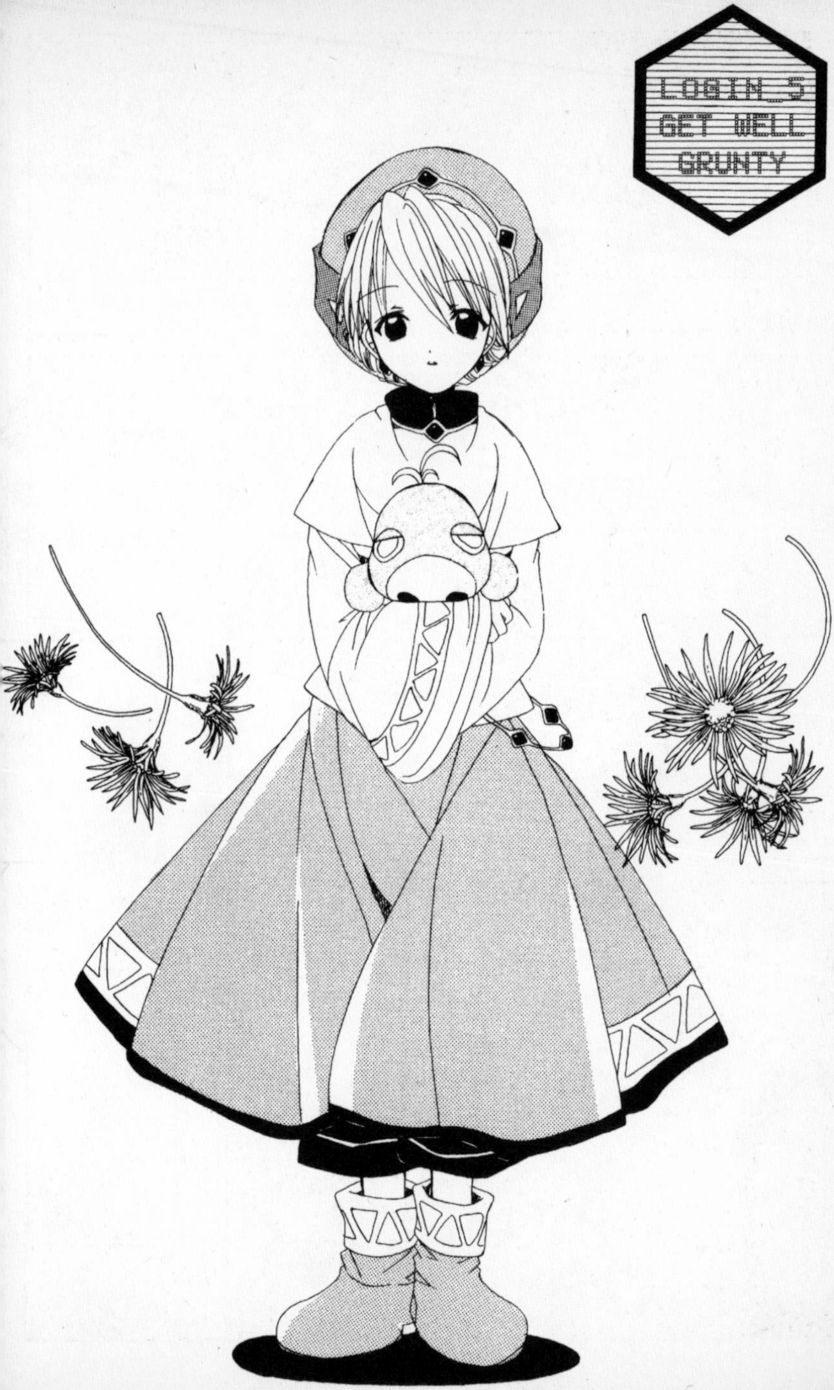
LOGIN_5
GET WELL
GRUNTY

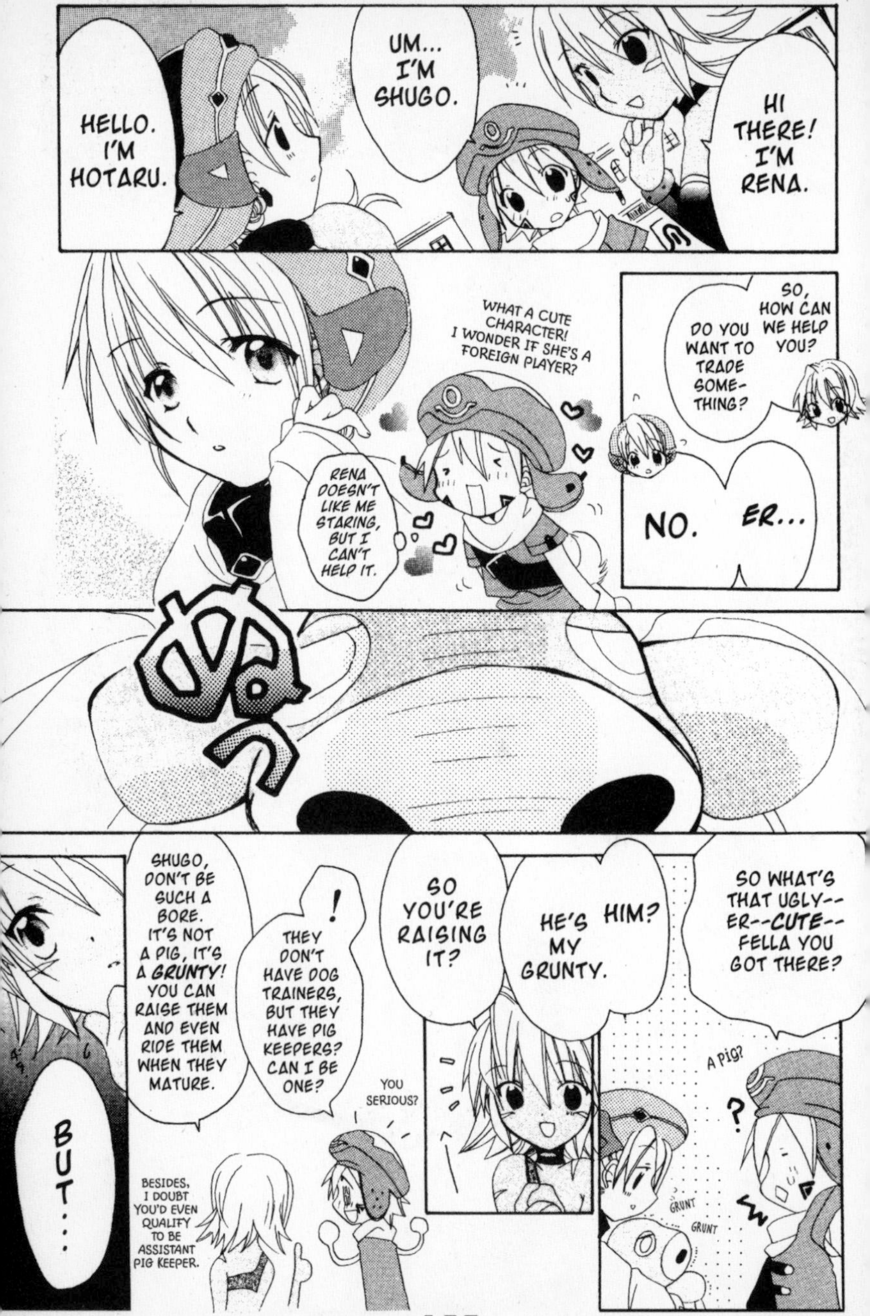
HI THERE! I'M RENA.
UM... I'M SHUGO.
HELLO. I'M HOTARU.
SO, HOW CAN WE HELP YOU?
DO YOU WANT TO TRADE SOMETHING?
ER...
NO.
WHAT A CUTE CHARACTER! I WONDER IF SHE'S A FOREIGN PLAYER?
RENA DOESN'T LIKE ME STARING, BUT I CAN'T HELP IT.
ぬっ
SO WHAT'S THAT UGLY--ER--*CUTE*--FELLA YOU GOT THERE?
A PIG?
?
GRUNT
GRUNT
HIM?
HE'S MY GRUNTY.
SO YOU'RE RAISING IT?
YOU SERIOUS?
!
THEY DON'T HAVE DOG TRAINERS, BUT THEY HAVE PIG KEEPERS? CAN I BE ONE?
SHUGO, DON'T BE SUCH A BORE. IT'S NOT A PIG, IT'S A *GRUNTY*! YOU CAN RAISE THEM AND EVEN RIDE THEM WHEN THEY MATURE.
BESIDES, I DOUBT YOU'D EVEN QUALIFY TO BE ASSISTANT PIG KEEPER.
BUT...

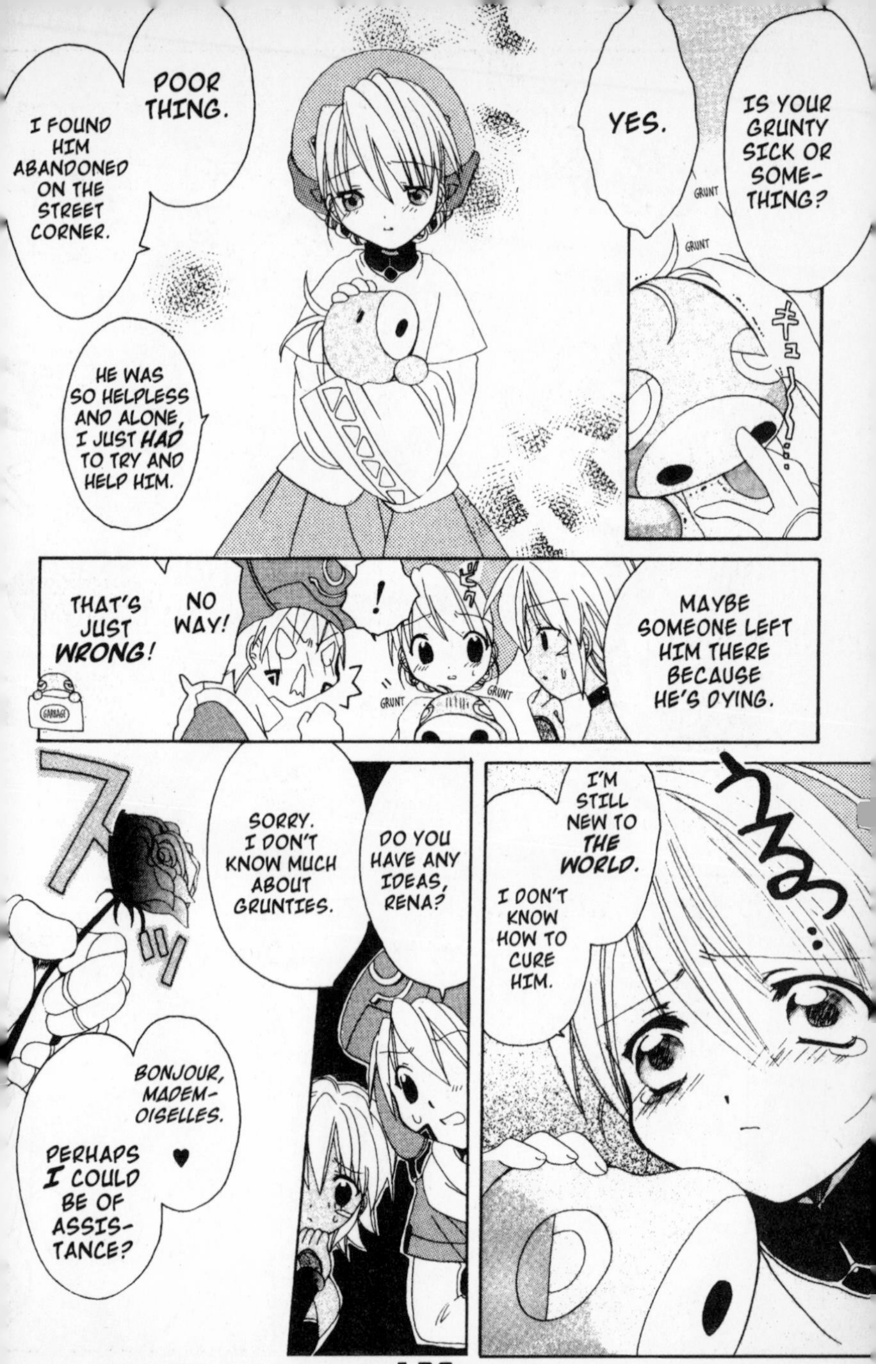
IS YOUR GRUNTY SICK OR SOME-THING?
YES.
GRUNT
GRUNT
POOR THING.
I FOUND HIM ABANDONED ON THE STREET CORNER.
HE WAS SO HELPLESS AND ALONE, I JUST **HAD** TO TRY AND HELP HIM.
MAYBE SOMEONE LEFT HIM THERE BECAUSE HE'S DYING.
!
GRUNT
GRUNT
NO WAY!
THAT'S JUST **WRONG**!
GARBAGE
I'M STILL NEW TO **THE WORLD**.
I DON'T KNOW HOW TO CURE HIM.
DO YOU HAVE ANY IDEAS, RENA?
SORRY. I DON'T KNOW MUCH ABOUT GRUNTIES.
BONJOUR, MADEM-OISELLES.
PERHAPS **I** COULD BE OF ASSIS-TANCE? ♥

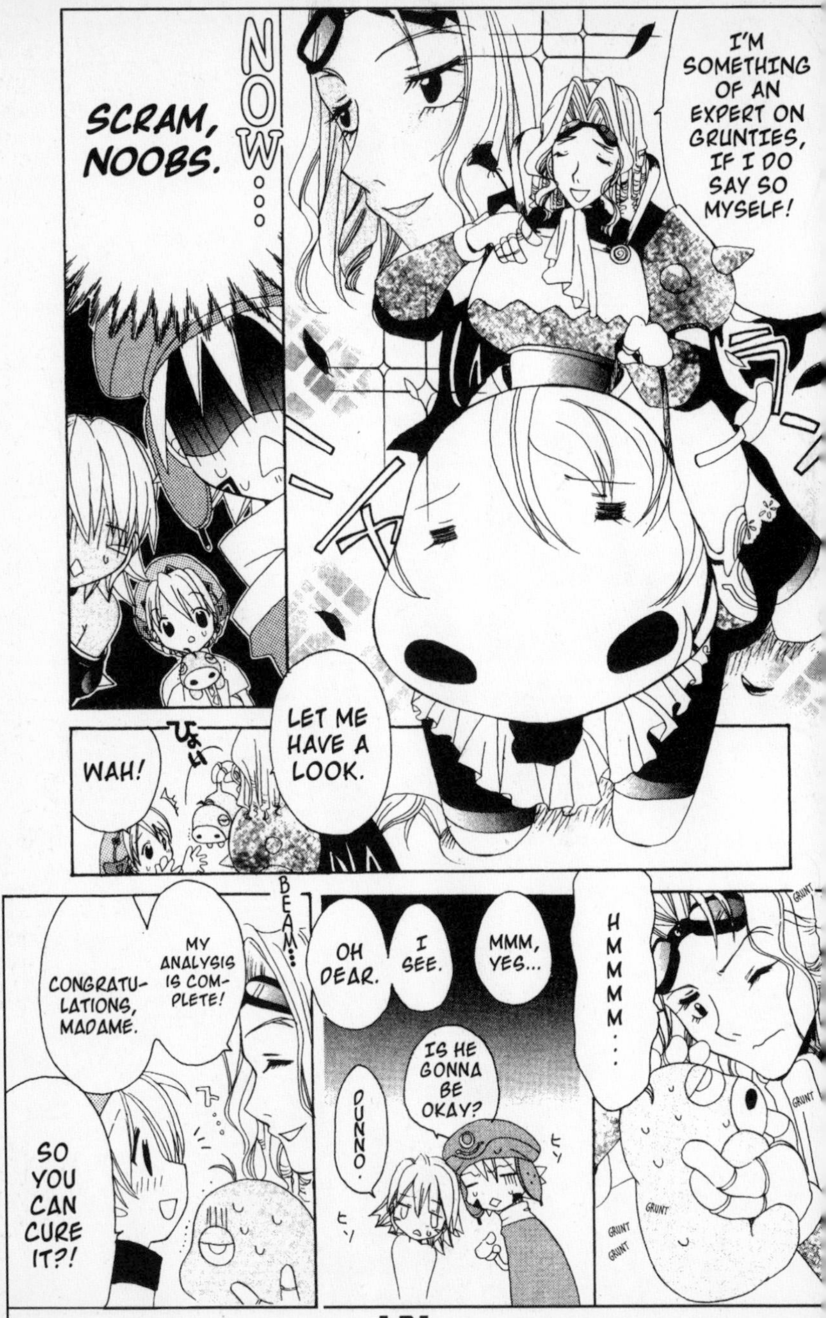
I'M SOMETHING OF AN EXPERT ON GRUNTIES, IF I DO SAY SO MYSELF!
NOW...
SCRAM, NOOBS.
LET ME HAVE A LOOK.
ひょい
WAH!
HMMMMM...
GRUNT
GRUNT
GRUNT
GRUNT
GRUNT
MMM, YES...
I SEE.
OH DEAR.
IS HE GONNA BE OKAY?
DUNNO.
BEAM...
MY ANALYSIS IS COMPLETE!
CONGRATULATIONS, MADAME.
SO YOU CAN CURE IT?!

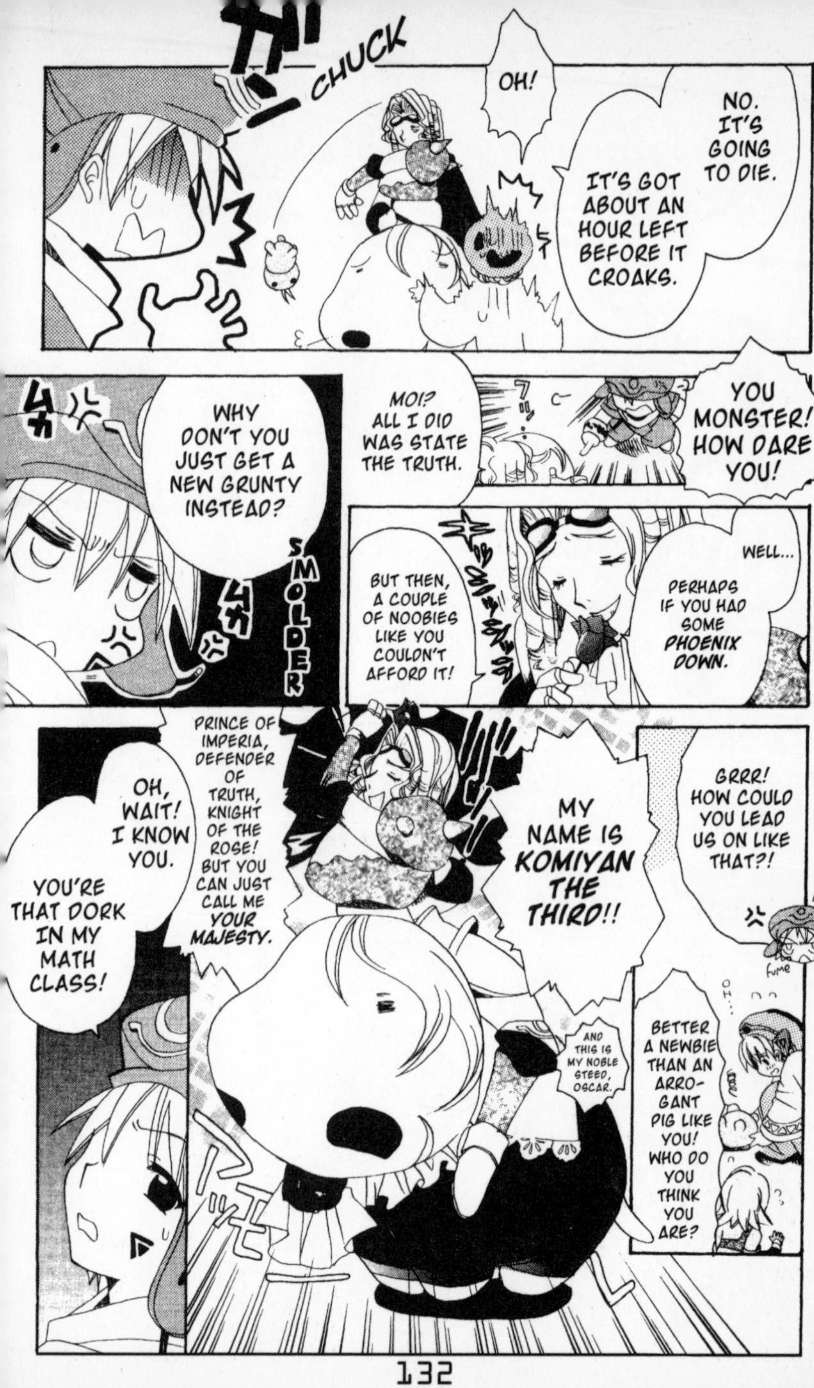
CHUCK
OH!
NO. IT'S GOING TO DIE.
IT'S GOT ABOUT AN HOUR LEFT BEFORE IT CROAKS.
YOU MONSTER! HOW DARE YOU!
MOI? ALL I DID WAS STATE THE TRUTH.
WELL...
PERHAPS IF YOU HAD SOME **PHOENIX DOWN.**
BUT THEN, A COUPLE OF NOOBIES LIKE YOU COULDN'T AFFORD IT!
WHY DON'T YOU JUST GET A NEW GRUNTY INSTEAD?
SMOLDER
GRRR! HOW COULD YOU LEAD US ON LIKE THAT?!
FUME
FUME
BETTER A NEWBIE THAN AN ARROGANT PIG LIKE YOU! WHO DO YOU THINK YOU ARE?
OH...
MY NAME IS **KOMIYAN THE THIRD!!**
PRINCE OF IMPERIA, DEFENDER OF TRUTH, KNIGHT OF THE ROSE! BUT YOU CAN JUST CALL ME **YOUR MAJESTY.**
AND THIS IS MY NOBLE STEED, OSCAR.
OH, WAIT! I KNOW YOU.
YOU'RE THAT DORK IN MY MATH CLASS!

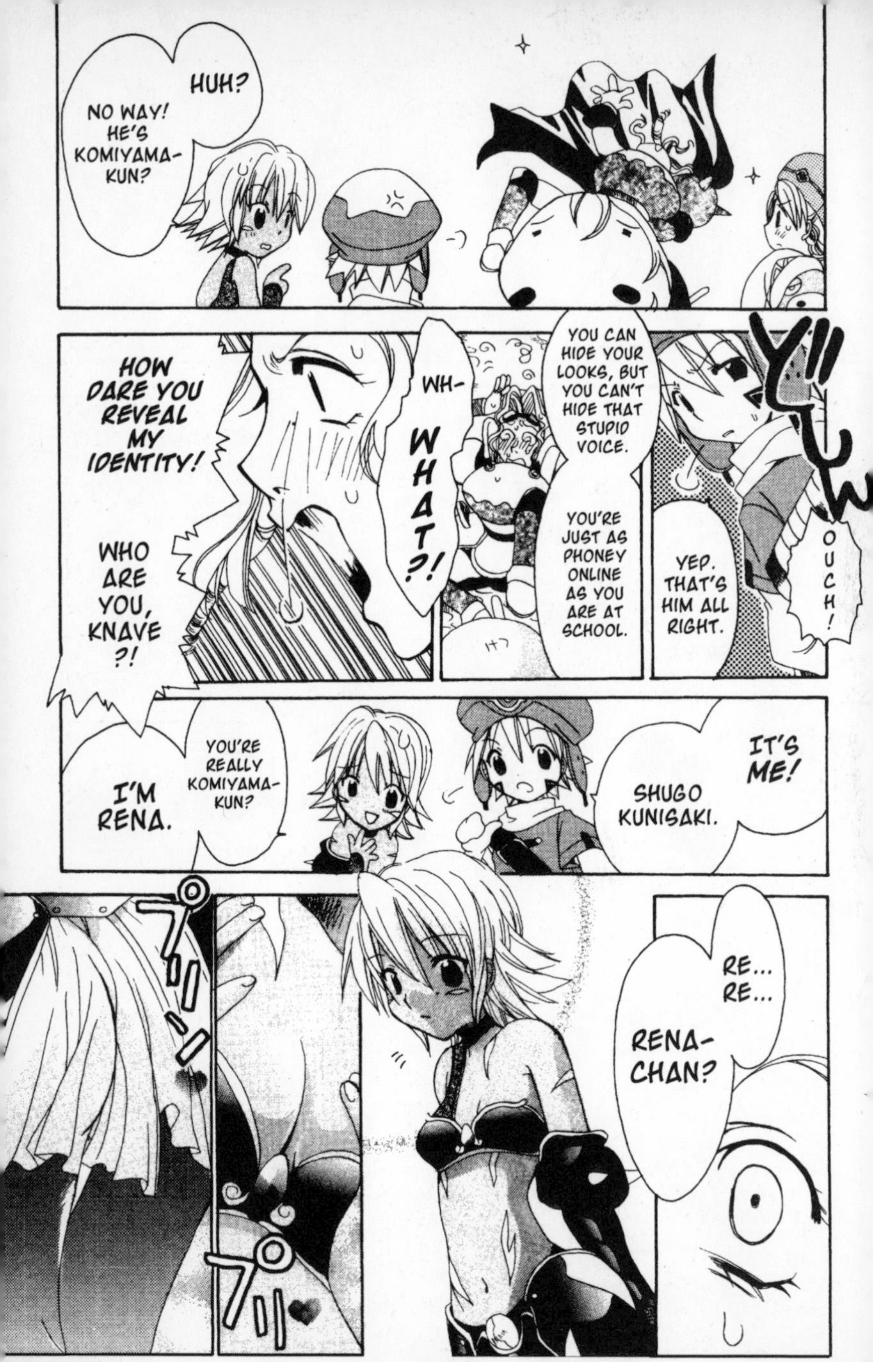
HUH?
NO WAY! HE'S KOMIYAMA-KUN?
OUCH!
YEP. THAT'S HIM ALL RIGHT.
YOU CAN HIDE YOUR LOOKS, BUT YOU CAN'T HIDE THAT STUPID VOICE.
YOU'RE JUST AS PHONEY ONLINE AS YOU ARE AT SCHOOL.
WH-
WHAT?!
HOW DARE YOU REVEAL MY IDENTITY!
WHO ARE YOU, KNAVE?!
IT'S ME!
SHUGO KUNISAKI.
YOU'RE REALLY KOMIYAMA-KUN?
I'M RENA.
RE... RE...
RENA-CHAN?

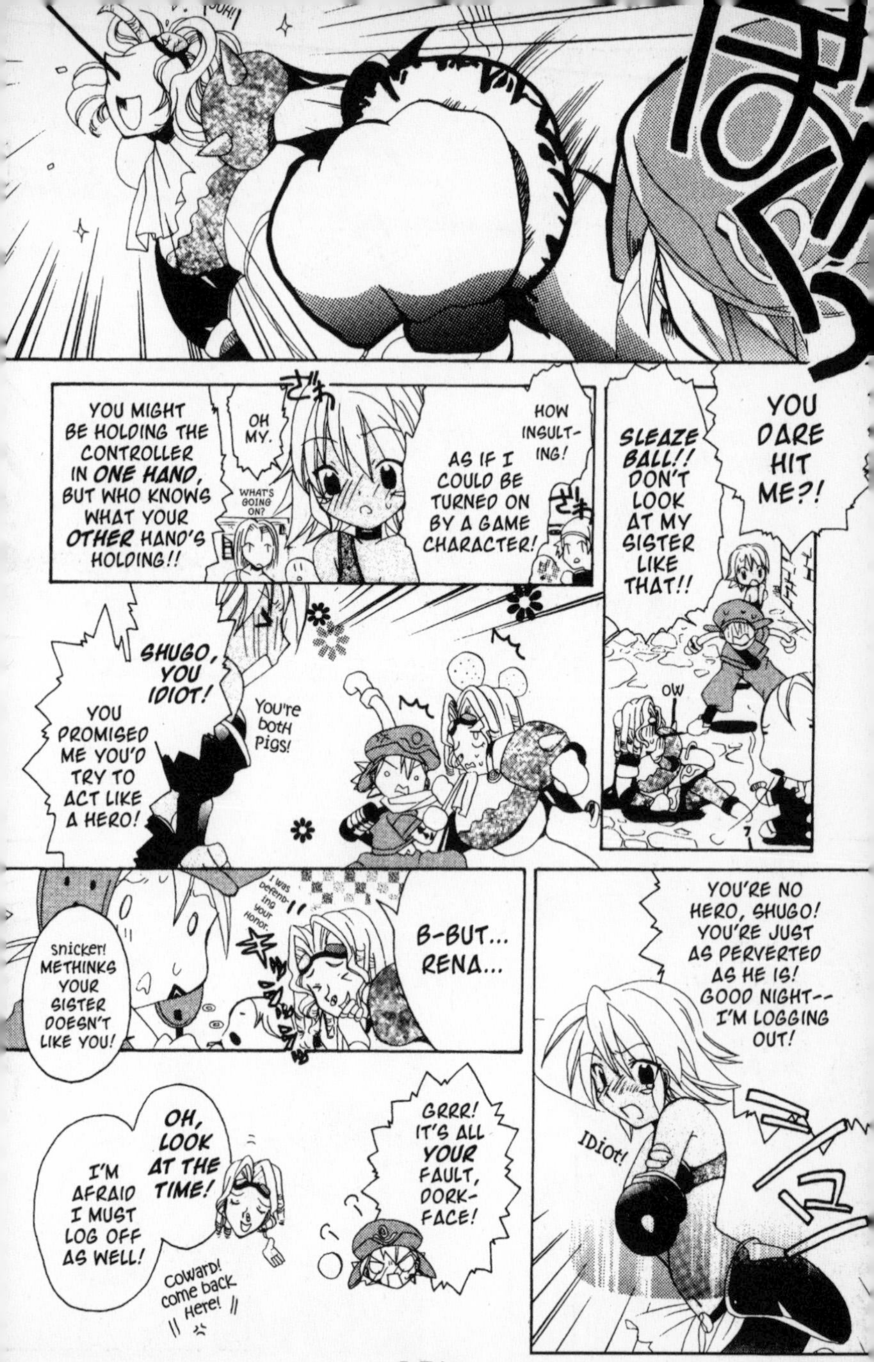
YOU DARE HIT ME?!
SLEAZE BALL!! DON'T LOOK AT MY SISTER LIKE THAT!!
OW
HOW INSULTING!
AS IF I COULD BE TURNED ON BY A GAME CHARACTER!
OH MY.
YOU MIGHT BE HOLDING THE CONTROLLER IN ONE HAND, BUT WHO KNOWS WHAT YOUR OTHER HAND'S HOLDING!!
WHAT'S GOING ON?
You're both pigs!
SHUGO, YOU IDIOT!
YOU PROMISED ME YOU'D TRY TO ACT LIKE A HERO!
YOU'RE NO HERO, SHUGO! YOU'RE JUST AS PERVERTED AS HE IS! GOOD NIGHT-- I'M LOGGING OUT!
Idiot!
B-BUT... RENA...
I was defending your honor.
snicker! METHINKS YOUR SISTER DOESN'T LIKE YOU!
GRRR! IT'S ALL YOUR FAULT, DORK-FACE!
OH, LOOK AT THE TIME!
I'M AFRAID I MUST LOG OFF AS WELL!
Coward! come back Here!

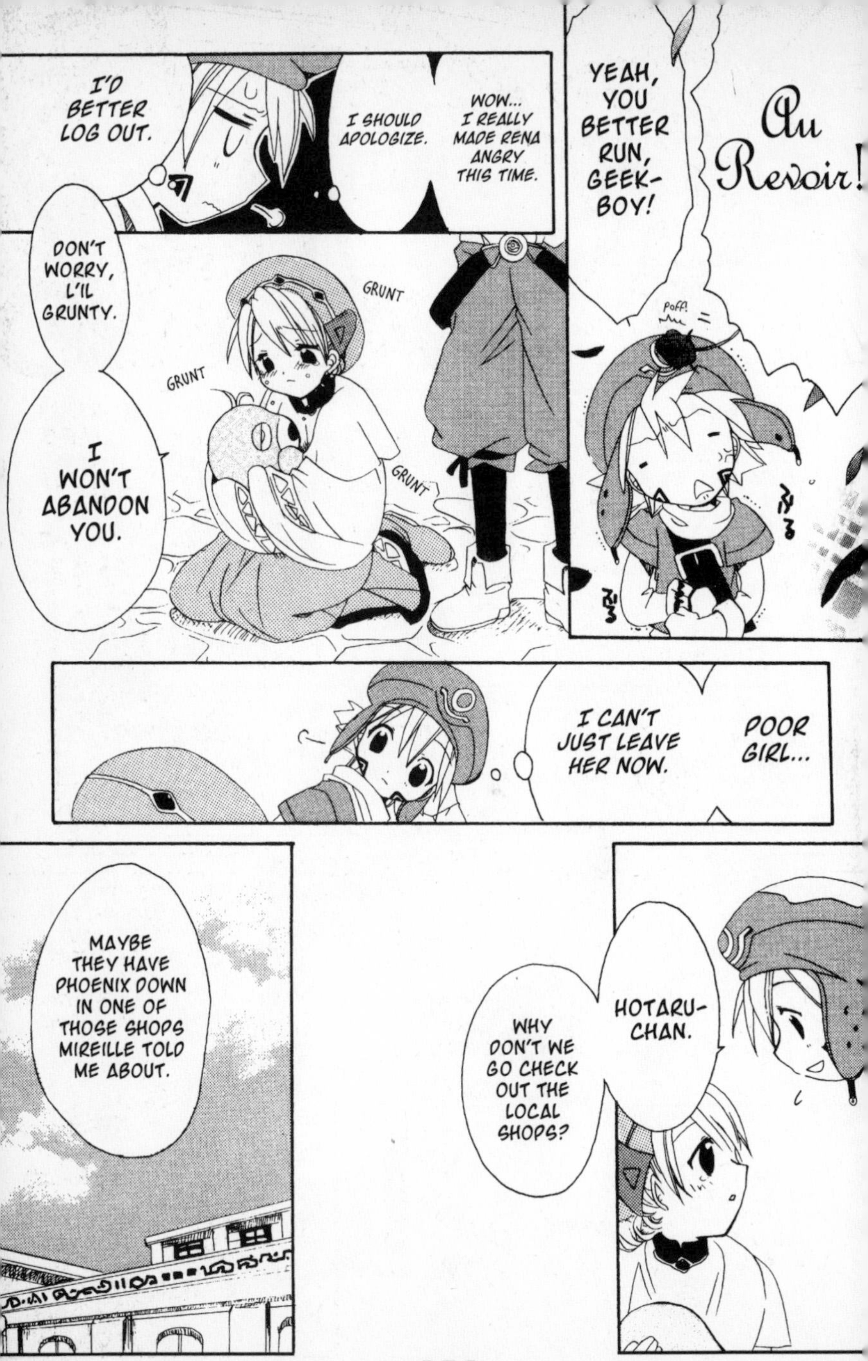
Au Revoir!
YEAH, YOU BETTER RUN, GEEK-BOY!
Poff!
WOW... I REALLY MADE RENA ANGRY THIS TIME.
I SHOULD APOLOGIZE.
I'D BETTER LOG OUT.
GRUNT
DON'T WORRY, L'IL GRUNTY.
GRUNT
GRUNT
I WON'T ABANDON YOU.
POOR GIRL...
I CAN'T JUST LEAVE HER NOW.
HOTARU-CHAN.
WHY DON'T WE GO CHECK OUT THE LOCAL SHOPS?
MAYBE THEY HAVE PHOENIX DOWN IN ONE OF THOSE SHOPS MIREILLE TOLD ME ABOUT.

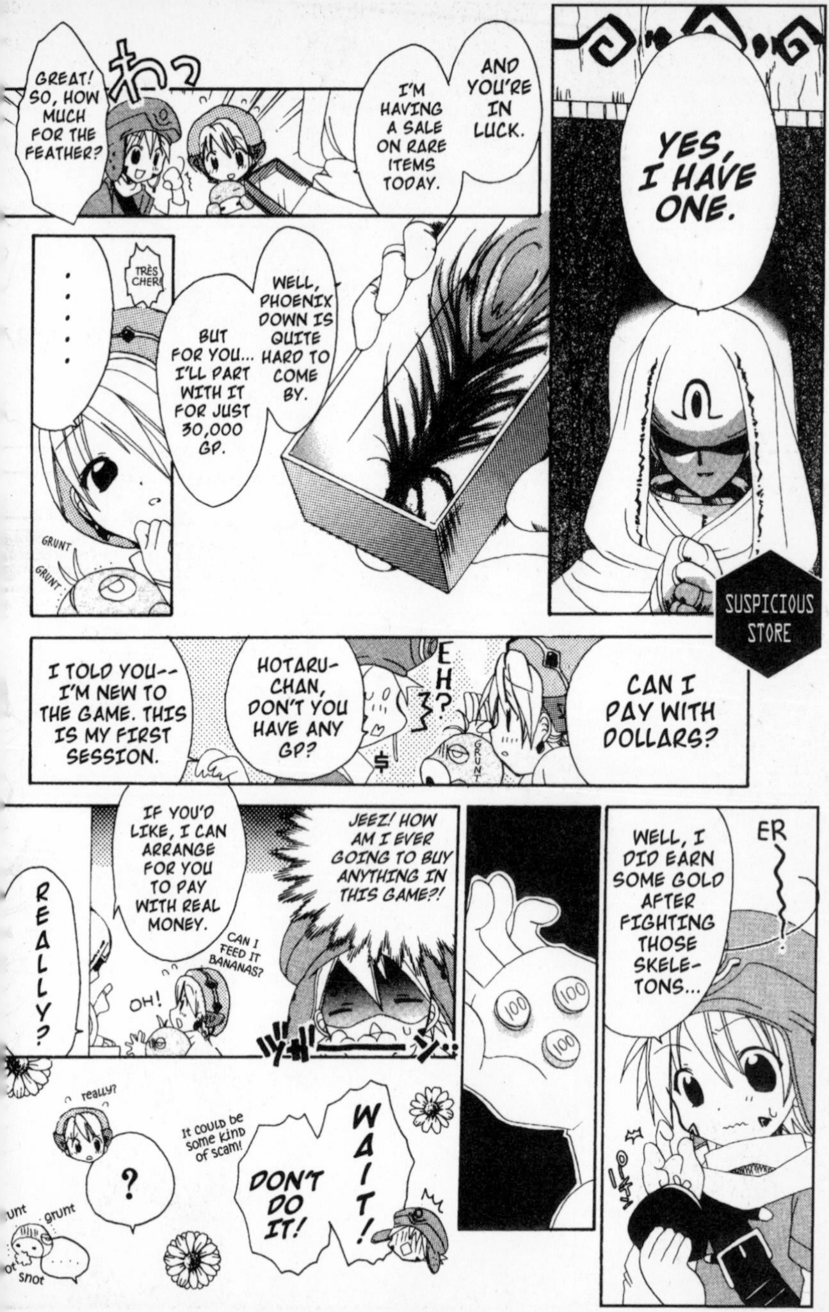
YES, I HAVE ONE.
AND YOU'RE IN LUCK.
I'M HAVING A SALE ON RARE ITEMS TODAY.
わっ
GREAT! SO, HOW MUCH FOR THE FEATHER?
SUSPICIOUS STORE
WELL, PHOENIX DOWN IS QUITE HARD TO COME BY.
BUT FOR YOU... I'LL PART WITH IT FOR JUST 30,000 GP.
TRÈS CHER!
......
GRUNT
GRUNT
CAN I PAY WITH DOLLARS?
GRUNT
EH?
HOTARU-CHAN, DON'T YOU HAVE ANY GP?
I TOLD YOU-- I'M NEW TO THE GAME. THIS IS MY FIRST SESSION.
ER~!
WELL, I DID EARN SOME GOLD AFTER FIGHTING THOSE SKELETONS...
100
100
100
JEEZ! HOW AM I EVER GOING TO BUY ANYTHING IN THIS GAME?!
IF YOU'D LIKE, I CAN ARRANGE FOR YOU TO PAY WITH REAL MONEY.
CAN I FEED IT BANANAS?
OH!
REALLY?
WAIT!
DON'T DO IT!
It could be some kind of scam!
really?
?
grunt
snot
...

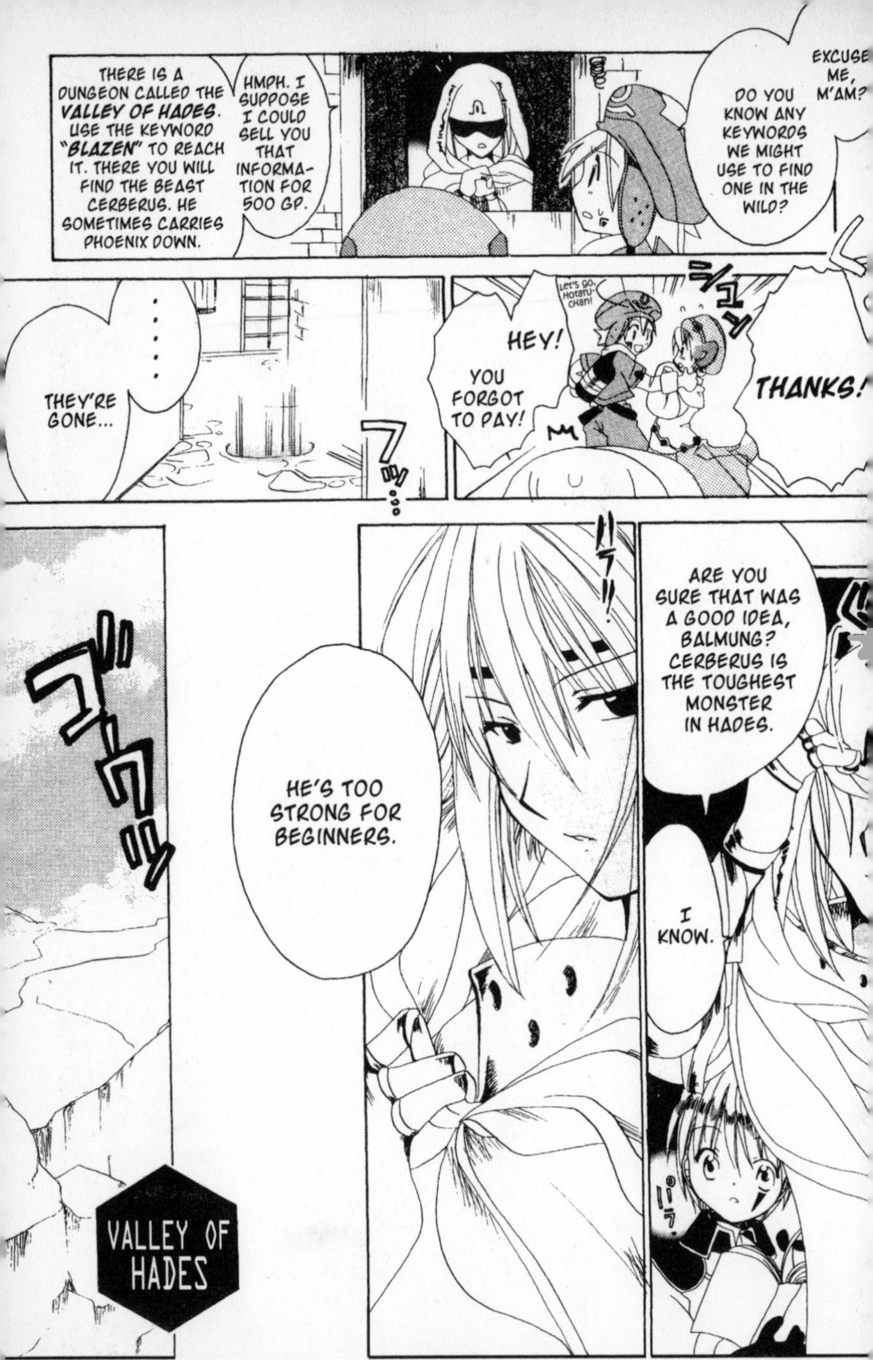
EXCUSE ME, M'AM?
DO YOU KNOW ANY KEYWORDS WE MIGHT USE TO FIND ONE IN THE WILD?
HMPH. I SUPPOSE I COULD SELL YOU THAT INFORMATION FOR 500 GP.
THERE IS A DUNGEON CALLED THE VALLEY OF HADES. USE THE KEYWORD "BLAZEN" TO REACH IT. THERE YOU WILL FIND THE BEAST CERBERUS. HE SOMETIMES CARRIES PHOENIX DOWN.
THANKS!
LET'S GO, HOTARU-CHAN!
HEY!
YOU FORGOT TO PAY!
......
THEY'RE GONE...
ARE YOU SURE THAT WAS A GOOD IDEA, BALMUNG? CERBERUS IS THE TOUGHEST MONSTER IN HADES.
I KNOW.
HE'S TOO STRONG FOR BEGINNERS.
VALLEY OF HADES

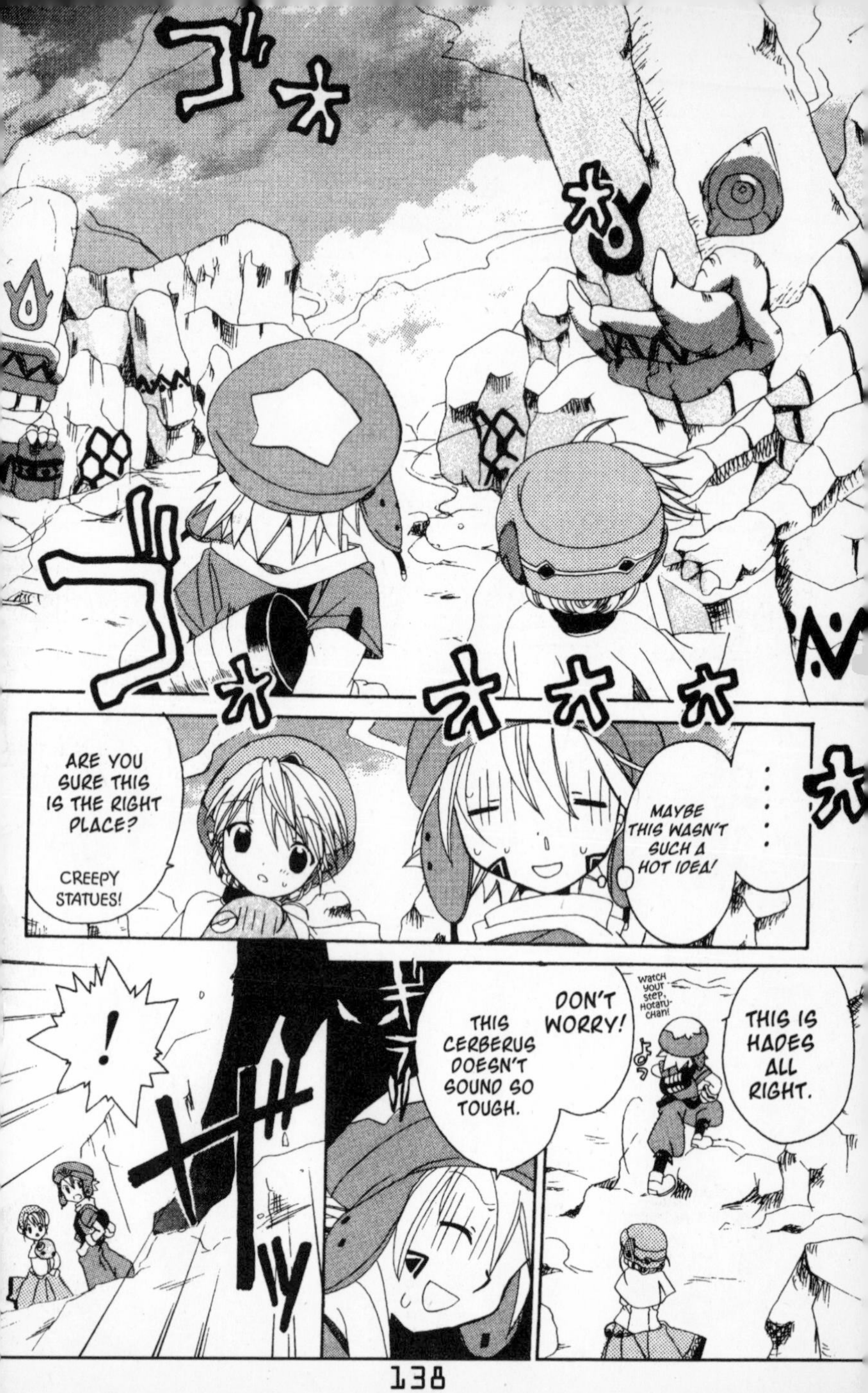

MAYBE THIS WASN'T SUCH A HOT IDEA!
ARE YOU SURE THIS IS THE RIGHT PLACE?
CREEPY STATUES!
THIS IS HADES ALL RIGHT.
Watch your step, Hotaru-chan!
DON'T WORRY!
THIS CERBERUS DOESN'T SOUND SO TOUGH.
!

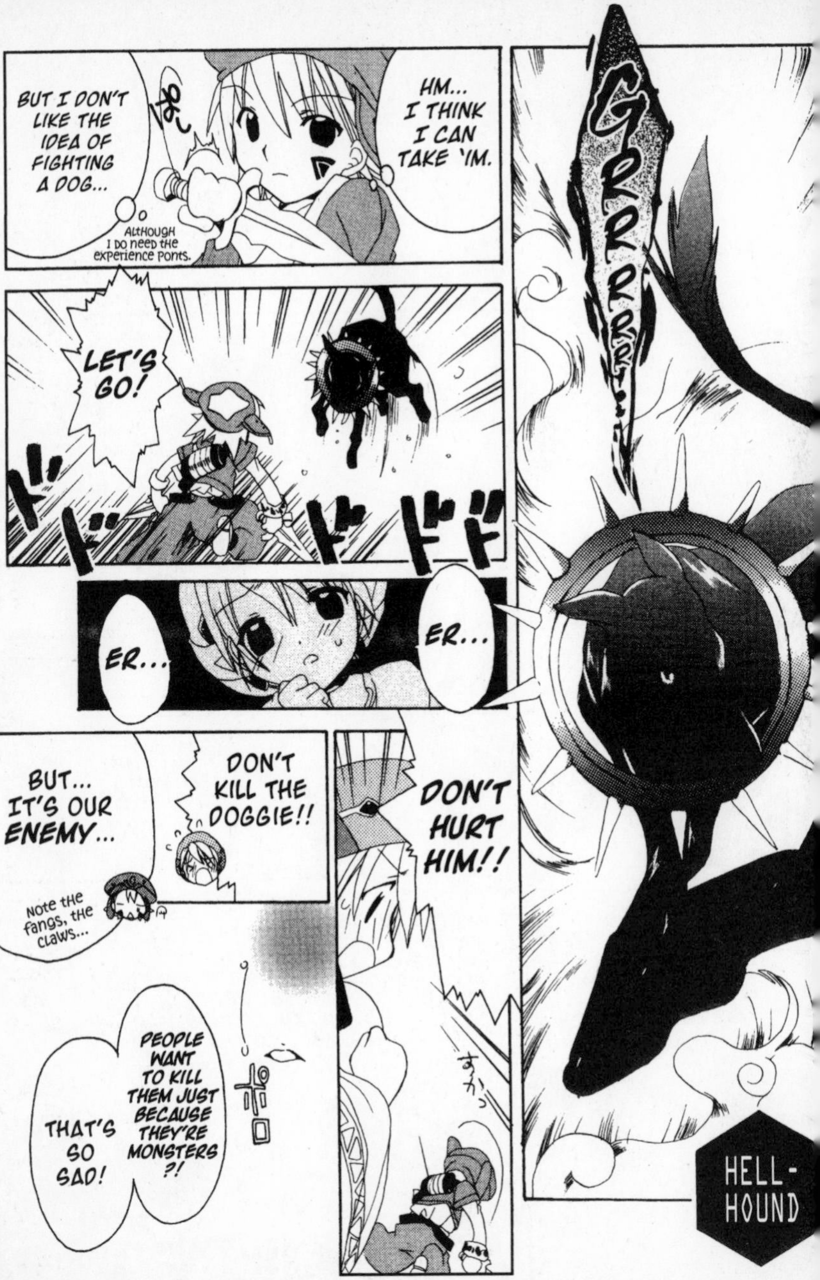
GRRRRRRR...
HELL-HOUND
HM... I THINK I CAN TAKE 'IM.
BUT I DON'T LIKE THE IDEA OF FIGHTING A DOG...
ALTHOUGH I DO NEED THE EXPERIENCE PONTS.
LET'S GO!
ER...
ER...
DON'T HURT HIM!!
DON'T KILL THE DOGGIE!!
BUT... IT'S OUR ENEMY...
Note the fangs, the claws...
PEOPLE WANT TO KILL THEM JUST BECAUSE THEY'RE MONSTERS?!
THAT'S SO SAD!

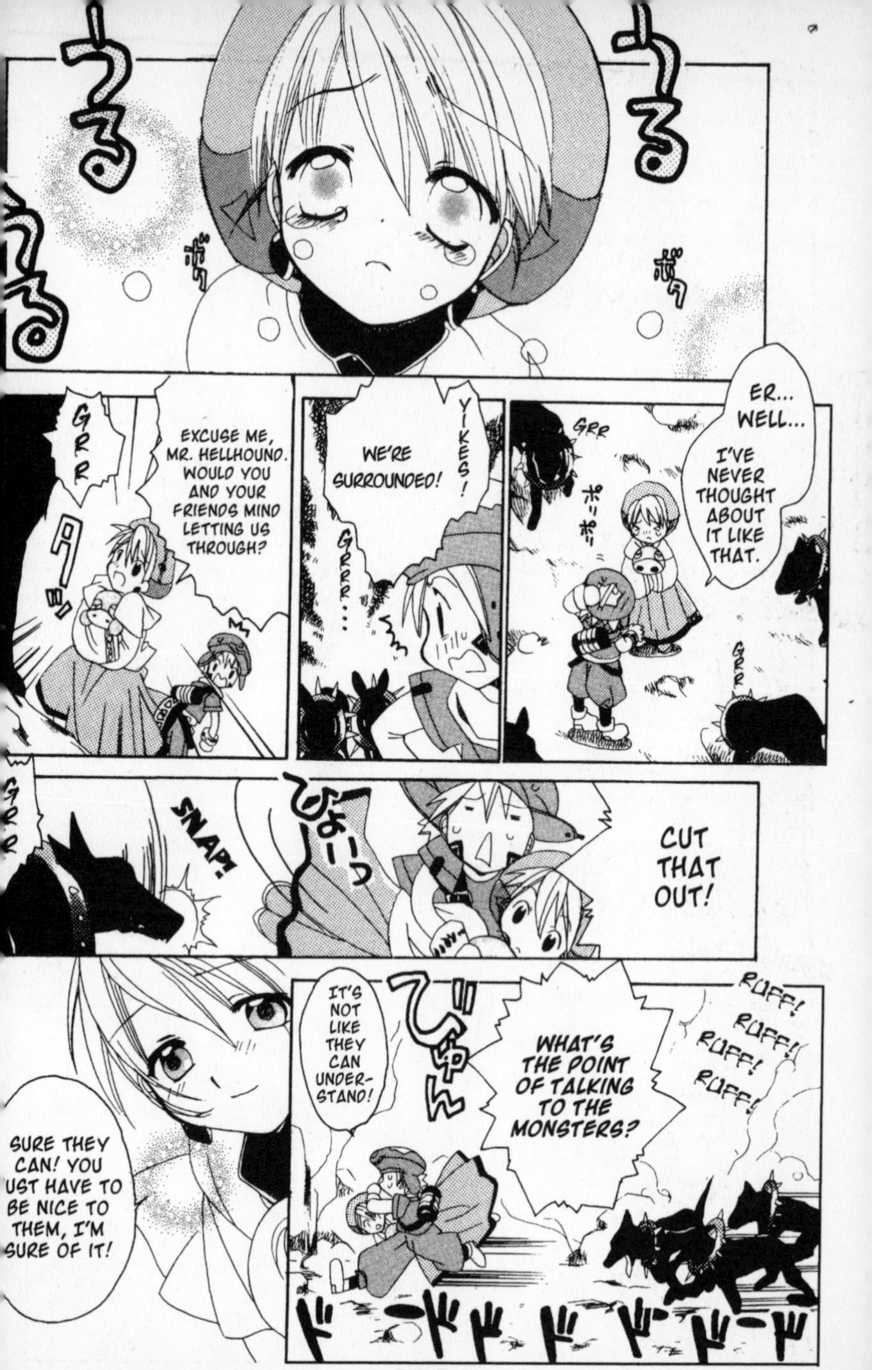
うる
うる
ER... WELL...
I'VE NEVER THOUGHT ABOUT IT LIKE THAT.
GRR
GRR
YIKES!
WE'RE SURROUNDED!
GRRR...
GRR
EXCUSE ME, MR. HELLHOUND. WOULD YOU AND YOUR FRIENDS MIND LETTING US THROUGH?
CUT THAT OUT!
SNAP!!
GRRR
RUFF!
RUFF!!
RUFF!
RUFF!
WHAT'S THE POINT OF TALKING TO THE MONSTERS?
IT'S NOT LIKE THEY CAN UNDER-STAND!
SURE THEY CAN! YOU UST HAVE TO BE NICE TO THEM, I'M SURE OF IT!

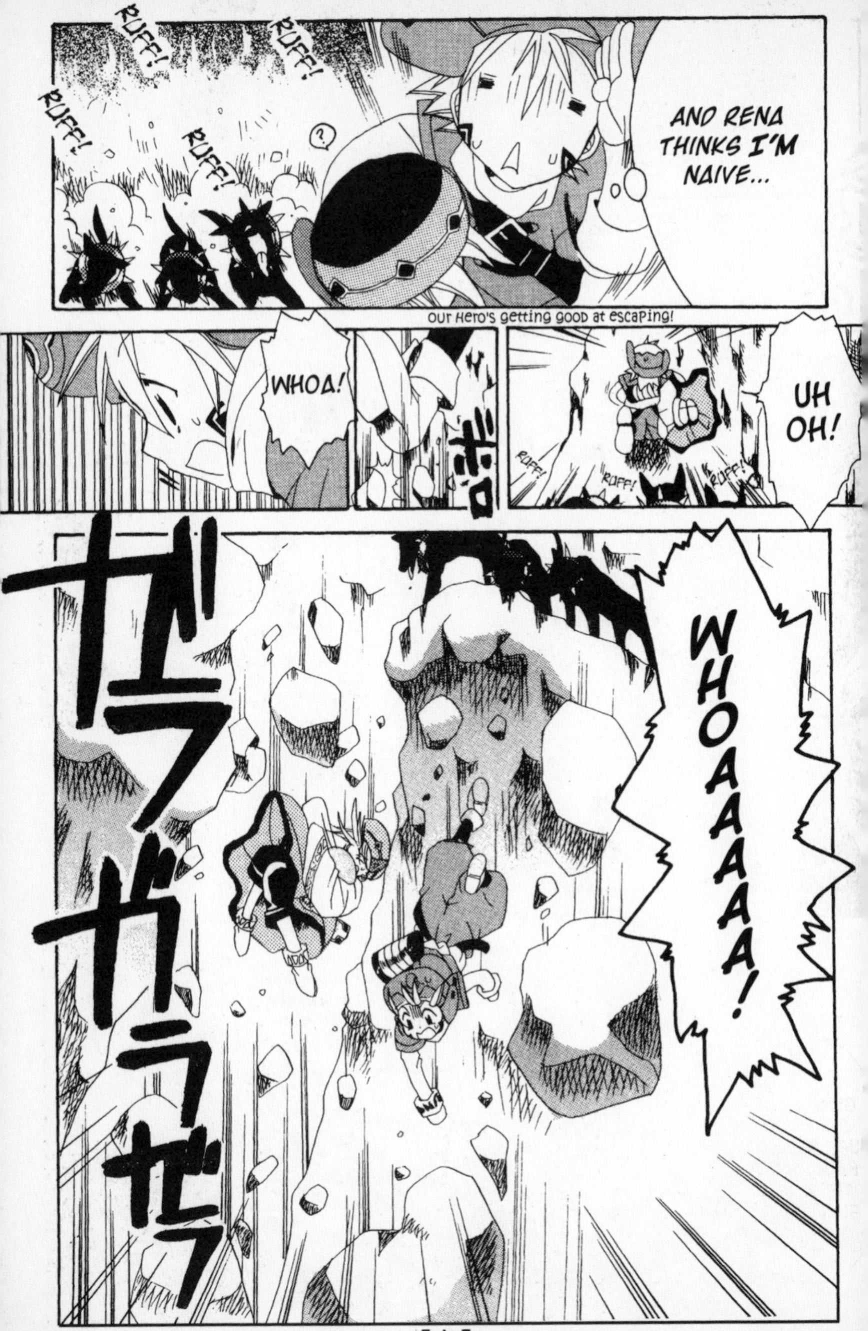
AND RENA THINKS I'M NAIVE...
RUFF! RUFF! RUFF! RUFF!
Our Hero's getting good at escaping!
UH OH!
RUFF! RUFF! RUFF!
ボロ
WHOA!
WHOAAAAAA!
ガラガラガラ

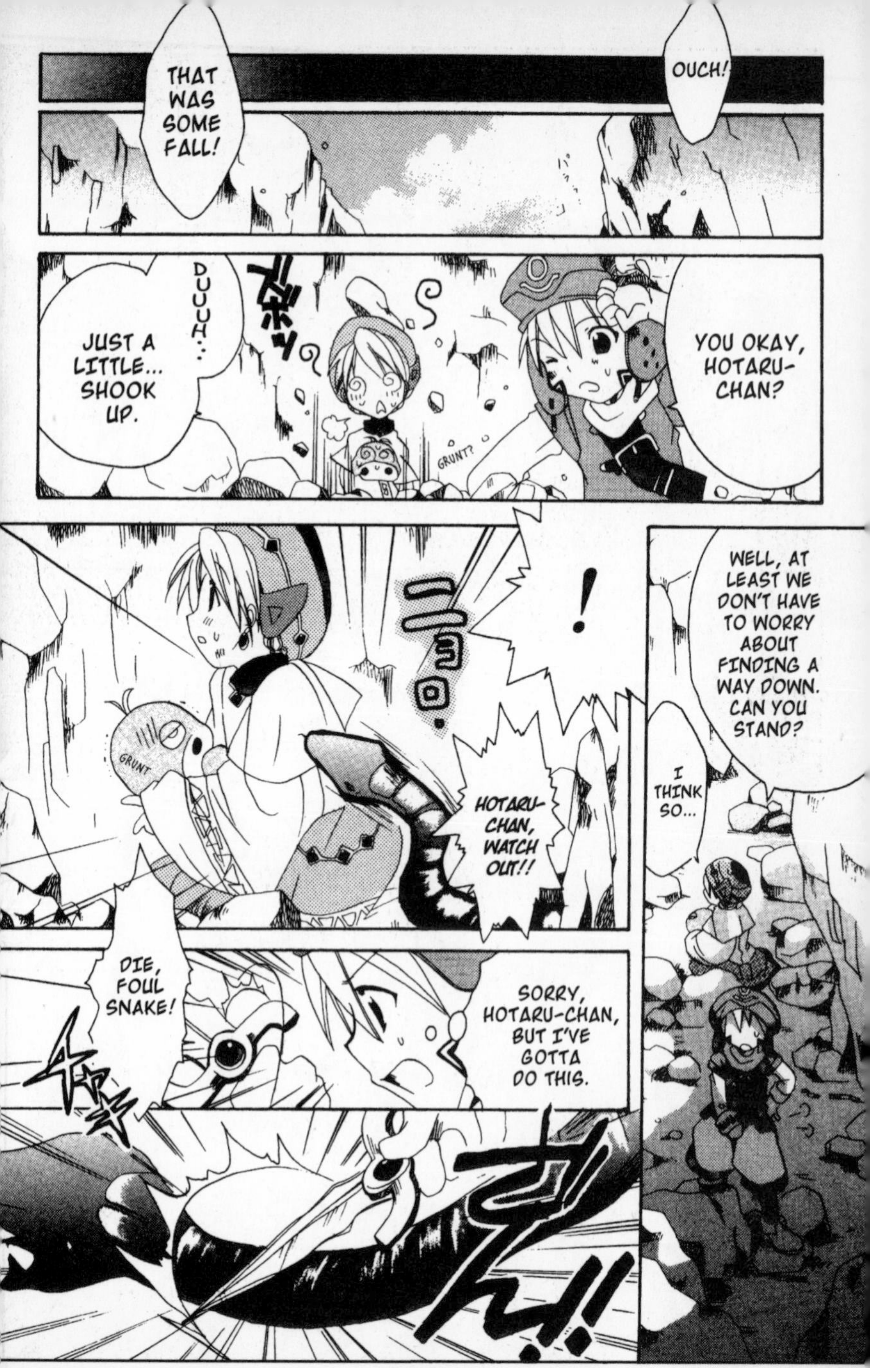
OUCH!
THAT WAS SOME FALL!
YOU OKAY, HOTARU-CHAN?
GRUNT?
DUUUH...
JUST A LITTLE... SHOOK UP.
WELL, AT LEAST WE DON'T HAVE TO WORRY ABOUT FINDING A WAY DOWN. CAN YOU STAND?
I THINK SO...
!
HOTARU-CHAN, WATCH OUT!!
GRUNT
SORRY, HOTARU-CHAN, BUT I'VE GOTTA DO THIS.
DIE, FOUL SNAKE!

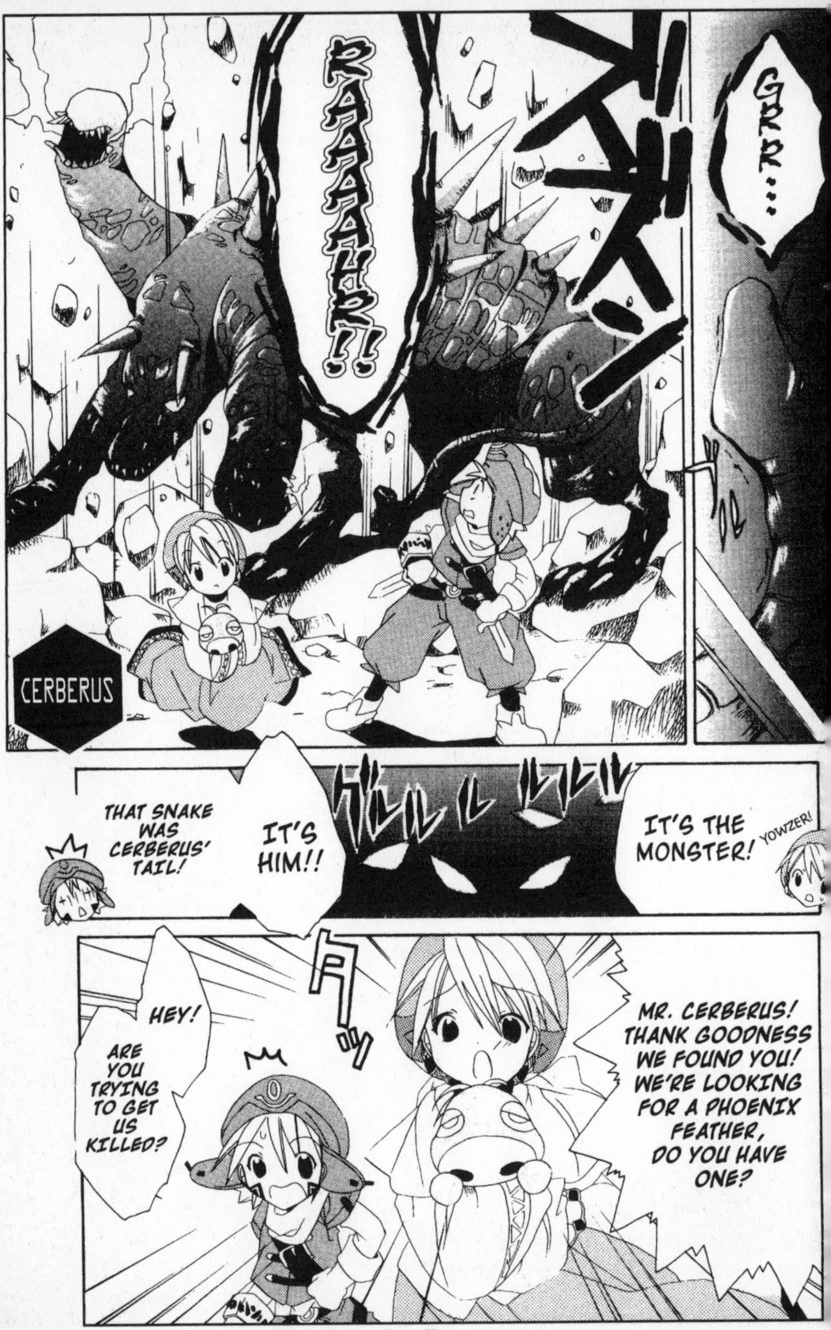
GRRR...
RAAAAAHR!!
CERBERUS
IT'S THE MONSTER!
YOWZER!
IT'S HIM!!
THAT SNAKE WAS CERBERUS' TAIL!
MR. CERBERUS! THANK GOODNESS WE FOUND YOU! WE'RE LOOKING FOR A PHOENIX FEATHER, DO YOU HAVE ONE?
HEY!
ARE YOU TRYING TO GET US KILLED?

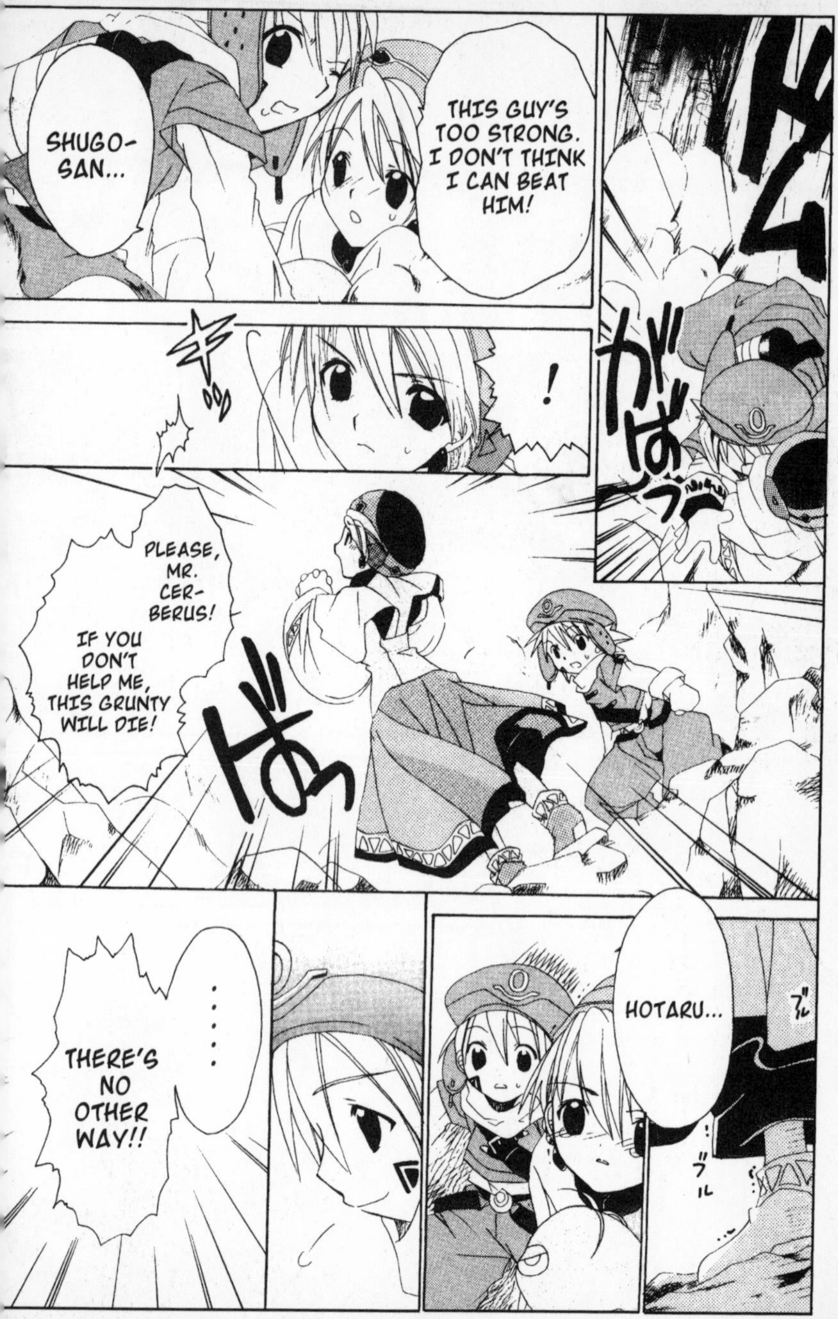
がばっ
THIS GUY'S TOO STRONG. I DON'T THINK I CAN BEAT HIM!
SHUGO-SAN...
!
PLEASE, MR. CERBERUS!
IF YOU DON'T HELP ME, THIS GRUNTY WILL DIE!
ばっ
ブル
HOTARU...
ブル
......
THERE'S NO OTHER WAY!!

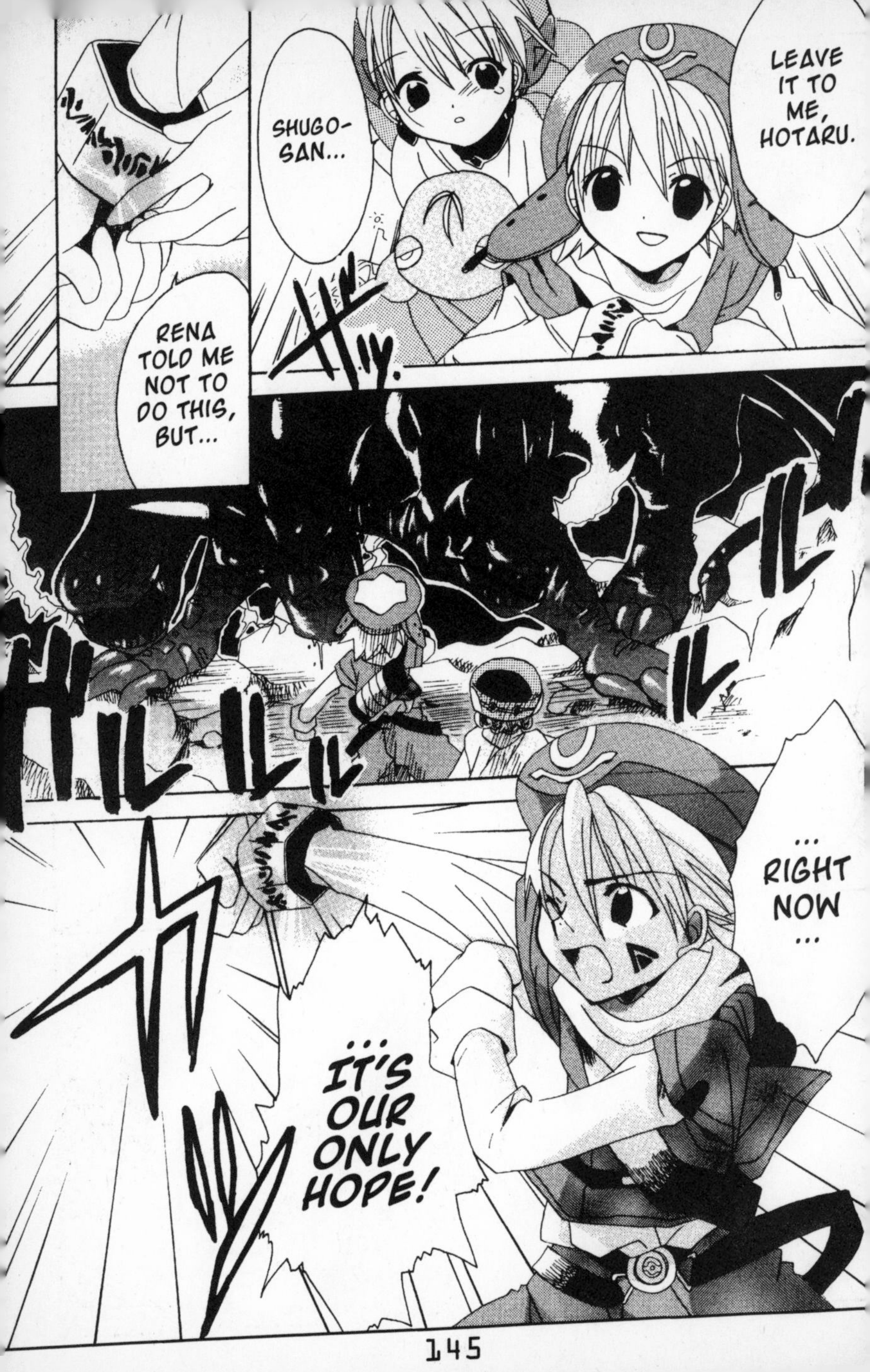
LEAVE IT TO ME, HOTARU.
SHUGO-SAN...
RENA TOLD ME NOT TO DO THIS, BUT...
...RIGHT NOW...
...IT'S OUR ONLY HOPE!

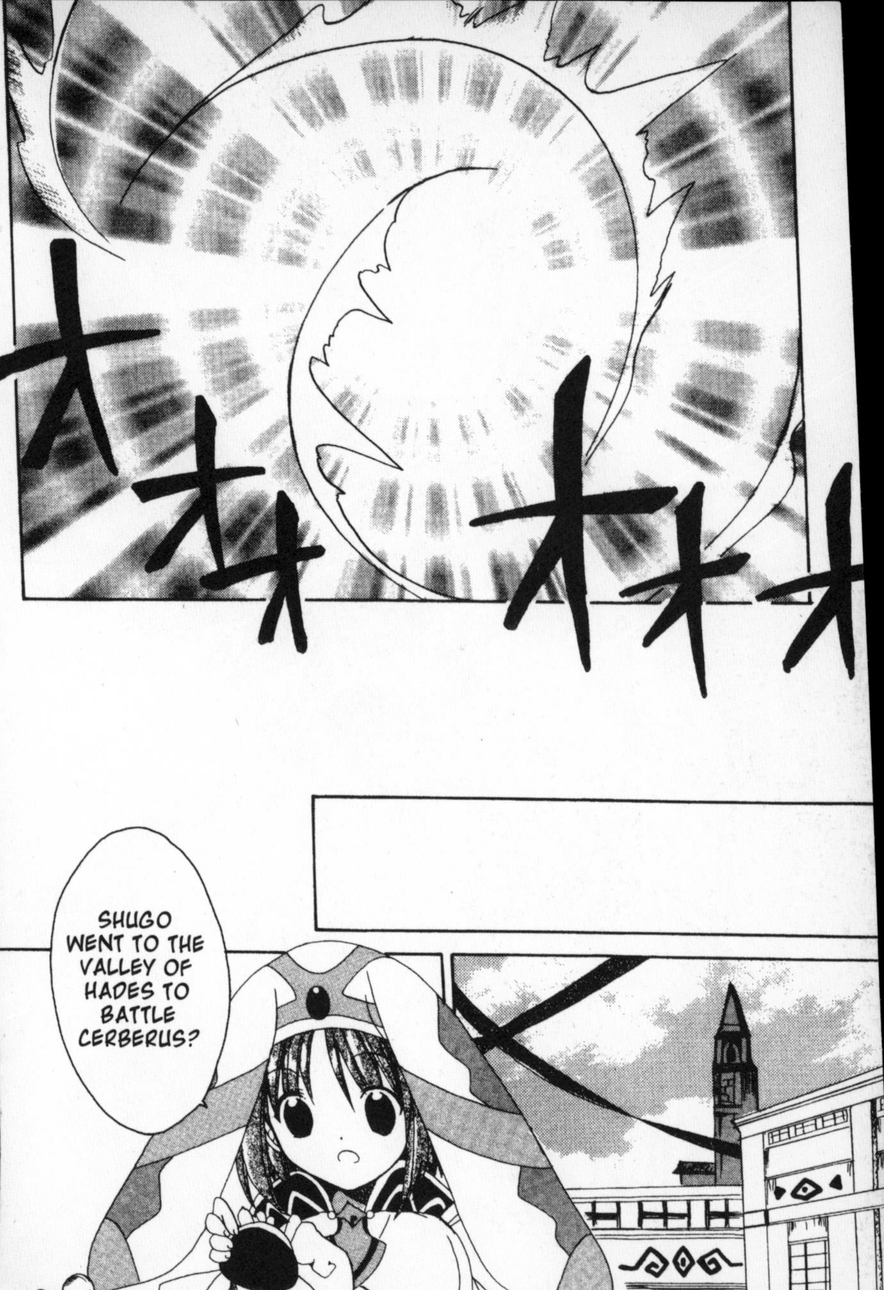
オオオオオオ
SHUGO WENT TO THE VALLEY OF HADES TO BATTLE CERBERUS?

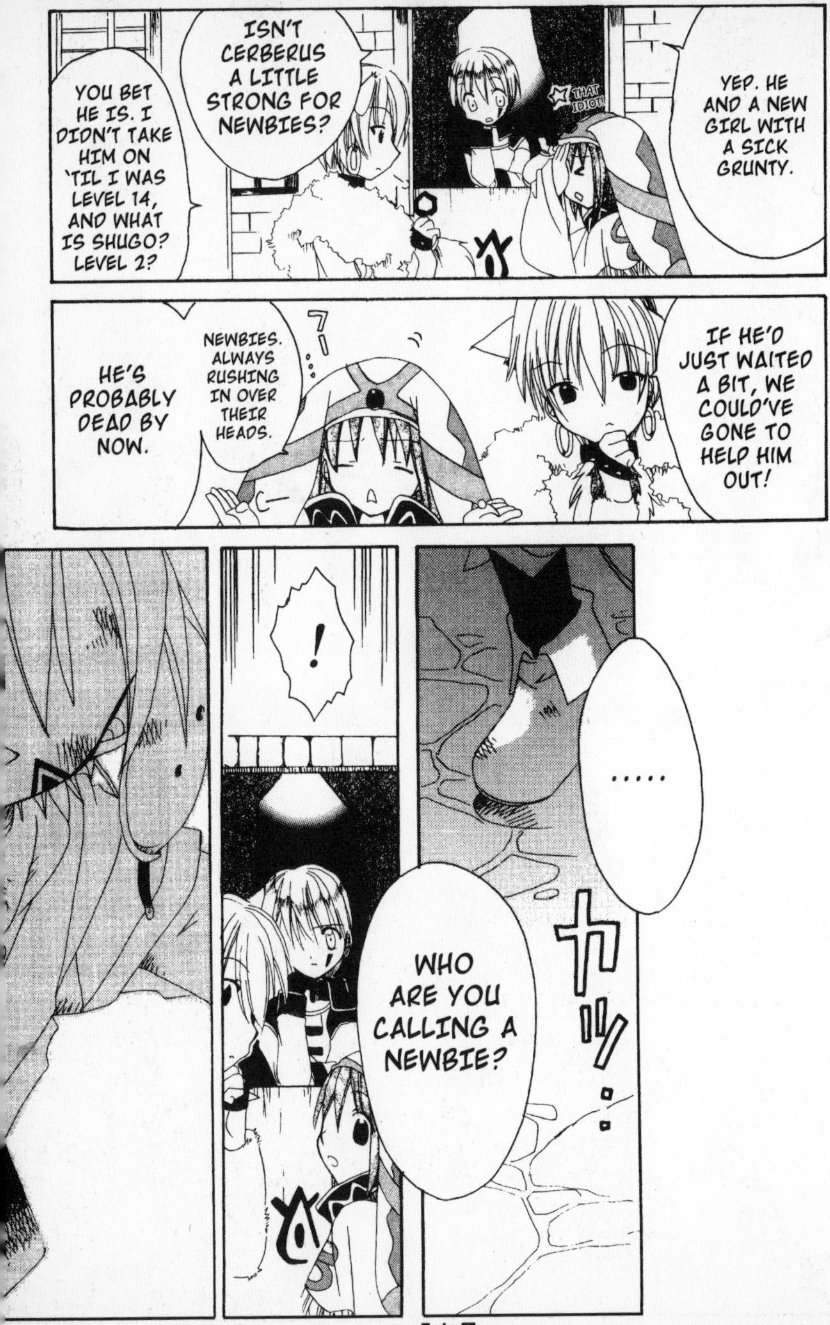
YEP. HE AND A NEW GIRL WITH A SICK GRUNTY.
THAT IDIOT!
ISN'T CERBERUS A LITTLE STRONG FOR NEWBIES?
YOU BET HE IS. I DIDN'T TAKE HIM ON 'TIL I WAS LEVEL 14, AND WHAT IS SHUGO? LEVEL 2?
IF HE'D JUST WAITED A BIT, WE COULD'VE GONE TO HELP HIM OUT!
NEWBIES. ALWAYS RUSHING IN OVER THEIR HEADS.
HE'S PROBABLY DEAD BY NOW.
.....
WHO ARE YOU CALLING A NEWBIE?
!

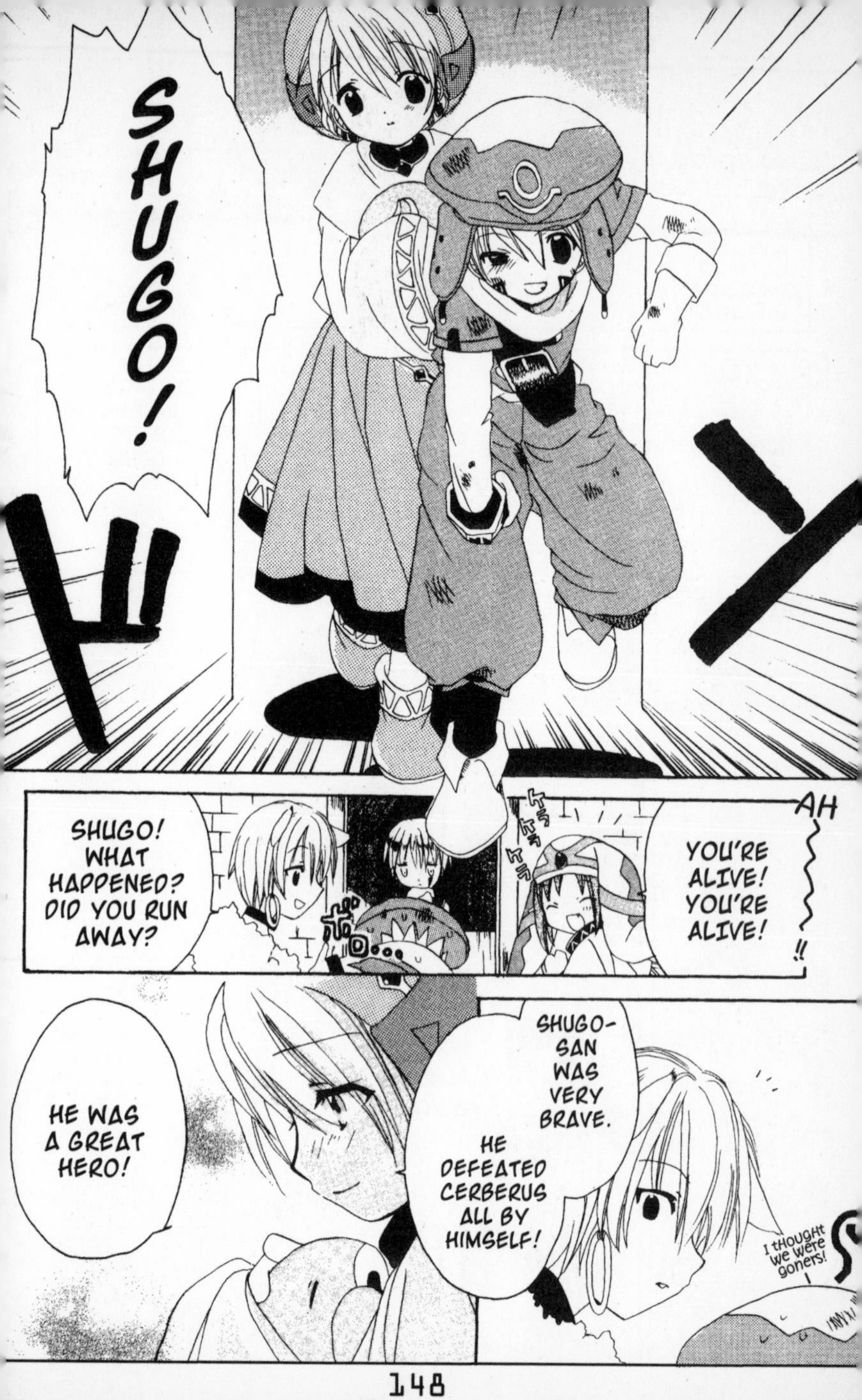
SHUGO!
ドン
AH~~~!!
YOU'RE ALIVE! YOU'RE ALIVE!
ケラケラ
SHUGO! WHAT HAPPENED? DID YOU RUN AWAY?
ボロ...
SHUGO-SAN WAS VERY BRAVE.
HE DEFEATED CERBERUS ALL BY HIMSELF!
I thought we were goners!
HE WAS A GREAT HERO!

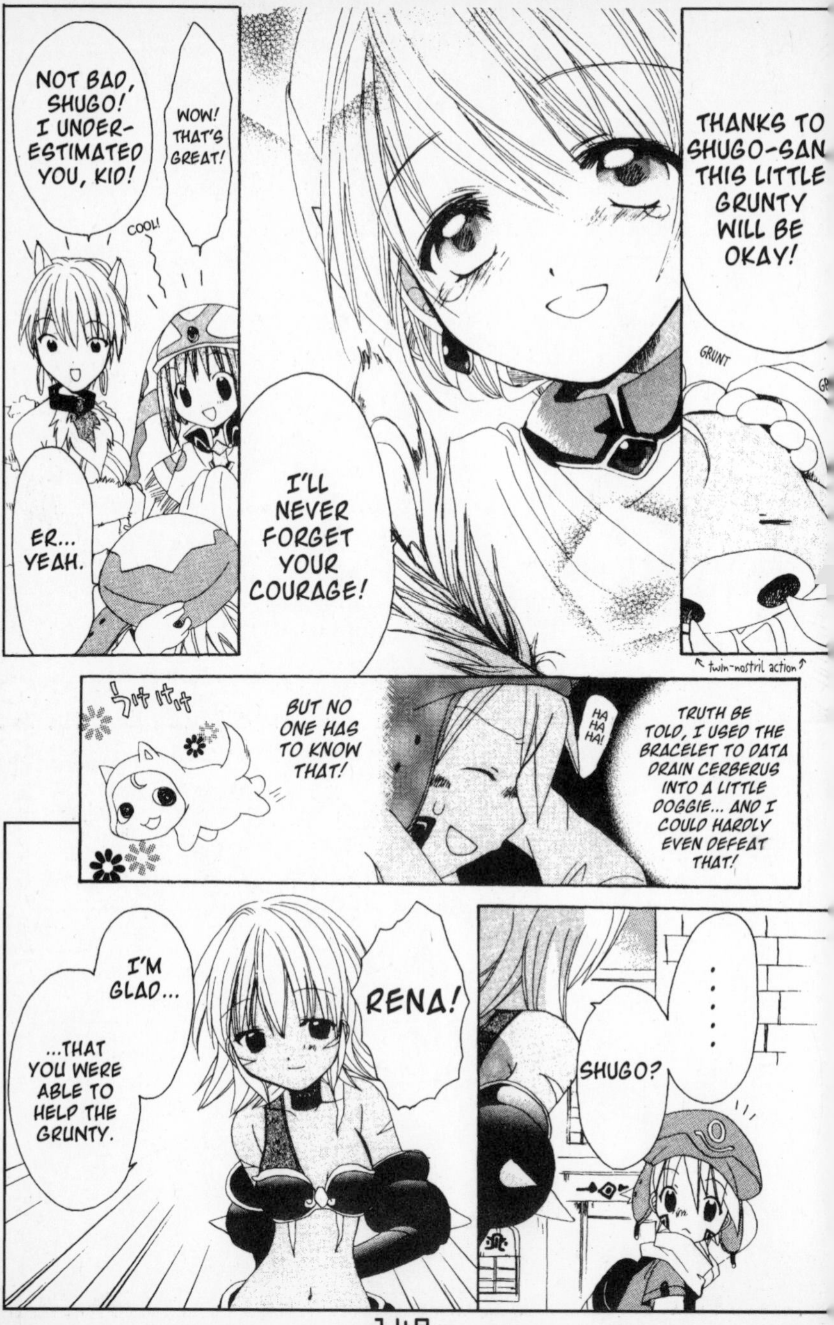
THANKS TO SHUGO-SAN THIS LITTLE GRUNTY WILL BE OKAY!
GRUNT
↖ twin-nostril action ↗
I'LL NEVER FORGET YOUR COURAGE!
WOW! THAT'S GREAT!
NOT BAD, SHUGO! I UNDER-ESTIMATED YOU, KID!
COOL!
ER... YEAH.
TRUTH BE TOLD, I USED THE BRACELET TO DATA DRAIN CERBERUS INTO A LITTLE DOGGIE... AND I COULD HARDLY EVEN DEFEAT THAT!
HA HA HA!
BUT NO ONE HAS TO KNOW THAT!
うけけけ
......
SHUGO?
RENA!
I'M GLAD...
...THAT YOU WERE ABLE TO HELP THE GRUNTY.

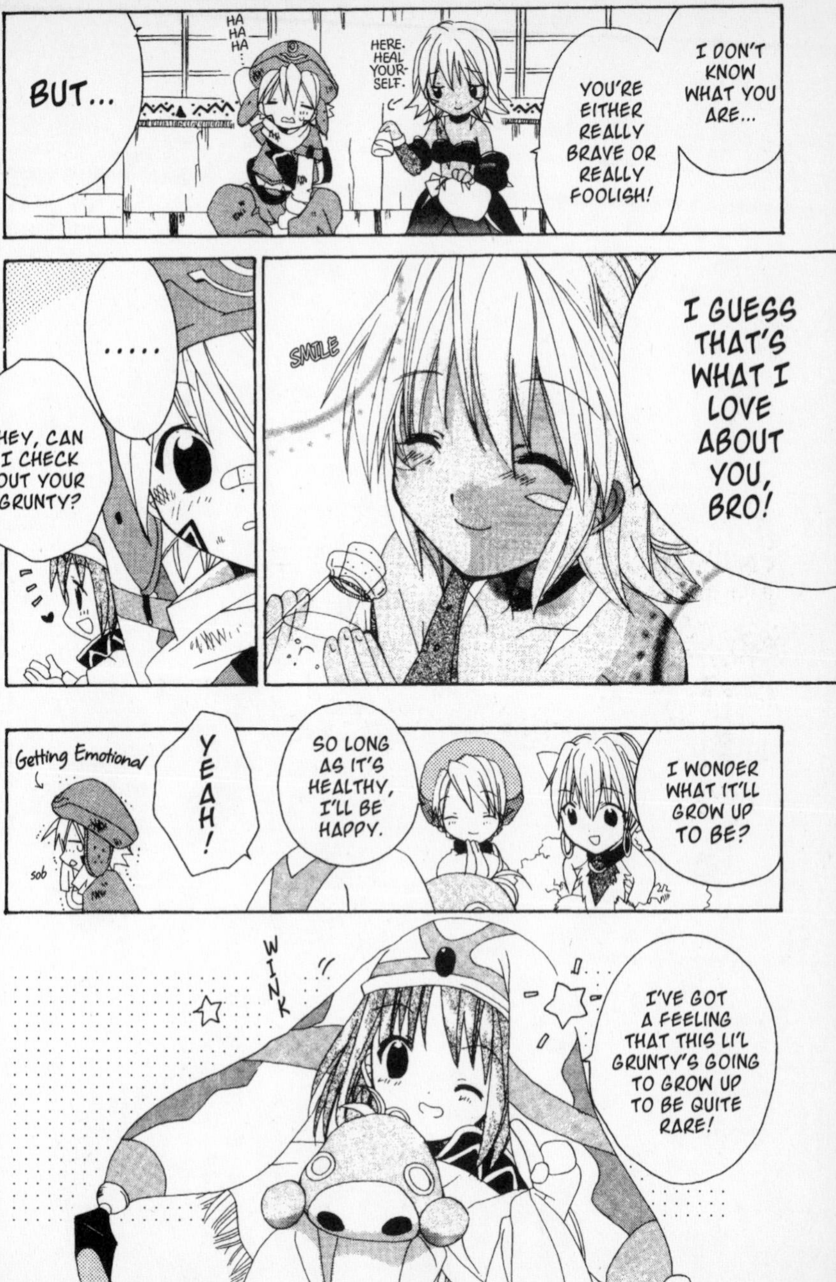

I DON'T KNOW WHAT YOU ARE...
YOU'RE EITHER REALLY BRAVE OR REALLY FOOLISH!
HERE. HEAL YOURSELF.
HA HA HA...
BUT...
I GUESS THAT'S WHAT I LOVE ABOUT YOU, BRO!
SMILE
.....
HEY, CAN I CHECK OUT YOUR GRUNTY?
I WONDER WHAT IT'LL GROW UP TO BE?
SO LONG AS IT'S HEALTHY, I'LL BE HAPPY.
YEAH!
Getting Emotional
sob
I'VE GOT A FEELING THAT THIS LI'L GRUNTY'S GOING TO GROW UP TO BE QUITE RARE!
WINK

NEW GENERATION ONLINE

THE WORLD

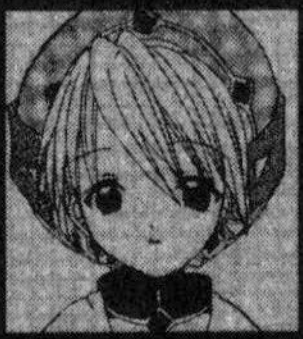

SUBJECT: THANK YOU SO MUCH!

SENDER: HOTARU

GREETINGS!

HELLO. I REALLY WANTED TO THANK YOU FOR THE OTHER DAY. THANKS TO YOU, MY GRUNTY'S QUITE HEALTHY NOW. HE'S ACTUALLY EATING A LOT!
IT WAS SO COOL OF YOU TO HELP, SHUGO.

I'D LOVE TO VISIT THE JAPANESE GAME SERVER AGAIN.

PLEASE SAY HI TO EVERYONE FOR ME!

CHEERS,
HOTARU

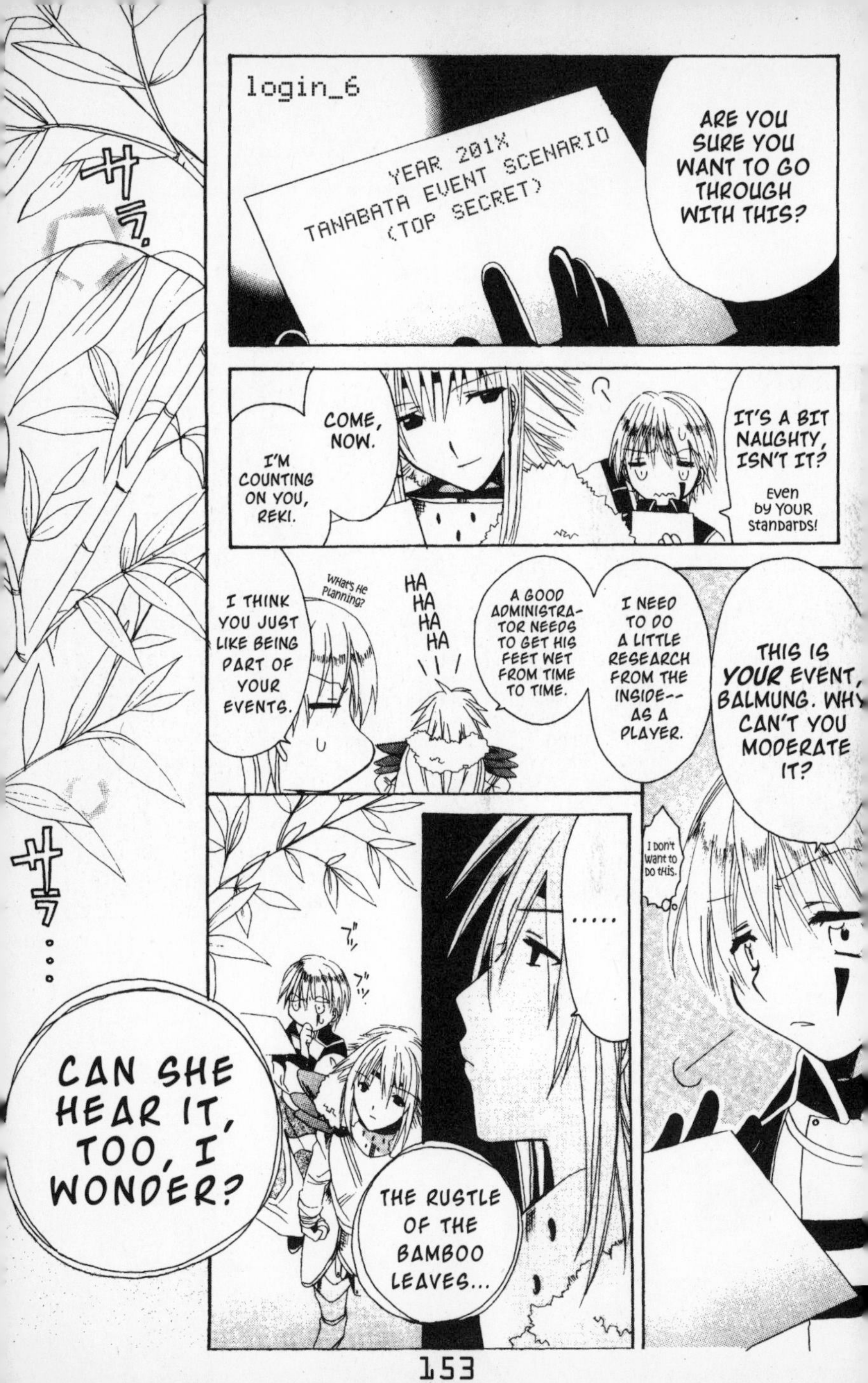
login_6
YEAR 201X
TANABATA EVENT SCENARIO
(TOP SECRET)
ARE YOU SURE YOU WANT TO GO THROUGH WITH THIS?
IT'S A BIT NAUGHTY, ISN'T IT?
Even by YOUR standards!
COME, NOW.
I'M COUNTING ON YOU, REKI.
THIS IS *YOUR* EVENT, BALMUNG. WHY CAN'T YOU MODERATE IT?
I NEED TO DO A LITTLE RESEARCH FROM THE INSIDE--AS A PLAYER.
A GOOD ADMINISTRATOR NEEDS TO GET HIS FEET WET FROM TIME TO TIME.
HA HA HA HA
What's he planning?
I THINK YOU JUST LIKE BEING PART OF YOUR EVENTS.
I don't want to do this.
.....
ブツ
ブツ
THE RUSTLE OF THE BAMBOO LEAVES...
サラ。
サラ…
CAN SHE HEAR IT, TOO, I WONDER?

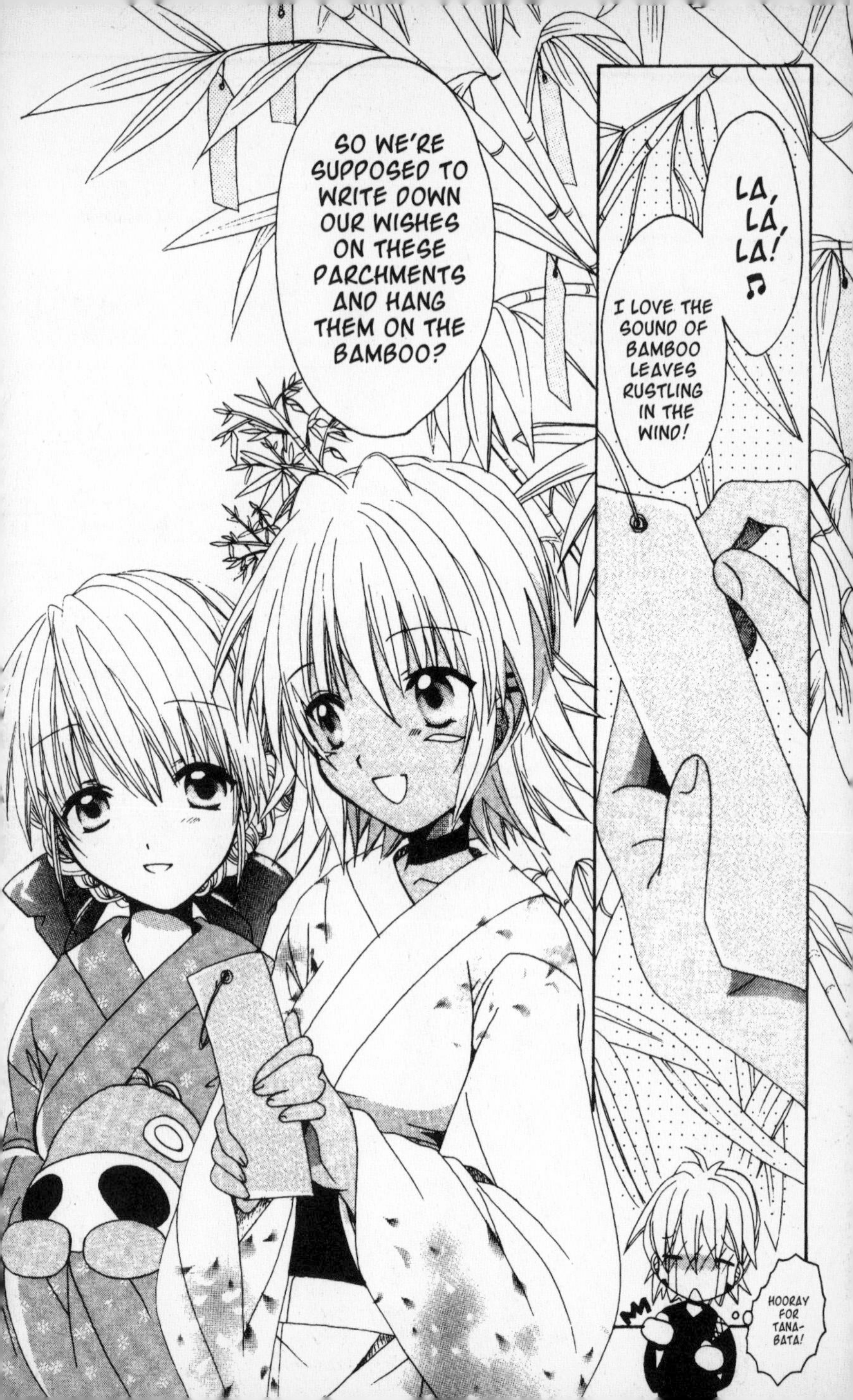
LA, LA, LA! ♫
I LOVE THE SOUND OF BAMBOO LEAVES RUSTLING IN THE WIND!
HOORAY FOR TANA-BATA!
SO WE'RE SUPPOSED TO WRITE DOWN OUR WISHES ON THESE PARCHMENTS AND HANG THEM ON THE BAMBOO?

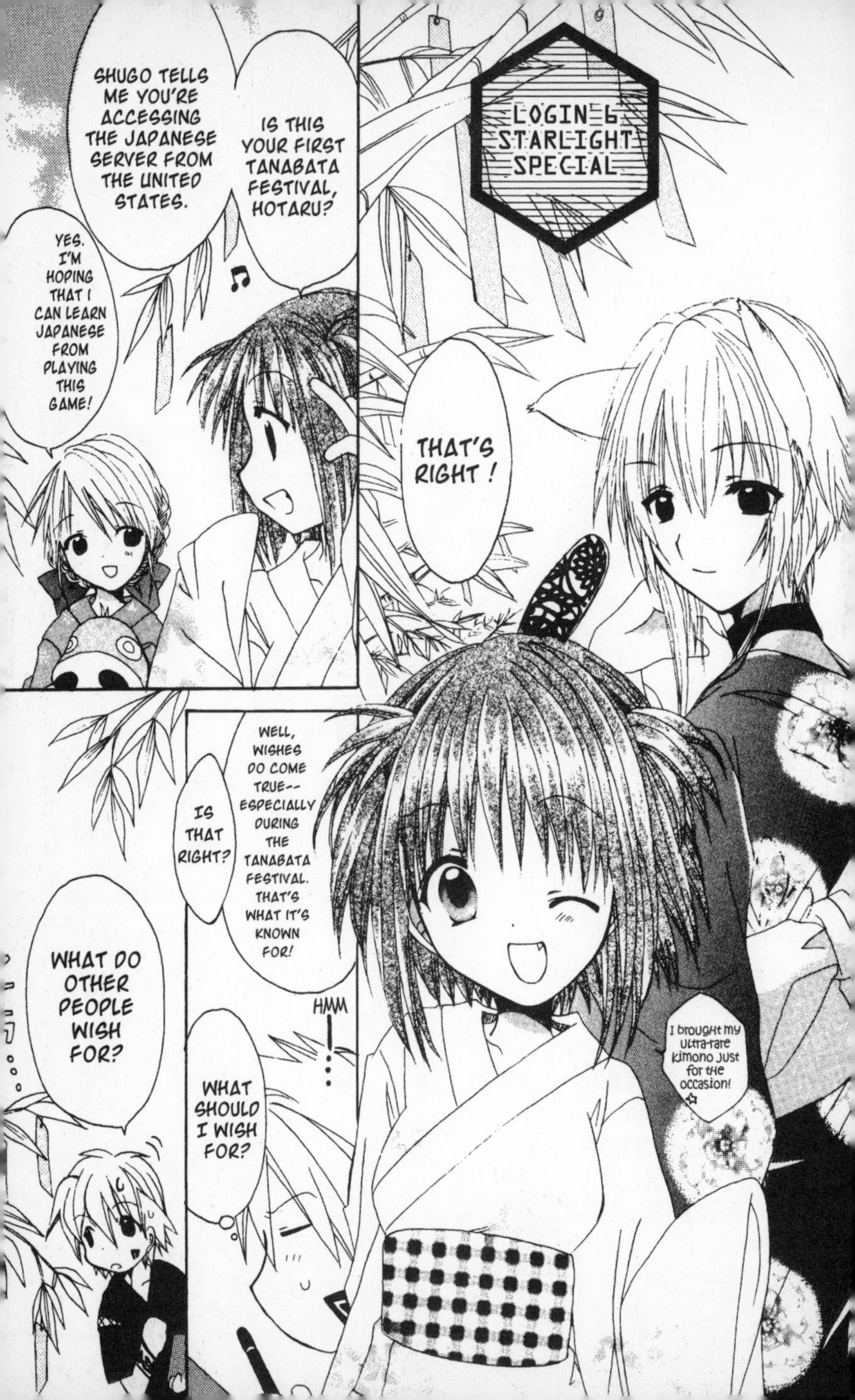
LOGIN 6 STARLIGHT SPECIAL
THAT'S RIGHT!
I brought my ultra-rare kimono just for the occasion! ☆
IS THIS YOUR FIRST TANABATA FESTIVAL, HOTARU?
SHUGO TELLS ME YOU'RE ACCESSING THE JAPANESE SERVER FROM THE UNITED STATES.
YES. I'M HOPING THAT I CAN LEARN JAPANESE FROM PLAYING THIS GAME!
WELL, WISHES DO COME TRUE-- ESPECIALLY DURING THE TANABATA FESTIVAL. THAT'S WHAT IT'S KNOWN FOR!
IS THAT RIGHT?
WHAT DO OTHER PEOPLE WISH FOR?
HMM
WHAT SHOULD I WISH FOR?

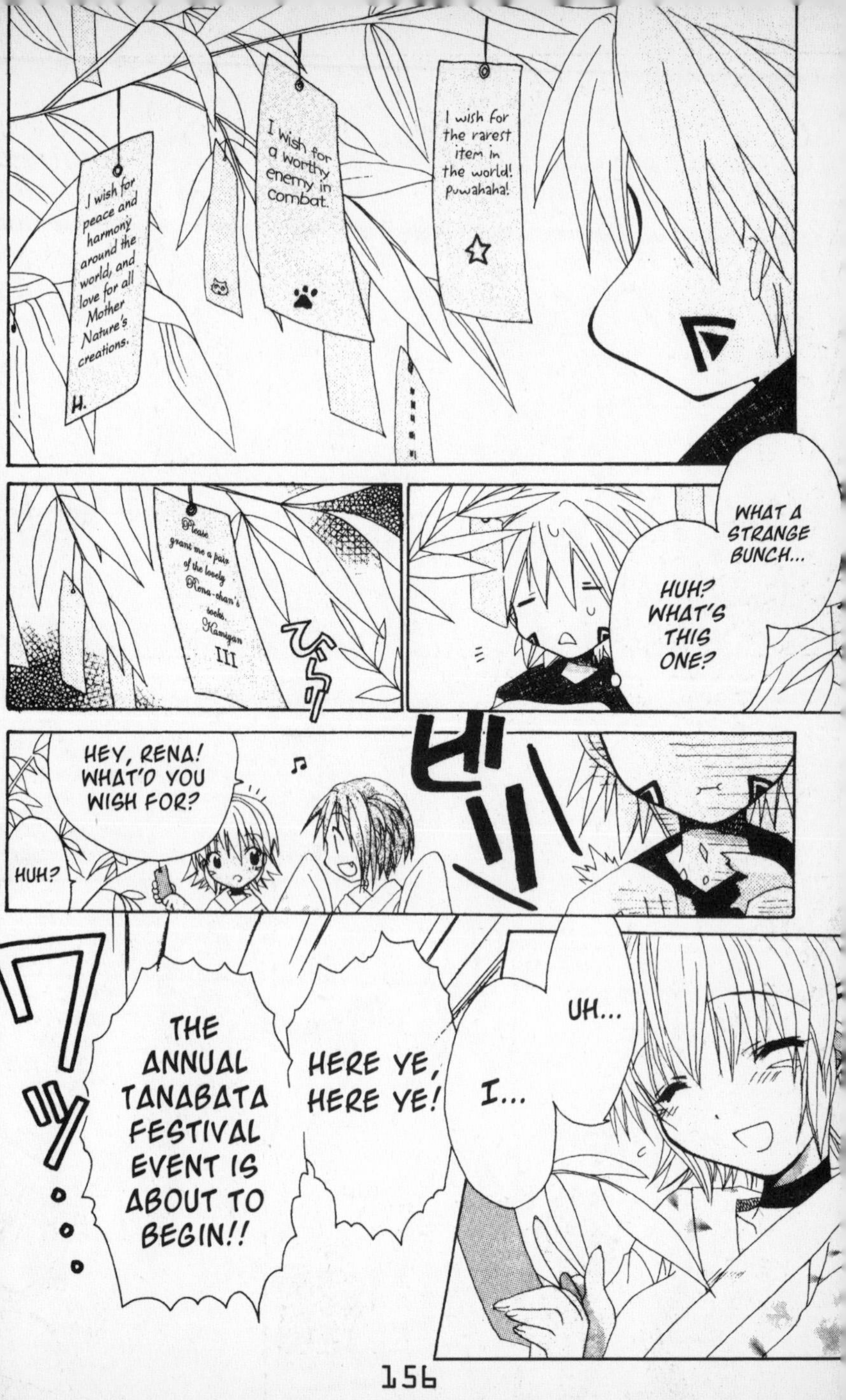
I wish for the rarest item in the world! puwahaha!
I wish for a worthy enemy in combat.
I wish for peace and harmony around the world, and love for all Mother Nature's creations. H.
WHAT A STRANGE BUNCH...
HUH? WHAT'S THIS ONE?
Please grant me a pair of the lovely Rena-chan's socks. Kamiyan III
ひら
ビリッ
HEY, RENA! WHAT'D YOU WISH FOR?
HUH?
UH...
I...
HERE YE, HERE YE!
THE ANNUAL TANABATA FESTIVAL EVENT IS ABOUT TO BEGIN!!
ワッ...

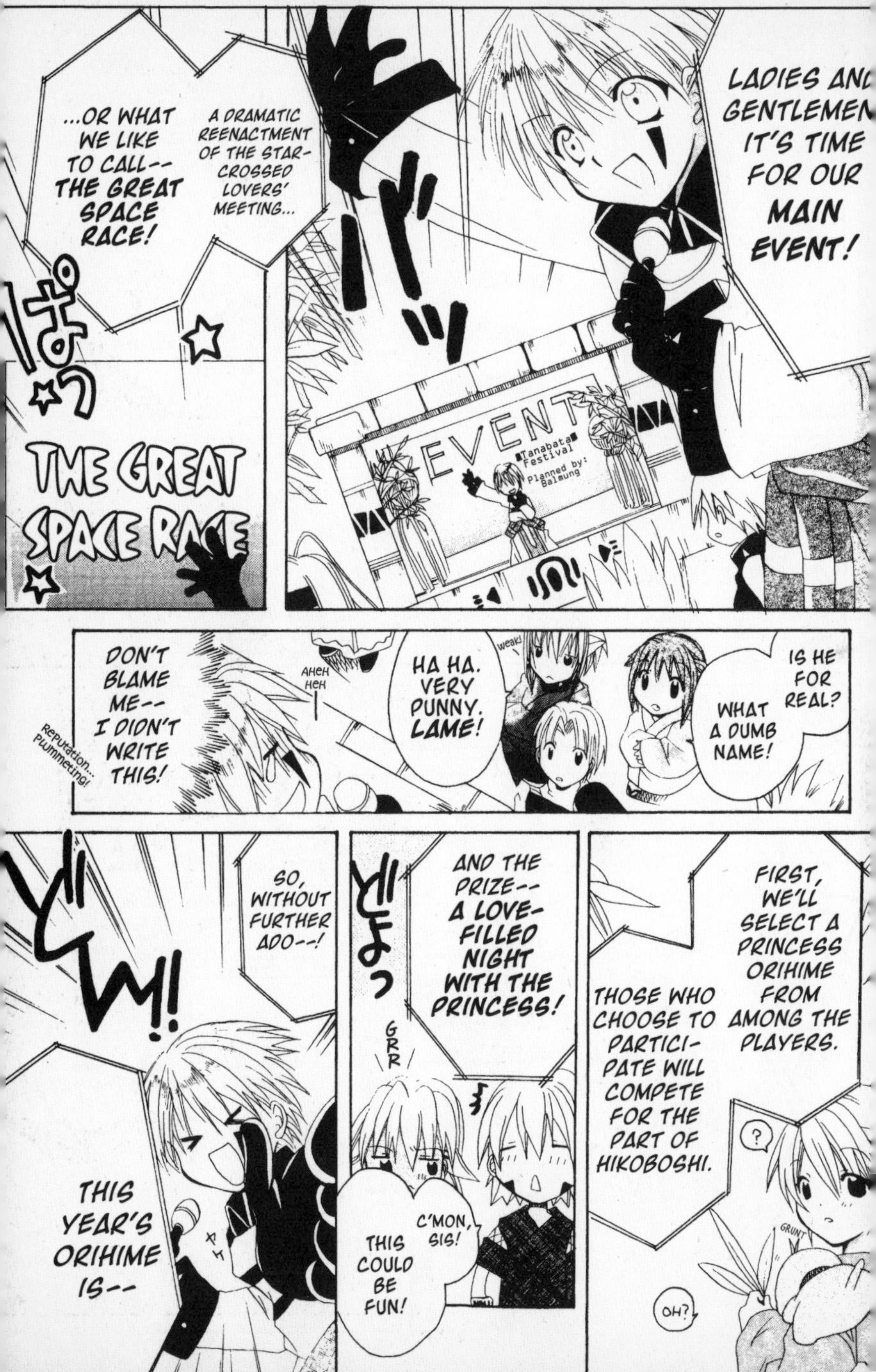
LADIES AND GENTLEMEN IT'S TIME FOR OUR MAIN EVENT!
A DRAMATIC REENACTMENT OF THE STAR-CROSSED LOVERS' MEETING...
バッ
EVENT
Tanabata Festival
Planned by: Balmung
...OR WHAT WE LIKE TO CALL-- THE GREAT SPACE RACE!
ぱっ
THE GREAT SPACE RACE
IS HE FOR REAL?
WHAT A DUMB NAME!
weak!
HA HA. VERY PUNNY. LAME!
AHEH HEH
DON'T BLAME ME-- I DIDN'T WRITE THIS!
Reputation... Plummeting!
FIRST, WE'LL SELECT A PRINCESS ORIHIME FROM AMONG THE PLAYERS.
THOSE WHO CHOOSE TO PARTICIPATE WILL COMPETE FOR THE PART OF HIKOBOSHI.
?
GRUNT
OH?
AND THE PRIZE-- A LOVE-FILLED NIGHT WITH THE PRINCESS!
どよっ
GRR
C'MON, SIS!
THIS COULD BE FUN!
SO, WITHOUT FURTHER ADO--!
どん!!
THIS YEAR'S ORIHIME IS--

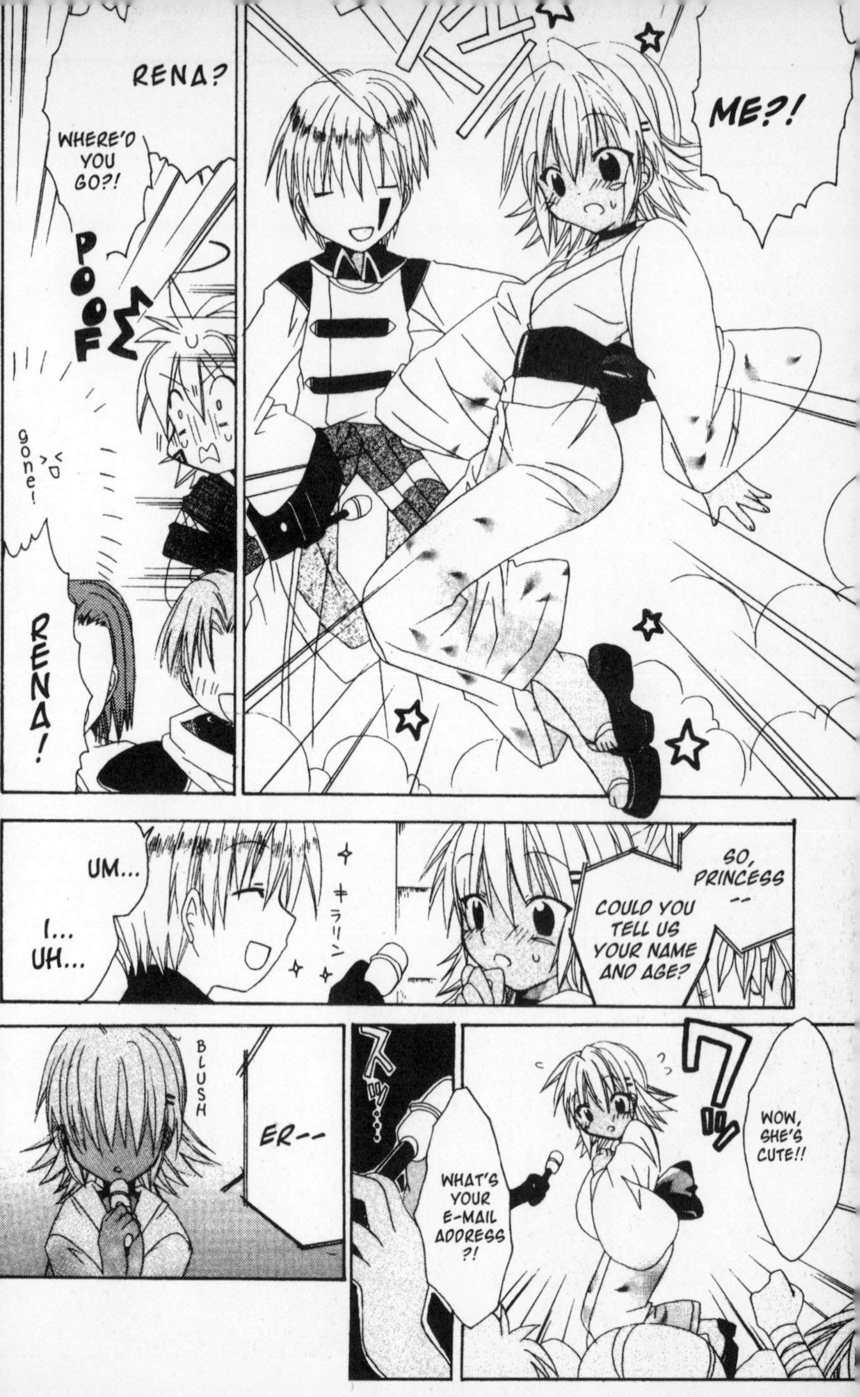
ME?!
RENA?
WHERE'D YOU GO?!
POOF
gone!
RENA!
SO, PRINCESS --
COULD YOU TELL US YOUR NAME AND AGE?
キラリン
UM...
I... UH...
WOW, SHE'S CUTE!!
WHAT'S YOUR E-MAIL ADDRESS?!
ER--
BLUSH

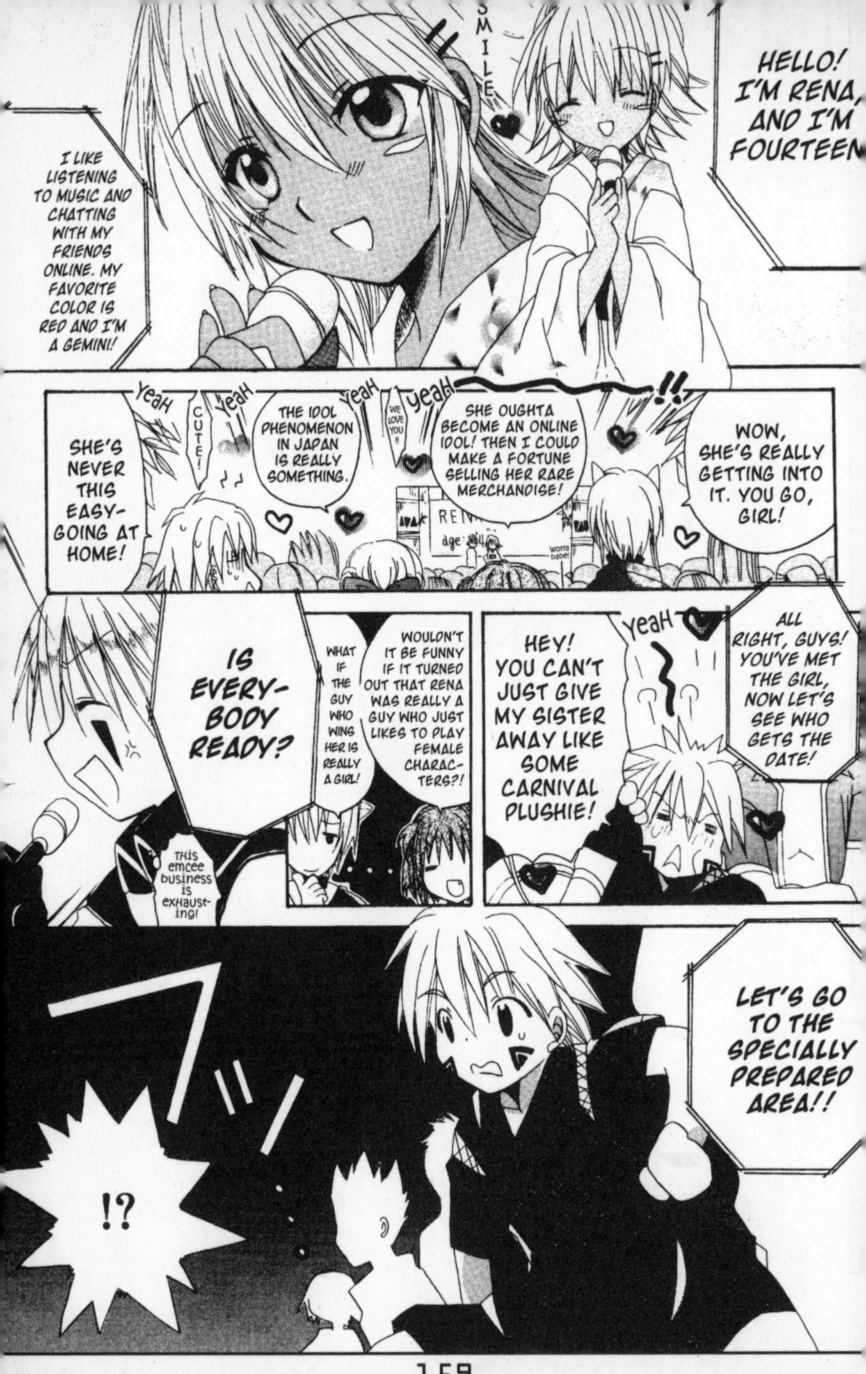
SMILE
HELLO! I'M RENA, AND I'M FOURTEEN
I LIKE LISTENING TO MUSIC AND CHATTING WITH MY FRIENDS ONLINE. MY FAVORITE COLOR IS RED AND I'M A GEMINI!
WOW, SHE'S REALLY GETTING INTO IT. YOU GO, GIRL!
yeaH!!
SHE OUGHTA BECOME AN ONLINE IDOL! THEN I COULD MAKE A FORTUNE SELLING HER RARE MERCHANDISE!
WE LOVE YOU!!
yeaH
THE IDOL PHENOMENON IN JAPAN IS REALLY SOMETHING.
yeaH
CUTE!
yeaH
SHE'S NEVER THIS EASY-GOING AT HOME!
wotta babe!
ALL RIGHT, GUYS! YOU'VE MET THE GIRL, NOW LET'S SEE WHO GETS THE DATE!
yeaH
HEY! YOU CAN'T JUST GIVE MY SISTER AWAY LIKE SOME CARNIVAL PLUSHIE!
WOULDN'T IT BE FUNNY IF IT TURNED OUT THAT RENA WAS REALLY A GUY WHO JUST LIKES TO PLAY FEMALE CHARACTERS?!
WHAT IF THE GUY WHO WINS HER IS REALLY A GIRL!
IS EVERY-BODY READY?
THIS emcee business is exhaust-ing!
LET'S GO TO THE SPECIALLY PREPARED AREA!!
!?

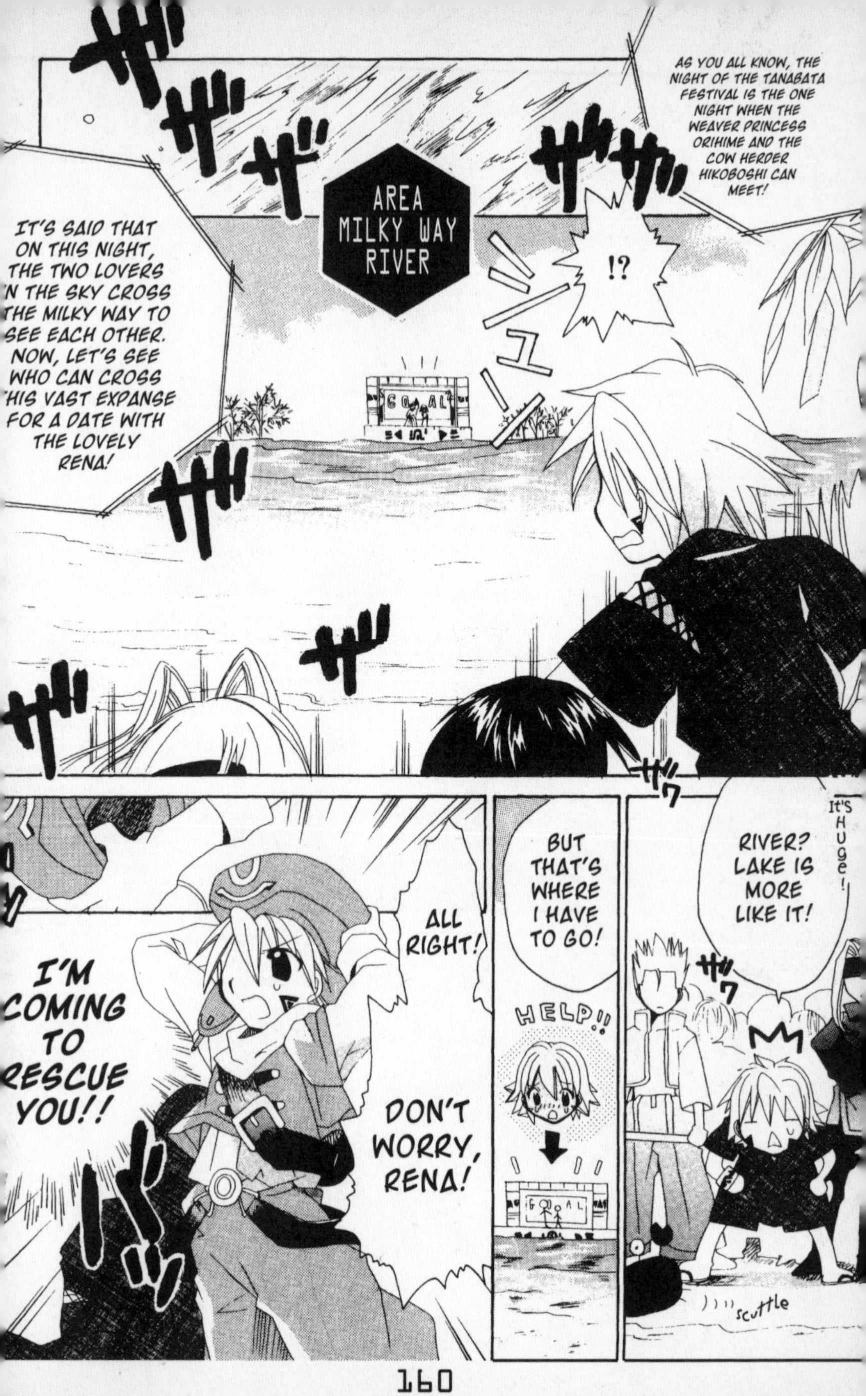

AS YOU ALL KNOW, THE NIGHT OF THE TANABATA FESTIVAL IS THE ONE NIGHT WHEN THE WEAVER PRINCESS ORIHIME AND THE COW HERDER HIKOBOSHI CAN MEET!
AREA MILKY WAY RIVER
IT'S SAID THAT ON THIS NIGHT, THE TWO LOVERS IN THE SKY CROSS THE MILKY WAY TO SEE EACH OTHER. NOW, LET'S SEE WHO CAN CROSS THIS VAST EXPANSE FOR A DATE WITH THE LOVELY RENA!
!?
GOAL
RIVER? LAKE IS MORE LIKE IT!
It's Huge!
BUT THAT'S WHERE I HAVE TO GO!
HELP!!
GOAL
scuttle
ALL RIGHT!
DON'T WORRY, RENA!
I'M COMING TO RESCUE YOU!!

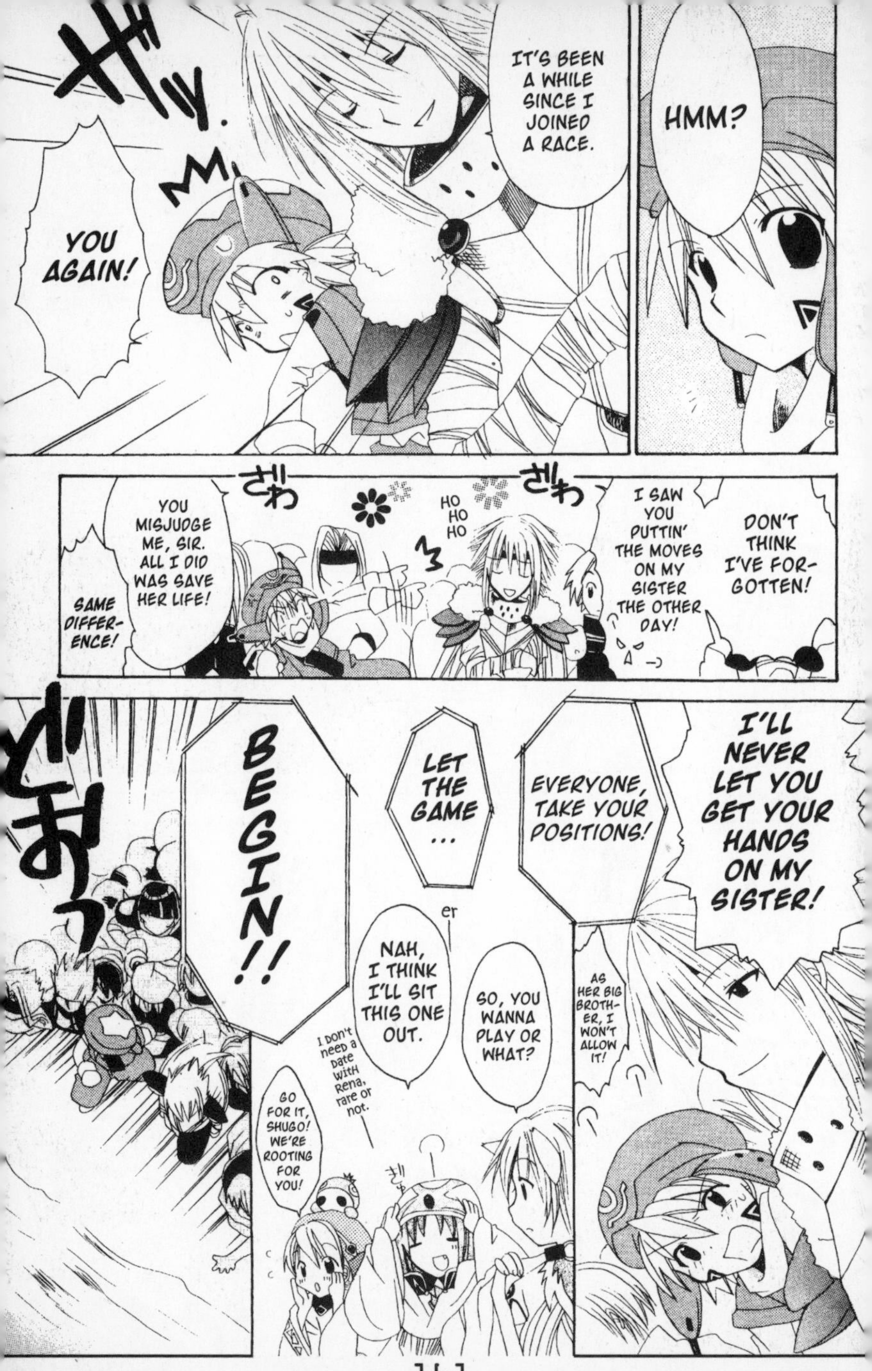
HMM?
IT'S BEEN A WHILE SINCE I JOINED A RACE.
ザッ
MM!
YOU AGAIN!
DON'T THINK I'VE FOR-GOTTEN!
I SAW YOU PUTTIN' THE MOVES ON MY SISTER THE OTHER DAY!
ざわ
HO HO HO
ざわ
YOU MISJUDGE ME, SIR. ALL I DID WAS SAVE HER LIFE!
SAME DIFFER-ENCE!
I'LL NEVER LET YOU GET YOUR HANDS ON MY SISTER!
AS HER BIG BROTH-ER, I WON'T ALLOW IT!
EVERYONE, TAKE YOUR POSITIONS!
LET THE GAME ...
SO, YOU WANNA PLAY OR WHAT?
er
NAH, I THINK I'LL SIT THIS ONE OUT.
I don't need a date with Rena, rare or not.
GO FOR IT, SHUGO! WE'RE ROOTING FOR YOU!
BEGIN!!
どぉっ

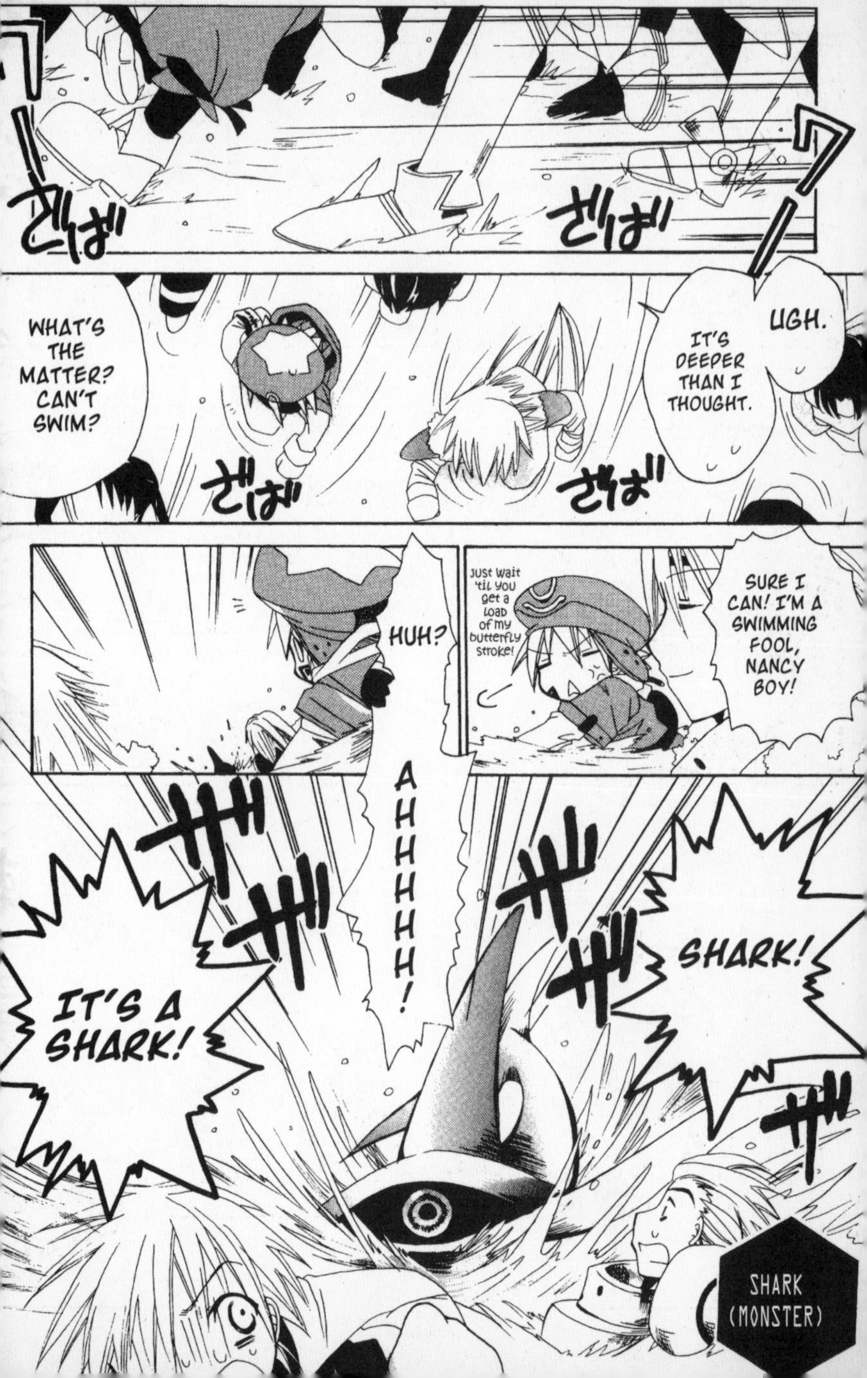

ざば
ざば
UGH.
IT'S DEEPER THAN I THOUGHT.
ざば
ざば
WHAT'S THE MATTER? CAN'T SWIM?
SURE I CAN! I'M A SWIMMING FOOL, NANCY BOY!
Just wait 'til you get a load of my butterfly stroke!
HUH?
AHHHHHH!
ザザ
SHARK!
ザザ
IT'S A SHARK!
ザ
SHARK (MONSTER)

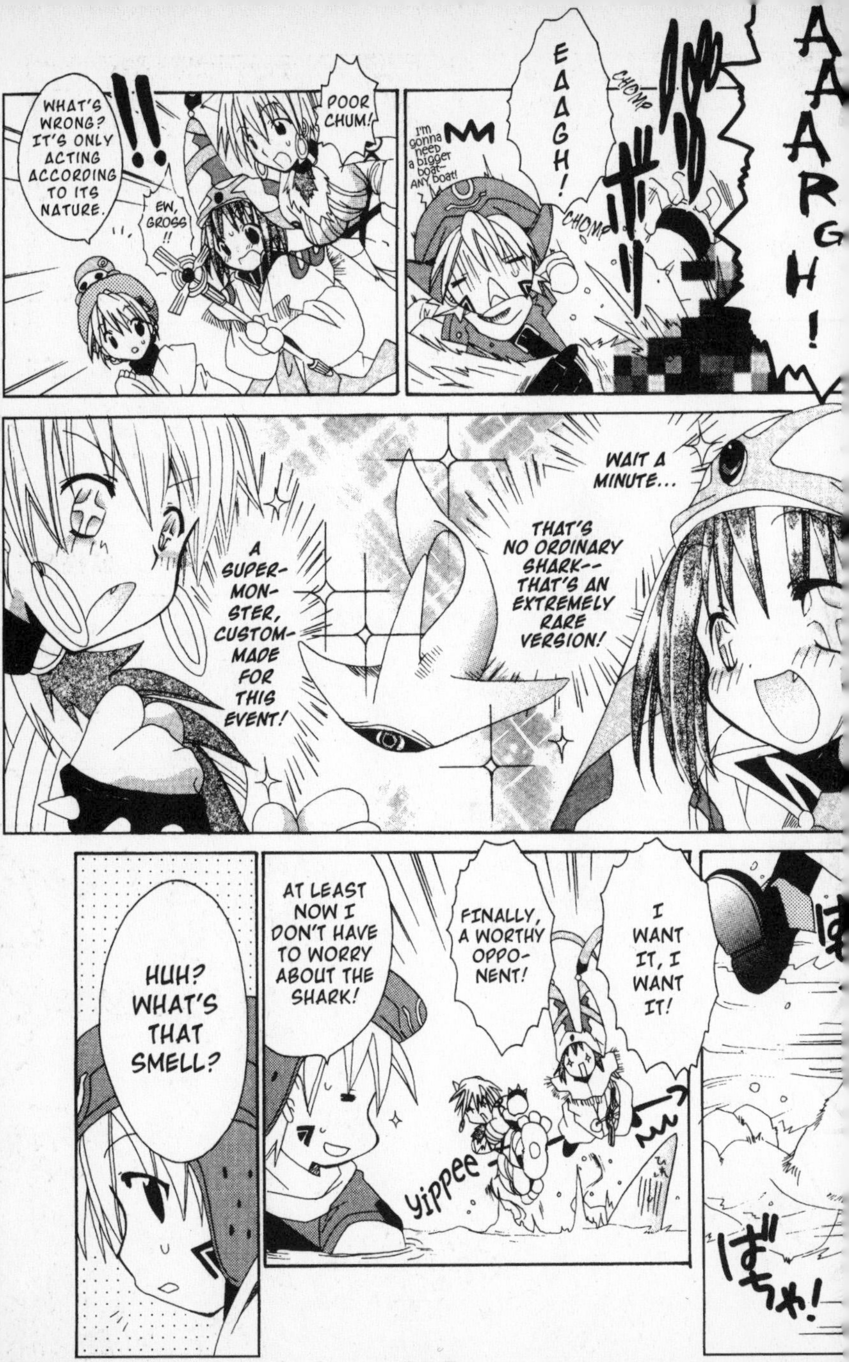
AAAARGH!
CHOMP
CHOMP
EAAGH!
I'm gonna need a bigger boat--ANY boat!
POOR CHUM!
!!
WHAT'S WRONG? IT'S ONLY ACTING ACCORDING TO ITS NATURE.
EW, GROSS!!
WAIT A MINUTE...
THAT'S NO ORDINARY SHARK--THAT'S AN EXTREMELY RARE VERSION!
A SUPER-MONSTER, CUSTOM-MADE FOR THIS EVENT!
ばちゃ!
I WANT IT, I WANT IT!
FINALLY, A WORTHY OPPONENT!
yippee
AT LEAST NOW I DON'T HAVE TO WORRY ABOUT THE SHARK!
HUH? WHAT'S THAT SMELL?

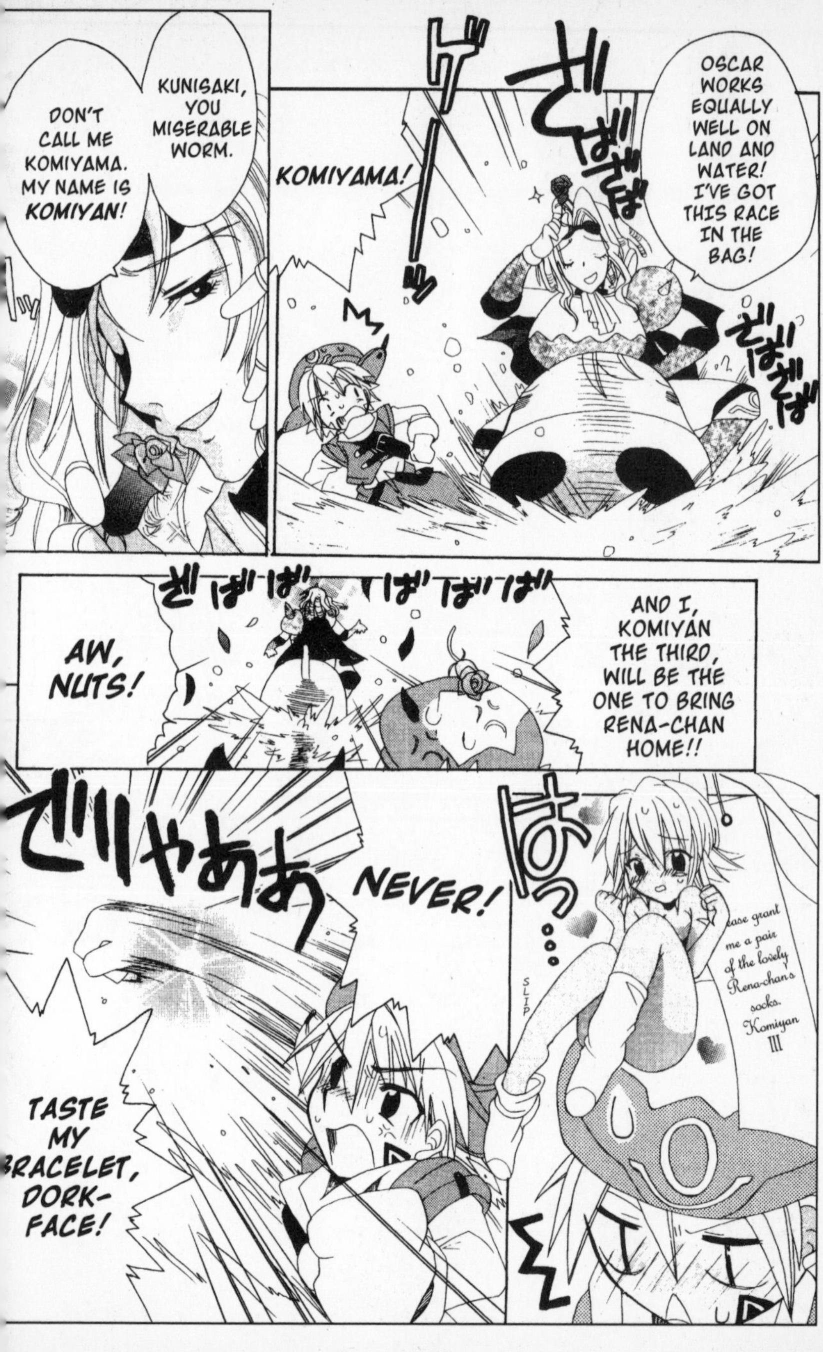
OSCAR WORKS EQUALLY WELL ON LAND AND WATER! I'VE GOT THIS RACE IN THE BAG!
ざばざば
ざばざば
KOMIYAMA!
KUNISAKI, YOU MISERABLE WORM.
DON'T CALL ME KOMIYAMA. MY NAME IS KOMIYAN!
ざばばば ばばばば
AND I, KOMIYAN THE THIRD, WILL BE THE ONE TO BRING RENA-CHAN HOME!!
AW, NUTS!
はっ…
SLIP
ease grant me a pair of the lovely Rena-chan's socks. Komiyan III
でりゃあああ
NEVER!
TASTE MY RACELET, DORK-FACE!

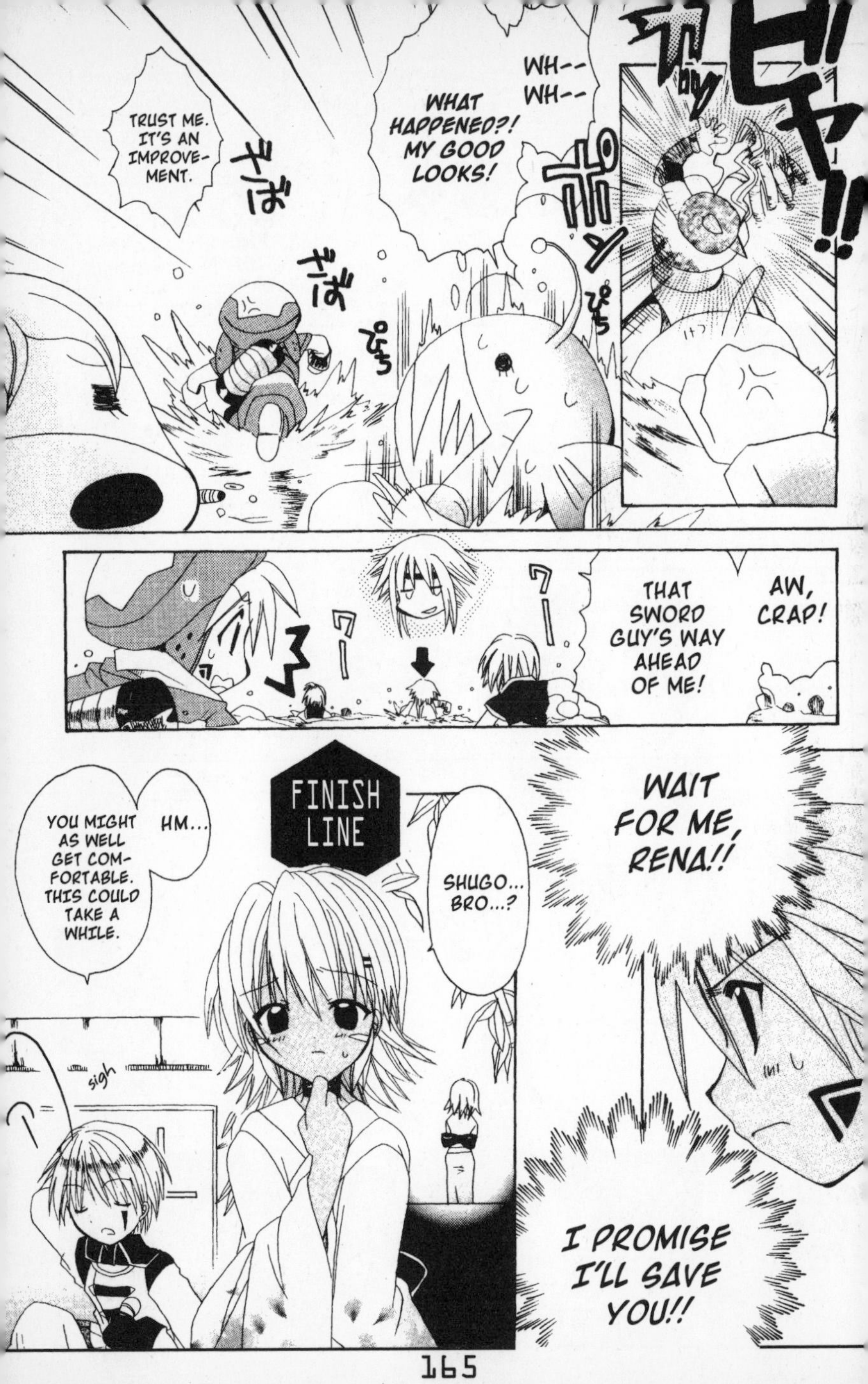
ビギャ!!
ポン
ぴち
WH-- WH--
WHAT HAPPENED?! MY GOOD LOOKS!
TRUST ME. IT'S AN IMPROVEMENT.
ざば
ざば
ぴち
AW, CRAP!
THAT SWORD GUY'S WAY AHEAD OF ME!
WAIT FOR ME, RENA!!
I PROMISE I'LL SAVE YOU!!
FINISH LINE
SHUGO... BRO...?
HM...
YOU MIGHT AS WELL GET COMFORTABLE. THIS COULD TAKE A WHILE.
sigh

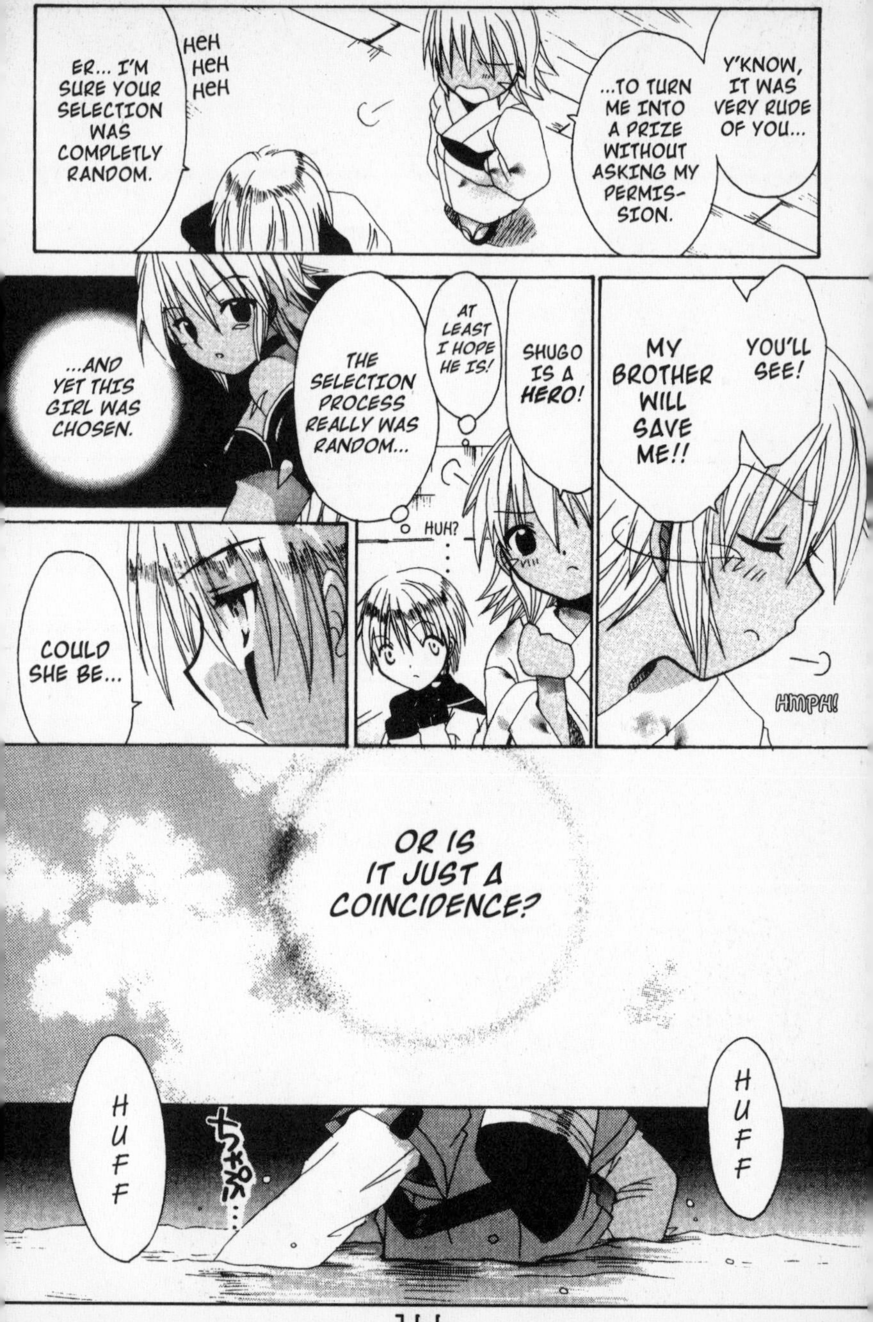
Y'KNOW, IT WAS VERY RUDE OF YOU...
...TO TURN ME INTO A PRIZE WITHOUT ASKING MY PERMISSION.
HEH HEH HEH
ER... I'M SURE YOUR SELECTION WAS COMPLETLY RANDOM.
YOU'LL SEE!
MY BROTHER WILL SAVE ME!!
HMPH!
SHUGO IS A HERO!
AT LEAST I HOPE HE IS!
THE SELECTION PROCESS REALLY WAS RANDOM...
HUH?
...
...AND YET THIS GIRL WAS CHOSEN.
COULD SHE BE...
OR IS IT JUST A COINCIDENCE?
HUFF
HUFF
ちゃぷ…

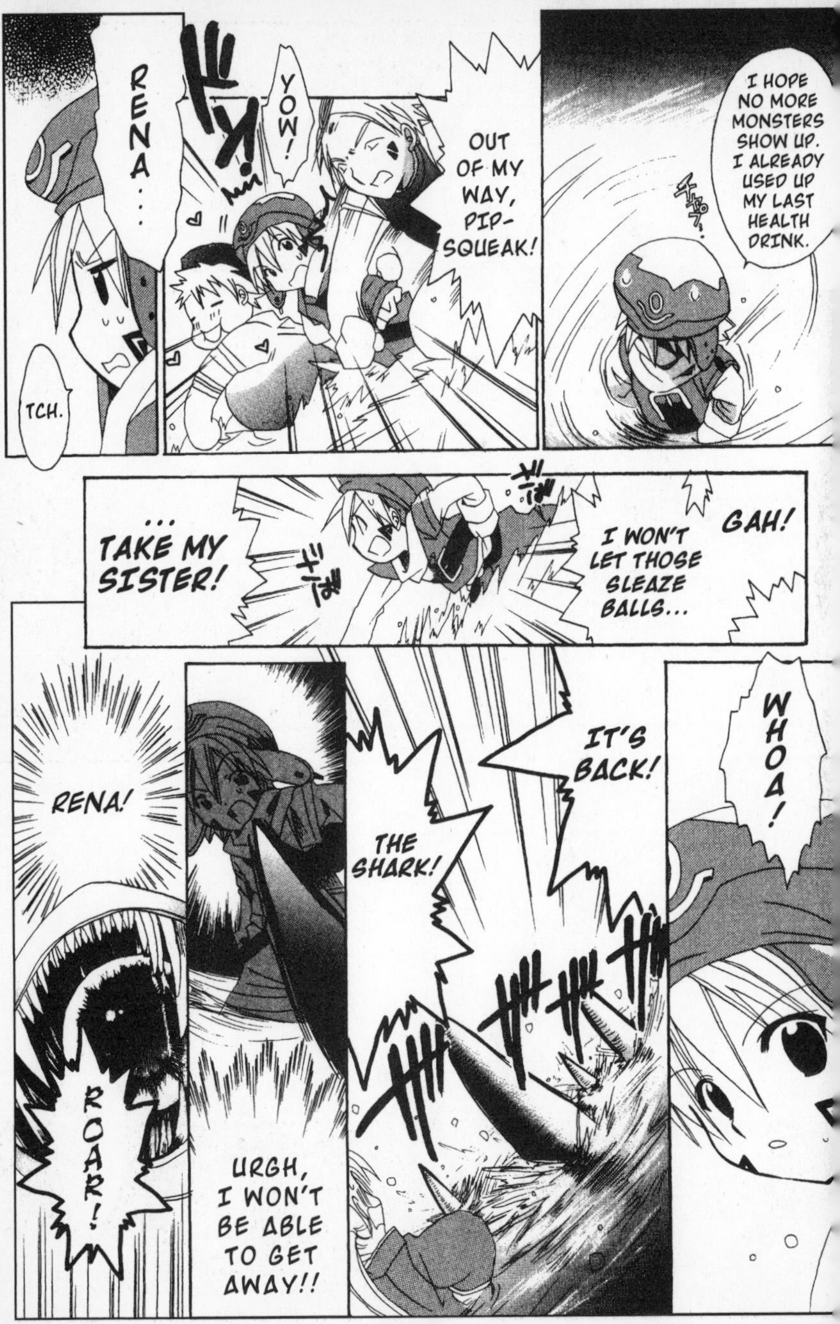
I HOPE NO MORE MONSTERS SHOW UP. I ALREADY USED UP MY LAST HEALTH DRINK.
OUT OF MY WAY, PIP-SQUEAK!
YOW!
RENA...
TCH.
GAH!
I WON'T LET THOSE SLEAZE BALLS...
...TAKE MY SISTER!
WHOA!
IT'S BACK!
THE SHARK!
RENA!
URGH, I WON'T BE ABLE TO GET AWAY!!
ROAR!

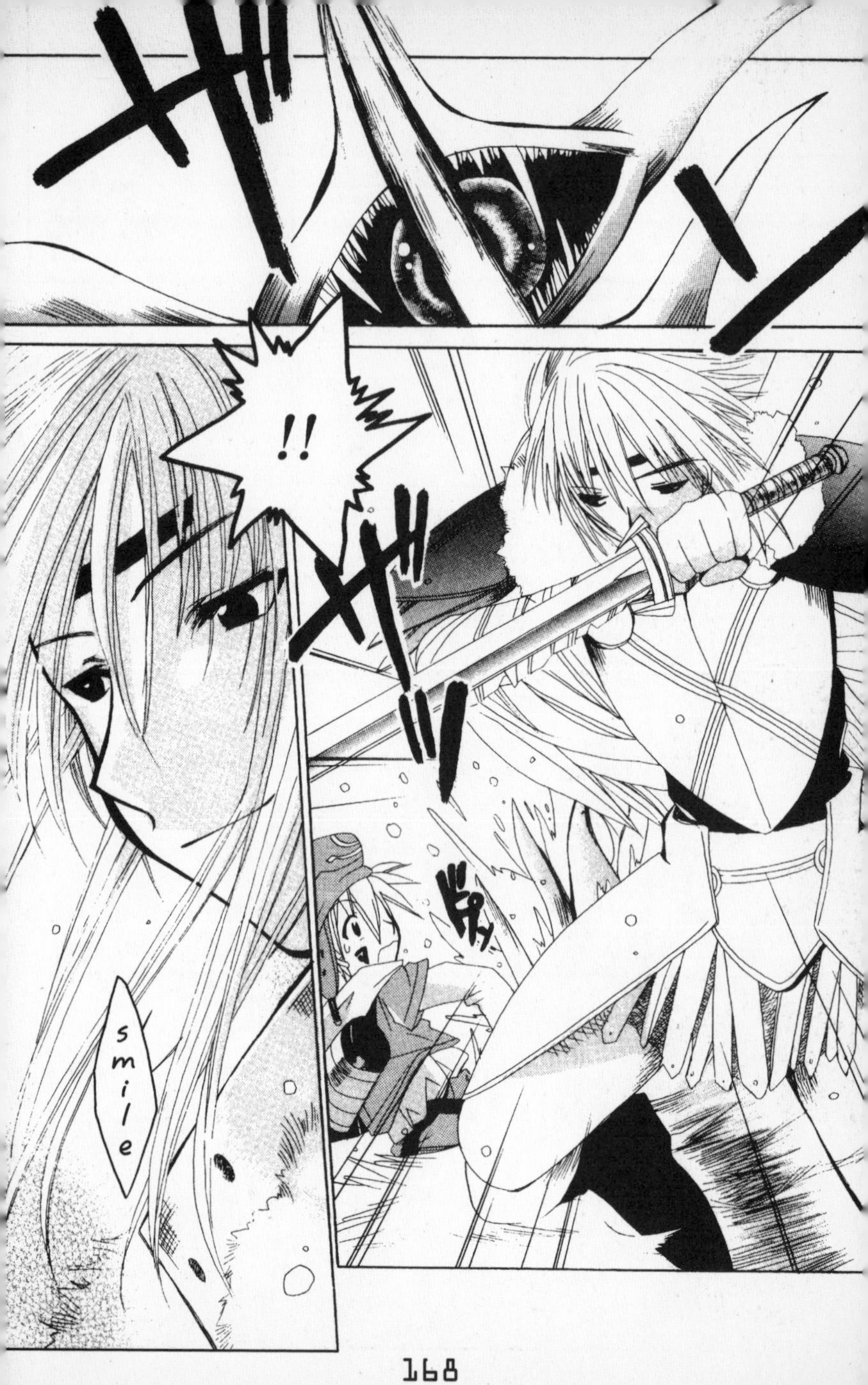
!!
smile

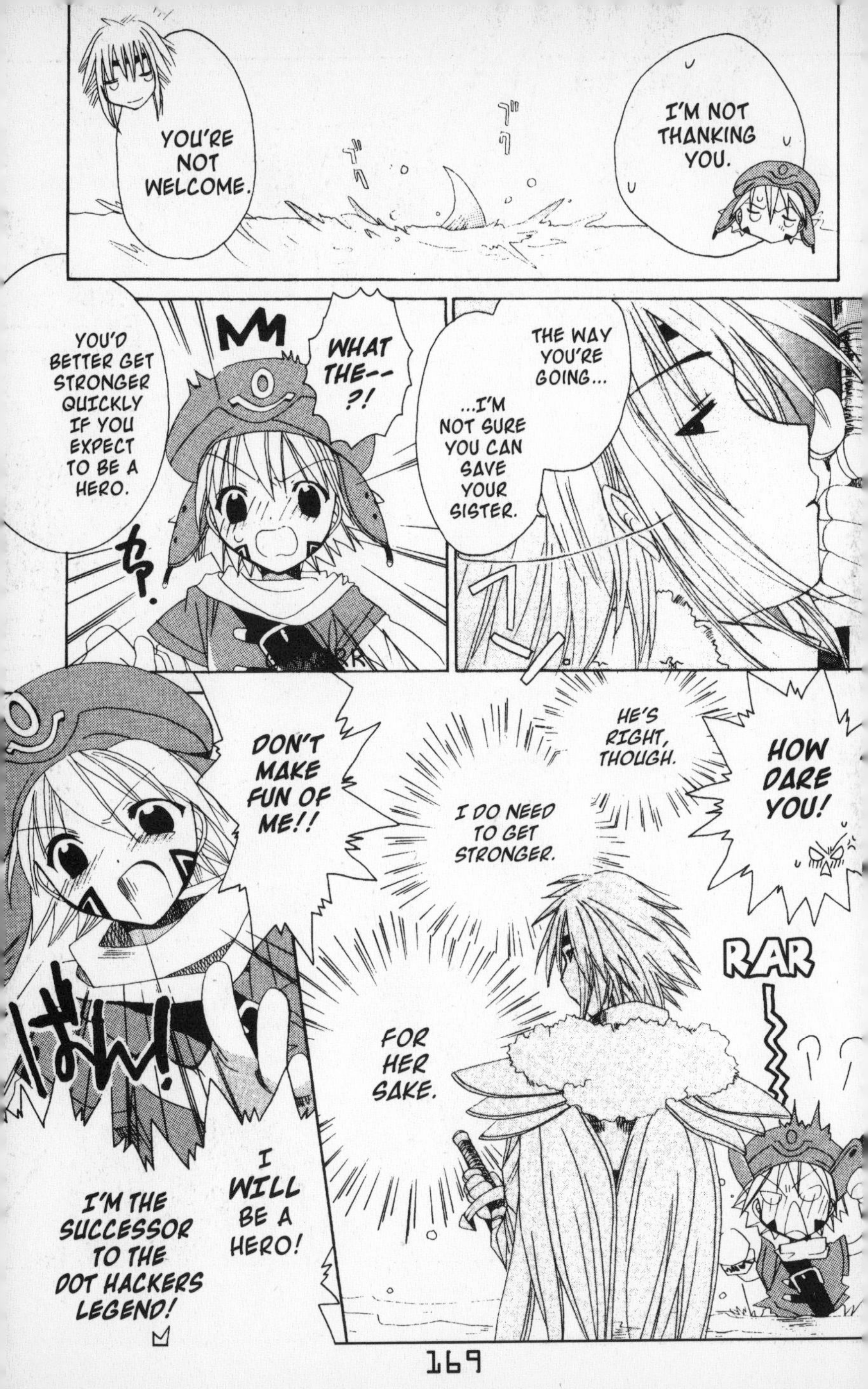
I'M NOT THANKING YOU.
YOU'RE NOT WELCOME.
THE WAY YOU'RE GOING...
...I'M NOT SURE YOU CAN SAVE YOUR SISTER.
WHAT THE--?!
YOU'D BETTER GET STRONGER QUICKLY IF YOU EXPECT TO BE A HERO.
HOW DARE YOU!
RAR
HE'S RIGHT, THOUGH.
I DO NEED TO GET STRONGER.
FOR HER SAKE.
DON'T MAKE FUN OF ME!!
I WILL BE A HERO!
I'M THE SUCCESSOR TO THE DOT HACKERS LEGEND!

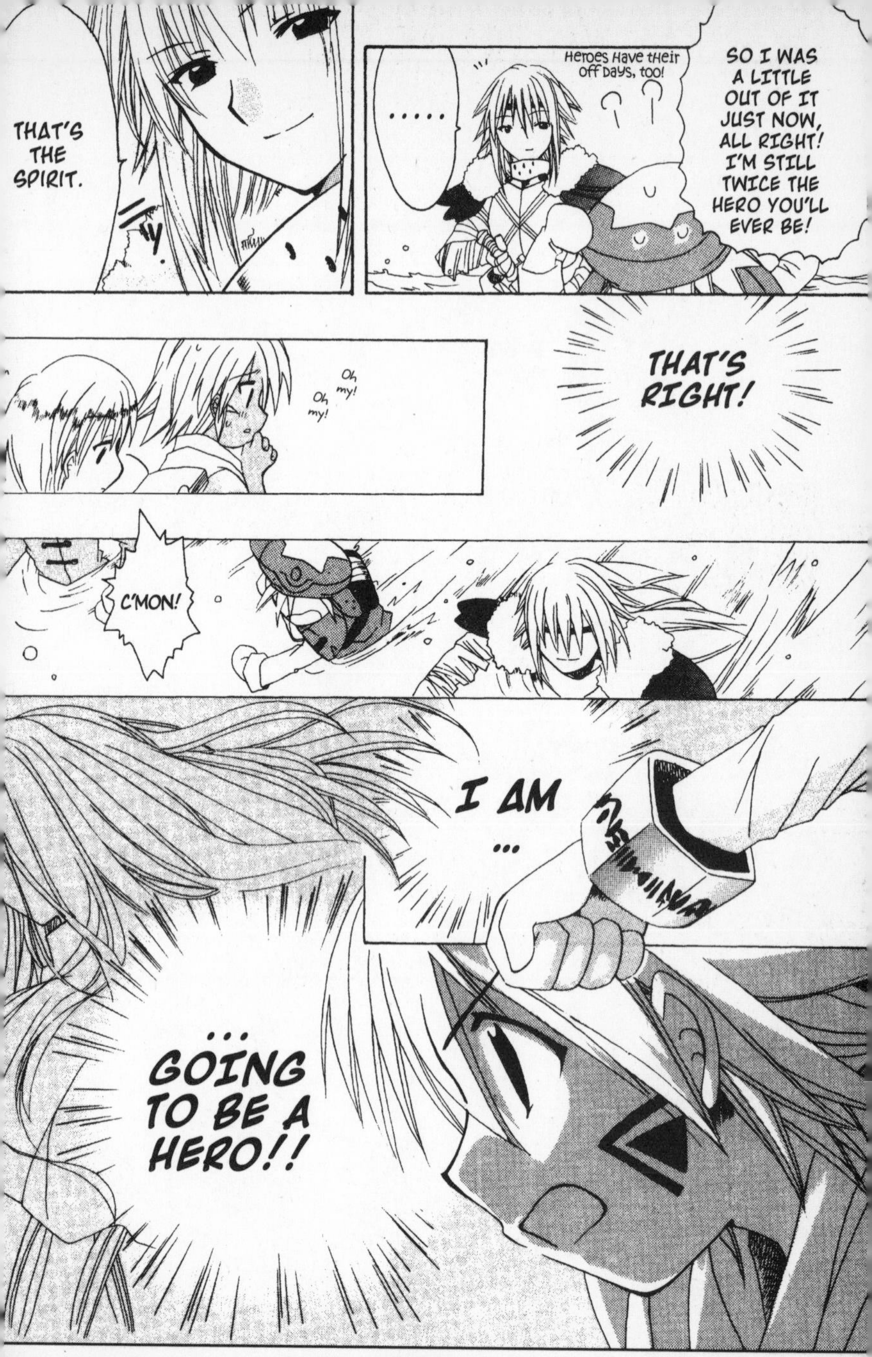
SO I WAS A LITTLE OUT OF IT JUST NOW, ALL RIGHT! I'M STILL TWICE THE HERO YOU'LL EVER BE!
Heroes have their off days, too!
.....
THAT'S THE SPIRIT.
THAT'S RIGHT!
Oh my!
Oh my!
C'MON!
I AM ...
... GOING TO BE A HERO!!

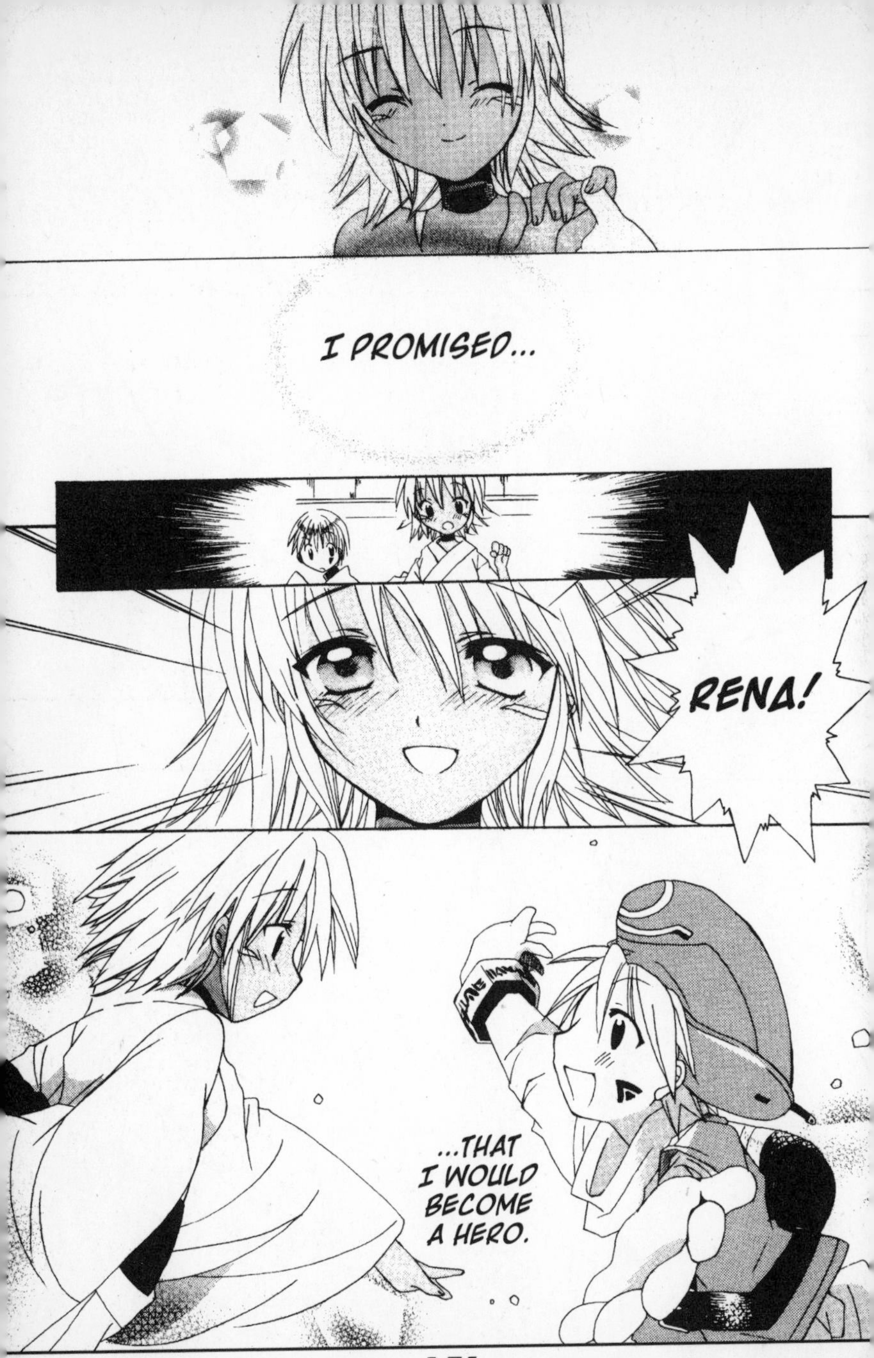
I PROMISED...
RENA!
...THAT I WOULD BECOME A HERO.

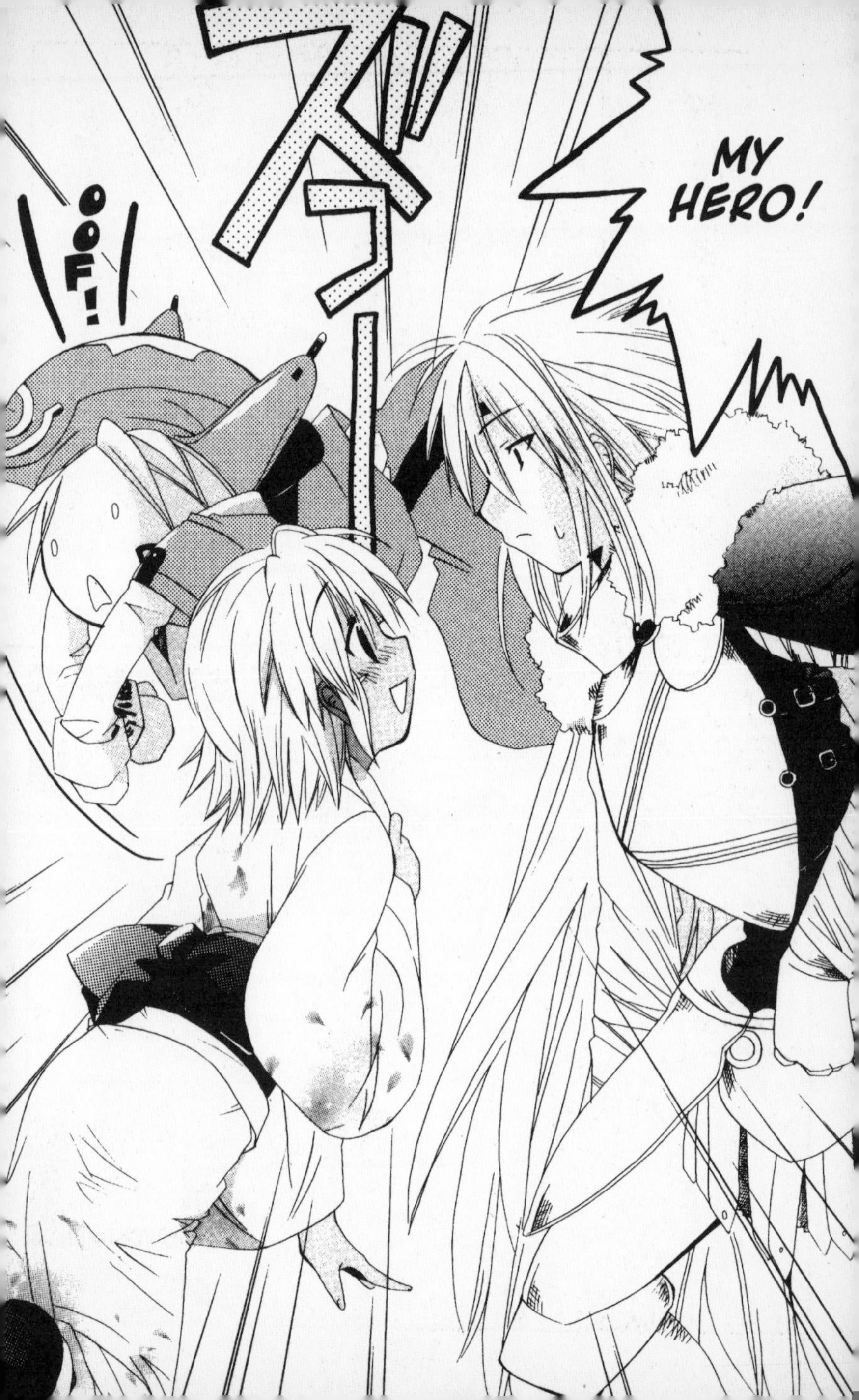

MY HERO!
ズゴッ
OOF!

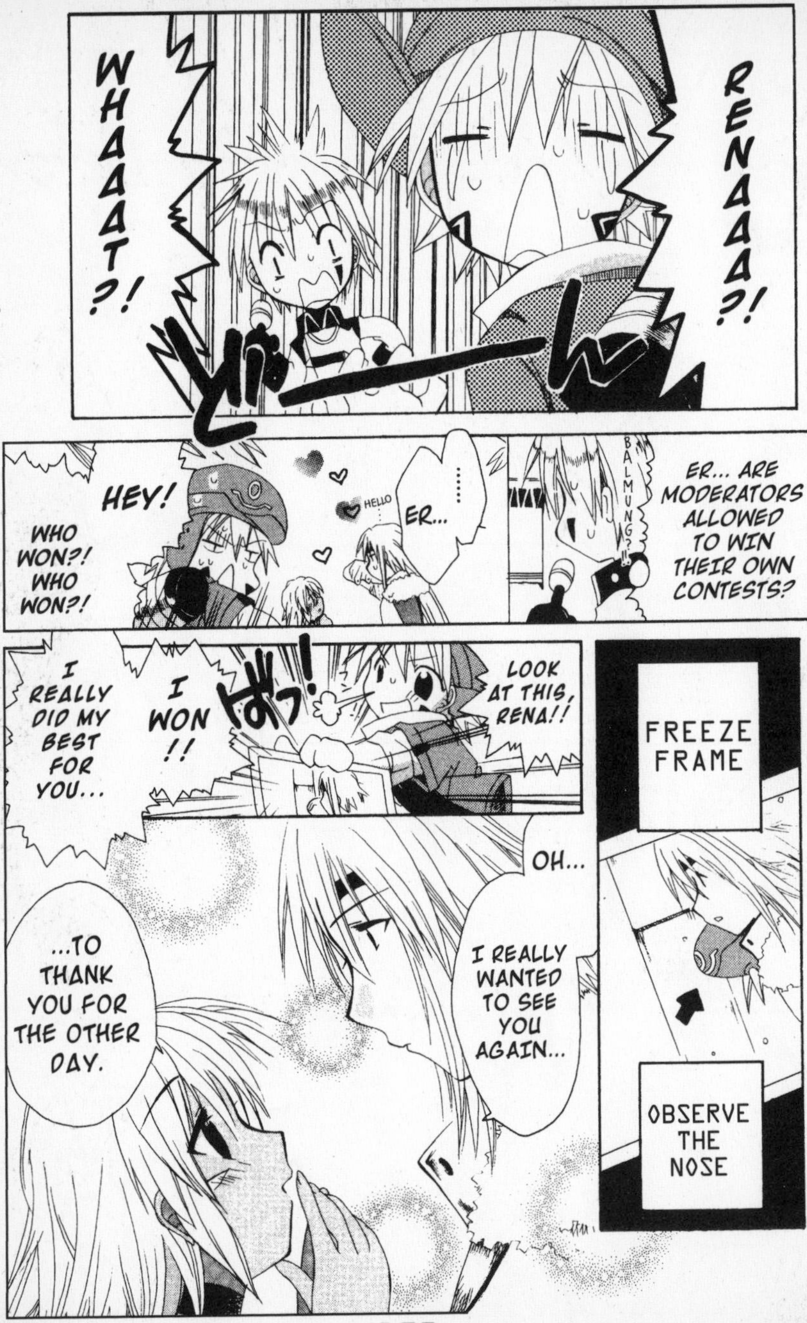
RENAAAA?!
WHAAAAT?!
BALMUNG?!
ER... ARE MODERATORS ALLOWED TO WIN THEIR OWN CONTESTS?
......
ER...
HELLO
HEY!
WHO WON?! WHO WON?!
FREEZE FRAME
OBSERVE THE NOSE
LOOK AT THIS, RENA!!
I WON!!
I REALLY DID MY BEST FOR YOU...
OH...
I REALLY WANTED TO SEE YOU AGAIN...
...TO THANK YOU FOR THE OTHER DAY.

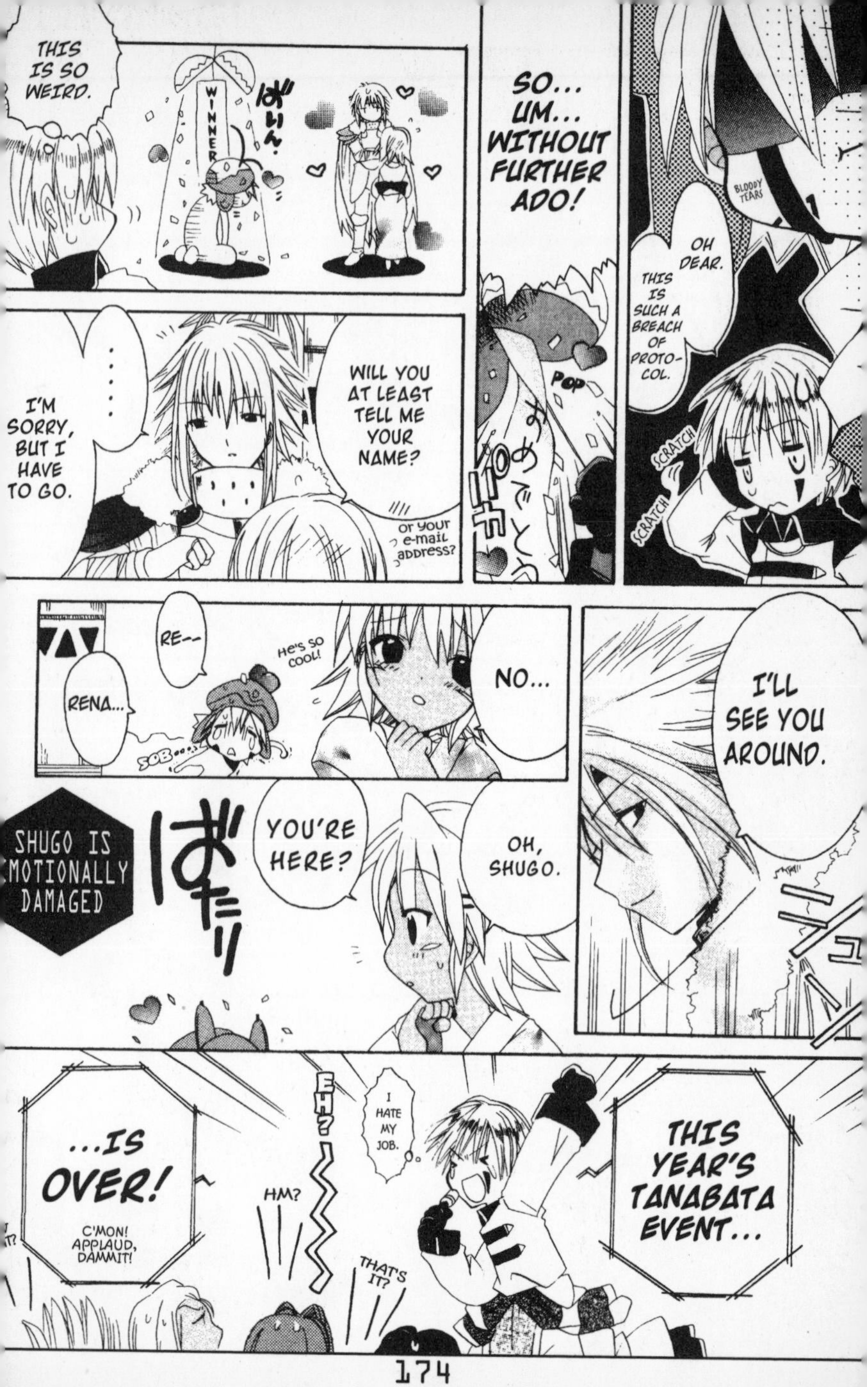
BLOODY TEARS
OH DEAR.
THIS IS SUCH A BREACH OF PROTOCOL.
SCRATCH
SCRATCH
SO... UM... WITHOUT FURTHER ADO!
POP
おめでとう
THIS IS SO WEIRD.
WINNER
ぱいん!
WILL YOU AT LEAST TELL ME YOUR NAME?
Or your e-mail address?
......
I'M SORRY, BUT I HAVE TO GO.
I'LL SEE YOU AROUND.
NO...
He's so cool!
RE--
RENA...
SOB...
OH, SHUGO.
YOU'RE HERE?
ぱたり
SHUGO IS MOTIONALLY DAMAGED
THIS YEAR'S TANABATA EVENT...
I HATE MY JOB.
EH?
HM?
THAT'S IT?
...IS OVER!
C'MON! APPLAUD, DAMMIT!

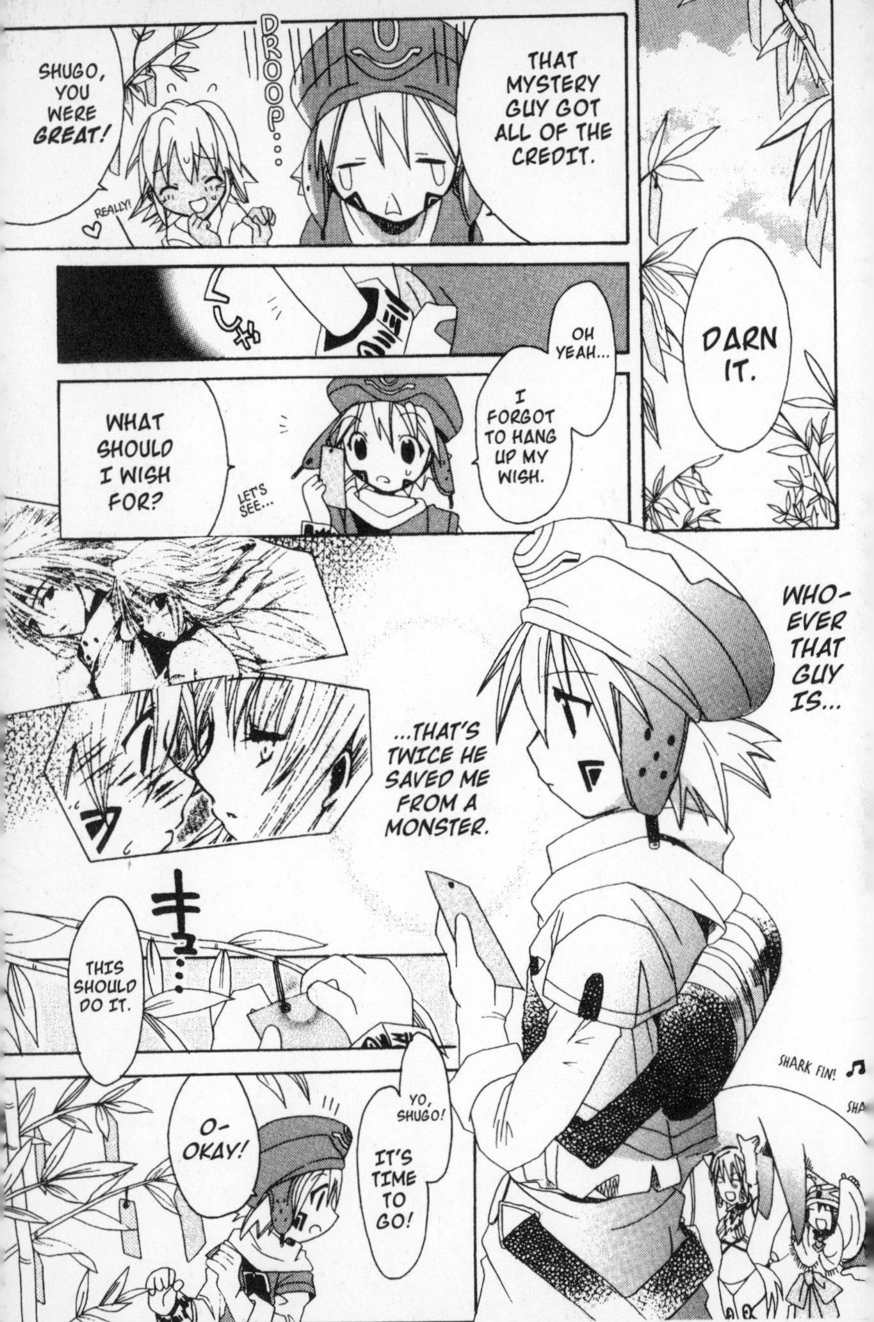
DARN IT.
THAT MYSTERY GUY GOT ALL OF THE CREDIT.
DROOP...
SHUGO, YOU WERE GREAT!
REALLY!
OH YEAH...
I FORGOT TO HANG UP MY WISH.
WHAT SHOULD I WISH FOR?
LET'S SEE...
WHO-EVER THAT GUY IS...
...THAT'S TWICE HE SAVED ME FROM A MONSTER.
SHARK FIN!
SHA
THIS SHOULD DO IT.
YO, SHUGO!
IT'S TIME TO GO!
O-OKAY!

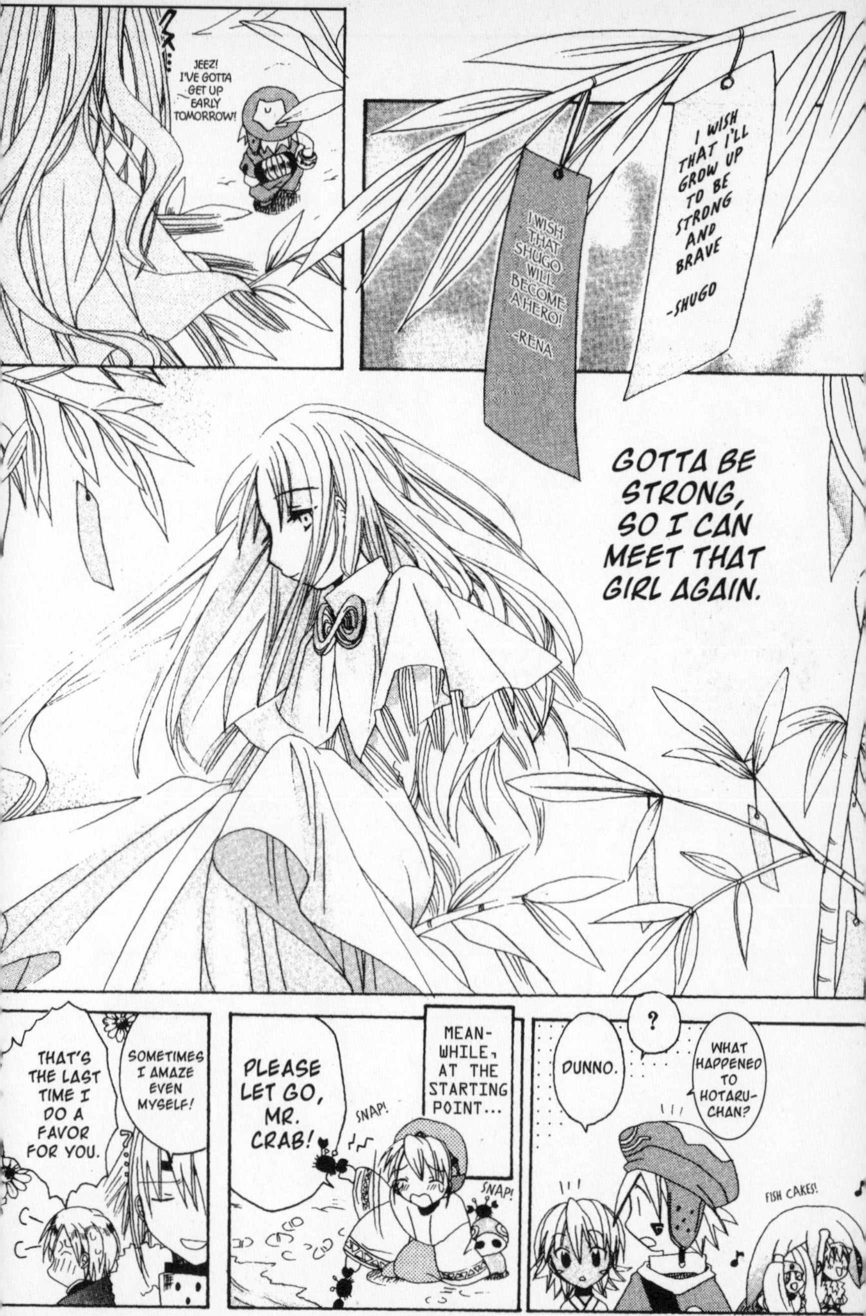
I WISH THAT I'LL GROW UP TO BE STRONG AND BRAVE -SHUGO
I WISH THAT SHUGO WILL BECOME A HERO! -RENA
JEEZ! I'VE GOTTA GET UP EARLY TOMORROW!
GOTTA BE STRONG, SO I CAN MEET THAT GIRL AGAIN.
?
WHAT HAPPENED TO HOTARU-CHAN?
DUNNO.
FISH CAKES!
MEAN-WHILE, AT THE STARTING POINT...
PLEASE LET GO, MR. CRAB!
SNAP!
SNAP!
SOMETIMES I AMAZE EVEN MYSELF!
THAT'S THE LAST TIME I DO A FAVOR FOR YOU.

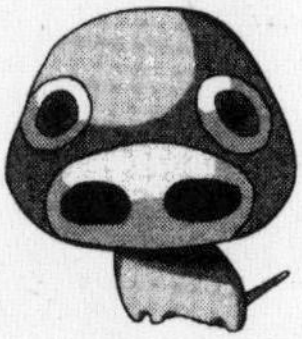

NEW GENERATION ONLINE

THE WORLD

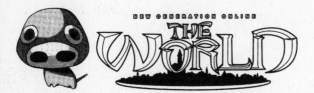

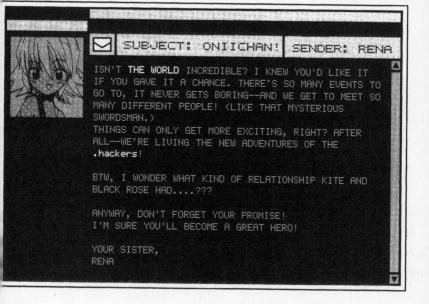

SUBJECT: ONIICHAN! SENDER: RENA

ISN'T **THE WORLD** INCREDIBLE? I KNEW YOU'D LIKE IT IF YOU GAVE IT A CHANCE. THERE'S SO MANY EVENTS TO GO TO, IT NEVER GETS BORING--AND WE GET TO MEET SO MANY DIFFERENT PEOPLE! (LIKE THAT MYSTERIOUS SWORDSMAN.)
THINGS CAN ONLY GET MORE EXCITING, RIGHT? AFTER ALL--WE'RE LIVING THE NEW ADVENTURES OF THE **.hackers**!

BTW, I WONDER WHAT KIND OF RELATIONSHIP KITE AND BLACK ROSE HAD....???

ANYWAY, DON'T FORGET YOUR PROMISE!
I'M SURE YOU'LL BECOME A GREAT HERO!

YOUR SISTER,
RENA

Last year we began a great undertaking--
a melding of anime, manga and video
game unlike anything seen before.
We called our child .hack!
Our baby's been very good to us.
The project turned out better than we ever
imagined and is now a hit around the world.

Thanks to everyone for your hard work!

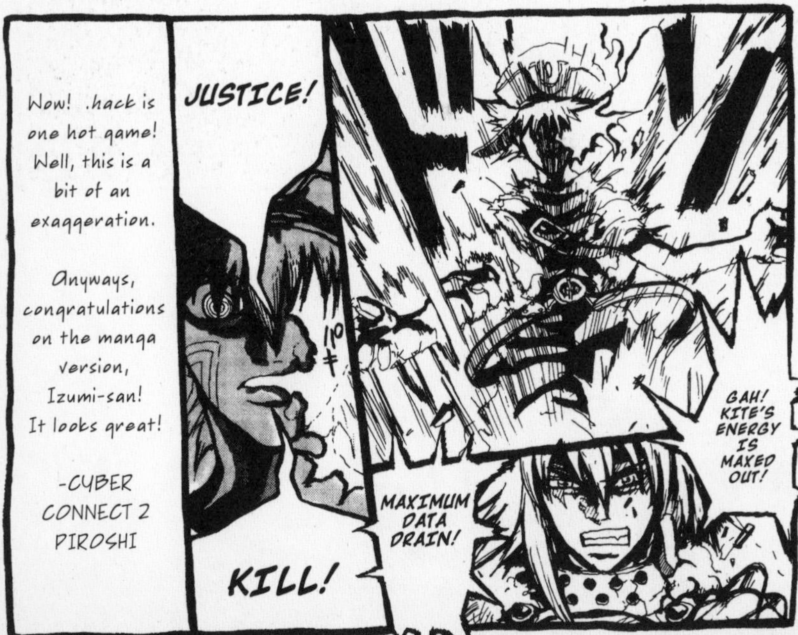
GAH! KITE'S ENERGY IS MAXED OUT!
MAXIMUM DATA DRAIN!
JUSTICE!
KILL!
Wow! .hack is one hot game! Well, this is a bit of an exaggeration.
Anyways, congratulations on the manga version, Izumi-san! It looks great!
-CYBER CONNECT 2 PIROSHI

どっと吐く@コミック版

DEEP SIGH @ COMIX

☆

I never would have made it this far without all of your support. Thank you so much! I am so grateful to be part of Project .hack as the manga artist. I love both the game and the anime, so it was such an honor. Thank you for reading it!

But the story's not over yet! I hope you'll come back for volume 2! Thanks President Matsuyama! Thanks Hamazaki-san and all of my staff! I couldn't have done it without you! I love you all!

THANKS
MUNE MARINO-SAN
RURU HARUTA
☆ BUDAN-NA
YUSEIMARU KATSURA-CHAN
SAGIRI SUDA-SAN
SEIKO TODA-SAN
YUINA MIZUMUZUKI-CHAN

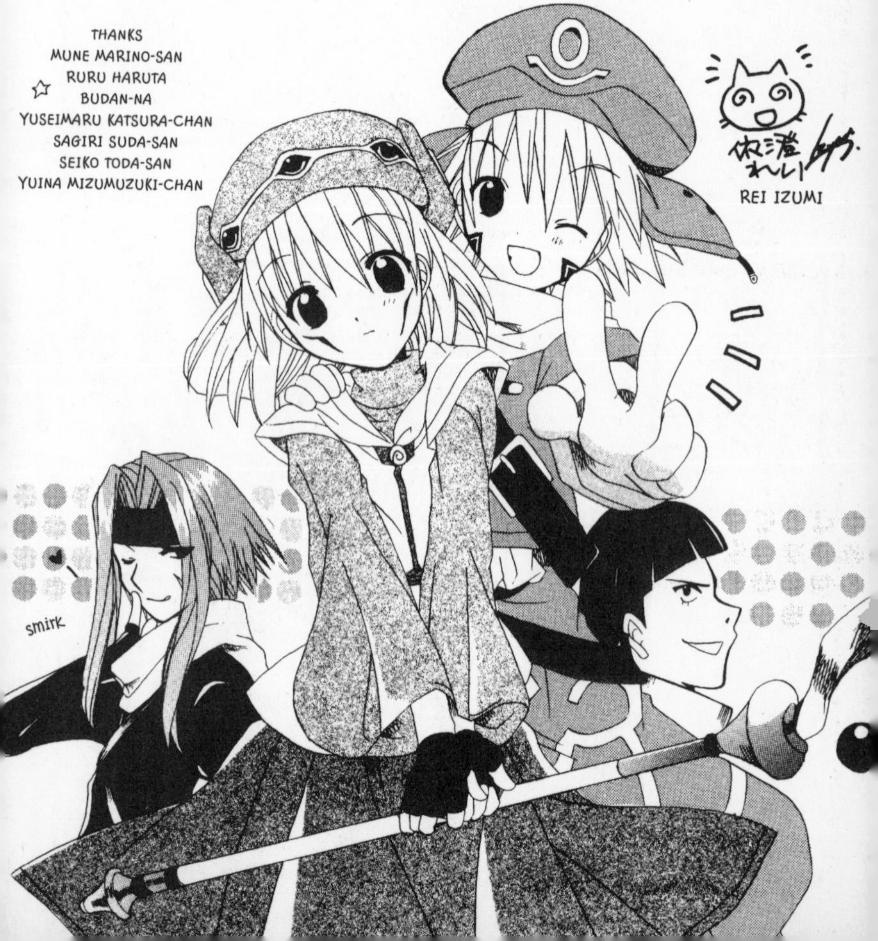
依澄れい
REI IZUMI
smirk

どっと吐く@コミック版
DEEP SIGH @ COMIX

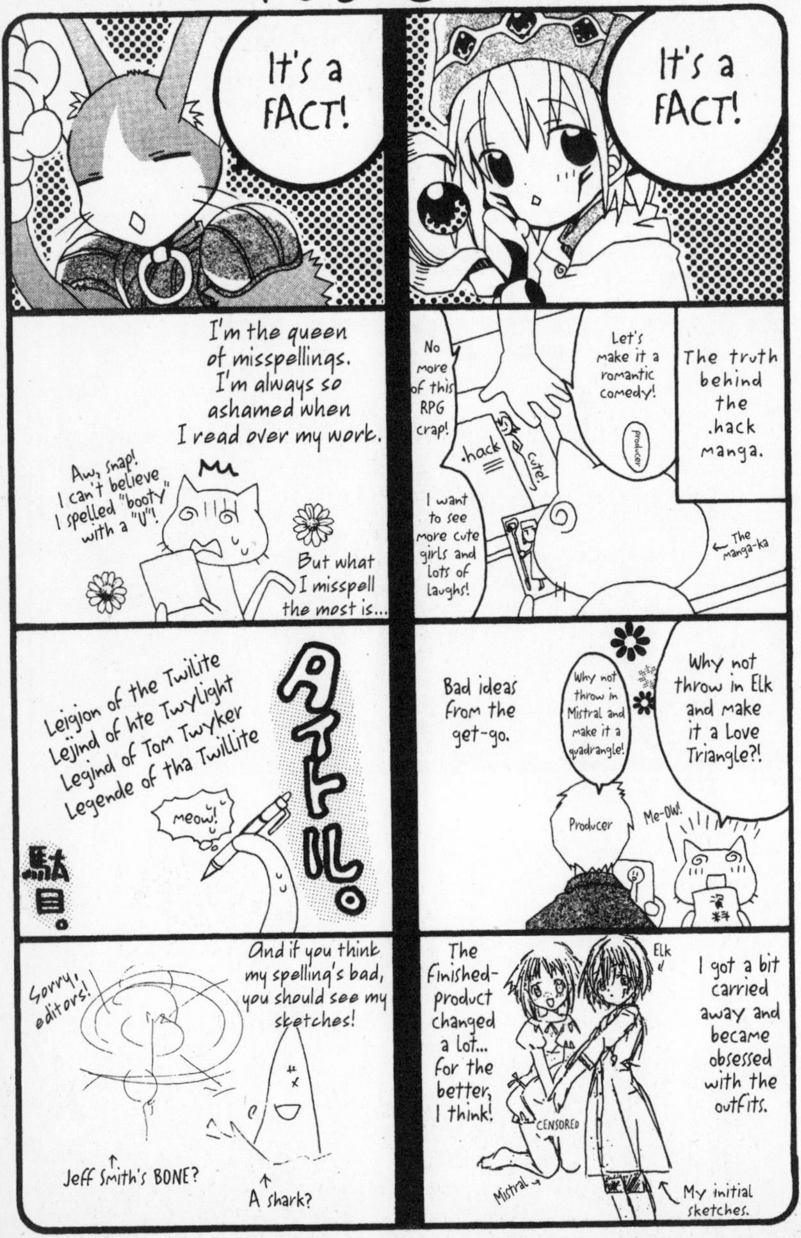
It's a FACT!
It's a FACT!
The truth behind the .hack manga.
Let's make it a romantic comedy!
producer
No more of this RPG crap!
.hack
cute!
I want to see more cute girls and lots of laughs!
← The manga-ka
I'm the queen of misspellings. I'm always so ashamed when I read over my work.
Aw, snap! I can't believe I spelled "booty" with a "U"!
But what I misspell the most is...
Why not throw in Elk and make it a Love Triangle?!
Why not throw in Mistral and make it a quadrangle!
Bad ideas from the get-go.
Producer
Me-OW!
タイトル。
Leigion of the Twilite
Lejind of hte Twylight
Legind of Tom Twyker
Legende of tha Twillite
meow!
駄目。
I got a bit carried away and became obsessed with the outfits.
Elk
The finished-product changed a lot... for the better, I think!
CENSORED
Mistral →
My initial sketches.
And if you think my spelling's bad, you should see my sketches!
Sorry, editors!
Jeff Smith's BONE?
A shark?

SUBJECT: .HACK VOLUME 2

SENDER: SHUGO

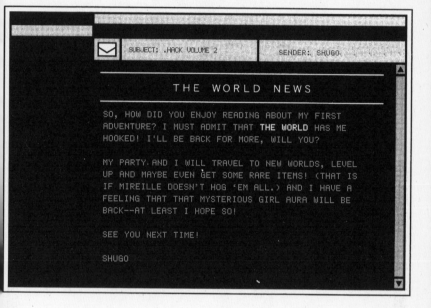

THE WORLD NEWS

SO, HOW DID YOU ENJOY READING ABOUT MY FIRST ADVENTURE? I MUST ADMIT THAT **THE WORLD** HAS ME HOOKED! I'LL BE BACK FOR MORE, WILL YOU?

MY PARTY AND I WILL TRAVEL TO NEW WORLDS, LEVEL UP AND MAYBE EVEN GET SOME RARE ITEMS! (THAT IS IF MIREILLE DOESN'T HOG 'EM ALL.) AND I HAVE A FEELING THAT THAT MYSTERIOUS GIRL AURA WILL BE BACK--AT LEAST I HOPE SO!

SEE YOU NEXT TIME!

SHUGO

ACCESS TO LOGIN_volume 2.

.hack

ドットハック//たそがれのうでわでんせつ

//黄昏の腕輪伝説

漫画
IZUMI REI
依澄れい

1

原作
HAMAZAKI TATSUYA
浜崎達也

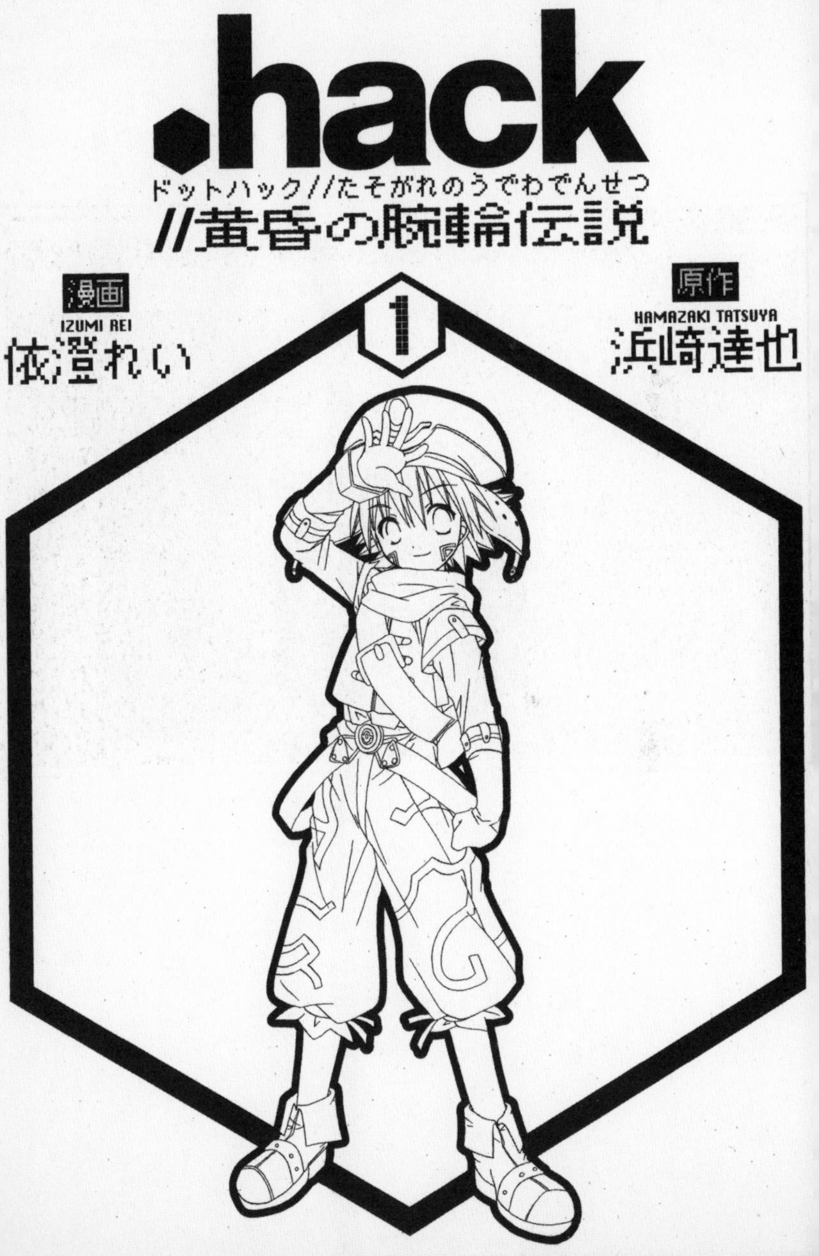

.hack

//黄昏の腕輪伝説

1

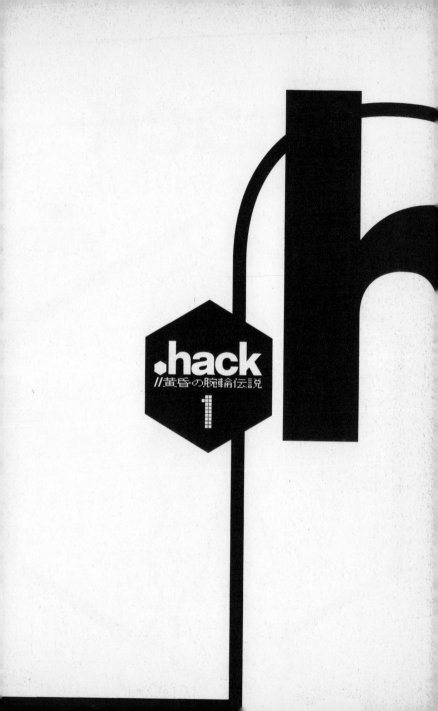

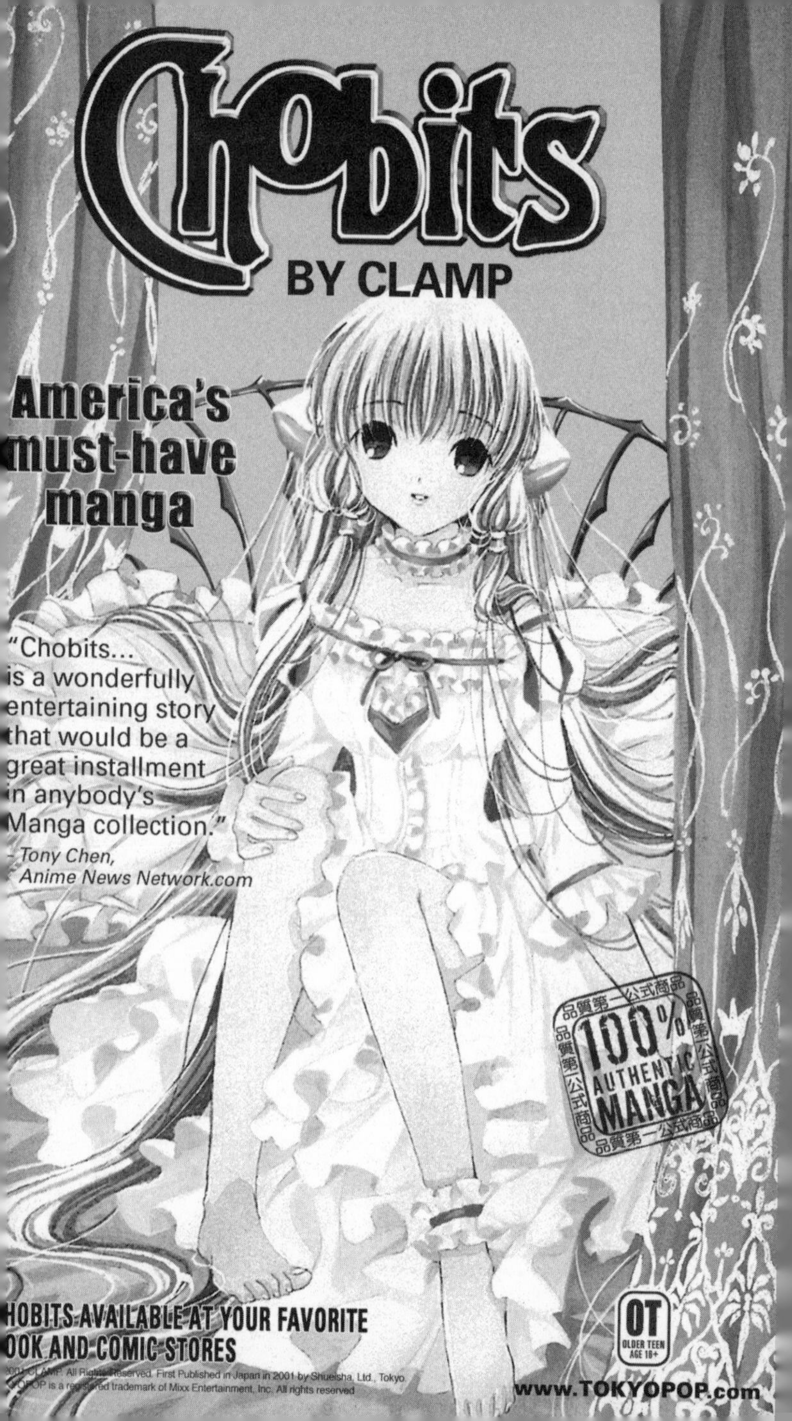
Chobits
BY CLAMP
America's must-have manga
"Chobits... is a wonderfully entertaining story that would be a great installment in anybody's Manga collection."
- Tony Chen, Anime News Network.com
品質第一公式商品
100% AUTHENTIC MANGA
HOBITS AVAILABLE AT YOUR FAVORITE
OOK AND COMIC STORES
OT
OLDER TEEN AGE 16+
www.TOKYOPOP.com

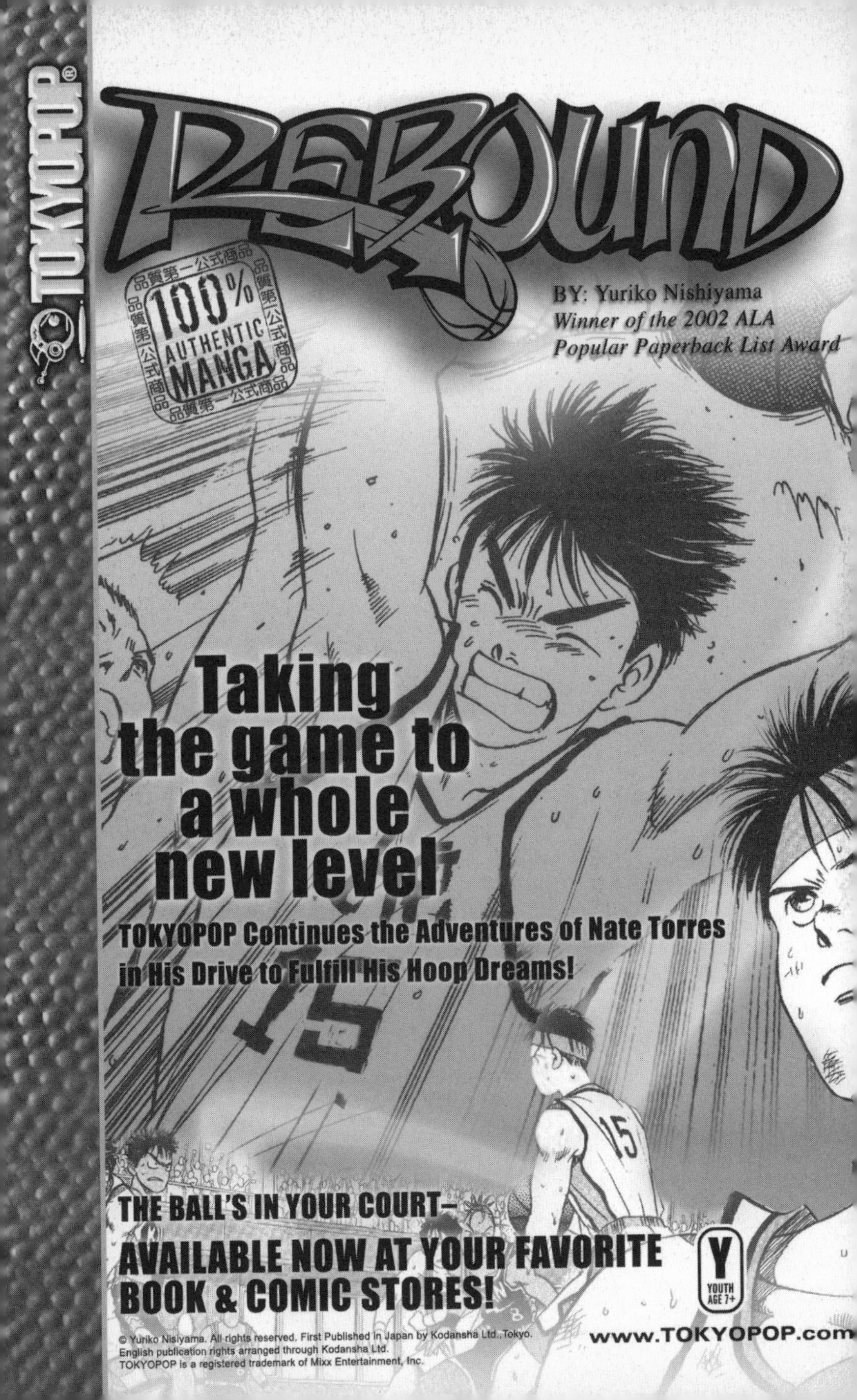
TOKYOPOP®
REBOUND
100% AUTHENTIC MANGA
BY: Yuriko Nishiyama
Winner of the 2002 ALA Popular Paperback List Award
Taking the game to a whole new level
TOKYOPOP Continues the Adventures of Nate Torres in His Drive to Fulfill His Hoop Dreams!
15
THE BALL'S IN YOUR COURT–
AVAILABLE NOW AT YOUR FAVORITE BOOK & COMIC STORES!
Y YOUTH AGE 7+
www.TOKYOPOP.com
© Yuriko Nisiyama. All rights reserved. First Published in Japan by Kodansha Ltd., Tokyo.
English publication rights arranged through Kodansha Ltd.
TOKYOPOP is a registered trademark of Mixx Entertainment, Inc.

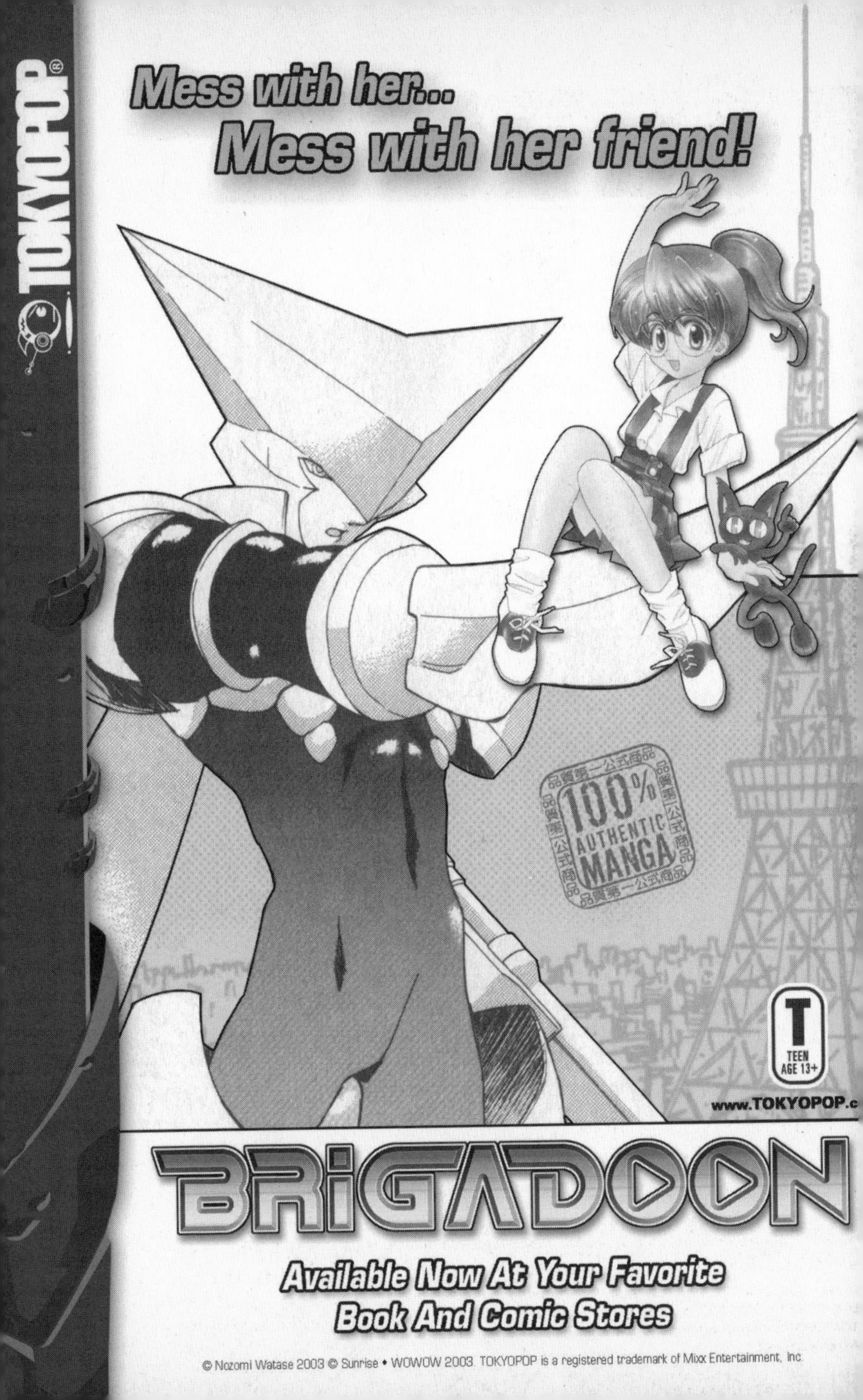
TOKYOPOP
Mess with her...
Mess with her friend!
100% AUTHENTIC MANGA
T
TEEN AGE 13+
www.TOKYOPOP.c
BRIGADOON
Available Now At Your Favorite
Book And Comic Stores
© Nozomi Watase 2003 © Sunrise • WOWOW 2003. TOKYOPOP is a registered trademark of Mixx Entertainment, Inc.

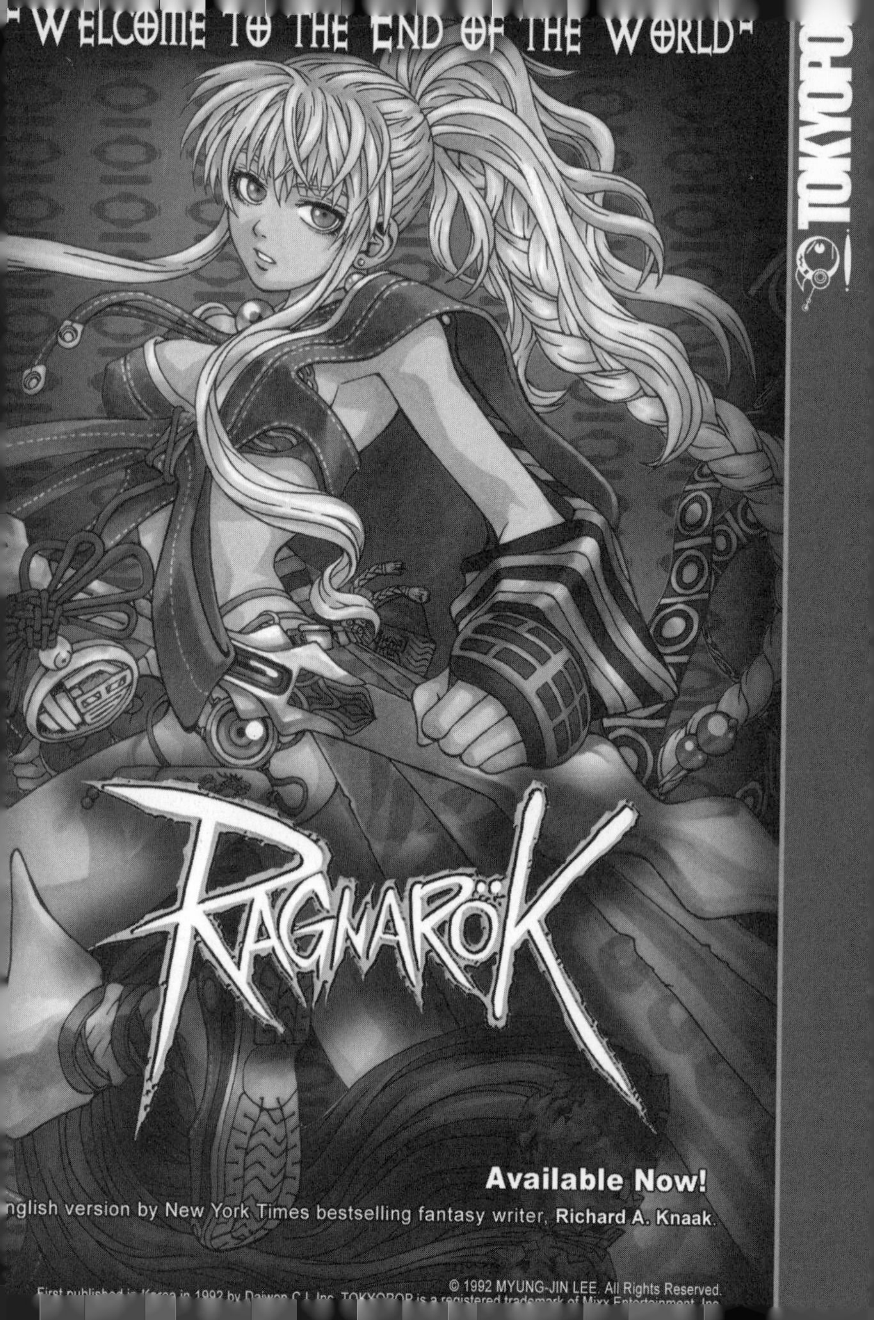

WELCOME TO THE END OF THE WORLD
RAGNARÖK
Available Now!
nglish version by New York Times bestselling fantasy writer, Richard A. Knaak.
© 1992 MYUNG-JIN LEE. All Rights Reserved.

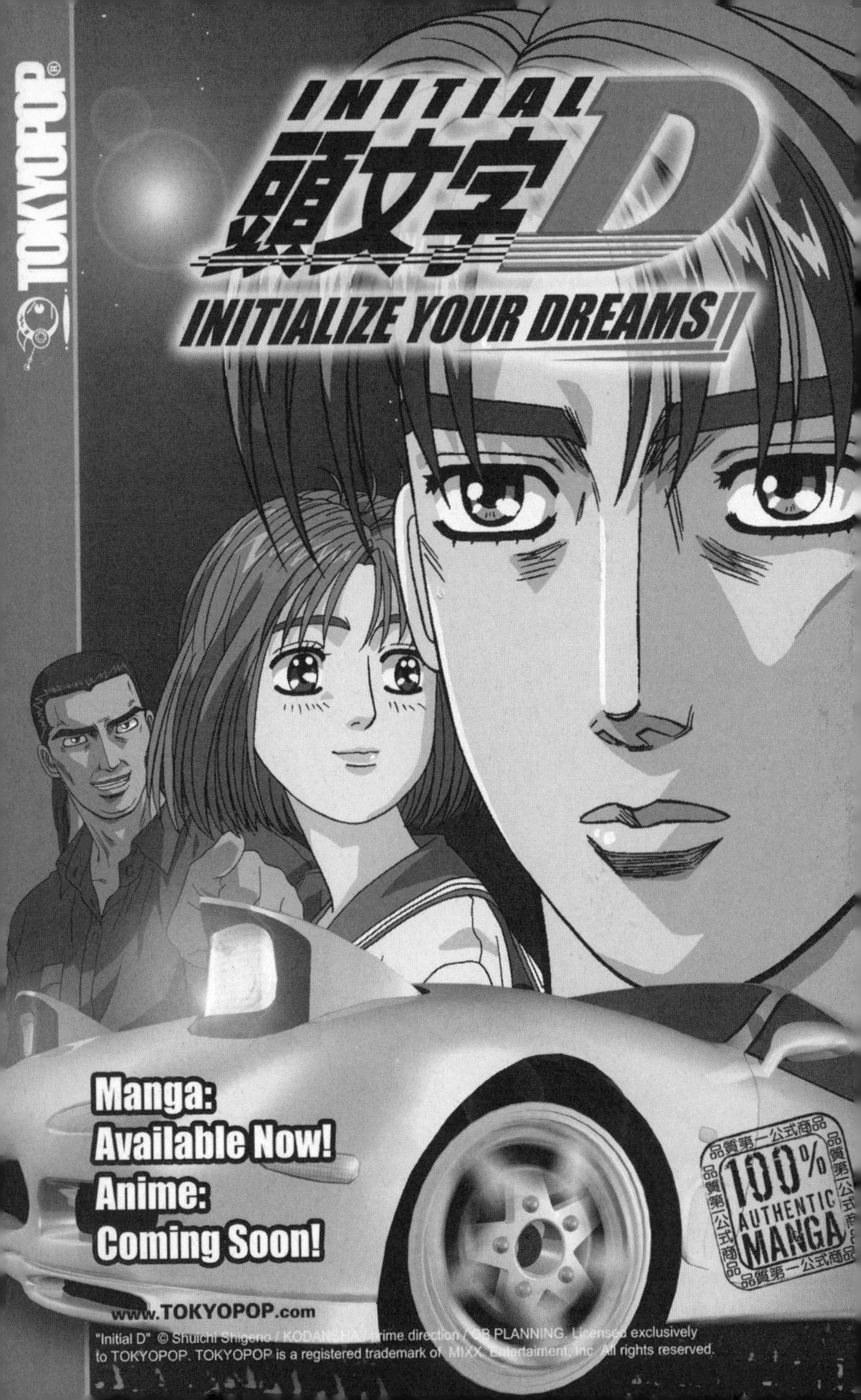
TOKYOPOP
INITIAL
頭文字D
INITIALIZE YOUR DREAMS!!
Manga:
Available Now!
Anime:
Coming Soon!
品質第一公式商品
100% AUTHENTIC MANGA
www.TOKYOPOP.com
"Initial D" © Shuichi Shigeno / KODANSHA / prime direction / OB PLANNING. Licensed exclusively to TOKYOPOP. TOKYOPOP is a registered trademark of MIXX Entertainment, Inc. All rights reserved.

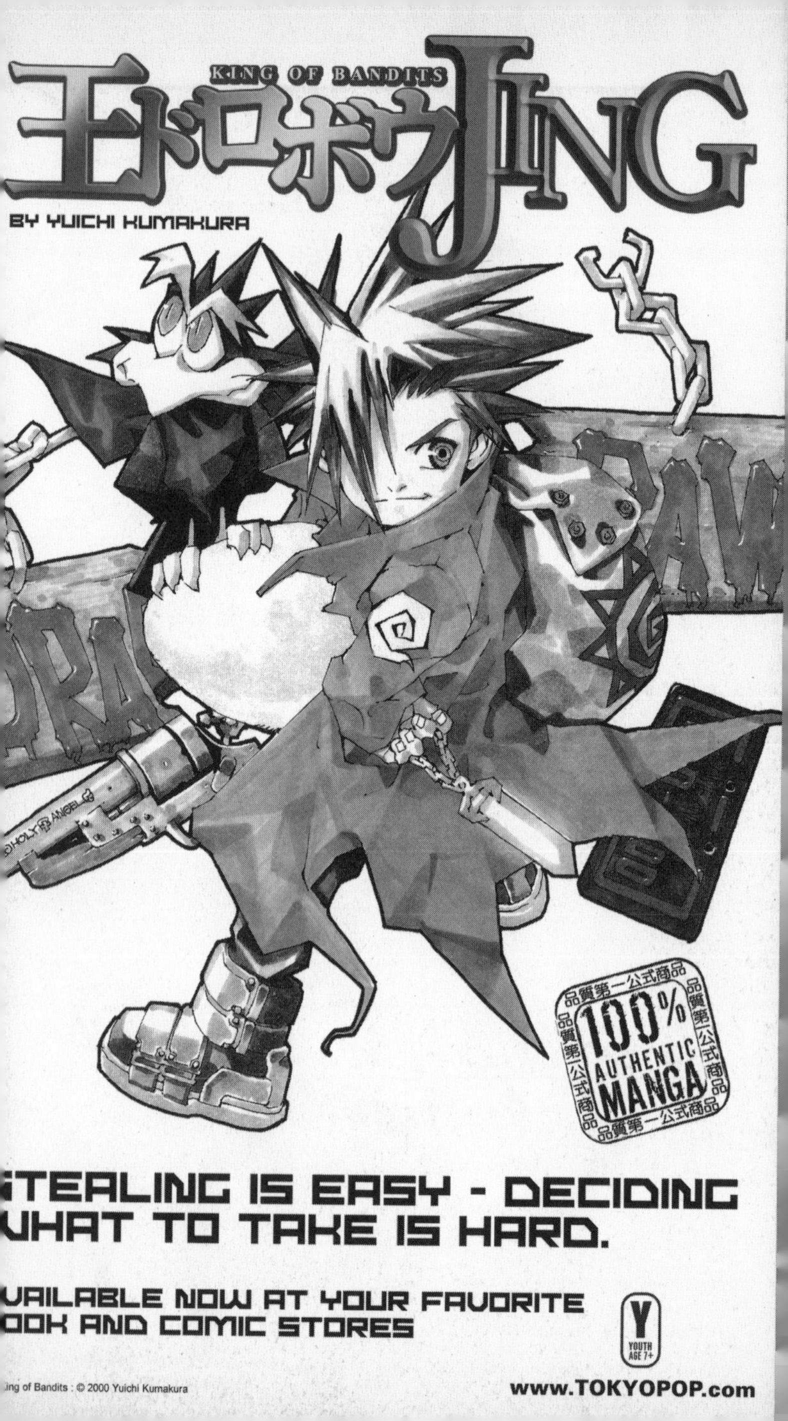
KING OF BANDITS
王ドロボウ JING
BY YUICHI KUMAKURA
品質第一公式商品
100% AUTHENTIC MANGA
TEALING IS EASY - DECIDING
HAT TO TAKE IS HARD.
VAILABLE NOW AT YOUR FAVORITE
OOK AND COMIC STORES
Y
YOUTH AGE 7+
ing of Bandits : © 2000 Yuichi Kumakura
www.TOKYOPOP.com